Standpoint Autotheory
*Writing Embodied Experiences and
Relational Artistic Practices*

Publication Series of the
Academy of Fine Arts Vienna
Volume 28

Standpoint Autotheory
*Writing Embodied Experiences and
Relational Artistic Practices*

Edited by Ana de Almeida
and Mariel Rodríguez

Sternberg Press

Contents

Preface by the Rectorate

Academia is discourse and debate in shared spaces—spaces that can vary from physical learning spaces to workshops, laboratories, and studios, from digital spaces to spaces of individual thought and probably more. Spaces of thought can be immaterial forms of shared imagination in and through which common intellectual experiences indeterminately grow and develop further with unforeseeable temporalities. Even if we cannot see or measure them: we still know about their existence and their infinite productivity. (Sometimes our best thoughts emerge from half-conscious moments of the squandering of time: drifting through space, being only half-awake or dreaming.) But such spaces can also have material concretizations. Books are precisely this: spaces for shared intellectual experience, gathering shared insights and potentials for further reasoning. Therefore, of course, the extended space of academia, and of the Academy of Fine Arts Vienna specifically, is of great concern for our culture of intellectual production. This is the Publication Series of the Academy, which has, by now, led to twenty-eight publications, covering the wide field of research and debate that the Academy stands for.

In this book, Ana de Almeida and Mariel Rodríguez present specific perspectives on the connections between art and theory, individual biography and history. Much of this reflects—directly and indirectly—the institutional history of the Academy, its intellectual legacies and thematic passions.

We would like to thank the editors, authors and peer reviewers for their contributions, and, as always, we are grateful to all the partners for their committed support, especially Sternberg Press.

Ana de Almeida and Mariel Rodríguez

La auto-cosa
Writing Together through Institutions,
Artistic Practices,
and Critical Imagination

Arriving

Perhaps it was the safety offered by the distance of the chair removed by the organizers before the meeting that made me seek eye contact to my right rather than looking at the person seated directly to my left, their shoulder way too close for my emotional state, a mix of excitement and anxiety. The organizers had practically filled the room with rows of silver-legged black chairs, divided by an aisle down the middle, which were occupied by some forty people, students as well as teaching and administrative staff. She looked back at me and smiled tenderly, a young woman with curly brown hair wearing a white blouse with long, green, leaflike ornaments. It was a pleasant smile, and I convinced myself that this was also a pleasant room—wood-tiled floor, white walls, and simple but generous windows—an absolute relief after having had to lean all my weight and press as hard as I could against the giant wooden door to enter this ornate, orangish neoclassical building.[1]

I, in turn, remember holding a small notebook and pen. It was an important day, marking the start of my long-coveted studies at a European university. Everything was novel and exciting. Just a few weeks earlier, I had traveled to Vienna for the entrance exam, and from there everything went quickly. I was accepted into the program, heralding the beginning of years intertwined with this institution, the Academy of Fine Arts. Nervous energy mingled with excitement in my body. My attentive ears tried to catch every linguistic nuance, intonation, and dialect, in an attempt to confirm what I had learned in my German lessons. My gaze roamed the room, searching for familiar faces among the teachers and students who had tested me weeks before, wondering who my new friends would be. I exchanged glances with a woman with the kindest eyes wearing elegant vintage clothes. She sat to my left; we exchanged smiles and looks of anticipation.

Soon the two of us would be asked to walk down the aisle formed by the sequence of chair-wide empty spaces. At the front, we, the two *I*s of this essay, members of the incoming year of the new Master in Critical Studies program, waited our turn to present ourselves.

In early autumn 2011, the "Uni brennt" protests of 2009–10 were still reverberating through the halls of the Academy of Fine Arts Vienna. The massive protests against the effects of the homogenized curricula and the removal of democratic structures in Austrian universities, sparked by the implementation of the Bologna Process, had started at the main building of the Academy at Schillerplatz, where we were currently introducing ourselves. A public meeting

1 In 2022, our colleague Philipp Muerling protested the continued lack of accessibility at the front entrance of the Academy of Fine Arts Vienna even after major renovations. Elizabeth Spouse, "Protect People, Not Monuments: Make the Academy Accessible for Everyone! An Interview with Philipp Muerling," Improper Activities, December 4, 2022, https://improperwalls.com /improperdoseyouneed/2022/1/29/protect-people-not-monuments.

in front of the building was followed by the occupation of the Academy's assembly hall.[2] The occupiers protested the implementation of a neoliberal education economy, which included the credit transfer system among European higher education institutions and the BA/MA system, of which our shiny Master in Critical Studies was now the gloomy face. Not an easy start, one must say—to be part of a "program [which] is primarily oriented towards those critical positions that have been inspired by, among others, Gender Studies, Post- and Decolonial Studies, Subaltern Studies, Cultural Studies and Queer Studies, but also by the Frankfurt School, Poststructuralism and Deconstruction,"[3] and at the same time representing a reform process that treats knowledge as a tradable commodity and "correlates to the principles of the all-embodying privatization and commodification within neoliberal capitalism."[4]

The two *I*s of this essay were deliberating. One *I* wondered how to position herself before the contradiction of enrolling in a post-Bologna program after years of actively protesting its implementation in her hometown of Lisbon by attending meetings, painting banners, and demonstrating.[5] Was keeping her chin up, despite the resentment of some fellow students and having professors indirectly close off art classes for Master in Critical Studies students the price to pay for this ambivalence?[6] The other *I*, in turn, thought she had found a righteousness in the protesters' critique not only of university reforms but also of the racist and sexist policies of exclusion in which they were embedded.[7] She now knew that the 2008 university amendment and the "abolishment" of tuition fees in Austria didn't apply to her.[8] Newly arrived from Mexico, she had to bear with the excitement of the first *I*—an unburdened EU citizen who for a moment was silly to think she had arrived in her long-yearned-for welfare utopia—while she, the second-class citizen *I*, sighed, as if predicting that the tuition invoice she held in her hands was only the first of many challenges custom-made for migrants to come.

During the first week, navigating the institution became the primary focus. After submitting my academic documents at the registrar's office, where the atmosphere was everything but welcoming, I walked down the hall and noticed something scribbled on the wall in pencil—"I am Canadian and I want to study here"—which brought a smile to my face, dispelling my earlier despondency.[9] Before exiting the building, I peeked into the assembly hall, perhaps to rekindle an appreciation for this prestigious institution, home to works by Rembrandt and a triptych by Hieronymus

2 Lina Dokuzović and Eduard Freudmann, "Squatting the Crisis: On the Current Protests in Education and Perspectives on Radical Change," *eipcp*, November 2009, https://eipcp.net/projects/creatingworlds /dokuzovic-freudmann/en.html.

3 "Master in Critical Studies: Curriculum," Academy of Fine Arts Vienna, accessed August 12, 2024, https://www.akbild.ac.at/en/studies/study-programs /copy_of_master-in-critical-studies?set_language=en.

4 Dokuzović and Freudmann, "Squatting the Crisis."

5 Natália Faria, "Estudantes saem hoje à rua para pedir o fim de Bolonha, das propinas e dos exames nacionais," *Jornal Público*, March 24, 2009, https://www .publico.pt/2009/03/24/portugal/noticia/estudantes-saem-hoje-a-rua -para-pedir-o-fim-de-bolonha-das-propinas-e-dos-exames-nacionais-1370603.

6 For more on the tensions between the Master in Critical Studies, the Bologna Process, and access to art classes, see Marwa Abou Hatab, Ana de Almeida, Diedrich Diederichsen, Vasilena Gankovska, Moira Hille, Laura Nitsch, and Constanze Ruhm, "Einfach dranbleiben: 10 Jahre Critical Studies – Eine Roundtable-Diskussion zum Master," in *Big Critical Energy*, ed. Leonie Huber, Valerie Ludwig, and Andrea Zabric (Vienna: Schlebrügge.Editor, 2021), 52–64.

7 Dokuzović and Freudmann, "Squatting the Crisis."

8 Rosemarie Blasi, *Kritik am Bologna-Prozess aus der Sicht der Studierenden* (Munich: Grin, 2011); European Students' Union, *Bologna with Student Eyes 2009*, https://esu-online.org/wp-content/uploads/2024/06/Bologna-With-Student -Eyes_2009_565284.pdf; Hans Pechar and Angela Wroblewski, "Die Auswirkungen von Bologna auf die Lage der Studierenden in Österreich," *Zeitschrift für Hochschulentwicklung*, no. 2 (June 2011): 6.

9 For a critique of the obstacles in the registrar's office, such as the questioning of language skills and competencies as discriminatory treatment, see Abou Hatab et al., "Einfach dranbleiben."

Bosch. The marble columns and ceiling frescos exuded history and ostentation. I attempted to connect with the surroundings. Examining a relief, I read inscriptions honoring Kaiser Leopold I, the Academy's founder, and Franz Joseph I, the building's creator. However, flanking these reliefs were two inscriptions that read: "Kaiser Leopold I, who expelled the Jews from Vienna," and "Franz Joseph I, who triggered WWI." Since the typography, color, and texture of these inscriptions mimicked the reliefs, they could be easily overlooked. I later discovered that this was a work by Platform History Politics.[10] The walls of this building loudly proclaim that there is more than meets the eye. They are the surfaces on which I find the first script, the first lesson on the politics of visibility—a topic that will become constitutive for my work. I know I am in a good place to study.

Publishing

Coffee was savored at Café Nil during a rendezvous with you, my partner, and me—new friends in the making. Hours drifted away in conversation. You shared your ideas about exploring feminist critiques of representation through fanzines and how growing up in Mexico and witnessing the recent wave of violence against women was always in the back of your thoughts.[11] I shared my project about my father's photos, connecting them to the revolutions in Portugal and Czechoslovakia.

Yes, I remember. I was surprised by the simplicity of your departure point as the daughter of a Portuguese dad and a Czech mom. The photo albums we all have at home made me think of all the possible ways this project can open up complex topics. An "inter-revolutionary space," you called it, and you were sure you found it there, inside a cardboard box full of photographs.[12]

There was an interesting symmetry in the big plans we had for our international and intergenerational projects. You came from the winding pathways of the big-name disciplines, the solemn letters and humanities, eager to meander from the epicenter of writing toward a growing interest in drawing and painting. I, in turn, a trained artist who had completed a rather classical academic education in painting, was ready to find my way from an entirely practice-based language of visual arts to a practice of writing, then still unknown to me.

When did we start cooking up the idea of making a book?

Two *I*s walk into a bar. One *I* says: Almost thirteen years have passed since the day we met at the welcome presentation for the students of the Master in Critical Studies. I wonder how it happened that you now sometimes think about leaving Austria and I feel like I got stuck here? I never wanted to come to Vienna, I didn't like being here, I felt I had accidentally landed here, at the bottom of a Biedermeier well. I hated the language, the sky, the trees. I felt miserable for a long time. And you were my sunshine, the glowing one, with the power to hold your life in your own hands, the one who

10 The intervention was removed during the restoration and redevelopment of the main building at Schillerplatz. Eduard Freudmann, "'Swastikas? Ornaments!' as a Continuity of Repression: History-Political Conditions of a Public Art and Educational Institution," trans. Lina Dokuzović, *an-academy*, October 2010, https://transversal.at/transversal/1210/freudmann/en.

11 Mariel Rodríguez, "In Search of Independence | Machismo and Narcopolitics: Past and Present Violent Subjectivities in Mexico" (MA thesis, Institute for Art and Cultural Studies, Academy of Fine Arts Vienna, 2014).

12 Ana de Almeida, "From the Collection to the Archive: A Reflection on the Production of Images in the 1974–1989 Inter-revolutionary Space between the Carnation and the Velvet Revolutions" (PhD project, Institute for Art and Cultural Studies, Academy of Fine Arts Vienna, 2014–), https://www.akbild.ac.at/en/research/center-for-doctoral-studies/dissertation-and-phd-projects/current-dissertation-projects/from-the-collection-to-the-archive-a-reflection-on-the-production-of-images-in-the-1974-1989-inter-revolutionary-space-between-the-carnation-and-the-velvet-revolutions?set_language=en.

had decided to come to Austria, who had sat in an airplane to come to an interview, who, seven thousand kilometers away, had already learned the language with joy and discipline. I fed from your positive attitude in the first years, from your ease in making friends, from the reports of city explorations, your excursions to swim in the Danube, your trips to the mountains. I was awestruck by the way you opened your heart to the human and nonhuman beauties of this place, and I admired your investment in perfecting the language and how fast you showed results. Within a couple of months, you were already using the expression *aber selbstverständlich!* But now you are often fed up. After all these years of your artistic and academic successes being accompanied by never-ending obstacles in dealing with the bureaucratic maze of Vienna's immigration department, by wasting time and investing money in visa renewals, by becoming the exotic half of romantic relationships, by threats of deportation, it seems we switched places. I was able to build a safe place on the foundations of my EU citizenship.

You asked me: *When did we start cooking up the idea of making a book?* I think it was somewhere in the middle. Where we stood when both of us were suddenly unsure of where we were, unsure if we wanted to stay or leave, unsure if being in Austria made us closer to being *Austrian* or closer to being *Portuguese* or *Mexican* than we ever were, the middle between art practice and writing.

The first *I* slowly takes a sip of her drink and thinks to herself: I wonder which artists' books and writings bored Renée Green as she longed to read something about living as an artist?[13] My memory brings me back to 2012. We discovered an announcement looking for art students interested in an internship at Salon für Kunstbuch, a bookstore and project by the artist Bernhard Cella, which back then was still located in a charming but unheated souterrain on Mondscheingasse. Both of us applied and were accepted. During the internship, we catalogued and explored self-published booklets, fanzines, and books without ISBNs, discussing the ones that caught our attention. We also contributed to Cella's salon by researching, collecting, and, at the end of our internship, exhibiting no-ISBN and artists' books from Mexico and Portugal. We gleaned valuable insights from this experience. One of them was the prevalence of unpaid internships in the arts, which perpetuated a system favoring those privileged enough to forgo paid employment during their studies. This obscured the financial realities of pursuing a career in art and culture, while widening the gap between the students who could fully devote themselves to their studies and those who needed to work for money. It also enforced the myth of artistic work as a sort of personal realization that can be remunerated with symbolic capital. *Do what you love.* And employ your knowledge of and connections in the Portuguese and Mexican artists' book and fanzine scenes to produce unpaid content for big-name cultural institutions such as the 21er Haus (now Belvedere 21).[14] This internship left us with a bittersweet feeling but also allowed us to recognize our shared interest in artists' writing practices, editing, and projects that, through individual voices and personal narratives, could say something about politics, the economy, or social struggles—something bigger than the biographies and perspectives of the authors themselves.

13 Renée Green, "Other Planes, Different Phases, My Geometry, Times, Movements: Becomings Ongoing," in *Other Planes of There: Selected Writings* (Durham, NC: Duke University Press, 2014), 1.

14 See Ana de Almeida, "Dependent Publishing: An Overlook on Contemporary Self-Publishing Practices in Portugal," accessed July 30, 2024, https://www.anadealmeida.com/?edependent; and Mariel Rodríguez, "Edita: Self-Publishing Practices in *Contemporary Mexico*," accessed July 30, 2024, https://marielrodriguezrodriguez.com/?Edita.

We dreamed of starting our own independent publishing house for artists' books in Vienna. We budgeted, brainstormed, and decided to go for it. We bought a secondhand Risograph, drafted a mission statement, named our association Transatlantica: Internationaler Kunst- & Kulturverein zugunsten ausgedruckter Medien (Transatlantica: International Art and Cultural Association in Favor of Printed Media), and designed a logo that resembled a shipping container. Transatlantica was meant to be both a publishing house and an annual publication. The focus was to publish projects by our contemporaries that we found inspiring, as well as original texts in Portuguese and Spanish, bypassing the usual review and translation protocols.

Standpoint Autotheory: Writing Embodied Experiences and Relational Artistic Practice belongs to this long story of wanting to foreground the texts that embrace us, the positions by artists who write that surround us. We do not intend to present an overarching view of all forms of self-reflexive practice produced in the context or through the influence of the Academy of Fine Arts Vienna. Instead, this book can be understood as an affective map of the discussions, cooperations, and ways of doing art that inspire the editors' views on the topic. The way we write is not only informed by the writings of others; it is sustained by them, entangled in them, inseparable from them. In this sense, this anthology is a form of continuing the dialogue with peers, students, and teachers, especially artists for whom writing is a fundamental part of their practice. Instead of proposing a classical chapter division, each showcasing a different theme, the structure of the book is closer to a mapping exercise where topics overlap, intersect, and expand on one another.

Searching for a Subject

In 2012, a seminar in the summer semester organized by the Academy and Kunsthaus Bregenz was offered by Jens Kastner and Max Jorge Hinderer Cruz. We and our fellow students in the master's program were invited to discuss relevant texts as preparation for a symposium titled "Art and Ideology Critique after 1989."[15] Both seminar and symposium reconstructed central arguments of the critique of ideology by analyzing the role of its central writings since 1968 in and outside the art field. We also looked at the reformulation of these texts in artistic practices between 1989 and 1991 and beyond. The seminar was hosted in a fancy villa in Bregenz. I read bell hooks for the first time—the title essay from her book *Art on My Mind: Visual Politics* (1995).[16] It contains enormous knowledge, but not the type you can distill into bullet points. The power of the text emanates from the very fabric of its writing. Instead of relying on scholarly conventions, it draws its strength from the intimate details of hooks's path to becoming an artist—the teachers and role models that illuminated the way so she could claim the strength to contradict the common internalized belief that Black folks cannot be artists because "you could not eat art."[17] The text is both literary and autobiographical while at the same time deeply reflective on the politics of seeing, how processes of recognition and defamiliarization can help understand and change "how we perceive the visual, how we write and talk about it."[18] Through a micropolitics of the gaze, she gives an

15 The symposium took place at Kunsthaus Bregenz in cooperation with Eva Birkenstock, Diedrich Diederichsen, Max Jorge Hinderer Cruz, and Ruth Sonderegger.

16 bell hooks, "Art on My Mind," in *Art on My Mind: Visual Politics* (New York: New Press, 1995), 1–9.

17 hooks, 1.

18 hooks, 2.

account of "representation as a crucial location of struggle."[19] This text spoke to me more than the other texts in the seminar, and greatly impacted my writing and artistic practice. Kastner often included such self-reflexive feminist texts in his syllabi. In his seminars on aesthetics and the sociology of art, we discussed Latin American decolonial theory, reading authors such as Gloria Anzaldúa and Maria Lugones.

With the writings of various authors swirling around in our heads, we returned to Vienna and to Rosi, our second-hand Risograph duplicator that worked properly—until it didn't. The machine left us, but the idea of the thing prevailed. Yes, the *thing* that we and so many people around us were doing. We first gave it the nickname *la auto-cosa* (the self-thing), and then we asked, *qué cosa* is this thing all about?

We started by calling it *autoethnography*, a term we became acquainted with in "Ethnographic Imagination and Artistic Practices," a seminar on research methodologies taught by Anette Baldauf in the summer semester of 2013. We learned that autoethnography, characterized by incorporating personal narratives and individual voices into scientific and cultural accounts, emerged as a qualitative research method in the late twentieth century, and was primarily embraced by anthropologists. However, the exploration of the self and the personal extends beyond anthropology, permeating various fields of knowledge production in the social sciences and humanities, including ethnography, sociology, psychology, and philosophy. Interestingly, the expression of subjectivity within scientific endeavors was traditionally confined to the artistic realm, which granted permission for artists to infuse their subjectivity into their work. In stark contrast, the sciences maintained an objective distance from personal narratives, feelings, and experiences. The prevailing view deemed discussions about oneself as unscientific, emphasizing the dichotomies embedded in scientific objectivity such as subject-object, rational-emotional, public-private, and concrete-abstract.

The incorporation of the personal can nevertheless happen on different levels of the relational. Autoethnography can focus on the prism of personal experience or unfold through insider ethnographies, when the ethnographer belongs to the group being studied. This requires the researcher to identify with the group and calls for special attention to methodology. As individuals and researchers, we are always part of different communities. In "Writing against Culture" (1991), the anthropologist Lila Abu-Lughod argues that "the relationship between feminism and anthropology might better be understood as the result of diametrically opposed processes of self-construction through opposition to others—processes that begin from different sides of a power divide."[20] While anthropologists stand on the side of power, feminists stand in a position of resistance and opposition. Studying scientific voices' conflicted relationship to Otherness, Abu-Lughod coined the term "halfies" to refer to "people whose national or cultural identity is mixed by virtue of migration, overseas education, or parentage."[21]

Thinking about how to study culture, according to Abu-Lughod, both feminists and halfies are concerned with distance. How can the researcher produce knowledge if she is enmeshed within the object of study? Since "for halfies, the Other is in certain ways the self,"[22] how can one ignore the connections between a researcher who is both a Turkish

19 hooks, 3.
20 Lila Abu-Lughod, "Writing against Culture," in *Recapturing Anthropology: Working in the Present* (Santa Fe, NM: School of American Research Press, 1991), 467.
21 Abu-Lughod, 466.
22 Abu-Lughod, 468.

migrant in Austria and a textile artist, among other identities, and the creative work behind the sartorial knowledge brought by other immigrants from Turkey to Austria? What does the study of transnational industrial practices reveal about the gendered division of labor across geographies? Which patterns emerge through the knowledge transfers among disciplines, professions, and crafts, and between the private and public spheres? This is the focus of Elif Süsler-Rohringer, whose contribution to this publication, "The Persistence of Patterns: From Strong Subjectivity to Local and Global Sartorial Exchanges," acknowledges the fundamental divide that states of mobility introduce to anthropological research through the defamiliarization of ethnoscapes, as "the *ethno* in ethnography takes on a slippery, nonlocalized quality," in the words of Arjun Appadurai.[23] Süsler-Rohringer focuses on her own positioning in relation to subjective histories told from an actor-centered perspective, casting a sharp look on the research *field*—the long underestimated and unexamined *where* of anthropology, as Akhil Gupta and James Ferguson have described it—by presenting the domestic space as the unacknowledged place where creativity happens.[24]

We gradually learned how the concept of objectivity, central to scientific inquiry, was dismantled as personal accounts started to gain prominence owing to their overt engagement and political potential. In 2012, during Pascal Jurt's summer seminar "Militant Investigation," we studied and discussed the strategies employed "in places as diverse as social movements in Argentina, job centers in [the Berlin district of] Neukölln, Mayday parades, in radical left-wing anthologies, but also in the field of art production."[25] The skepticism toward traditional scientific accounts that echoed across different disciplines was influenced by feminist critiques of representation. In the United States, the claims of the women's liberation movement, part of the second wave of feminism from 1960 to 1980, were encapsulated by the slogan: "the personal is political." The emergence of women's consciousness-raising groups, like the New York Radical Women or W.I.T.C.H.—"a radical feminist group employing guerrilla-theater actions to call attention to sexism"[26]—played a crucial role in propagating women's emancipation through political activism, especially targeting the experiences of white middle-class women fighting for gender equality in terms of bodily autonomy, abortion, contraception, and equal pay. In the first anthology she edited, *Sisterhood Is Powerful* (1970), Robin Morgan argued that history was predominantly narrated from a male perspective, systematically erasing the involvement and significance of women. Morgan introduced the term "herstory" to emphasize the need to recognize women's experiences and contributions throughout history, challenging the male-centric narratives that historically dominated knowledge production.[27] These movements were relevant but proved insufficient in radically contesting oppressive structures for categories of women other

23 Arjun Appadurai, *Modernity at Large: Cultural Dimensions of Globalization* (Minneapolis: University of Minnesota Press, 1996), 48.

24 Bruno Latour, *Reassembling the Social: An Introduction to Actor-Network-Theory* (Oxford: Oxford University Press, 2005); Akhil Gupta and James Ferguson, "Discipline and Practice: 'The Field' as Site, Method, and Location in Anthropology," in *Anthropological Locations: Boundaries and Grounds for a Field Science*, ed. Akhil Gupta and James Ferguson (Berkeley: University of California Press, 1998), 2.

25 Pascal Jurt, "Militante Untersuchung," Academy of Fine Arts Vienna, summer 2012, https://campus.akbild.ac.at/akbild_online/ee/ui/ca2/app /desktop/#/slc.tm.cp/student/courses/129553?$ctx=lang=de&$scrollTo=toc _overview. Translations are by the authors unless noted otherwise.

26 "The anagram was adaptable, representing Women's International Terrorist Conspiracy from Hell, Women Inspired to Commit Herstory, Women Interested in Toppling Consumer Holidays, etc." Robin Morgan, "Activism," accessed November 5, 2024, https://www.robinmorgan.net/activism/.

27 Robin Morgan, ed., *Sisterhood Is Powerful: An Anthology of Writings from the Women's Liberation Movement* (New York: Vintage, 1970).

than white, binary, and other normative ones. The spread of emancipatory and anti-colonial movements in geographies with a colonial background led to a specific conjuncture that allowed for the rise of a multiracial feminism. These targeted not only equality among genders but also social justice. The scholar and poet Becky Thompson writes, "During the 1970s, women of color were involved on three fronts—working with white-dominated feminist groups; forming women's caucuses in existing mixed-gender organizations; and developing autonomous Black, Latina, Native American, and Asian feminist organizations."[28]

Un/learning

When I first stepped onto the second floor of the Academy's Semperdepot for "Post-Conceptual Art Practices," I knew I wanted to stay. The course consisted of a rich program of lectures, performances, discussions, student presentations, and excursions both inside and outside the institution.[29] Led by Marina Gržinić, the class was exhilarating and full of lively discussions. That evening, we read photocopied fragments of Trinh T. Minh-ha's *Woman, Native, Other* (1989) that had been distributed around the tables. We engaged in a loud collective reading. At some point, we arrived at this passage:

No matter which side i belong to, once i step down into the mud pit to fight my adversary, i can only climb out from it stained. This is the story of the duper who turns her/himself into a dupe while thinking s/he has made a dupe of the other. The close dependency that characterizes the master-servant relationship and binds the two to each other for life is an old, patent fact one can no longer deny.

Thus, insofar as I/i understand how "sexism dehumanizes men," I/i shall also see how "my racism must dehumanize me" (Pence). The inability to relate the two issues and to feel them in my bones, has allowed me to indulge in the illusion that I will remain safe from all my neighbors' problems and can go on leading an undisturbed, secure life of my own. Hegemony and racism are, therefore, a pressing feminist issue; "as usual, the impetus comes from the grassroots, activist women's movement." Feminism, as Barbara Smith defines it, "is the political theory and practice that struggles to free all women. … Anything less than this vision of total freedom is not feminism, but merely female self-aggrandizement.[30]

Trinh emphasizes the interconnectedness of various social oppressions—particularly sexism and racism—and the consequences of engaging in adversarial relationships. Taking sides, ignoring or obliterating the interplay between these relationships, leads to a shared degradation. In the name of personal security, no one is spared the risk of reproducing exactly what they are criticizing. To address hegemony and racism as feminist issues, according to Kimberlé Crenshaw, is to recognize how "ignoring difference *within* groups

28 Becky Thompson, "Multiracial Feminism: Recasting the Chronology of Second Wave Feminism," *Feminist Studies* 28, no. 2 (Summer 2002): 338.

29 "The Studio for Post-Conceptual Art Practices (PCAP), at the Institute of Fine Arts, Academy of Fine Arts Vienna, […] consists (with the Erasmus visiting students that come to the art studio usually for a semester) of approximately 50 students and is open to different interventions into art, community, technology, politics and the social. The collaboration of the students, professor, and teaching assistants results in art, activist, and community-based projects strongly connected with contemporary theory and interventional logic in social and political spaces. Activism, politics, and theory are of utmost importance for how we deal with visual practices and politics of representation in PCAP." "About Us," PCAP class website, accessed November 5, 2024, https://m1.antville.org /tags/-%20About%20us/.

30 Trinh T. Minh-ha, *Woman, Native, Other: Writing Postcoloniality and Feminism* (Bloomington: Indiana University Press, 1989), 95 (emphasis added).

contributes to tension *among* groups."[31] These tensions can be addressed through an intersectional perspective. Gržinić, serious and defiant, spoke to us about the process of internalizing colonial oppression and the racial epidermal schema as the bodily embodiment of racial discrimination: white people will never know what it means to be Black. In a loud, almost militant tone, she said: "Look around, we are all racists! We don't acknowledge it, but we are, deep inside, racists." My skin crawled. The room was silent. The class, as usual, had already gone past its scheduled end. We were hungry and tired. The session finished soon after this statement.

I left the building with Gržinić's words and Trinh's ideas tumbling around in my head, confronted with the fact of my long-denied racism. Walking by Lehargasse, I saw holes in the facade of the building commissioned by Franz Joseph I, holes left by machine-gun bullets during the Second World War, historical memory protected by glass, indicating Austria's history of racism and anti-Semitism. What does *my* story have to do with all that? As a white upper-middle-class Mexican cis woman—*una mestiza*—living in Austria, my positionality had changed. Regarding Western social markers such as class, ethnicity, sexual preference, and appearance, I had been spared the experience of standing on the more vulnerable side of the power divide. I grew up hearing (and repeating) the idea that we, Mexicans, acknowledge classism and not racism, under the spell—in Nina Hoechtl's words— of *el delirio güero* (white delusion). How can Mexicans be racists if we feel North American racism is exercised against *us*? How can *we* be racists when Mexico had one of the "earliest" abolitionist movements in 1821? The blindness to Mexican racism has been historically constructed. Under the pretext of *mestizaje*, Mexico, as well as almost all other

Latin American countries, claims to have eradicated differences through mixture. Mestizaje is the mortar that binds the fictive concept of Latin America and the foundation for the reproduction of privilege.[32]

Yes, but let us return to how the emergence of voices previously marginalized in academic discourse added another layer to the evolving *auto-cosa* narrative. Both personal experience and an array of non-Western positions had been deemed irrelevant for critical discourse, which indicates the gaps in knowledge production. During the 1960 and 1970s, various movements were informed by the decolonial impulses in the Caribbean and Africa. An awareness of the limits of hegemonic European and North American discourse and the growing power of anti-colonial movements also gave rise to new forms of scholarship based on the experiences of people from colonized territories and histories. In 1961, Frantz Fanon published *The Wretched of the Earth*, examining colonialism as a psychopathology that affects all members of society, albeit in different ways.[33] In the book, he challenged prevailing views of the master-slave dynamic and considered embodied perspectives.

Toward the end of the 1970s, a groundbreaking critique emerged from the field of literary studies that shed new light on how discourse has the power to distort reality while also emphasizing scholars' solipsism when writing about the "other." Edward Said's *Orientalism* (1978) pointed to persistent

31 Kimberlé Crenshaw, "Mapping the Margins: Intersectionality, Identity Politics, and Violence against Women of Color," *Stanford Law Review* 43, no. 6 (July 1991): 1242, https://doi.org/10.2307/1229039.

32 These reflections are the focus of Mariel Rodríguez, "Mestizaje(s): Gender, Alterity and Internal Colonialism in Mexican Visual Cultures" (PhD diss. project, Institute for Art and Cultural Studies, Academy of Fine Arts Vienna, 2014–), https://www.akbild.ac.at/en/research/center-for-doctoral-studies/dissertation-and-phd-projects/mestizaje-s.

33 Frantz Fanon, *The Wretched of the Earth*, trans. Richard Philcox (New York: Grove Press, 2004).

tropes in visualizing Eastern and Arab cultures, contributing to a reevaluation of the binary of social relations. Said analyzed "orientalism" as a self-referential Western scholarly tradition, a style of thought based on the distinction between East and West, Orient and Occident. Orientalism operates as a corporate institution dedicated to propagating this distinction. One of Said's main arguments has to do with the dynamics of alterity: *us* produces *them* always from an oppositional perspective. A negative identity construction implies that the Other must be everything I am not—otherwise, we wouldn't be so different. In this volume, the creation of alterity, rooted in oppositional social and cultural dynamics, is evident in Mai Ling's feminist approach to orientalism, which challenges colonial perspectives on Asian femininity, and in the contributions by Nina Hoechtl and Verena Melgarejo Weinandt. Across these positions, there is a shared effort to decolonize identity by acknowledging the intersectionality of gender, race, and class.

When you write about becoming aware of the ignorance of your inherent racism, I am reminded of Renée Green's expression "ongoing becomings."[34] I like the way this expression entails a state of permanent mutability and permanent beginning. My research on revolutions has given me an Arendtian passion for the concept of radical beginnings,[35] and I find that Green's words have the capacity of not only summoning a state of permanent change but also conveying the idea that you become aware of these changes retrospectively. *You have to leave the island in order to see the island.*[36] Only when you look over your shoulder do you see who you've become. And while you are busy looking back, reflecting, analyzing, narrating your last steps, your feet are probably already taking you in a new direction.

Green was a professor at the Academy of Fine Arts Vienna from 1997 until 2002, preceding Gržinić as the head of the conceptual art class. I've met some of her former students, and I wonder how much of her art, writings, and teaching was preserved in them after she moved back to the US. Perhaps something remained within the walls of this institution? The same question applies, of course, to other instructors. A teaching institution such as the Academy is a place of passage for most people who are, were, and will be affiliated with it. Do we find here, next to the bad ghosts of Hitler, Kaiser Leopold I, and the others whom the Platform History Politics has summoned in their critical séances, also friendly ghosts in the form of traits left by critical thinking, reverberations left by the sound of emancipative words, eerie energy left by moments of commoning?

Good and bad ghosts are also present in Nina Hoechtl's contribution, "A Visual Glossary, Expanded: *Delirio güero* (White Delusion)," as well as in her overall artistic practice. As cofounder of the Secretariat for Ghosts, Archival Politics and Gaps, Hoechtl has dealt with the "ghosts of nationalist socialist ideologies, ghosts of colonial fantasies and old and new ghosts of feminist agency."[37] Her work is in constant dialogue with past, present, and future ghosts. In this volume, she invokes the delusional hauntings left by white saviors in Mexico, the country she relocated to. The text evolves as a reflection on the "politics of location" implied in her position

34 Green, "Other Planes, Different Phases."

35 Hannah Arendt, *On Revolution* (London: Penguin Books, 2006).

36 José Saramago, *O conto da ilha desconhecida* (Lisbon: Assíro & Alvim, 1997).

37 Nina Hoechtl, "Hauntings in the Archive!," accessed November 6, 2024, http://www.ninahoechtl.org/works/hauntings-in-the-archive/; Sekretariat für Geister, Archiv-Politiken und Lücke (SKAGL) is a project by Nina Hoechtl and Julia Wieger, accessed November 6, 2024, http://www.skgal.org/.

as a "halfie."[38] As an Austrian artist and researcher working in Mexico, *la güera* belongs to a genealogy of white saviors that can be traced back to the failed attempt to establish an Austrian monarchy in the Americas. In her text, these and other stories are narrated in the form of a self-reflexive glossary entry to elucidate her video *DELIRIO GÜERO WHITE DELUSION. 2211, 2018, 1825 and Back* (2018).

When I think of Green's passage through the Academy, I am thinking less of her leaving behind a legacy in the academic sense of a master-to-apprentice transfer of genius and knowledge. Rather, I prefer to think that her voice is a pebble lying at the base of a fluid but general understanding of situatedness in relation to identity politics as a potential category, not a fixed one. Or as Stuart Hall puts it, "Perhaps instead of thinking of identity as an already accomplished fact, which the new cultural practices then represent, we should think, instead, of identity as a 'production,' which is never complete, always in process, and always constituted within, not outside, representation."[39] It is a relational mix of imagination, history, and creolization. It is not about the future, about ultimately realizing how labels have switched; it is not about achieving a new category, collecting identities. It is about the process of becoming. This is contained in Cana Bilir-Meier's appeal: "Tell your own stories, become a storyteller." In her contribution, "Becoming a Storyteller: Methodologies in Collaborative, Activist, Artistic, and Archival Work in Remembering," Bilir-Meier focuses on identity production as an ongoing collaboration among those directly affected by racism, anti-Semitism, police violence, and right-wing terror. These (always partial) identities defined by affectedness, far from being given labels, are complex and dynamic categories that have to be built together and reclaimed as the foundation for visibility and agency. Through a self-determined practice of telling one's own story against imposed dominant narratives, one is not—one becomes. And becoming together is the actual act of resistance; it is activist work, it is an act of solidarity, and it is poetic practice.

But how can resistance take place in an academic context through art and research? Recall Linda Tuhiwai Smith's claim that "the word itself, 'research' is probably one of the dirtiest words in the indigenous world's vocabulary." How can we still conduct research when the term "is inextricably linked to European imperialism and colonialism"?[40] The shift from a "damage-centered" to a "desire-focused" perspective on research, as proposed elsewhere by Eve Tuck and K. Wayne Yang, is adopted by Bilir-Meier in an effort to transition to forms of research that stem from social, political, and communal needs and seek to distance themselves from Europe's continued history of exploiting communities.[41] In Moira Hille's seminar on artistic research in the summer semester of 2019, this shift of perspective was addressed, along with the transformative potential of posthumanist research positions that urge for the development of "a critique of science that focuses on interspecies relations."[42] In the seminar, texts by Linda Tuhiwai Smith and Anna Lowenhaupt Tsing provided

38 Adrienne Rich, "Notes toward a Politics of Location" (1984), in *Blood, Bread, Poetry: Selected Prose, 1979–1984* (New York: Norton, 1986), 210–31.

39 Stuart Hall, "Cultural Identity and Diaspora," in *Selected Writings on Race and Difference*, ed. Paul Gilroy and Ruth Wilson Gilmore (Durham, NC: Duke University Press, 2021), 222.

40 Linda Tuhiwai Smith, *Decolonizing Methodologies: Research and Indigenous Peoples* (London: Zed Books, 1999), 1.

41 Eve Tuck and K. Wayne Yang, "R-Words: Refusing Research," in *Humanizing Research: Decolonizing Qualitative Inquiry with Youth and Communities*, ed. Django Paris and Maisha T. Winn (London: SAGE Publications, 2014), 223–48.

42 Moira Hille, "Artistic Research," Academy of Fine Arts Vienna, summer 2019, https://campus.akbild.ac.at/akbild_online/ee/ui/ca2/app/desktop/#/slc.tm.cp/student/courses/143955?$scrollTo=toc_overview.

a framework to think about the resonances among critiques from Indigenous studies and the philosophy of science.[43]

Here, for example, Karen Barad's concepts of "diffraction" and "interference" (which she uses interchangeably) are displaced from the field of classical physics onto the social realm. Barad describes Donna Haraway's critique of reflexivity and suggestion that "diffraction can serve as a useful counterpoint to reflection: both are optical phenomena, but whereas reflection is about mirroring and sameness, diffraction attends to patterns of difference," and continues by challenging linear and reflective notions of writing, advocating instead for an approach that recognizes the entanglements and interferences of processes that make meaning. For Barad, "diffraction involves reading insights through one another in ways that help illuminate differences as they emerge: how different differences get made, what gets excluded, and how those exclusions matter."[44] Diffraction contrasts with mere reflection by emphasizing how differences emerge through "intra-actions," prompting writers like Bilir-Meier to consider the material and discursive forces shaping their work.

Here, in *Standpoint Autotheory*, situated and process-based artistic practices are part of all the contributions since they deal with questions of identity through different strategies.[45] Verena Melgarejo Weinandt, in "A Deep Dive into the (Collective) Self: Creating Autohistoria-teoría with the Performative Alter Ego Pocahunter," and Mai Ling, in "Who Is Mai Ling? Challenges of Anonymity and Practice of Care," deal with the self through the creation of alterity. Melgarejo Weinandt turns to the dialectics of embodied knowledge through working with her alter ego, Pocahunter—a figure who emerges as the artistic materialization of internalized and embodied (*incorporadas*) external projections that had a formative role in constructing her identity. At the same time, through a newfound agency, this alter ego has the capability of reinscribing itself into the performing body and becomes active in constructing a self-determined identity. Through this artistic process of constitutive alterity production, Melgarejo Weinandt participates in the critique of the violent and supremacist subject established through Cartesian secularized universalism and the critique of epistemic violence against subjects who produce embodied and nonrational knowledge. In this sense, Pocahunter—a new thinking, feeling, and acting body, created in collaboration with others—expresses herself through an embodied practice that shapes identity through conveying what is self-determined, what is overdetermined, and what is common.

If Melgarejo Weinandt works with a constant movement between the auto and the alter, Mai Ling, in turn, only speaks and writes as Mai Ling. Although sharing a strategy of counter-appropriation of problematic pop-cultural stereotypes, the collective opts for a strategy of obfuscation of individual stories. Their approach recalls Rosi Braidotti's understanding of

43 Smith, *Decolonizing Methodologies*; Anna Lowenhaupt Tsing, *The Mushroom at the End of the World: On the Possibility of Life in Capitalist Ruins* (Princeton, NJ: Princeton University Press, 2015).

44 Karen Barad, *Meeting the Universe Halfway: Quantum Physics and the Entanglement of Matter and Meaning* (Durham, NC: Duke University Press, 2007), 29, 30.

45 These practices are clearly present in the program of some courses at the Academy. See, for example, the description of the studio "Art and Space | Spatial Strategies" led by Iman Issa since 2020: "The studio for Art and Space | Spatial Strategies (prev. Sculpture and Spatial Strategies) centers around developing an understanding of space in all of its facets including physical, temporal, social and historical. Through a concentration on technology, material, technique, process, context, and site, the studio offers a working group and a practical think tank to think through and undertake art presentations that are reflexive of their relationship to their sources, presentations and wider implications." "Art and Space | Spatial Strategies," Academy of Fine Arts Vienna, accessed July 30, 2024, https://www.akbild.ac.at/en/institutes/fine-arts/studios/art-and-space/spatial-strategies?set_language=en.

"nomadism" to reimagine the writer as an ever-evolving entity, unbound by fixed identities. This nomadic perspective encourages a dynamic, boundary-crossing writing practice that acknowledges the multiplicity of voices and experiences. The nomadic approach embraced by Mai Ling points to the creation of an identity that is fluid and collective and rests on contingency. As Braidotti writes: "The nomadic consciousness combines coherence with mobility. It aims to rethink the unity of the subject, without reference to humanistic beliefs, without dualistic oppositions, linking instead body and mind in a new set of intensive and often intransitive transitions."[46] Mai Ling also deals with embodied practices of the self and the pain inflicted by processes of othering and violent determination over their bodies. Nevertheless, the *Is* conveyed in Mai Ling are opaque selves that work together in what we propose calling *anti-vulnerability processes*. Like many existing biological forms of aggregated life, their members change permanently, as does their shape.

Questioning Identities

Two *Is* walk into a bar. One says: Remember when you used to work in a bar like this? The other replies: Which one?

During my first years in Vienna, I worked in different places, including some bars and restaurants. However, as a *drittstaatsangehörige Arbeitskraft* (third-state foreign worker), it was not always easy to land a job. You need someone to agree to do the required procedures to obtain a job permit from the AMS (Arbeitsmarktservice, Labor Market Service). This permit needs to be renewed every year, for a fee of around twenty euros. Although it may not sound like much, not everyone is willing to put up the money. After my first year working in a café, I had a talk with my employer. She told me they were happy with my work but it was somewhat of a burden to deal with this permit. She took a sip of her *Ingwer-Limo* and with an awkward smile asked if I was in a relationship with someone from the EU. I mumbled yes, to which she replied, "Oh, that's perfect! Maybe you can marry and get your papers. That would make everything much easier on our side."

I see, says the first *I*, sitting at the counter all this time, listening carefully. She takes another sip of her drink before adding: You question the way I talk about *ongoing becomings*, suggesting that they implicitly always represent emancipatory or self-determined ways of becoming. I feel you are asking, *what if I end up becoming the other that I don't want to be?*

Yes! What if my work ends up being instrumentalized in ways in which I am complicit? Since the 1990s, "Hal Foster warns artists against the essentializing dangers of self-othering, cautions curators about the temptation of taking for granted the political amidst the subaltern, and alerts cultural institutions to the patronizing inclination lurking behind the endeavor to 'give voice' to the Other(s)."[47] For him, the main risk is to fall into the "*realist assumption*: that the other, here postcolonial, there proletarian, is in the real, not in the ideological, because he or she is socially oppressed, politically transformative, and/or materially productive. Often this realist assumption is compounded by a *primitivist fantasy*: that the other has access to primal psychic and social processes from which the white (petit) bourgeois subject is

46 Rosi Braidotti, *Nomadic Subjects: Embodiment and Sexual Difference in Contemporary Feminist Theory* (New York: Columbia University Press, 1994), 31.

47 Mariel Rodríguez, curatorial text for the "Field Within" exhibition brochure, xE – Exhibition Space of the Academy of Fine Arts Vienna, July–September 2019.

blocked."[48] But you are also telling me that any identity or particularity must recognize itself within the relational system of forces in which it is inscribed.

I like to think that delving into the rabbit hole of identity is the way to arrive at a negotiation table to discuss your ideas, aspirations, projects, desires, and fears. It is a table you can sit at only if you come from a place of "radical honesty," as Mai Ling puts it. You lay yourself bare, on your own terms, to speak from a place of transparency instead of vulnerability. You have to position yourself because you cannot negotiate with others if you don't know where you are or where your interlocutors are sitting. How do you know in which direction to talk? How do you know where the ones you are talking to are, how near or far?

The thing with this table is that you can constantly switch places or sit on two or more chairs at the same time. You can stand still for a moment, and as soon as you start negotiating with others, you realize you have to situate yourself again.

From that perspective, the "primitivist fantasy" seems to fade away. To talk about the self from the position of the self-ethnographer is not the product of a gift that provides special *access* to knowledge production. The texts we bring together in this book show how self-reflexivity as a methodological approach opens up a space to think in terms of interrelatedness, entanglements, genealogies, and legacies. They show how identity can be negotiated on different terms, be it forms of entangled history, multidirectionality, nomadism, or situated universalism, or how it can be employed with specific collective goals in mind under forms of strategic essentialism.[49]

In the twenty-first century, the development of racial capitalism creates "combat zones" as spaces where people come together to try to subvert the imposed order.[50] These zones are often marked by experiences of migration and displacement. In the current volume, Olena Khoroshylova, andrea ancira, and Sanja Lasić each deal with violent processes of forced displacement due to war, extractivism, and the lasting consequences of armed conflicts on social organization and the realm of collective emotions. Khoroshylova recounts how, while being driven away from her home in Ukraine, she suddenly and unexpectedly encountered a physical space of collective memory—the German forced-labor camp her grandmother had been taken to from Ukraine during the Second World War. In this space, social strategies for adapting to a new environment overcame the violence inflicted, despite its long-lasting effects. Through this encounter, Khoroshylova builds a bridge between her grandmother's experience of women's collaborative survival strategies and her own as a refugee displaced by the ongoing

48 Hal Foster, "The Artist as Ethnographer?," in *The Return of the Real* (Cambridge, MA: MIT Press, 1996).

49 For more on these terms, see, respectively, Sebastian Conrad and Shalini Randeria, "Einleitung: Geteilte Geschichten – Europa in einer postkolonialen Welt," in *Jenseits des Eurozentrismus: Postkoloniale Perspektiven in den Geschichts- und Kulturwissenschaften*, ed. Sebastian Conrad, Shalini Randeria, and Regina Römhild, 2nd ed. (Frankfurt: Campus Verlag 2013), 34; Michael Rothberg, *Multidirectional Memory: Remembering the Holocaust in the Age of Decolonization* (Stanford, CA: Stanford University Press 2009); Braidotti, *Nomadic Subjects*; Nora Sternfeld, "Situierter Universalismus: Warum der Partikularismus der Befreiung und der Universalismus, in den sie sich befreit, keine Gegensätze sind," in *After Europe: Beiträge zur dekolonialen Kritik*, ed. Julian Warner (Berlin: Verbrecher, 2021), 67–78; and Gayatri Chakravorty Spivak, "Subaltern Studies: Deconstructing Historiography," in *Selected Subaltern Studies*, ed. Ranajit Guha and Gayatri Chakravorty Spivak (Oxford: Oxford University Press, 1988), 13. For more on the many pitfalls of identity politics as well as positive references to collective identity—and the political and historical developments of ways to relate to it—see Jens Kastner and Lea Susemichel, *Identitätspolitiken: Konzepte und Kritiken in Geschichte und Gegenwart der Linken* (Münster: Unrast, 2022).

50 Mary Louise Pratt, *Imperial Eyes: Travel Writing and Transculturation* (London: Routledge, 1992).

large-scale Russian attacks on Ukraine. In the research project *Sevdah of Lost Identity* (2018–), Sanja Lasić navigates a net of severed and re-woven relationships to her home country, Bosnia-Herzegovina, while addressing her eating disorders and PTSD as manifestations of the toll that war and forced displacement have taken on her mental health. By articulating a voice shaped at the intersection of the myriad languages she has learned—or has had to learn—in a state of mobility, through singing the musical genre *sevdah,* Lasić can rewrite the lines of her own story that, like those of many others, was painfully ruptured by trauma at an early age. Both authors, from different perspectives, find in lost ancestors the interlocutors needed to situate their own experience and address the lack of archives with storytelling and speculative narration.

Family genealogy is inscribed and marked by affect and a body politics of knowledge determined by national belonging, social mobility, language, everyday practices, tradition, and dissidence. Engaging with this normative social unit can be a powerful method for estimating social and political conjunctures from the perspective of their influence in the aesthetic realm. The contributions by andrea ancira, Cana Bilir-Meier, Nina Hoechtl, and Lena Ditte Nissen stem from artistic practices and research on vernacular and family archives. They provide a glimpse into the affective, emotional, memorial, oneiric, and sometimes traumatic forms of embodied histories of familial and geographical backgrounds. The different ways the artists work with these archives—by searching, collecting, caring, and activating—belong to an archaeology of memory. They weave narratives from fragments and debris—situated narratives of empowerment or disempowerment, militancy or flight. These narratives share a common space at the crossroads of the realms of the private, affective, and embodied, as well as the official, national, and institutional. They are narratives of reappropriation through acts of making history private.

Decolonizing

The inclusion of the self has always been present in the work of artists—for instance, in autobiographical accounts.[51] In contrast, the systemic approach undertaken by the methods of standpoint and autotheory allows for an integration not only of autobiographical information but of affects, relationships, personal stories, and embodied experience as significant sources of information to study social, cultural, and political events. Moreover, the critical stance and poetics fostered by taking lived experience as a point of departure for knowledge production becomes the source for articulating counter-discourses that question notions of objectivity, neutrality, and universality.[52]

The texts included in this volume are various manifestations of radical self-reflexive attitudes present in different modes of thinking and practice, such as autoethnography, practices of the self, *autohistoria-teoría*, standpoint theories, "strong objectivity" and situated knowledge, narrativity and storytelling, radical positioning, performative philosophy, autofiction, and thinking-feeling, as well as other methods that, through the interrogation of embodied experiences,

51 A noteworthy seminar at the Academy of Fine Arts Vienna on the relation of art and artists with diary writing, autofiction, and daily exercises was "Jogger, Jogis und Journale: Tagebücher und andere Exerzitien," held by Diedrich Diederichsen and Julia Pennauer in the winter semester of 2019.

52 Stacey Young, *Changing the Wor(l)d: Discourse, Politics, and the Feminist Movement* (New York: Routledge, 1997).

illuminate the connections between the personal and the political, the individual and the communal.[53]

In the contributions, we can see that decolonial thought urgently questions identity construction as a relational phenomenon inscribed in hierarchical power structures. This view is the product of a detached ethos that characterizes the logics of dominion required by colonial subjects. To overthrow the fantasy of the detached researcher who remains objective, to produce only transparent thought and the separation between what is logical, reasonable, and verifiable from that which is charged with emotion, constantly changing, belonging to the realm of nature (and evil forces), we need to look at the various pieces of history and identity that form our beings. To decolonize our universes of meaning, it is necessary to abandon the Cartesian solipsism of the mind-body divide to regain access to the registers of memory, the oneiric, and the imaginary, which have been lost to colonial domination.

In a 2020 conversation, Renée Green and Iman Issa, who that year became a professor at the Academy, discussed the term *decolonize*. Issa states that she thinks of identity "as something that one needs to claim, a manner of existing socially and politically in the world that is not ascribed but earned. It is also almost always contingent and rarely ever essential." Together they think about the term not as fixed but as having different valences throughout time, and about the need to see it under the prism of different modes of existence, therefore necessarily building and rethinking new relations to it on a permanent basis. Thus, identity becomes indissociable from decolonizing and, conversely, this relationship also ensures that what one understands by decolonizing depends on the way one understands identity. As Issa points out, "This idea that decolonizing institutions is to fill them with objects, people, and things that bear and act out the markers of their 'specific identities' contrasted with that 'bland' dominant one feels like securing colonialism with metal bolts rather than decolonizing anything."[54]

I look at the texts that flow into this book and see constellations forming. Questions flow through them, aggregate in them, entangle with them, diverge from and question each other. Andrea ancira's study of the Guatemalan Civil War brings a perspective to memory and mourning from a standpoint within the country. In "Unlearning the Archive: A River as Trace," ancira finds affective and embodied ways of producing cartography and subsequently a speculative space for memory. Navigating her family's history, ancira becomes an archivist who handles photographs, radio recordings, and various guerrilla artifacts. But instead of reproducing the authoritarian task of expropriation for preservation, she opens up the archive through a disorienting map as a space for collective mourning.

Involving the archive thus becomes an opportunity for exercising historical and political responsibility; by letting it speak, by activating its voices and its silences, one can take a stance. In "Attempt to Situate: Speak or Let Speak?," Lena

53 For more on these terms—practices of the self, autohistoria-teoría, standpoint theories and strong objectivity, thinking-feeling (*sentipensar*)—see, respectively, Michel Foucault, "Self Writing," in *Ethics: Subjectivity and Truth*, ed. Paul Rabinow, trans. Robert Hurley et al. (New York: New York Press, 1994), 207–22; Gloria Anzaldúa, *Light in the Dark / Luz en lo oscuro: Rewriting Identity, Spirituality, Reality*, ed. AnaLouise Keating (Durham, NC: Duke University Press, 2015); Donna Haraway, "Situated Knowledges: The Science Question in Feminism and the Privilege of Partial Perspective," *Feminist Studies* 14, no. 3 (1988): 575–99; Sandra Harding, "Stronger Objectivity for Sciences from Below," in *Objectivity and Diversity: Another Logic of Scientific Research* (Chicago: University of Chicago Press, 2015); and Orlando Fals Borda, *Una sociología sentipensante para América Latina*, ed. Víctor Manuel Moncayo (Mexico City: Siglo XXI Editores, 2015).

54 Iman Issa, "Conversation with Renée Green on the Term 'Decolonize'" (2020), accessed March 18, 2024, http://imanissa.com/writings.

Ditte Nissen is aware of the morally compromised position of an implicated subject, as both speaking about and letting the archive of her perpetrator family members speak is charged with great ambivalence.[55] Should the violence of their words remain forever silent, or can (re)listening prompt reflection, especially among those with implicated positions? This question concerns the possibility of moving away from guilt into responsibility by transforming the relationship to memory.

By decentralizing her research at the Usumacinta River bordering Mexico and Guatemala, ancira's text approaches Stephanie Misa's "An Altar for the Fleshy Tongue," also part of this anthology. In discussing her mother tongue and how colonized communities ensured its survival, Misa also chooses a strategy of decentralization, dedicating her research to a language erased by colonialism. She moves between Bisaya, spoken in the central region of the Philippines, and the only recordings of a Tasmanian First Nation's language. Confronted with a technical inscription and reproduction medium that leaves these recordings in a liminal space between imprinting and erasure, Misa finds the body to be the archive where languages are held, "the tongue as the site where language leaves the body and enters the world." Misa's text *slows time*, which is the mode of the archive and the premise we need to permeate and be permeated by the experiences of others.

Writing

Many of our collaborative writing exercises have stemmed from how we've conceptualized and documented our various projects. I think of the many texts written by Gudrun Ingenthron, our invented overachieving curatorial persona.[56]

Our shared interest in the theme of the present book was already evident in "Field Within," an exhibition conceived by Ingenthron around 2016 that you curated for xE in 2019.[57] The seeds of our collaborative writing were sown. "Field Within" was our first exploration into recent expressions of the ethnographic turn in contemporary art. Cana Bilir-Meier, Stephanie Misa, and Verena Melgarejo Weinandt were also part of that exhibition.

In his 1982 essay "Self Writing," Michel Foucault explores the transformative power that writing can have on one's identity.[58] Through his archaeological method, he traces and reconstructs a range of practices—including diary keeping, writing confessions, letters, and autobiographies—through which individuals have engaged in self-examination and self-transformation throughout time. In a different paper from the same year, Foucault proposes a genealogy of the technologies of the self, from Greco-Roman philosophy and the early Roman Empire to Christianity. From his analysis of these historical periods and their modes of thought, he concludes that the maxim "Know yourself" eventually came to obscure the most basic principle of "Take care of yourself."[59] Foucault gave different reasons for this "inversion between the hierarchy of

55 Michael Rothberg, *The Implicated Subject: Beyond Victims and Perpetrators* (Stanford, CA: Stanford University Press, 2019), 36.

56 Gudrun Ingenthron was a persona embodied through the curatorial collective formed by Ana de Almeida, Mariel Rodríguez, and Catalina Ravessoud (also a former Master in Critical Studies student). Ingenthron was active between 2013 and 2019. Her aim was to put all our expertise, curricula, contacts, ideas, and talents together to create a persona: a talented young curator, probably German or from a German-speaking country, who could speak eight languages and had degrees in art, Greek history, the humanities, philosophy, and critical studies.

57 "Field Within," curated by Mariel Rodríguez, Academy of Fine Arts Vienna, accessed July 30, 2024, https://www.akbild.ac.at/en/museum-and -exhibitions/Exhibit/exhibitions-events/current-exhibitions/2019/field-within?set _language=en.

58 Foucault, "Self Writing."

59 Michel Foucault, "Technologies of the Self," in *Technologies of the Self: A Seminar with Michel Foucault*, ed. Luther H. Martin, Huck Gutman, and Patrick H. Hutton (Amherst: University of Massachusetts Press, 1988), 22.

the two principles of antiquity," such as the importance given to morality in Christianity, whose legacy is present in the modern values attributed to self-knowledge.[60] He traces these transitions from the perspective of Western European philosophical traditions, starting from the modern period, when attention turns toward knowledge of the cognizant subject while practices of care are practically forgotten. This might be one of the reasons Ruth Sonderegger initially felt uneasy with our invitation to contribute to this volume. Western philosophy, as she writes, has historically been responsible for disseminating Eurocentrism, racism, and anti-Semitism, while claiming the authority to do so in the name of producing knowledge about the subject. The late writings of Foucault thus contribute to a broader exploration of the relationship between power, knowledge, and the individual by emphasizing the significance of writing as a form of caring for the self. For him, writing as an art of oneself has "an ethopoietic function: it is an agent of the transformation of truth into ethos."[61]

I think it is important to examine not only the relationship between artistic practices and writing but also the connection between artistic practices and reading. The anthropologist Kamala Visweswaran lays this out in terms of the connection between ethnography and literature. She reflects on their functions by thinking of ethnography as literature and literature as ethnography. Interestingly, the relation between the two is not found in autobiography or other potentially documentary literary forms. Instead, she finds ethnography to be closer to fiction, for both share a constructivist logic in their—of course different—world-making practices. "Ethnography, like fiction, no matter its pretense to present a self-contained narrative or cultural whole, remains incomplete and detached from the realms to which it points."[62]

During the winter semester in 2013/14, Anette Baldauf, Sonderegger, and Jakob Krameritsch offered a writers' workshop to inspire the process of writing along with improving our writing skills. This workshop addressed writing as a means of storytelling.[63] I enjoyed the workshop, as it allowed me to take my experiments with writing seriously. Or maybe it was the other way around, allowing me to take writing less seriously and letting play become part of the process. I embraced experimentation and let alternative writing methods influence my practice. Moreover, the workshop helped me realize that the anxiety of facing a blank page is a common experience that can be overcome through creative writing exercises and consistent practice.

Incorporating writing as a form of research has become integral to our practice, and writing as a collaborative process has played a significant role in this. Through collective writing, I've discovered that I can achieve things that I couldn't on my own. But I must say, it works well specifically because you are my interlocutor. Perhaps it's the many common experiences that have brought us to collaborate or the synergy that comes from having common goals. While I'm not entirely sure of the exact reasons, I do know that I genuinely enjoy the process of writing with you.

Writing is active thinking—tracing and connecting the dots. In this sense, in the art of writing self-reflexivity is a

60 Foucault, 22.

61 Foucault, "Self Writing," 209.

62 See Kamala Visweswaran, *Fictions of Feminist Ethnography* (Minneapolis: University of Minnesota Press, 2003), 1.

63 "If we approach the writing of a dissertation as a means of storytelling, what story do we want to convey? What are some of the devices that support us in the making of a compelling story? What happens when we redirect our research imagination and fictionalize our project? How does fiction—critical fiction, fictocriticism, speculative fiction—help us to grasp the wider significance of our conceptual framework and research question? Finally, how do we integrate these devices into our everyday writing, the writing of articles, essays, chapters or even grant proposals?" Writers' Workshop, Academy of Fine Arts Vienna, 2013/14.

form of documentation and attitude to research in which the curiosity in one's own positioning and situatedness can speak about topics broader than the self. As Gloria Anzaldúa proposes, writing is the activity that most effectively allows for opening up a space to handle difficult emotions produced by the wounds inflicted on us, our communities, and our ancestors. In this respect, the idea of writing oneself into research is tightly linked to healing; it traverses all the texts in this volume.[64]

This is an anthology of texts by artists who write. And they do so in different ways. Through writing, one can access different registers of identity, memory, and emotion, producing texts open to polyvocality and combining various forms of knowledge that navigate history, autobiography, mythology, and personal observations, an ideal medium to deal with the aftermath of extreme violence, both inflicted and perpetrated. It is a glimpse into the many worlds and world-making processes that take place through art and, in this specific narration, establish a dialogue through their encounters in Vienna.

64 Anzaldúa, *Light in the Dark*, 1; Gloria Anzaldúa, *Borderlands / La Frontera: The New Mestiza* (San Francisco: Aunt Lute Books, 2012).

Literature

Abou Hatab, Marwa, Ana de Almeida, Diedrich Diederichsen, Vasilena Gankovska, Moira Hille, Laura Nitsch, and Constanze Ruhm. "Einfach dranbleiben: 10 Jahre Critical Studies – Eine Roundtable-Diskussion zum Master." In *Big Critical Energy*, edited by Leonie Huber, Valerie Ludwig, and Andrea Zabric, 52–64. Vienna: Schlebrügge.Editor, 2021.

Abu-Lughod, Lila. "Writing against Culture." In *Recapturing Anthropology: Working in the Present*, edited by Richard G. Fox, 137–62. Santa Fe, NM: School of American Research Press, 1996.

Anzaldúa, Gloria. *Borderlands / La Frontera: The New Mestiza*. San Francisco: Aunt Lute Books, 2012.

Anzaldúa, Gloria. *Light in the Dark / Luz en lo oscuro: Rewriting Identity, Spirituality, Reality*, edited by AnaLouise Keating. Durham, NC: Duke University Press, 2015.

Appadurai, Arjun. *Modernity at Large: Cultural Dimensions of Globalization*. Minneapolis: University of Minnesota Press, 1996.

Barad, Karen. *Meeting the Universe Halfway: Quantum Physics and the Entanglement of Matter and Meaning*. Durham, NC: Duke University Press, 2007.

Blasi, Rosemarie. *Kritik am Bologna-Prozess aus der Sicht der Studierenden*. Munich: Grin, 2011.

Braidotti, Rosi. *Nomadic Subjects: Embodiment and Sexual Difference in Contemporary Feminist Theory*. New York: Columbia University Press, 1994.

Conrad, Sebastian, Shalini Randeria, and Regina Römhild. "Einleitung: Geteilte Geschichten – Europa in einer postkolonialen Welt." In *Jenseits des Eurozentrismus: Postkoloniale Perspektiven in den Geschichts- und Kulturwissenschaften*, 2nd ed., edited by Sebastian Conrad, Shalini Randeria, and Regina Römhild, 32–70. Frankfurt: Campus Verlag, 2013.

Crenshaw, Kimberlé. "Mapping the Margins: Intersectionality, Identity Politics, and Violence against Women of Color." *Stanford Law Review* 43, no. 6 (1991): 1241–99. https://doi.org/10.2307/1229039.

Dokuzović, Lina, and Eduard Freudmann. "Squatting the Crisis: On the Current Protest in Education and Perspectives on Radical Change." *eipcp*, November 2009. https://eipcp.net/projects/creatingworlds/dokuzovic-freudmann/en.html.

European Students' Union. *Bologna with Student Eyes 2009*. https://esu-online.org/wp-content/uploads/2024/06/Bologna-With-Student-Eyes_2009_565284.pdf.

Fals Borda, Orlando. *Una sociología sentipensante para América Latina*. Edited by Víctor Manuel Moncayo. Mexico City: Siglo XXI Editores, 2015.

Fanon, Frantz. *The Wretched of the Earth*. Translated by Richard Philcox. New York: Grove Press, 2004.

Foster, Hal. "The Artist as Ethnographer?" In *The Return of the Real*, 171–204. Cambridge, MA: MIT Press, 1996.

Foucault, Michel. "Self Writing." In *Ethics: Subjectivity and Truth*, edited by Paul Rabinow, translated by Robert Hurley et al., 207–22. New York: New York Press, 1994.

Foucault, Michel. "Technologies of the Self." In *Technologies of the Self: A Seminar with Michel Foucault*, edited by Luther H. Martin, Huck Gutman, and Patrick H. Hutton, 16–49. Amherst: University of Massachusetts Press, 1988.

Freudmann, Eduard. "'Swastikas? Ornaments!' as a Continuity of Repression: History-Political Conditions of a Public Art and Educational Institution." Translated by Lina Dokuzović. *an-academy*, October 2010. https://transversal.at/transversal/1210/freudmann/en.

Green, Renée. "Other Planes, Different Phases, My Geometry, Times, Movements: Becomings Ongoing." In

Other Planes of There: Selected Writings, 1–18. Durham, NC: Duke University Press, 2014.

Gupta, Akhil, and James Ferguson. "Discipline and Practice: 'The Field' as Site, Method, and Location in Anthropology." In *Anthropological Locations: Boundaries and Grounds for a Field Science*, edited by Akhil Gupta and James Ferguson, 1–46. Berkeley: University of California Press, 1998.

Hall, Stuart. "Cultural Identity and Diaspora." In *Selected Writings on Race and Difference*, edited by Paul Gilroy and Ruth Wilson Gilmore, 257–71. Durham, NC: Duke University Press, 2021.

Haraway, Donna. "Situated Knowledges: The Science Question in Feminism and the Privilege of Partial Perspective." *Feminist Studies* 14, no. 3 (1988): 575–99.

Harding, Sandra. "Stronger Objectivity for Sciences from Below." In *Objectivity and Diversity: Another Logic of Scientific Research*. Chicago: University of Chicago Press, 2015.

hooks, bell. "Art on My Mind." In *Art on My Mind: Visual Politics*, 1–9. New York: New Press, 1995.

Kastner, Jens, and Lea Susemichel. *Identitätspolitiken: Konzepte und Kritiken in Geschichte und Gegenwart der Linken*. Münster: Unrast, 2022.

Latour, Bruno. *Reassembling the Social: An Introduction to Actor-Network-Theory*. Oxford: Oxford University Press, 2005.

Pechar, Hans, and Angela Wroblewski. "Die Auswirkungen von Bologna auf die Lage der Studierenden in Österreich." *Zeitschrift für Hochschulentwicklung*, no. 2 (June 2011): 1–14.

Pratt, Mary Louise. *Imperial Eyes: Travel Writing and Transculturation*. London: Routledge, 1992.

Rich, Adrienne. "Notes toward a Politics of Location." In *Blood, Bread, Poetry: Selected Prose, 1979–1984*, 210–31. New York: Norton, 1986.

Rothberg, Michael. *The Implicated Subject: Beyond Victims and Perpetrators*. Stanford, CA: Stanford University Press, 2019.

Rothberg, Michael. *Multidirectional Memory: Remembering the Holocaust in the Age of Decolonization*. Stanford, CA: Stanford University Press, 2009.

Saramago, José. *O conto da ilha desconhecida*. Lisbon: Assírio & Alvim, 1997.

Spivak, Gayatri Chakravorty. "Subaltern Studies: Deconstructing Historiography." In *Selected Subaltern Studies*, edited by Ranajit Guha and Gayatri Chakravorty Spivak, 3–32. Oxford: Oxford University Press, 1988.

Sternfeld, Nora. "Situierter Universalismus: Warum der Partikularismus der Befreiung und der Universalismus, in den sie sich befreit, keine Gegensätze sind." In *After Europe: Beiträge zur dekolonialen Kritik*, edited by Julian Warner, 67–78. Berlin: Verbrecher, 2021.

Thompson, Becky. "Multiracial Feminism: Recasting the Chronology of Second Wave Feminism." *Feminist Studies* 28, no. 2 (Summer 2002): 336–60.

Smith, Linda Tuhiwai. *Decolonizing Methodologies: Research and Indigenous Peoples*. London: Zed Books, 2012.

Tsing, Anna Lowenhaupt. *The Mushroom at the End of the World: On the Possibility of Life in Capitalist Ruins*. Princeton, NJ: Princeton University Press, 2015.

Tuck, Eve, and K. Wayne Yang. "R-Words: Refusing Research." In *Humanizing Research: Decolonizing Qualitative Inquiry with Youth and Communities*, edited by Django Paris and Maisha T. Winn, 223–48. London: SAGE Publications, 2014.

Visweswaran, Kamala. *Fictions of Feminist Ethnography*. Minneapolis: University of Minnesota Press, 2003.

Young, Stacey. *Changing the Wor(l)d: Discourse, Politics, and the Feminist Movement*. New York: Routledge, 1997.

Olena Khoroshylova

Sofa, Zimmer, Wohnung
Forced Migration and Women in Partnerships

On January 5, 2023, during a seven-hour drive with my two young children back "home" to Upper Austria, I thought about the impending first anniversary of our forced migration—an experience that was meant to last only a few weeks. Two significant changes stood out from the past year: a growing reluctance to regard houses and buildings as home, and my evolving friendship with two female refugees, who have become crucial partners in living through this displacement.

We were returning from a brief trip to Belgium, where my best friend, her twelve-year-old disabled daughter, and another close female companion had sought refuge from the ongoing Russian war in Ukraine. Eventually they were sheltered in an opulent villa with an extensive maze of rooms, adorned with an elegant English garden. However, many events unfolded before they reached that point. In late February 2022, Oksana and her daughter, Vira, were still in Kyiv, despite the incessant bombings.[1] While the news was forecasting

Kyiv's imminent downfall, Oksana conducted daily online art therapy sessions for children, providing a semblance of normalcy amid the chaos. Two weeks later, witnessing the impact of the continuous shelling on her daughter's mental state, Oksana made the difficult decision to leave. The next day, they maneuvered through the immense crowds in Kyiv's main railway station, boarding a train to Lviv in western Ukraine. The train was so full that they had to stand for the entire sixteen-hour journey. That same day I tried to arrange Oksana's onward journey to Europe.[2] However, upon finalizing the arrangements, I discovered that she required not two but three seats, as another female friend was now traveling with them. Thus commenced their six-month partnership in exile. It was at this point that I first noticed the changes in women's choices and strategies in times of urgency.[3]

Since March 2022, Ukrainian refugees have found shelter in Austria and other countries of the EU. Different from the previous years, when people were forced to move owing to wars in Syria, Afghanistan, and other regions, Ukrainians were immediately granted the right to work and relocate themselves and their families within the EU as they chose. I later would learn that the differences in access, and consequently in status, of Ukrainians and other refugees

1 Names have been changed.

2 Although Ukraine is in Europe, I use the term "Europe" to refer to the countries west of Ukraine to stay true to the way my Ukrainian friends and I refer to them colloquially, which mirrors our perception of Ukraine as existing in a liminal space compressed between two outsides: what we understand as Europe and Russia.

3 While one might debate the definition of "women" in the context of the latest refugee waves (for example, the United Nations' focus since 2015 on the gender-specific challenges and risks refugee and migrant women and girls face), this text frames women as a foundation for solidarity rather than a UN- or state-defined category. These solidarity networks can be built among people entering the country legally or illegally as well as based on self-determined categories. For more on the UN's studies, see "Women Refugees and Migrants," UN Women Europe and Central Asia, accessed March 7, 2023, https://eca.unwomen.org/en /news/in-focus/women-refugees-and-migrants-0.

in many EU countries occurred through the activation of the Temporary Protection Directive of the European Commission. This measure, adopted following the conflicts in the former Yugoslavia in the 1990s, was triggered for the first time on March 4, 2022, to offer "quick and effective assistance to people fleeing the war in Ukraine."[4]

I heard about these differences here and there, but they became shockingly clear three months after my arrival in Austria. I was helping the Berlin-based artist Alicja Rogalska with childcare while she finished installing a work in the outdoor exhibition "What Can be Done? Solidarity Practices," curated by Michaela Geboltsberger in Traiskirchen,[5] a town that is home to the Bundesbetreuungsstelle für Asylwerber (Federal Office of Assistance for Asylum Seekers) and the largest refugee camp in Austria.[6] Rogalska's work, *Alterations*—a collaboration with Zahra Akbari, Bashirahmad Hasanzadeh, Roya Nasrati, Obaidullah Shirzad, Paulina Semkowicz, and Margot Handler—dealt with the recognition (or lack thereof) of foreign work qualifications and university degrees in Austria, and the obstacles this creates for refugees.[7] As artistic interventions in public space, many works in the show dealt with displacement, visibility versus invisibility, and the condition of being a refugee. Changes in Austrian refugee policy were a constant topic in this town, where people have arrived in waves since 1956. The biggest and still current concern was about the people who had arrived from Iraq and Syria in 2015; a report from that year by Amnesty International attests to the degrading treatment of refugees in Traiskirchen.[8]

As I drove to Upper Austria, I kept thinking: 1956 Hungary, 1968 Czechoslovakia, 1973 Chile, 1982 Poland, 1989 Romania, the 1990s the Balkans, 1999 Afghanistan, later Iraq and Syria … 2022 Ukraine. What distinguishes us displaced people?

What was going on politically in Austria each time masses of desperate people fled to this country? I reminded myself that a defining aspect of the forced migration wave I'm part of is its gender ratio, which sets it apart from previous migrations. Ukrainian martial law restricts men from leaving Ukraine. Along with instances of illegal border crossings, there are a limited number of legal exceptions permitting men to exit the country. According to the United Nations, 73 percent of individuals fleeing Ukraine are women.[9]

Apparently, the self-perception of Ukrainian women who arrive in Vienna is far removed from that of the "refugee." These self-images emphasize a geographical and cultural proximity to Austria and might express negative attitudes toward refugees from other countries. A study published by the University of Vienna in September 2022 shows that this perception—which distances Ukrainian women from other refugees in Austria—has become common.[10] Nevertheless, upon my arrival in Austria as a refugee, I was swiftly confronted with political and administrative structures that

4 "Temporary Protection," European Commission, accessed March 7, 2023, https://home-affairs.ec.europa.eu/policies/migration-and-asylum/common -european-asylum-system/temporary-protection_en.

5 "What Can Be Done? Practices of Solidarity," Kunst im öffentlichen Raum Niederösterreich, accessed March 7, 2023, https://koernoe.at/en/project/what -can-be-done-practices-of-solidarity.

6 "Erstaufnahmestelle Ost," Stadtgemeinde Traiskirchen, accessed March 7, 2023, https://www.traiskirchen.gv.at/portrait-traiskirchen /erstaufnahmezentrum/.

7 For more on *Alterations*, see "What Can Be Done?"; and Helga Kusolitsch, "Alicja Rogalska," June 30, 2022, https://helgakusolitsch.at/2022/06/30/9629/.

8 *Quo vadis Austria? Die Situation in Traiskirchen darf nicht die Zukunft der Flüchtlingsbetreuung in Österreich werden* (Vienna: Amnesty International Österreich, 2015), https://www.amnesty.at/media/1928/research-traiskirchen.pdf.

9 "Women Refugees and Migrants."

10 Sieglinde Rosenberger and Anna Lazareva, "'Ich wollte auf Urlaub und nicht als Geflüchtete nach Österreich kommen': Vertriebene Ukrainerinnen in Wien" (research report, Universität Wien, Vienna, September 2022), https://inex .univie.ac.at/fileadmin/user_upload/p_inex/Rosenberger-Lazareva-Bericht _Ukraine_Vertriebene_.pdf.

delineated the essence of being a refugee: defining my needs, outlining my limitations, and mapping out the steps toward my integration. It soon became evident that this archetype of the refugee scarcely acknowledges my identity as a woman or my responsibility as a caregiver, attributes me with marginal intelligence and skills, and displays a limited comprehension of the drastic change between my recent past—when I was working and nurturing children alongside my male partner within the communal setting of family and friends—and my current isolation from these networks of mental and material support.

In the meantime, a political desire for seemingly simple solutions—aimed at controlling refugees by confining them to predictable living and behavioral frameworks—drives authorities to compartmentalize the rights and obligations of displaced women, including their need for shelter, financial support, work, and integration into the host society. Nevertheless, these processes remain closely linked to a preconceived, static, and gender-neutral notion of the "refugee."[11] A tension emerges between the actual nature of something and its design or portrayal. The construct of the refugee, while initially providing a sense of security through state-backed support and physical safety, also triggers a profound sense of dismay by extinguishing hopes of returning home and restoring life to its former state.

Intersection

Back to my road trip. The name on the highway sign buzzed with familiarity. Though I was driving this route for the first time, my memory pushed forth the words "Nürnberg, Fürth, Waldstraße 99, Flößaustraße 20," as if recollecting the address for an important meeting. Finally, I could clearly visualize the page where I had read this. My pulse quickened—I was speechless. I recognized it as the place where my grandmother Kovalyova Maria Fedorivna was held by the Nazis as a forced laborer during the Second World War. From 1942 to 1945, she lived in the barracks at Waldstraße 99 in Fürth, Germany. Every single day, she and the other prisoners had to walk forty minutes to the military factory at Flößaustraße 20. The fact that I knew the damn address by heart, just as she did, made me consider changing my itinerary to confront my desire to be a witness.

Surname, first name, patronymic: Kovalyova Maria Fedorivna.

Year of birth: March 26, 1927.

Place of residence at the time of exile: Dnipro region, Krynychky district, the village of Khutir Batkivka.

Place of residence in Germany: From 9 July 1942 was registered in Fürth, Flößaustraße 20, and from 25 January 1944 in Fürth, Waldstraße 99, a camp.

Length of stay: Two years and nine months.

Date of release: May 20, 1945.

Country of residence: Ukraine.

I, Kovalyova Maria Fedorivna, maiden name Fedorenko, was living with my family in the village of Khutir Batkivka, Krynychky district, Dnipro region, at the outbreak of the war. There were four children in the family, me and my three younger sisters. […]

The territory of our district was occupied from August 8, 1941, to October 28, 1943. We were captured by the

11 See "Gender," UN Refugee Agency Integration Handbook, last updated March 9, 2024, https://www.unhcr.org/handbooks/ih/age-gender-diversity /gender; "Flucht und Gender," Netzwerk Fluchtforschung, accessed March 7, 2023, https://fluchtforschung.net/arbeitskreise/flucht-und-gender/.

advancing troops, but then they left and only the rear areas remained. We could not evacuate because we had no idea where to go.

[…]

In June 1942, I was taken to Germany. A week before departure, we passed a medical examination. […]

In the evening, the headman [of the village] came to us and warned us that we were leaving tomorrow, and ordered us to pack our things. In the morning, a cart came to pick up all the girls one by one.

[…]

We were taken to the train. My father came with me, and the other girls were accompanied by their relatives. We were put into a freight car.[12]

At the age of fifteen, my grandmother Kovalyova Maria Fedorivna was taken from Ukraine to Germany to perform forced labor. She was in the city of Fürth from 1942 to 1945 as an *Ostarbeiterin*, an unpaid worker in a Nazi military factory.[13] Almost sixty years later, when I was fifteen myself, I conducted an in-depth interview with her about her experience for a school publication. Though the interview started as a student assignment, it quickly became an opportunity to catch up on missed dialogues. During family gatherings or kitchen chats, we never spoke about "Germany"—the name our family gave to this period of my grandmother's life. Legitimizing questions that were previously off-limits, the interview opened a door to the historical and political context of a typical working-class family in Ukraine in the early 2000s.

The conversations I had with my grandmother during that time—and there were many, as we started to meet regularly—were intimate and brought us closer. At the time, I didn't realize that these were significant encounters. Now, twenty years later, memories of them still move me. For me, a Ukrainian forced migrant with two small children residing in Austria because of a war initiated by Russia, the experience of interviewing my grandmother has become an invaluable bridge connecting history, politics, and culture.

I recorded the series of interviews by hand, striving to capture every word and ensuring I wrote down the exact phrases she used. It seemed that within these precise formulations I might reveal some kind of hidden code that divulged what she experienced but did not want to mention in front of her grandchild. The interview was rich in details, facts, and chronology of the typical experience that she, as a forced woman laborer from the east, had in Germany during the Second World War. The text proved valuable, and not only to me. In 2005, it was published in the anthology *Tsei bil u sertsi ne vshchukhaye: Zbirka uchnivskykh referativ* (This Heartache Never Subsides: A Collection of Student Essays). According to some sources, the text was subsequently transferred to a German archive, but I haven't been able to confirm this yet.

I stopped the car and searched on Google Maps for Flößaustraße 20 and Waldstraße 99 in the city of Fürth. From my interviews with Maria, I knew these addresses were within walking distance of each other, so the plan was to find a nearby hotel and attempt to follow the same path she had. The next morning, the kids stayed in the hotel's playroom while

12 Olena Kovalyova, "Poloneni viyny" [Captives of war], in *Tsei bil u sertsi ne vshchukhaye: Zbirka uchnivskykh referativ* [This heartache never subsides: A collection of student essays], ed. Serhiy Baturyn and Lyubov Sochka (Lviv: Kalvaria, 2005), 115–20. Kovalyova is the author's maiden name. Quotations have been translated by the author unless stated otherwise.

13 *Ostarbeiter/in* was a term given by Nazis to forced laborers from "the east," namely Ukraine and neighboring areas.

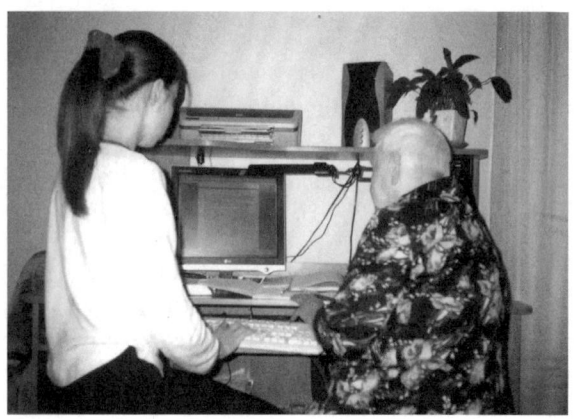

Fig. 1 Interviewing Maria in 2004

I went to the address of the barracks. It was freezing, and I thought of the wooden clogs Maria had mentioned, picturing for a moment how she might have walked in them. I parked the car in a shopping-center parking lot and began to search for the building. Google suggested that I was in the right place, but I still couldn't figure out the exact location of the building with the number 99. I wandered in different directions, almost losing hope of finding the address. Suddenly, I turned around and looked at the entire complex from a distance. It was a wide, simple, rectangular, boxlike building without any type of architectural style or specific design. Inside, small shops and labyrinthine corridors were visible. The building looked like a replica of the shopping center that was built near our house in Kryvyi Rih in the late 2000s. The same blend of architectural indifference and economic efficiency had produced almost identical structures in two different contexts. Near the central entrance, without any indication of the street name, the number 99 was barely visible. It was already clear that I would not find any visual hint of what the barracks looked like or what happened there in the 1940s, whether it had been demolished or rebuilt. I stood in front of the door through which the past could not be seen. "From the outset, the now legendary [...] reconstruction of the country," writes W. G. Sebald, "after the devastation wrought by Germany's wartime enemies, a reconstruction tantamount to a second liquidation in successive phases of the nation's own past history, prohibited any look backward."[14]

Illuminated Rooms, Darkened Windows: Living through Displacement

Upon arrival, we were counted. As far as I can remember, there were ninety of us. [...] We were all accommodated together in one room at Waldstraße 99. [...] The house we lived in had two floors. I don't know what was on the first floor, because we always went straight up the stairs to the second floor. There was a large room on the second floor that was quite illuminated, but at night we had to cover the windows with black paper so that the light would not be visible during the bombing. The room had tables, wardrobes, and beds that stood by the windows. The beds were wooden, bunk beds with mattresses and bedding. The room was washed and cleaned every day, and the linen was changed once a week. We were lucky that there were no cockroaches, mice, or rats in the room, which could spread diseases. Later, for convenience, we were transferred to Flößaustraße, so as not to have to walk

14 W. G. Sebald, *On the Natural History of Destruction*, trans. Anthea Bell (New York: Random House, 2003), 7.

across the city every day. There we were accommodated on the fourth floor. The living conditions were the same.[15]

The privilege of having had this conversation with Maria opened a completely new perspective on my own experience of forced migration and that of other women. Namely, how the typologies of housing for forced women migrants are interconnected with their strategies for survival, adaptation, and socialization.

In the summer of 2022, I wandered through the corridors of the University of Arts Linz. I planned to propose a course for the next semester and was interested in getting to know the university. In the large hall on the first floor, student posters and flyers were hung haphazardly. One, in an attempt to find affordable accommodation, succinctly declared "Sofa, Zimmer, Wohnung" (sofa, room, apartment). It occurred to me that these three words encapsulated my entire route as a refugee from Ukraine to Austria. Moreover, they serve as a concise representation of the shelter typologies encountered by migrant women—and correspondingly, the scenarios in which they find themselves.

It is difficult to call these new spaces home. Consequently, they are often described only by their spatial characteristics: "I was given a bed," "We were allocated a separate room," "We were provided with an apartment." In these temporary spaces, trajectories through the private realms of bedroom, bathroom, and kitchen, as well as the outer spaces of socialization, are being established. The new forced routine is painful, exposed, vulnerable, and disorienting, pushing individuals toward self-reflection and self-discovery. The feeling of alienation in places you didn't choose to be is familiar to me. Each point of light in the celestial tapestry of

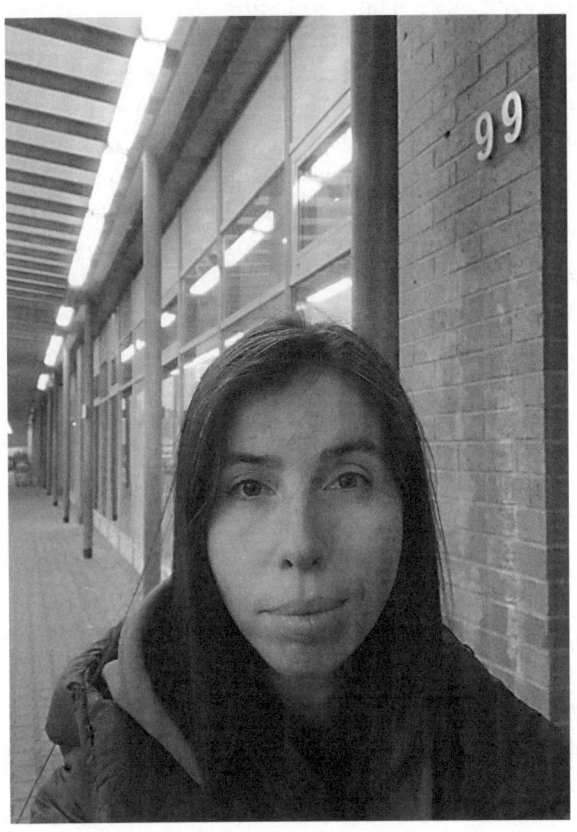

Fig. 2 My visit to Waldstraße 99, Fürth, January 2023

15 As a fifteen-year-old, I wondered what these bombings inside Germany could be. After all, Germany was the aggressor—did they attack themselves? Much later, from Sebald's *On the Natural History of Destruction*, I learned that this had to do with the Allied bombings of the civilian population.

forced migration not only represents a life uprooted from its native constellation but also testifies to the void left behind in both physical and mental space.

Looking deeper at the reverberations between spaces and people, I focused on the living conditions, preferences, and borders that forced women migrants might (or might not) build in communal settings, ranging from someone's couch to shared living at a shelter. But at the same time, I wanted to explore the disruptions in the everyday life of women refugees. This was the starting point for the artistic-research course "Sofa, Zimmer, Wohnung: How the Loss of Living Routine Affects Forced Migrated Women," which I conducted with the sociologist Daryna Pyrogova at the University of Arts Linz between October 2023 and February 2024.

Under Pyrogova's guidance, students conducted in-depth interviews with almost a dozen forced migrant women from Ukraine and three from Iran. The experience of Ukrainian women refugees was a focus of the research—but not limited to it—because this wave of migration was recent and included so many women. The course was an extension of Pyrogova's research with Oleksandra Tarkhanova, a Swiss colleague of Ukrainian origin, which "sheds light on the particular conditions under which Ukrainians made their migration decisions and illustrates how this case of displacement allows focusing on the decision-making process when many external constraints faced by other migrant populations are absent."[16] This was the context for the students' interviews, which they conducted independently.

At the start of the course, I was seeking a different reflection, a different mirror than the one I had been looking into; there, I was eager to see what the participants would discover. I feared delving into this experience alone, and had the overwhelming desire to view it through the broader perspective offered by the experiences of other migrant women, and not just those from Ukraine. The method we planned for the artistic research was influenced, across time, by my interview of Maria, and created a new layer of "missed dialogues" with forced migrants. For example, an artist from Iran made an unexpected discovery during the course—which, although it might have seemed obvious to outsiders, the artist hadn't yet considered. Interviewing their aunt, the student learned that she could never return to Iran due to the danger of being persecuted for leaving illegally twenty years ago. This realization was contrasted with the experiences of Ukrainian women who had briefly visited Ukraine to reconnect with places, family, and friends, but who still had to remain in Austria for the safety of themselves and their children.

According to the typologies I selected to represent certain experiences and their scenarios, Maria was given a sofa to sleep on and, periodically in 1943 and 1944, visited an apartment (*Wohnung*) to work for a German woman. From Maria's testimony, I also learned that the forced women laborers were relocated from one address to another. For most people, the sudden loss of domestic routine is itself quite painful, whether it be an apartment that accidentally burned down because an iron was left on or a house that was destroyed by an air-raid bomb. In these situations, the psyche tries to hold on to objects that once represented home. Toni Alberti, another seminar participant, called this phenomenon "gravity," and created a poetic confession accompanied by a digital phantom. First shown with a projector and later printed on paper, the work conjures mixed feelings. It evokes something that could have been created manually in a material form or,

16 Oleksandra Tarkhanova and Daryna Pyrogova, "Forced Displacement in Ukraine: Understanding the Decision-Making Process." *European Societies* 26, no. 2 (2023): 481–500, doi:10.1080/14616696.2023.2280680.

conversely, might not have left the confines of digital reality. This effect enhances the ambivalence of the migrant in discerning reality from the phantoms of the world left behind.

Another approach was taken by Carlotta Borcherding and the performer Veronika Maidukova, who had to flee Ukraine. In an interview with Borcherding, Maidukova described how, when rushing to leave her home, she took only the things she couldn't live without, which included her dance leotards, instead of more practical items. Photographing a performance by Maidukova, Borcherding documents her fundamental need to be a dancer and the pain of choosing what of her former self to leave behind. The photo series illustrates the states of self-reinvention by a forced women migrant within not only the physical boundaries of new housing but also the inner rooms of self-reflection.[17]

In October 2023, Alberti and Borcherding displayed the artistic projects they developed following cross-disciplinary research. The exhibition took place in the windows of a typical one-room ground-floor apartment in central Kyiv that had been partially vacated by its occupants after the onset of the full-scale invasion in 2022. The space itself—essentially just a sofa, room, and apartment—embodied the three housing typologies that formed the starting point of their exploration. The works could be seen in the windows by passersby only in the evening, emphasizing the absence of its residents.

Cooperation

Stopping at Waldstraße 99, I recalled several episodes from Maria's experiences in the barracks. I was grateful to finally match the description with this location.

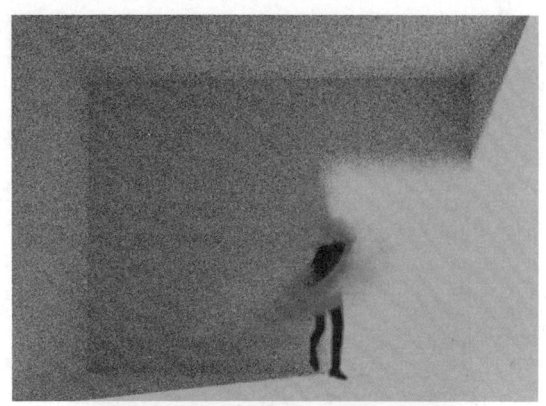

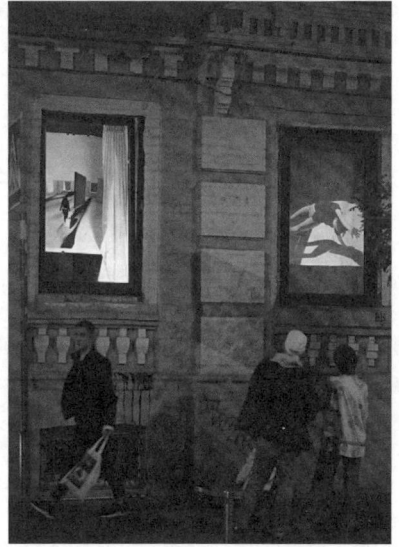

Fig. 3 Toni Alberti, *Gravity (1/3)*, 2023. Digital collage.
Fig. 4 "Sofa, Zimmer, Wohnung," exhibition view, Kyiv, October 2023.

17 See Carlotta Borcherding, "untitled (2023)," accessed March 7, 2023,
https://carlottaborcherding.cargo.site/.

All this time, the girls I left the village with stuck together, tried to always do the same jobs, help each other, share all the crumbs we had. […]

Apart from the clothes we arrived in, we had nothing else. We wore the same clothes in winter and summer. Over time the shoes wore out too and we were given wooden shoes. It was something like a wooden block with a belt attached to it. Since we had no other shoes, we had to wear them in any weather. Our feet were very cold in winter, and we tried to get to the factory quickly so that our feet did not have time to freeze. After a few years, we had almost no clothes left, everything was worn out to the hilt. The clothes looked like rags. One day we noticed that the military overcoats had woolen linings on them, which could be used to make something for ourselves. Since only the girls and I worked with the finished overcoats, and only we could cut off these linings unnoticed, while the Germans went to lunch we stayed and cut them off. Then we would tie them to our belts and take them out of the factory in the evening. When we got home, we would distribute the cut pieces to everyone. The girls started making clothes from them. I made a sundress and a blouse. Everyone was so happy to have warm clothes that they didn't even want to think about the possibility of being found out. But that's exactly what happened. A month later, my friend and I were spotted. We were sent to a labor camp in Langenzenn as a punishment. I was placed in an isolated cell there for about two months. The most terrifying two months of my life.

My grandmother didn't want me to make an audio recording of her telling her story. She harbored a sense of shame linked to the act of theft, perceiving it as unacceptable even under the circumstances. But the narrative held importance, prompting my desire to document it. However, it was a challenge to acquire further details. The barrier was breached when I asked about the fate of the stolen items. It seemed to me that it wasn't a seventy-seven-year-old woman who responded, but rather the teenage girl who had so desperately believed in their childish plan.

My grandmother's story was typical for forced migrant women survivors in Ukraine. Interestingly, cooperation was a key aspect of her communal dwelling in barracks, which connects the experiences of the current generation to those of my grandmother's generation. While not directly comparable, the cases are still related.

Everywhere, I encountered more and more stories of Ukrainian women "sticking together" to better survive in exile. The range of resilient alliances that I and many other women have been forming exceeds what was expected or imagined by the host countries and the women themselves.

What can we uncover about the fresh wave of Ukrainian migration through looking at the actual experience of forced migration? Exploring the coping mechanisms that women employed, such as shared budgets, co-parenting, and communal living, reveals a profound resilience and adaptability. Shared budgets help pool financial resources, making it easier to handle economic challenges. Co-parenting arrangements allow for shared childcare, easing the burden on individual mothers. Communal living provides emotional support and a sense of community, which are crucial for psychological well-being in exile. Through these practices, Ukrainian women demonstrate a powerful capacity for creating supportive networks that enhance their collective survival and integration in new environments.

Communes and Communal Ways of Reassembling Routine

Architects believe that buildings, space, and accommodations play a significant role in shaping behavior. Early modernists actively experimented with the design of communal dwellings, envisioning them as stimuli for the formation of communes. Such projects were often designed with large shared and public spaces and a minimization of private spaces, thereby encouraging shared leisure activities.[18] However, to accommodate refugees, entirely different architectural precedents were realized—for instance, the typically private architecture of the Austrian suburbs and rural areas became the foundation for certain forms of communal coexistence.

In March 2022, a friend and I, along with her son, found ourselves in a former farmhouse in the mountains in Upper Austria, having been generously offered a house to accommodate two families. I'd felt that my children and I weren't considered a family since my partner wasn't with us, so during my journey out of Ukraine, I searched for a female friend with whom I could navigate the challenges abroad. I later noticed that many of my female Ukrainian friends and acquaintances fleeing the war did the same. By the summer of 2022, my friend and I were prepared to expand our partnership with one more "family."

During the first six months of the mass exodus of Ukrainian women to the EU, as I began my research, I heard stories of living in repurposed gymnasiums and school classrooms. Such massive shelters with countless beds, often featured in news reports during the initial three months of the invasion, could instill fear and dissuade women in Ukraine who were deliberating whether to leave. When I stayed in some of these shelters with my children while traveling, I had the opportunity to speak with the women living there and observe their new routines.

The farmhouse in Upper Austria was my primary safe space, my "base." Every two to three months, I visited Ukraine for a few days or a week. I spoke with different women at various periods of their displacement. During a trip with my children toward the end of spring 2022, we had to make a long stop in Poland as we awaited a bus transfer. Following the advice of volunteers, we went to a shelter for some rest—a large sunlit room with alternating rows of cots and passageways. Each bed had a pillow and mattress; there were signs indicating play and quiet zones; acrobatic mats were stacked in one corner. All this revealed itself when we settled into the space. However, what was not immediately apparent, and only became clear after some observation, was that the women and children were interacting. Children played among themselves; mothers were helping one another and seemed calm. Someone gathered the children and put away the games and toys with them before lunch; someone started organizing a common table for snacks. It was as if they were keeping a collective eye on the entire space. It looked more like a well-organized hive than a waiting room where people pretend to ignore each other. Here, on the contrary, they seemed to intuitively know how to act together effectively. After spending half a day there, I was so immersed in this wave of routine and predictability, and a kind of childlike bliss, that I found myself picturing where in the hall I would settle with my children if we stayed longer.

18 "House Commune," Constructivism-Kharkiv, accessed March 7, 2023, https://constructivism-kharkiv.com/en/should-know/house-commune.

Contrary to the assumption that these shelters are uncomfortable, some of the women expressed feeling at ease within the supportive community and were in no hurry to move out. Their main reasons were along the lines of "We are fine together," "What will I do alone?," and "The children are busy with each other." As long as these women had functioning co-parenting arrangements and strong non-romantic partnerships, they preferred to live communally rather than independently.[19]

The shelter provided a sense of security and community that many of these women found essential. The communal environment fostered a shared responsibility for childcare, easing the burdens on individual mothers and creating a supportive network. This experience highlighted the importance of social bonds and collective support in coping with the challenges of forced migration.

Curtain Call

It is six in the morning in Fürth. I am slowly driving from Waldstraße 99 to Flößaustraße 20, mimicking a walking pace. Outside, the temperature is -16°C, and there is a pleasant rhythm of old and new apartment buildings from the turn onto Flößaustraße to the former military factory. Seeing a heavy four-story constructivist building with brutalist features, I feel a bit nervous. I suspect it was constructed by the Nazis. I am surprised that, unlike bombed civilian targets and the destruction of Nuremberg, this military complex remains.

"To be sure, a cityscape is not made of flesh," Susan Sontag writes. "Still, sheared-off buildings are almost as eloquent as bodies in the street."[20] The same applies to those that are not ruined. "The expansion of the iconography of suffering to the destroyed environment of human existence," as described by the philosopher, writer, and curator Borys Philonenko in his preface to the recent Ukrainian translation of Sontag's book, overlooks one aspect—the iconography of surviving architectural witnesses.[21] Both Google Maps and the street signage suggest that the former Nazi military factory now functions as a business center. Located at the same address, restored and cleaned, the building affirms the truth of Maria's stories.

From the corner of Flößaustraße and Neumannstraße, I video-called my parents to share this sensitive moment. We were happy and emotional, barely able to hold back tears.

In April 1945, about twenty of us gathered and descended into the basement where we hid from bullets and waited to be freed. There was nothing to eat. I suggested to the girls that we go out and look for something edible, but no one wanted to go, everyone was scared. After much persuasion, only Dusya agreed. We went and dug up some potatoes, beets, and cabbage in the Germans' garden. We took a pot from the house and made borscht on bricks.[22] With the prepared borscht, we headed back to the basement. As we were approaching the entrance, I heard a powerful explosion. I turned back and saw Dusya lying

19 I assume that some women have found romantic partnerships, but in this text I'd like to praise the phenomenon of non-romantic partnerships specifically. I have often encountered this type of bond, which is remarkably strong and reliable, even in the absence of a romantic component.

20 Susan Sontag, *Regarding the Pain of Others* (New York: Farrar, Straus and Giroux, 2003), 8.

21 Borys Philonenko, preface to Susan Sontag, *Sposterezhennya za bolem inshykh*, trans. Yaroslava Strikha (Kharkiv: ist publishing, 2023), 19. The Ukrainian edition was published recently in the context of the ongoing war.

22 "Ukrainian borscht is a traditional dish that is cooked with broth combined with beetroot, sugar beet or fermented beet juice." In 2022, it was added to the "list of intangible cultural heritage in need of urgent safeguarding." "Culture of Ukrainian Borscht Cooking," UNESCO Intangible Cultural Heritage, accessed March 7, 2023, https://ich.unesco.org/en/USL/culture-of-ukrainian-borscht-cooking-01852.

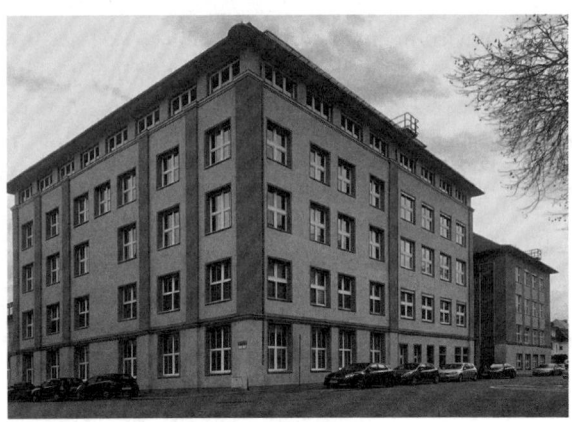
Fig. 5 Flößaustraße 20, Fürth, January 2023

on the ground, dead. I started calling out to the girls, not understanding what had happened. Then I realized that a shell fragment had hit her directly in the back of the head. Only because I was much shorter than her, I survived once again. I was still mechanically holding the pot of borscht in my hands. Someone ran up, took the borscht from me, and carried it to the basement. By that time, it was clear that Dusya was already dead. Someone began to search for boards and straw. We made a box, dug a shallow hole, and buried her in the Germans' garden.

When it becomes impossible to hold on to things that embody home, or when only a few such items remain in your possession, what else can you cling to in order to feel connected to your former self? Perhaps the only anchor is the people who share a common experience with you, whose presence affirms the continuity of your former self within your current reality—even when you can no longer express or assert yourself through your previous skills or ways of being.[23]

The first stage of my refugee experience compelled me to connect with the experiences of other Ukrainian women to understand what was happening to me. I was interested in how women would choose partnerships with other women, among other lifesaving strategies. I chose the interview method with another goal in mind—to relate this experience to that of my grandmother. Back when I researched her wartime experience, I thought I was retelling her story for future generations. Now, at the age of thirty-five, I find myself telling it once more—this time to myself, as part of my own narrative.

When you blow on a dandelion in early autumn, some of the fluffy seeds might fly away in the breeze, while others, stubborn and deep-rooted, cling resolutely to the already half-empty head. This is what happens to people when the winds of war blow. But these are not individual entities flying away gracefully, equidistant from one another; instead, they form fast-paced and resilient partnerships during their flight. Since the start of Russia's full-scale aggression against Ukraine, I have been one of the many uprooted.

I have struggled to identify and articulate the problem, despite sensing it from the beginning. Now I understand that it revolves around disappearance and the (in)visibility of oneself and others. In this context, invisibility holds particular significance within Ukraine. We cannot afford to divert our attention away from the core events and people who are present. As a result, invisibility becomes both a means and a condition. Conscious partnerships make women visible—primarily to one another—which fundamentally changes everything.

23 *Crushed Hopes: Underemployment and Deskilling among Skilled Migrant Women* (Geneva: International Organization for Migration, 2012), https://publications.iom.int/system/files/pdf/crushed_hopes_3jan2013.pdf.

Literature

Amnesty International Österreich. *Quo vadis Austria? Die Situation in Traiskirchen darf nicht die Zukunft der Flüchtlingsbetreuung in Österreich werden.* Vienna: Amnesty International Österreich, 2015. https://www.amnesty.at/media/1928/research-traiskirchen.pdf.

International Organization for Migration. *Crushed Hopes: Underemployment and Deskilling among Skilled Migrant Women.* Geneva: International Organization for Migration, 2012. https://publications.iom.int/system/files/pdf/crushed_hopes_3jan2013.pdf.

Kovalyova [Khoroshylova], Olena. "Poloneni viyny." In *Tsei bil u sertsi ne vshchukhaye: Zbirka uchnivskykh referativ,* edited by Serhiy Baturyn and Lyubov Sochka, 115–20. Lviv: Kalvaria, 2005.

Rosenberger, Sieglinde, and Anna Lazareva. "'Ich wollte auf Urlaub und nicht als Geflüchtete nach Österreich kommen': Vertriebene Ukrainerinnen in Wien." Research report, Universität Wien, Vienna, September 2022. https://inex.univie.ac.at/fileadmin/user_upload/p_inex/Rosenberger-Lazareva-Bericht_Ukraine_Vertriebene_.pdf.

Sebald, W. G. *On the Natural History of Destruction.* Translated by Anthea Bell. New York: Random House, 2003.

Sontag, Susan, *Regarding the Pain of Others.* New York: Farrar, Straus and Giroux, 2003.

Sontag, Susan. *Sposterezhennya za bolem inshykh.* Translated by Yaroslava Strikha. Kharkiv: ist publishing, 2023.

Tarkhanova, Oleksandra, and Daryna Pyrogova. "Forced Displacement in Ukraine: Understanding the Decision-Making Process." *European Societies* 26, no. 2 (2023): 481–500. doi:10.1080/14616696.2023.2280680.

UN Refugee Agency Integration Handbook. "Gender." Updated March 9, 2024. https://www.unhcr.org/handbooks/ih/age-gender-diversity/gender.

Sanja Lasić

Sevdah of Lost Identity

My ongoing project *Sevdah of Lost Identity* started in 2018 as an inquiry into the musical and visual motifs of the traditional art and culture of my native country, Bosnia-Herzegovina (BiH). My research into *sevdalinka* songs first developed into performance and video pieces, and then continued in the form of drawings and collages inspired by handicrafts, specifically the folk art of *ćilim* (tapestry) and *vez* (cross-stitch). Through the project, I deal with identity, post-traumatic stress disorder, forced displacement, and intergenerational and unhealed trauma from an embodied female perspective. The project builds on my personal experience of the war in BiH in the 1990s, the subsequent postwar period, and the aftermath of forced displacement, which stripped away my sense of self. Driven by a desire to reclaim this lost identity, I delved into the history of BiH, ex-Yugoslavia, and the Balkans, gathering information about collective traditions, cultural heritage, and my own ancestral roots.

I look at elements and motifs of traditional heritage, research their meaning, and then use this knowledge within my own artistic practice.

My upbringing diverged significantly from that of my childhood classmates in Slovenia, my academic colleagues in Italy and Austria, and even my own parents. My life has been marked by these displacements and abrupt changes—a series of breakages and disruptions that have taken a toll on my mental health. Raised in a demanding migrant household, I navigated the complexities of living in the remnants of the former Yugoslavia, balancing traditional values with liberal ideals. These contrasting worlds often collided, leaving me feeling frustrated, voiceless, and without control. Against this tumultuous backdrop, *Sevdah of Lost Identity* emerged as a platform for exploring buried emotions in the aftermath of war. As the performance-studies scholar Diana Taylor asserts, "Trauma-driven performances offer victims, survivors, and human rights activists ways to address the society-wide repercussions of violent politics and also, indirectly, to relieve personal pain."[1]

"Sve će tvoja djeca da odšute,
   tužne dane, sate i minute"[2]

For us Balkan people, and especially for the people of BiH, sevdah holds a profound significance. It is not just a musical genre; more importantly, it is an emotional state connected to yearning for unfulfilled love, melancholy, despair, and nostalgia. It describes emotions that are often difficult to name

1 Diana Taylor, "Trauma and Performance: Lessons from Latin America," *PMLA* 121, no. 5 (October 2006): 1674.

2 "Forever silent your children will remain, / Filled with the sadness of every minute of every hour of every day." Damir Imamović, "Sarajevo," from the album *Dvojka*, 2016. Translations are by the author unless otherwise noted.

or that one is perhaps reluctant to speak out loud. Singing, music, and dance serve as outlets for its release, embodying both a curse and a remedy.

The word sevdah comes from the Arabic word *sawda*, meaning "black bile." Galen of Pergamon (129–200 AD), considered the leading physician of the ancient world, coined the term from the ancient Greek words for black (*melas*) and bile (*chole*). In *De usu partium* (On the Usefulness of the Parts of the Body, 165–75), Galen's most influential work, he names black bile as one of the four humors responsible for a melancholic mood. His work was translated into Arabic toward the end of the ninth century, shaping premodern medicine in Persia and influencing medicine in Spain and the Ottoman Empire up until the modern era. Through these crossed histories, the word *sawda* became *sevda,* which in modern Turkish means both love and a painful sort of love.[3] In the mid-nineteenth century, sevdah appeared in South Slavic oral culture, but its current meaning of melancholy developed in the twentienth century.[4] Another music genre that derives from sawda is the Portuguese fado, which relates to the idea of *saudade* (Portuguese for longing or nostalgia).

Sevdah or sevdalinka songs are a traditional genre of BiH folk music that is understood as regional rather than territorial, with traces in other former Yugoslavian countries as well. It is characterized by love songs that express deep emotions of pathos and nostalgia, as well as proclamations of unfulfilled love, loss, and longing. Traditionally, the songs are divided by gender—some are meant to be performed only by women, others only by men.[5] Today, these rules are broken by a number of contemporary sevdah singers, bands, performers, and songwriters, for whom the strict gender division is slowly fading away. The main themes in the songs are traditional messages of love between a man and a woman. But today, more sensitive and relevant topics are being addressed, such as forced marriage, sexual violence, depression, queer and feminist views, and ethnic questions, giving the songs a profound sociopolitical relevance beyond their emotionally charged qualities. They describe the historical times in which they were written, but since most don't have a known author or an exact date, they can be differentiated through linguistic characteristics or descriptions of historical events such as wars.[6] For my artistic project, these findings have been enlightening, helping me understand where I come from and how sevdah relates to my own pain, the frustrations of my own experiences with war, and my postwar identity within a shared historical context.

Therefore, *Sevdah of Lost Identity* stems from a need to understand what being Bosnian-Herzegovinian from Sarajevo, from the Balkans, and from the former Yugoslavia might mean. The title describes the particular atmosphere I associate with each of these identities—an atmosphere impacted by the beginning of the war, the way it became deeply inscribed in myself, and my relationship with my country of origin after having been forced to leave. How, in my everyday life, do I perceive, live, and connect to my native country from afar? This project seeks to unravel the intersection of individual experience with the collective memory of shared history within both BiH and the diaspora community. In my project, the yearning for the loved one—a common motif in sevdah—is metaphorically displaced to the longing for my

3 Damir Imamović, *Sevdah: A Journey through Three Centuries*, trans. Amira Sadiković with Christopher Biehl (Zenica: Vrijeme, 2016), 9–10.

4 Imamović, 12.

5 Munib Maglajlić, *101 sevdalinka* (Mostar: Prva književna komuna, 1978).

6 "Sevdah (full length documentary with English subtitles)," 1 h., 5 min., 59 sec., YouTube video, uploaded by Radni Rad on February 17, 2013, https://youtu .be/NSn0E8km3jw?feature=shared.

city and the feelings related to my memories before the war. It's the longing for an identity for my family, who did everything in their power to bring us to safety, relinquishing parts of themselves in the process. The project's objective is to shed light on my narrative, which reflects a broader experience, and to revive the vibrancy of colors, scents, and sounds lost along the way.

"Sarajevo, podno Trebevića,
u tebi je sinje more priča"[7]

I was born in Sarajevo, Yugoslavia, in 1987, amid an economic crisis that stemmed from the oil crisis of the late 1970s and escalated into several periods of heavy inflation, prompting factory workers to protest for higher wages. Unresolved economic issues amplified political tensions between the republics, which led to the dissolution of Yugoslavia in 1991.[8] Nonetheless, my parents remember the 1980s as a prosperous and hopeful time. They describe everyday life in Sarajevo as safe, and they saw their future connected only with success. Three years before I was born, they had both graduated from the Department of Architecture at the University of Sarajevo, where they had also met. That year they had also both worked at the Winter Olympics. Sarajevo was experiencing a cultural and artistic boom, attracting tourists from around the world to the Ottoman-era main square Baščaršija, one of the most recognizable landmarks in the city. My mother was working in an architecture studio, and my father was an entrepreneur in the field of outdoor products made of cement, such as concrete vases and fences. He was one of the few striving toward ideals of liberal thinking within the rigid political system of socialist Yugoslavia, which focused on collective ownership and collectivist values.[9] On the one hand, this system ensured social stability and a man-made sense of equality for the masses, but on the other it created profound gaps between rural and urban communities, ossified social systems, and offered few possibilities for personal growth and individualistic ways of thinking.[10]

Two years before I was born, my parents got married in a civil ceremony and moved into an apartment in Ilidža, a district in the southern part of the city. When I was two, my brother was born. My parents led a very conventional lifestyle: graduation, marriage, home, kids. Their social life was part of their urban lifestyle, spontaneously meeting friends for coffee, taking short trips to the hills of Trebević above Sarajevo, or going to a concert. My parents often reminisce about the sense of continuity in their life before the war. They had long-standing relationships with a local mechanic and a supermarket cashier, friends were scattered across the city, they had a regular bar. With the onset of war, everything came to an abrupt halt, forcing them to rebuild their lives from scratch.

7 "Sarajevo, beneath the hill of Trebević, / You carry a sea full of stories." Imamović, "Sarajevo."

8 Dejan Jović, *Yugoslavia: A State That Withered Away* (West Lafayette, IN: Purdue University Press, 2009).

9 Damirka Mihaljević, "Development of Political Culture in Bosnia and Herzegovina," *European Quarterly of Political Attitudes and Mentalities* 9, no. 3 (2020): 13.

10 Mihaljević, 14

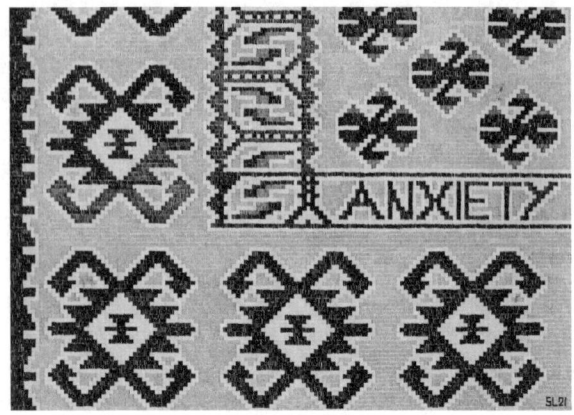

Fig. 6 Sanja Lasić, *Anxiety*, 2021. Black marker on paper, 50 × 70 cm.

"Ona dolazi, jednostavno osjetim
možda mi šapne snijeg sa grana
šta mi donosi, kusur od ljubavi
il' malo sreće minulih dana
ne znam kako, al' znam, ona dolazi"[11]

My parents often speak about their naivete in thinking the
war would not reach them because BiH's multiethnic and
cultural diversity goes back centuries—from the Neolithic
Butmir settlements and the Illyrian and Celtic people to
Germanic tribes and Slavs, including the formation of the
Kingdom of Bosnia, the invasion of the Ottomans, the settlement of Sephardic Jews expelled from Spain and Portugal,
and the annexation of Bosnian territory by the Austro-
Hungarian monarchy.[12]

I remember the day the siege of Sarajevo started. It was
a Sunday, and we were getting ready to go for a walk. I was

tying my brother's shoes when the news on TV showed men hiding behind a red brick wall and carrying big black guns. *Pam pam pam!* The early afternoon sounds of the muezzin's call to prayer and church bells were replaced by loud gunfire and shelling. The feeling was overwhelming and claustrophobic. The only creatures that seemed completely unbothered by the whole situation were the birds, still chirping in moments of silence between the shootings, flying over our heads as a reminder of life.

Im Jahr 2019 erlebte ich eine Phase schwerer Angstzustände und täglicher Panikattacken, die ein und halb Monate lang dauerten. Diese Erfahrung war mir nicht fremd, es geschah schon seit Jahren. Nur dieses Mal war es viel intensiver und es dauerte viel länger. Ich hatte das Gefühl, über dem Boden zu schweben und mich an nichts mehr festhalten zu können. Ich war wie ein Zombie, müde, erschöpft und in dauerhafter Angst, dass etwas Schlimmes passieren würde. Jeder Gedanke habe ich hinterfragt, ich

11 "She's coming, I can just feel it / Maybe the snow whispers to me from the branches / What does it bring me, crumbles of love / Or a bit of luck from the past few days / I don't know how, but I know, she is coming." Crvena Jabuka, "Tugo, nesrećo," from the album *Za sve ove godine*, 1987.

12 The Neolithic Butmir settlements were characterized by their unique handcrafted pottery and decorations featuring motifs of fertility and prosperous harvests. According to the artist and researcher Amila Smajović, this period is also relevant for the emergence of the craft of traditional BiH tapestries, which, similar to sevdah, developed into the cultural heritage that we know today with the arrival of the Ottomans and the introduction of additional materials and artistic motifs. I am working on several drawings that take inspiration from this visual folk tradition and its unique geometries, which are found on the tapestries themselves, through which I elaborate topics related to my BiH identity and the emotions connected to it. See "Rezultati znanstvenog istraživanja o simbolici motiva na bosanskom ćilimu: Autor Amila Smajović," 1 h., 18 min., 32 sec., YouTube video, uploaded by Central Network Live TV on December 9, 2021, https://www.youtube.com/watch?v=cQYOwEhz7B0; Nikola Pantelić, *Narodna umetnost Jugoslavije* (Belgrade: Jugoslovenka revija, 1984), 47–82; AhmetAlibašić, "History of Inter-religious Dialogue in Bosnia and Herzegovina," *Interdisciplinary Journal for Religion and Transformation in Contemporary Society* 6, no. 2 (2020): 344.

konnte mir selbst nicht ganz vertrauen, ich dachte, ich lebe in einer parallelen Welt. Ich konnte auch nicht mehr meinen eigenen Körper spüren, ich wusste nicht mehr, wem gehören meine Füße und Arme und sind meine Gedanken wirklich meine Gedanken. Der Auslöser für diese Episode war eigentlich eine Situation kleineren Ausmaßes (ein „normaler" Mensch würde auf sowas nicht reagieren).[13]

The siege of Sarajevo (*Opsada Sarajeva*) began on April 6, 1992. It was a prolonged blockade of the city, beginning shortly after a successful referendum for BiH's independence from Yugoslavia, and lasted until February 1996. Initially carried out by the JNA (Jugoslovenska Narodna Armija, the Yugoslav People's Army) and later by the Army of Republika Srpska, it was the longest siege on a European capital since the Second World War.

In the days after the war began, we took shelter in the cold and dark basement of the old Austro-Hungarian building where we lived. I still remember the smell of spring despite the suffocating feeling of our refuge. My light footfall on the concrete stairs to kindergarten had been replaced by the frantic footsteps of adults running down the marble stairway to the basement. At the end of April, my mother, my brother, and I escaped the besieged city. We found safety in a village called Renče, in the western part of Slovenia. My father, along with his parents, joined us about three or four months later; my mother hadn't had any contact with him during the time apart. From then on, my perception of colors, smells, and sounds lost its intensity. Everything prewar seemed more colorful, with more sounds and smells. Suddenly, it felt as if my life became black and white, suspended in a sort of heavy, sticky, blinding fog. I became anxious and sad. When I see myself in photos from the time before the war, I seem to be someone else, care-free and innocent, calm and happy. Twenty-nine years since the end of the siege of Sarajevo and the BiH war, I am still chasing after that "lost" child and lost feeling, my lost home, and trying to answer the question: Where do I belong?

The war left approximately one hundred thousand people dead and displaced over two million. A society emerged that was deeply segregated along ethnic lines. The war in BiH officially ended through the ratification of the General Framework Agreement for Peace in Bosnia and Herzegovina, also known as the Dayton Agreement, in December 1995; by February 1996, the paramilitary Serb troops had retreated from Sarajevo.[14] That summer, my family traveled to the city for the first time since the war. We drove for more than twenty hours from the Slovenian town of Vrtojba, where we lived at the time, crossing endless checkpoints in Croatian territory, passing through the newly divided territory of BiH, all the way down to Sarajevo. Every couple of hours someone in uniform stopped us, either police or military belonging to different ethnic groups, to control our passports and look through our things. Traveling by car, we had to avoid the countless mine areas and take roads that were still intact, which was a challenge as most of the routes had been destroyed at some

13 "In 2019, I experienced a period of severe anxiety and daily panic attacks that lasted for a month and a half. This experience wasn't anything new to me, it had been happening for years. Only this time it was much more intense and lasted much longer. I felt like I was floating above the ground and couldn't hold on to anything anymore. I was like a zombie, tired, exhausted and in constant fear that something very bad was going to happen. I questioned every thought, I couldn't fully trust myself, I thought I was living in a parallel world. I could no longer feel my own body, I no longer knew who owned my feet and arms and if my thoughts were really my thoughts. The trigger for this episode was actually a small-scale situation (a 'normal' person would have not reacted at all to something like this)." Quoted from a lecture-performance I realized at Brunnenpassage, Vienna, in October 2023, as part of *Sevdah of Lost Identity*.

14 Ana Mijić, "Identity, Ethnic Boundaries, and Collective Victimhood: Analysing Strategies of Self-Victimisation in Postwar Bosnia-Herzegovina," *Identities: Global Studies in Culture and Power* 28, no. 4 (2021): 473.

point during the fighting. Years later, my parents told me that they thought they would use this trip to assess the situation and figure out how to move back as soon as possible. This unfortunately did not happen because of several factors.

"Čija si?"[15]

Following the Dayton Agreement, BiH was divided into two largely ethnically homogeneous entities: the Serbian-dominated Republika Srpska and the Federation of Bosnia and Herzegovina (FB&H). Each had its own political structure and administrative organization and about half of the geographical territory. In 2000, through the International Court of Arbitration, the Brčko District was added as a neutral zone with its own administration within FB&B.[16] Soon after our trip, my father started to rebuild his cement factory in BiH, while my mother stayed in Slovenia and worked different odd jobs. Although he was in the same field as before, the socioeconomic landscape had completely changed and there were new rules in place based on the country's ethnic segregation. One-sided "(hi)stories" were taught in ethnically divided schools,[17] ethnic parties still dominated the political sphere, and ethnic divisions delineated the media landscape, while a law aimed at ensuring equal participation among the three constituent nations forced people to declare themselves either Bosniak, Croat, or Serb.[18] The belief in one's own cause, in one's own victimhood, was present on all three sides.[19] Almost thirty years after the war's end, the question of who was responsible remains pertinent.[20]

According to my parents, ethno-politics played a crucial role in their decision to sell my father's business and not move the family back to Sarajevo. His business was simply not welcome anymore based on his ethnic background, and my parents could not, nor did they want to, proclaim themselves anything other than Bosnian-Herzegovinians. Returning with two young children to a war-destroyed environment with fresh physical and psychological wounds, compared with Slovenia's stability, prosperity, and hope for a better life, made the idea of going back impossible. There is a saying among Bosnians: "Ne zna se kome je bilo gore, onima što su ostali ili onima što su otišli!" (It's unclear who had it worse, the ones who stayed or the ones who left!) Meaning that in both cases, life had to be rebuilt from scratch, and survival became everyone's central focus. No one was spared from fighting, struggling, or pain.

Both me and my brother have ethnically "neutral" names, which my parents chose to honor the mixture of their ethnic identities. My name often confuses people in pinpointing whether I am a victim or perpetrator of the Bosnian War. The question "Čija si?" is usually posed when I meet other BiH citizens, both at home and abroad.[21] Once we've established our ethnic backgrounds, our conversation expands to how we survived the war (did we flee or did we stay?) and the

15 "Whose are you?"

16 Mijić, "Identity, Ethnic Boundaries," 473.

17 Adila Pašalić-Kreso, "The War and Post-war Impact on the Educational System of Bosnia and Herzegovina," *International Review of Education* 54, nos. 3–4 (2008): 353–74.

18 Vedran Džihić, "Failing Promises of Democracy: Structural Preconditions, Political Crisis and Socioeconomic Instability in Bosnia and Herzegovina," *Southeastern Europe* 36, no. 3 (2012): 328–48.

19 Stef Jansen, "Remembering with a Difference: Clashing Memories of Bosnian Conflict in Everyday Life," in *The New Bosnian Mosaic: Identities, Memories and Moral Claims in a Post-war Society*, ed. Xavier Bougarel, Elissa Helms, and Ger Duijzings (London: Routledge, 2007), 193–208; Elissa Helms, *Innocence and Victimhood: Gender, Nation, and Women's Activism in Postwar Bosnia-Herzegovina* (Madison: University of Wisconsin Press, 2013).

20 Mijić, "Identity, Ethnic Boundaries," 473.

21 "Whose are you?" While the question asks about one's family lineage in terms of socioeconomic status, its implications in the aftermath of war are broader as it seeks to understand the individual's ethnic identity:

specifics of our losses (did we lose "just" our home or also people dear to us?). Only then can we move on to talk about the present, and sometimes even the future. I have concluded that the question of "Čija si?" is a result of deep trauma embedded in Bosnian-Herzegovinians that affects our lives perhaps more than we are aware, and influences the course of our future decisions. We are exposed to different and conflicting histories of the same event based on our ethnic background. In a post-conflict country such as BiH, public memory is reflected in the most common elements of social life, from school textbooks to music, further entrenching these differences.[22] For example, BiH pupils who are Serb Orthodox attend school that teaches the Serbian language. The students learn a one-sided history of the Bosnian War that highlights the losses and victories of ethnic BiH Serbs that either suffered or won, and completely excludes the other two ethnicities. The same pattern is repeated in schools attended only by BiH Croats or BiH Bosniaks.[23]

These divisions complicate a simple interaction with a fellow BiH citizen. We speak and behave differently based on each other's ethnicity; we are not relaxed, there is always tension and pain in our conversations. It is a sad reality.

In recent years, I learned that ethnic tensions existed even in my own family already before the war. According to my mother, my parents' union—the marriage of a Muslim woman and a Catholic man—was not welcomed by either of my grandmothers. The onset of war intensified these preexisting tensions, casting a long shadow over my childhood. Each side of my family, caught in the aftermath of the conflict, competed with claims of who was more victimized. Although my parents' marriage came together based on profound love, reflecting the Yugoslavian ideal of fostering a national identity, an average of only 12 percent of marriages in BiH were interethnic.[24] Nonetheless, I grew up with a solid sense of both of my ethnic backgrounds combined with the socialist ideology that my parents grew up with. This was celebrated during religious festivities. For example, my father would put up a Christmas tree as a reminder of his childhood in a Catholic household. Equally important would be to call my Muslim grandmother during Ramadan and Bajram to wish her luck and prosperity. Festivities like the New Year and Prvi Maj (May 1) were given more importance than religious holidays, which reflected my parents' upbringing and experience of socialist Yugoslavia. It was tough for my parents to convey to me and my brother the values of not only the geo-national view of our identity as postwar BiH citizens living in Slovenia but also the ethno-political aspects of it, which, during the war and especially after, divide rather than bring together the country. They largely managed to highlight the empowering aspects of our interfamily differences.

"U tebi su mnoge stare pjesme
O ljubavi što se pjevat' ne sm'je"[25]

I often ask myself: Is there anything within my own culture that could justify the amount of pain passed from generation to generation? Is there a way to heal from it all? Am I

22 Ignacio de la Torre, "Complexities about History Teaching and History Textbooks in Bosnia and Herzegovina," History and Memory Policies course, University of Tartu, 2014/15.

23 Heike Karge and Katharina Batarilo, *Reform in the Field of History in Education – Bosnia and Herzegovina. Modernization of History Textbooks in Bosnia and Herzegovina: From the Withdrawal of Offensive Material from Textbooks in 1999 to the New Generation of Textbooks in 2007/2008* (Braunschweig: Georg Eckert Institute for International Textbook Research, 2008), 16.

24 Mihaljević, 13.

25 "You carry so many old songs / But about love you are not allowed to sing." Imamović, "Sarajevo."

even allowed to do it from afar, from outside of my native country? Am I Bosnian-Herzegovinian enough to address these issues? In one study, the Viennese sociologist Ana Mijić analyzes the journey of Nadja, who fled Bosnia at the age of six for Vienna during the early months of the war. According to Mijić, "1.5 generation refugees" tend to experience feelings of rejection, non-belonging, and worthlessness—individuals who experienced forced migration in childhood, before their primary socialization was complete.[26] This applies to me as well—I arrived in Slovenia at the age of four and a half—and I address these feelings and questions regarding my identity through several of my works, not only *Sevdah of Lost Identity* but also the photo series *Jst sm* (2007), the drawing *Anxiety* (2021), the short video *Dženana* (2015), and many others.[27] Sevdah, and my research into the genre, offers me consolation and a safe space to answer, reflect on, and challenge some of these questions.

According to the singer Damir Imamović, the word sevdalinka first appeared "in the 9th volume of the Sarajevo-based magazine *Bosanska vila*, published on 15 May 1890, in the title *Patriotic sevdalinkas* (*Radoljubive sevdalinke*). Nikola T. Kašiković Sarajlija edited this magazine as a hotbed of Serbian nationalism in culture."[28] Sevdalinka was created by different populations who came to the territory of BiH and brought their own unique characteristics of song and lyrics. Besides the Arabic and Turkish influence of makam from the Ottoman Empire, we can detect influences of the Spanish romanso musical style brought by the Sephardic community, as well as melodic and poetic elements of the Slavic people who came from the former Roman area of Pannonia.[29] Sevdah reflects the sociopolitical history and geography of the region, both of which are intimately intertwined with the experiences and identity of its people. Thus, the interpretation and significance of sevdalinka evolve in tandem with the cultural and historical dynamics of the communities that cherish and perform these songs.

During the postwar period, musicians—particularly those influenced by Western genres—tended to maintain neutrality in political matters given their reliance on performing live across the former Yugoslav republics. However, an exception emerged in the form of turbo-folk music, which was deeply rooted in Balkan folk traditions, including sevdah. While I mainly encountered this genre during visits to the city of Banja Luka where my grandparents live, primarily in public spaces like bars and restaurants, I struggled to connect with it—both in terms of its lyrical content and the imagery often promoted through television programs of half-naked singers and dancers. In the 1990s, turbo-folk was everywhere—the scholar and curator Irena Šentevska summarizes that it was the "'soundtrack' of the Milošević regime. [… It] became the music of Serbia's isolation, a sexy accompaniment to Serbian porn nationalism or Balkan hardcore, a catalyst for pro-Fascist sentiment, even music of ethnic cleansing. Moreover, turbo-folk aided in redefining and homogenizing the Serbian national identity, and in denying war trauma in other parts of the former Yugoslavia."[30]

Imamović addresses the topic of the ethno-politics of the musical genre: "Sevdah was always political, thus, one needs

26 Ana Mijić, "(Non-)Belonging in the Context of War and Migration: Reconstructing the Self-Examinations of a 1.5 Generation Refugee," in *Global Processes of Flight and Migration: The Explanatory Power of Case Studies*, ed. Eva Bahl and Johannes Becker (Göttingen: Göttingen University Press, 2020): 186.

27 See my website, https://www.sanjalasic.com/.

28 Imamović, *Sevdah*, 44.

29 Imamović, 57, 60–61.

30 Irena Šentevska, "Turbo-Folk as the Agent of Empire: On Discourses of Identity and Difference in Popular Culture," *Journal of Narrative Theory* 44, no. 3 (Fall 2014): 418–19.

to be wary of the context."[31] According to Imamović, all aspects of each song—such as titles, sequence, and grouping with other songs—were normally linked to the political views of the publisher, while "the formal structuring of oral poetry would prove to be identical, irrespective of the ethno-religious identity of the characters or the performers, but content would still be the decisive criterion. For example, the very mention of 'Mara' (Maria) classified a song as Serb, 'Meyra' (Maryam) as Bosniak, and 'Kata' (Katarina) as Croat."[32]

"A kome su slane suze lile
Dok su bile zurle i borije"[33]

Ich suchte schließlich professionelle Hilfe und landete in der Praxis einer Neuropsychiaterin im 9. Wiener Bezirk. Nachdem sie sich meine Lebensgeschichte an-gehört hatte, kam sie zu dem Schluss, dass ich an einer Posttraumatische Belastungsstörung leide, die mit dem Krieg in meinem Heimatland, meinen Erfahrungen als Flüchtlingskind und dem Aufwachsen in einem Land, das sich meiner Identität gegenüber sehr feindlich ver-hielt, zusammenhängt. Meine erste Reaktion darauf war: „Oida, sind Sie verrückt!?" denn meine Familie und ich sind dem Schlimmsten entkommen, ich wuchs mit einem Dach über dem Kopf auf und ging zur Schule wie jedes andere Kind in meiner Altersgruppe. Sie erklärte mir weiter, dass ich aufgrund meines Alters, in dem sich meine Persönlichkeit gerade erst zu entwickeln begann, statt in einer stabilen und sicheren Umgebung aufzuwachsen, meine gesamte instabile Umgebung und die Geschehnisse wie ein Schwamm aufgesaugt habe. Wahrscheinlich war ich sowohl von den visuellen als auch von den akustischen

Merkmalen des Krieges betroffen, und ich war auch der emotionale Regulator für meine Eltern, die von der ganzen Sache traumatisiert waren.[34]

This excerpt is from a work I performed in Brunnenpassage in Vienna in October 2023 as part of *Sevdah of Lost Identity*. In the performance, I read an autobiographical text describing my childhood memories of the beginnings of the siege in Sarajevo and then sing a song. I weave together fragmented childhood memories with my current experiences of anxiety and PTSD, particularly the intense feelings of non-belonging. I shift between a childlike and adult perspective, utilizing two languages to express my thoughts and emotions. By delving into clinical diagnoses and therapeutic insights, I seek to gain a clearer understanding of my current mental state.

Traumatic events can cause emotional distress, anxiety, flashbacks, and sleep problems, but the symptoms usually slowly fade over time as the body and mind readapt to normality.[35] However, for some, like me, if the trauma repeats or is not addressed early on, these symptoms become chronic and significantly impair daily life, what modern psychiatry

---

31 Imamović, *Sevdah*, 44.

32 Imamović, 35.

33 "And whose salty tears were pouring / The same way flute and horn tune their sound." Imamović, "Sarajevo."

34 "I finally sought professional help and ended up in the practice of a neuropsychiatrist in Vienna's ninth district. After listening to my life story, she came to the conclusion that I suffer from post-traumatic stress disorder, which is related to the war in my home country, my experiences as a child refugee. My first reaction to this was: "Oh c'mon, that's crazy!" because my family and I escaped the worst, I grew up with a roof over my head and went to school like any other child in my age group. She further explained to me that, because of my age, when my personality was just beginning to develop, instead of growing up in a stable and safe environment, I absorbed my entire unstable environment and the events like a sponge. I was probably affected by both the visual and auditory features of the war, and I was also the emotional regulator for my parents, who were traumatized by the whole thing." Lecture-performance, Brunnenpassage, October 2023, part of *Sevdah of Lost Identity*.

diagnoses as post-traumatic stress disorder (PTSD), which in my case has resulted in a decades-long struggle with anxiety, an eating disorder, and phases of depression.[36] I experienced these recurring traumas throughout my childhood—witnessing war atrocities, undergoing forced displacement, fearing death, struggling to survive in unstable environments, and fear for my loved ones.

For the centerpiece of the performance, I sing an a cappella version of Damir Imamović's "Sarajevo" (2016). The song is a multifaceted history of the city, filled with different stories of its children affected by the war, a whole generation whose destiny was decided for us. The song holds a special place in my heart because it gave me the courage to tell my story in my own voice. The message of the song resonates through my entire body, grounding me through my personal experience, which often feels incredibly remote and imagined. Imamović beautifully manages to give us, the "forgotten" children of Sarajevo, a place in the city's history using our common language—the art of sevdah. In the performance, I sing in my native language and read the text in German because of its emotionally charged content. Among the five languages I speak, German is the last I learned, and the language that carries the least emotions for me. I am able to perform by creating a boundary, through the language, between the content and the emotions.

The performance itself was an important step toward regaining control, something I often feel I don't have. The psychologist Richard McNally has shown that narrating traumatic memories to others can help survivors actively engage with and reshape their past experiences, unlike the often overwhelming nature of intrusive traumatic memories. This narrative act allows survivors to gain control over the remnants of trauma, structure and order their recollections, and ultimately reconstruct their self-identity.[37] With the performance, I subconsciously created a space to speak about the traumatic experience of my childhood and not feel afraid when reliving it. By performing in German, I aim to selectively reveal and conceal aspects of myself; much like peeling away the layers of an onion, I expose fragments of memories and experiences.

Jst sm[38]

"Če kteri prstan kdaj se stre, to drug pač bo,
  moj prstan ne!" [39]

Language plays an important role in *Sevdah of Lost Identity* and in my everyday life. I live between German, English, Italian, Slovenian, and Bosnian, my native language. Between 1992 and 2001, my family relocated five times within Primorska, the western region of Slovenia. The distance between the villages we moved among was often no more than five kilometers. During this period, I attended

35 Debra Kaminer and Gillian Eagle, "Posttraumatic Stress Disorder and Other Trauma Syndromes," in *Traumatic Stress in South Africa* (Johannesburg: Wits University Press, 2010), 28–59.

36 Ellen L. Bassuk, Kristina Konnath, and Katherine T. Volk, *Understanding Traumatic Stress in Children* (Newton Centre, MA: National Center on Family Homelessness, 2006).

37 Richard J. McNally, "Are We Winning the War against Posttraumatic Stress Disorder?," *Science* 336 (2012): 872–74; cited in Joshua Pederson, "Speak, Trauma: Toward a Revised Understanding of Literary Trauma Theory," *Narrative* 22, no. 3 (2014): 339.

38 *Jst sem* (I am) is the title a series of ten self-portraits from 2007. In each photo I am holding a white sheet of paper with the words *Jst sem* followed by a different term each time ("I am a prisoner," "I am a good girl," "I am a baby," etc.). In this early work, I am questioning different identities that were given to me, asking myself which I really belong to.

39 "If any ring ever breaks, it will be someone else's, not my ring!" Simon Gregorčič, "Prstan," 1888. Gregorčič (1844 Vrsno–1906 Gorizia) was a Slovenian poet and priest.

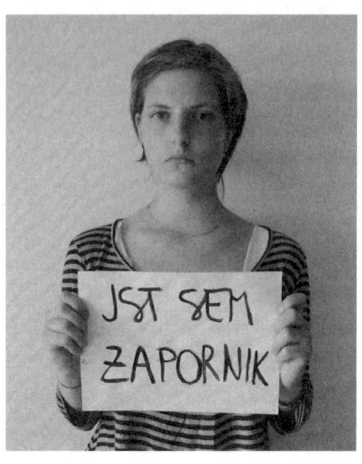

Fig. 7 Sanja Lasić, *Jst sem*, 2007. Digital photography, 30 × 40 cm.

four different elementary schools, consequently learning four distinct Slovenian dialects. Although the differences among these dialects were minor, they were significant within each community, serving as markers of collective identity. I was often teased by my peers for not speaking their village's dialect properly. While at school, I was continually corrected by teachers for not adhering closely enough to the official, more formal version of the Slovenian language. Arriving in the country as a refugee, I had to learn a new language (and dialects) not only for survival but also to fit in. I strove to perfect my language skills. I wanted to understand my environment and, most important, be understood and accepted as part of it. However, it's not just the language that makes you part of a specific community; it's also the customs and traditions, the use of everyday humor, and the perception of your environment based on your life experience. In 2002, my family obtained Slovenian citizenship because of my father's ancestors—his grandparents shared the same refugee experience as our family, but geographically reversed. Western Slovenia was harmed by fascist politics and hunger between the two world wars, and my great-grandparents escaped political persecution by finding refuge in Sarajevo, part of a large community of Slovenians from the border region with Italy. My grandfather struggled his whole life with his sense of identity and belonging in a similar way that I did; in Slovenia we were considered Bosnians, and in BiH we were considered Slovenians.

"Il tuo è un rosso relativo senza macchia d'amore"[40]

Although I grew up directly on the border with Italy in a community where most Slovenians also spoke Italian, mainly learning the language through television or working in Italy, I learned it only later when I studied in the Department for Fine Arts at the Artistic High School in Nova Gorica. Knowing the Italian language allowed me to later enroll in the Academy of Fine Arts in Milan. Little did I know that my persistence in this ongoing difficult process of integrating and acquiring language skills would be rewarded. At the academy in Milan, I was finally in a place where I felt I truly belonged. I encountered different Italian dialects and other cultures. I was among many other people whose home was somewhere else, and the city's vast multicultural landscape offered me a safe space for a diasporic identity I could now share with others. Here, I not only met people of different colors and ethnicities and learned about new languages but also encountered people who, like me, had experienced forced displacement owing to war, ethno-politics, or political

40 "Yours is a relative red without love's stain." Tiziano Ferro, "Rosso Relativo," from the album *Rosso Relativo*, 2001.

aggression. I was confronted with the socioeconomic gap between the wealthy and the poor. I was introduced to anarchism, attended exhibition openings, and visited art studios. Through these encounters, I learned a lot about myself, and started to confront my eating disorders and anxiety through my artistic work.

Slovenačka Bosanka / Bosanska Slovenka [41]

At fourteen, I developed anorexia, followed by a period of binge eating, which eventually led to struggling with bulimia for nearly a decade. Even though I wanted to stop I couldn't. Years later, I learned that my eating disorder, which still manifests today, is connected to a need for control. According to the sociologist Paula Saukko, "The interpretations of anorexia have usefully drawn critical attention to the sexist nature of body ideals and family structures and the dysfunctionality of (post)modern self-control. Still, interpretations of anorexia also often confirm the inherently pathological nature of anorexics, or women in general, as vain, overly dependent on others and their opinions, and prone to buttress general social compliance and conservatism." [42]

In the periods when I suffered from an eating disorder, I felt that I controlled nothing in my life, that power was held by people and events I didn't understand or think were connected to me. In my teenage years, being the older child and the daughter of the family meant my responsibilities included a specific way of behaving. I was not allowed to curse or talk when not addressed, and expressing my emotions through tantrums was out of the question. Crying was seen as hysterical, because one should be able to control their own emotions and thoughts in a calm and composed manner. Any type of thinking and behavior that differed from my parents or that was not aligned with the social group belonging to our BiH background was seen as unacceptable. I was expected to obtain good grades and excel in extracurricular activities such as sports. Failure in these areas was seen as the biggest shame for the family. From an early age, I strove to be perfect in everything I did. I became an overachiever and felt ashamed if I was seen as lazy or dumb.

The psychoanalyst Hilde Bruch established in 1973 the still prevalent notion that anorexia has its roots in "overpowering" family structures that do not allow the anorexic girl to become her "own self" but make her overly obedient, trying to live up to social and parental expectations to be pretty and good.[43] The intake of food was the only thing I subconsciously felt I could control: I decide whether I eat and therefore live or don't eat and therefore die. Saukko highlights a significant aspect of family dynamics, suggesting that the unresolved war traumas of fathers who fought in the Second World War could unconsciously impact their children, potentially contributing to conditions like anorexia nervosa. This echoes Bruch's theory of dysfunctional family dynamics in individuals with eating disorders. I too grew up with emotionally distant parents, whose own war trauma, depression, and anxiety manifested in a lack of communication and a rigid approach to parenting. This often created a demanding

41 In my video work *Slovenačka Bosanka / Bosanska Slovenka* (Slovenian Bosnian / Bosnian Slovenian, 2021), I sing a traditional song from Slovenia and add new lyrics in Bosnian and German. The work is described on my website: "The trauma caused by forced displacement is continuously elaborated in my work and my intention with this particular video is to show that, despite bad experience, I must accept the events and cherish my multi-cultural, social and political identities formed under these circumstances. The element of the mirror and 'the mask' in form of makeup suggest the never-ending hiding and revealing of these identities."

42 Paula Saukko, *Doing Research in Cultural Studies: An Introduction to Classical and New Methodological Approaches* (London: SAGE Publications, 2003), 3.

43 Saukko, 118–19.

and authoritarian dynamic. I learned to adapt to the emotional atmosphere of a room from a young age, anticipating and responding to the moods of adults to avoid conflict or punishment. People who grow up in an unstable environment often develop the skill of observing hand gestures and facial expressions to better read the nuances of what their conversation partners are communicating.[44] Although my parents provided us with an enormous amount of safety and stability considering the circumstances of that period, it is only now that I understand the extent of our family dysfunction in many areas of our everyday life. Bruch writes: "The patients were described as having been outstandingly good and quiet children, obedient, clean […]. The need for self-reliant independence, which confronts every adolescent, seemed to cause an insoluble conflict, after a childhood of robot-like obedience. They lack awareness of their own resources and do not rely on their feelings, thoughts and bodily sensations. […] Once this lack of autonomy has been defined, detailed histories will reveal subtle earlier indications of the deficits in autonomy and in initiative."[45]

After my PTSD diagnosis in 2019, I learned that "trauma expresses itself viscerally, through bodily symptoms, reenactments, and repeats," as Diana Taylor writes. "The fact that we cannot neatly separate trauma from posttraumatic stress points to the centrality of the reiterated effects that constitute the condition."[46] Eating disorders and PTSD have one thing in common: the sense of control over your body, your mind or thoughts, and your actions. Or perhaps better said, the loss of a control you cannot explain through words and speech. Taylor points out that a traumatic memory "is difficult to be organized on a linguistic level where arranging the memory in words and symbols leaves it to be organized on a somatosensory or iconic level: as somatic sensations, behavioral reenactments, nightmares and flashbacks."[47]

Eine andere lebhafte Erinnerung ist mit dem Tag unserer Flucht verbunden. Wir fuhren zunächst in die Nähe des Flughafens von Sarajevo. Dort angekommen, organisierten sie mehrere Busse, die uns zu dem Flugzeug brachten, das in Richtung Belgrad unterwegs war. Dies war das Flugzeug, das Waffen in die Stadt bringen und mit Zivilisten zurückfliegen sollte. Wir versuchten dreimal das Flugzeug zu erreichen. Beim ersten Mal, als wir in den Bussen zum Flugzeug in eine Schlange fuhren und die Fahrt endlos schien, wurden wir von den Scharfschützen beschossen. Der Bus vor uns als auch hinter uns wurde getroffen und ging in Flammen auf. Ich saß noch immer auf meinem Platz und beobachtete die ganze Szene, als meine Mutter mich hysterisch packte und mich anschrie, ich solle mich hinlegen, um nicht von einem Scharfschützen getroffen zu werden. Am nächsten Tag wurde es wegen weiterer schwerer Schießerei des Flughafens abgesagt und es gelang uns endlich beim dritten Mal. Wenn ich über diese Erinnerungen nachdenke, spüre ich es nie aus erster

44 The child takes the role of an adult and learns to suppress their own feelings to give space to the emotions of the parents. See Lindsay C. Gibson, *Adult Children of Emotionally Immature Parents: How to Heal from Distant, Rejecting, or Self-Involved Parents* (Oakland, CA: New Harbinger Publications, 2015).

45 Hilde Bruch, *Eating Disorders: Obesity, Anorexia and the Person Within* (New York: Basic Books, 1973), 255, quoted in Saukko, 122.

46 Taylor, "Trauma and Performance," 1675.

47 Taylor, 1675. The term "traumatic memory" was coined by the scholars Bessel van der Kolk and Onno van der Hart.

Perspektive bzw. als kleines Kind, sondern ich sehe all diese Bilder als erwachsene Person, die neben der kleinen Sanja sitzt und das Ganze beobachtet.[48]

I often experienced physical numbness during a panic attack—the feeling of not being able to recognize my own body, as if I was experiencing the event outside of myself. What helps once I realize it's a panic attack and not an actual dangerous situation is to re-ground myself. As Taylor writes, trauma is, by nature, performative, manifesting in both the individual and the social body.[49] I re-ground myself by feeling the floor with my bare feet or touching different parts of my body, my arms, my legs, my neck, in order to reconnect my brain with my body. It always feels as if the connection between my thoughts and my body gets lost for a while. An anxiety attack is physically exhausting and itself traumatizing. Over the years, I have acquired several useful tools that help me regain control when I begin to panic that I am losing control. Singing sevdah is one of them. The very act of singing is shown to have therapeutic results. The vibration of my voice, which I learned to pull from the bottom of my stomach, passes through my lungs and into the throat, then into my mouth, where I add the words. These vibrations are essential for stabilizing my breathing, my thoughts, and my tremors.

Finding the Voice

The very first sevdalinka "concerts" I gave were in my shower, trying to mimic the songs I found on YouTube. Since sevdah melodies are complex and quickly change from joyful to sad, this was a challenge. I needed to learn properly. I found support and inspiration in the singer and music teacher Nataša

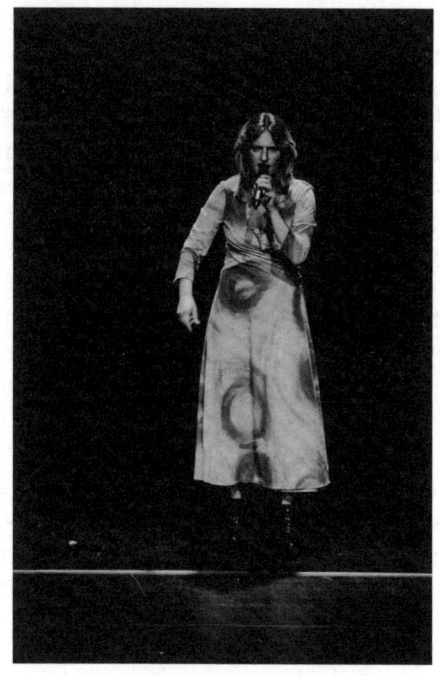

Fig. 8 Sanja Lasić, *Sevdah of Lost Identity*, 2021. Live performance at Studio Moliere Vienna as part of a project by Raw Matters.

48 "Another vivid memory is connected with the day of our escape. We first drove to the vicinity of the Sarajevo airport. Once there, they organized several buses to take us to the plane that was heading toward Belgrade. This was the plane that was supposed to bring weapons into the city and fly back with civilians. We tried to reach the plane three times. The first time, when we were driving in a queue of buses to the plane and the journey seemed like it would never end, we were shot at by the snipers. The bus in front of us as well as the bus behind us were hit and went up in flames. I was still sitting in my seat watching the whole scene when my mother grabbed me and hysterically screamed at me to lie down to avoid being hit by a sniper. The next day the trip was canceled due to even heavier gunfire at the airport, and we finally made it the third time. When I think about these memories, I never sense it from a first-person perspective or as a small child, but I see all these images as an adult sitting next to little Sanja and watching the whole thing." Lecture-performance, Brunnenpassage, October 2023, part of *Sevdah of Lost Identity*.

Mirković in Vienna and Damir Imamović in Sarajevo. The first lessons were especially hard because I had intense stage fright. I was determined to acquire additional tools to cope with the bodily effects of trauma alongside going to therapy, where I process the trauma through words. I also realized that I don't know how to sing sevdah since I was never directly exposed to the genre—I grew up outside of BiH, and my parents didn't listen to it at home. I was also keenly aware that I sing with a Slovenian accent, which made me feel more foreign than ever. Mirković and Imamović taught me not only the basics of singing (breathing exercises, posture, traditional techniques) but also how to acquire self-confidence and improve my skills despite my fear of being seen and heard. According to Rosi Braidotti, linguistic sites—not mother tongues—are the starting point. For her, "the polyglot considers the language not even as an instrument of communication but rather a site of symbolic exchange that links us together in a tenuous and yet workable web of mediated misunderstandings, which we call civilization."[50] Sevdalinka, through its melody, rhythm, and lyrics, started to heal me, and, quite literally, enabled me to have a voice.

"Ó gente da minha terra. Agora é que eu percebi.
Esta tristeza que trago. Foi de vós que recebi."[51]

During my studies in Milan, I spent one semester at the Faculty of Fine Arts in Lisbon as part of an exchange program. There, I discovered the music of fado, a genre that felt strangely familiar and soothing; years later, through my research on sevdah, I finally understood the immediate attraction. In Lisbon, I learned a basic level of Portuguese, which also enabled me to improve my conversational Spanish. I understood that the languages I live are not only a way of communicating but a way of feeling. For me, speaking different languages through the years developed into a way of singing. Through my artistic work and research, I started to understand the linguistic sites I inhabit not only in terms of the challenges they represent and the feelings of belonging or alienation they create but also in terms of the way they mediate my identity. I could regain power by understanding these languages in spatial terms (as sites) and learning how to move among them.

"Die Freiheit ist ein wundersames Tier und manche Menschen haben Angst vor ihr." [52]

The most difficult language I've learned is German, primarily through nearly a decade of working in bars in Vienna. I was exposed to Austrian dialects, and their singsong quality made it easier for me to process and memorize the language. Interestingly, I have trouble understanding standard German, like the one spoken in northern Germany, but I have no problem with German dialects from Switzerland or Liechtenstein. I believe this is due to their melody, which is similar to Italian.

"If you want my future, forget my past
If you wanna get with me, better make it fast." [53]

English is the language of everything in between. I started to learn it when I learned how to read. In Slovenia and other

49 Taylor, "Trauma and Performance," 1675.

50 Rosi Braidotti, *Nomadic Subjects: Embodiment and Sexual Difference in Contemporary Feminist Theory* (New York: Columbia University Press, 1994), 13.

51 "People of my land. It is now that I understand. This sadness that I carry. It is from you that I have received." Amália Rodrigues, "Ó gente da minha terra," 1950. Rodrigues (1920–1999) was a Portuguese poet and fado singer.

52 "Freedom is a wonderful beast, and some people are afraid of it." Georg Danzer "Die Freiheit," from the album *Die Freiheit*, 1984.

53 Spice Girls, "Wannabe," from the album *Spice* (1996).

Balkan countries, foreign television programs are subtitled, so I began learning English by listening to the language spoken on TV while reading the subtitles in Slovenian. I use English for academic and educational purposes and as a tool to be understood by a broader audience. Like German, it is a language that is not laden with emotions; therefore, it's a tool that helps me sort my thoughts in a pragmatic way.

> "Svijetu je svega dosta, ničeg
> željan nije osim glavnih junaka!" [54]

My native language, Bosnian, has been one of the rare stable elements in my life. It is the language that connects me to a feeling of ancestral identity and allows me to fully and naturally express my emotions and humor. It is the language of my parents, and I relate to it through their never-ending resilience and struggle not only to survive but also to plant new roots outside of our native country. As I was growing up, my family created an additional layer of languages. We would combine words from Bosnian and Slovenian and invent new phrases that would make sense only to the four of us.

> "Every morning I wake up in
> the middle of dreams I don't know.
> I search for answers only
> cause I really want to come home." [55]

In 2018, I came across the Croatian band Afion's rendition of "Anadolka."[56] Although I've heard many different versions of this song, their interpretation gave it a fresh feeling and a new message. From that moment on, "Anadolka" set the tone for my artistic practice and formed the basis for *Sevdah of Lost Identity*.

Oj djevojko, Anadolko, budi moja ti!
Ja ću tebi sevdalinke pjesme pjevati.
Hraniću te bademima, da mi mirišeš.
Pojiću te đul-šerbetom, da mi sevdišeš.
Ruse kose curo imaš, žališ li ih ti?
Aman, da ih žalim ne bih ti ih dala da ih mrsiš ti!
Bijelo lice curo imaš, žališ li ih ti?
Aman, da ga žalim ne bih ti dala da ga ljubiš ti!
Medna usta curo imaš žališ li ih ti?
Aman, da ih žalim ne bih ti dala da ih ljubiš ti![57]

In the song, Anadolka is being courted by a man. Their voices are interwoven in the lyrics. Anadolka embodies qualities desired in a bride: modesty, decorum in public, chastity (signifying her potential as a mother), physical attractiveness, education, and financial independence. She is expected to selflessly sacrifice for her family while maintaining a cheerful demeanor—which the scholar Danijela Majstorović calls a survival strategy for women in BiH, describing it as a form of "self-sacrificing micro-matriarchy" entrenched in Balkan tradition. This concept, rooted in rural, collectivist ideologies, perpetuates patriarchy's renewal. As Majstorović writes, "Women's self-sacrifice often leads to retreat into

54 "The world has had enough, it wants nothing more than true heroes!" Bijelo Dugme, "Glavni junak jedne knjige," from the album *Singlice* (1974–80).

55 In early 2018, I wrote, composed, and sang "Every Morning," and made an accompanying music video.

56 The author of the song is unknown, and versions can be found as a traditional song of Macedonia, Greece, Bulgaria, and Turkey, among other countries. See "Afion – Anadolka," 5:49, YouTube video, uploaded by Hame on August 31, 2009, https://www.youtube.com/watch?v=5WuOYGYt-Mw.

57 "Oh, girl, my Anadolka, be mine! / I will sing you sevdah songs. / I will feed you almonds, so you smell sweet to me. / I will give you rose sherbet, so you love me deeply. / Girl, you have lush hair, do you treasure it? / Oh, even if I treasure it, I wouldn't give it to you to tangle! / Girl, you have a fair face, do you treasure it? / Oh, even if I treasure it, I wouldn't give it to you to caress! / Girl, you have honeyed lips, do you treasure them? / Oh, even if I treasure them, I wouldn't give them to you to kiss!" Lyrics of "Anadolka," author unknown.

the private sphere and prioritization of motherhood, key survival tactics in the Balkan socio-economic landscape."[58]

I have interviewed several people—family, friends, and musicians from the sevdah industry—who consider "Anadolka" a "light" song with a simple message: a man is chasing a young girl who is refusing his love. My interpretation sees it as addressing much more than what it initially indicates. The true force of its lyrics should be taken seriously. For me, "Anadolka" represents the learning process I underwent about myself and a tool for navigating a black-and-white society constructed from rigid gender and ethnic roles and their negative impact on mental health. In my reading, "Anadolka" breaks from the traditional perspective of an obedient and voiceless female led by the patriarchy. Anadolka is aware of both her beauty (and the social upgrade of saying yes to this suitor) and the consequences that her decision carries. I realized she was a symbol of independence. In a society that often silences women, she possesses a powerful voice that challenges the status quo. Her courage inspired my own belief in myself, and I began to see how other female characters in sevdah songs help me find my own strength. Anadolka breaks free from an old ideology with the words: "Oh, even if I treasure it, I wouldn't give it to you to caress!" She is the embodiment of both the pain and the resilience that we, the people of BiH, pass from generation to generation.

According to the philosopher Isolde Charim, we live in a world characterized by a state of diversity that encompasses various cultures, lifestyles, and identities. She calls this a *pluralisierte Gesellschaft* (pluralized society) that challenges traditional concepts of identity, as individuals are increasingly influenced by multiple experiences and backgrounds, leading to a decline in fixed affiliations.[59] Charim examines the implications of this shift in Western societies across various domains, including religion, culture, political participation, political populism, and identity politics. Her ideas make me think of my own experience in relation to identity and the impossible task of isolating inherited identities as well as cultivated self-concepts. This constant exchange, growth, negation, and displacement continues to change in a world that demands that you proclaim yourself as just one singular entity. My experience of being stereotyped in the different places I've lived surely stems from a lack of understanding about the Balkans and a Eurocentric perspective that imagines us as peripheral. The universal human yearning for belonging and security often intersects with life's inevitable challenges, over which we have little to no control. For me, strength is found in honest conversations about sensitive topics shared with those who can truly listen. Once I started to share my personal story about the challenges of war, forced displacement, and the silent battles against anxiety and eating disorders, the world around me started to seem more kind. Through performance, visual art, and sevdah, I am gradually uncovering my true self. I envision the music and the tradition of sevdah gradually leading me to heal from the deep-seated wounds of intertwined collective and personal trauma. It is a process that will last a lifetime, but one that is a faithful companion in a world of uncertainty. By drawing on the experiences of my ancestors encoded within sevdalinka songs, I am encountering new forms of strength and wisdom. Sevdah has taught me that home is not merely a physical place, but a profound sense of belonging that can be cultivated within oneself, even from afar.

58 Danijela Majstorović, "Femininity, Patriarchy and Resistance in the Postwar Bosnia and Herzegovina," *International Review of Sociology* 21, no. 2 (July 2011): 288.

59 Isolde Charim, *Ich und die Anderen: Wie die neue Pluralisierung uns alle verändert* (Vienna: Zsolnay Verlag, 2018).

Literature

Alibašić, Ahmet. "History of Inter-religious Dialogue in Bosnia and Herzegovina." *Interdisciplinary Journal for Religion and Transformation in Contemporary Society* 6, no. 2 (2020): 343–64.

Bassuk, Ellen L., Kristina Konnath, and Katherine T. Volk. *Understanding Traumatic Stress in Children.* Newton Centre, MA: National Center on Family Homelessness, 2006.

Braidotti, Rosi. *Nomadic Subjects: Embodiment and Sexual Difference in Contemporary Feminist Theory.* New York: Columbia University Press, 1994.

Charim, Isolde. *Ich und die Anderen: Wie die neue Pluralisierung uns alle verändert.* Vienna: Zsolnay Verlag, 2018.

Džihić, Vedran. "Failing Promises of Democracy: Structural Preconditions, Political Crisis and Socioeconomic Instability in Bosnia and Herzegovina." *Southeastern Europe* 36, no. 3 (2012): 328–48.

Gibson, Lindsay C. *Adult Children of Emotionally Immature Parents: How to Heal from Distant, Rejecting, or Self-Involved Parents.* Oakland, CA: New Harbinger Publications, 2015.

Helms, Elissa. *Innocence and Victimhood: Gender, Nation, and Women's Activism in Postwar Bosnia-Herzegovina.* Madison: University of Wisconsin Press, 2013.

Imamović, Damir. *Sevdah: A Journey through Three Centuries.* Translated by Amira Sadiković with Christopher Biehl. Zenica: Vrijeme, 2016.

Jansen, Stef. "Remembering with a Difference: Clashing Memories of Bosnian Conflict in Everyday Life." In *The New Bosnian Mosaic: Identities, Memories and Moral Claims in a Postwar Society,* edited by Xavier Bougarel, Elissa Helms, and Ger Duijzings, 193–208. London: Routledge, 2007.

Jović, Dejan. *Yugoslavia: A State That Withered Away.* West Lafayette, IN: Purdue University Press, 2009.

Kaminer, Debra, and Gillian Eagle. "Posttraumatic Stress Disorder and Other Trauma Syndromes." In *Traumatic Stress in South Africa,* 28–59. Johannesburg: Wits University Press, 2010.

Karge, Heike, and Katharina Batarilo. *Reform in the Field of History in Education – Bosnia and Herzegovina. Modernization of History Textbooks in Bosnia and Herzegovina: From the Withdrawal of Offensive Material from Textbooks in 1999 to the New Generation of Textbooks in 2007/2008.* Braunschweig: Georg Eckert Institute for International Textbook Research, 2008.

Maglajlić, Munib. *101 sevdalinka.* Mostar: Prva književna komuna, 1978.

Majstorović, Danijela. "Femininity, Patriarchy and Resistance in the Postwar Bosnia and Herzegovina." *International Review of Sociology* 21, no. 2 (July 2011): 277–99.

Mihaljević, Damirka. "Development of Political Culture in Bosnia and Herzegovina." *European Quarterly of Political Attitudes & Mentalities* 9, no. 3 (2020): 13–15.

Mijić, Ana. "Identity, Ethnic Boundaries, and Collective Victimhood: Analysing Strategies of Self-Victimisation in Postwar Bosnia-Herzegovina." *Identities: Global Studies in Culture and Power* 28, no. 4 (2021): 472–91.

Mijić, Ana. "(Non-)Belonging in the Context of War and Migration: Reconstructing the Self-Examinations of a 1.5 Generation Refugee." In *Global Processes of Flight and Migration: The Explanatory Power of Case Studies,* edited by Eva Bahl and Johannes Becker, 185–200. Göttingen: Göttingen University Press, 2020.

Pantelić, Nikola. *Narodna umetnost Jugoslavije.* Belgrade: Jugoslovenka revija, 1984.

Pašalić-Kreso, Adila. "The War and Post-war Impact on the Educational System of Bosnia and Herzegovina." *International Review of Education* 54, nos. 3–4 (2008): 353–74.

Pederson, Joshua. "Speak, Trauma: Toward a Revised Understanding of Literary Trauma Theory." *Narrative* 22, no. 3 (2014): 333–53.

Saukko, Paula. *Doing Research in Cultural Studies: An Introduction to Classical and New Methodological Approaches*. London: SAGE Publications, 2003.

Šentevska, Irena. "Turbo-Folk as the Agent of Empire: On Discourses of Identity and Difference in Popular Culture." *Journal of Narrative Theory* 44, no. 3 (Fall 2014): 413–41.

Taylor, Diana. "Trauma and Performance: Lessons from Latin America," *PMLA* 121, no. 5 (October 2006): 1674–77.

Torre, Ignacio de la. "Complexities about History Teaching and History Textbooks in Bosnia and Herzegovina." History and Memory Policies course, University of Tartu, 2014/15.

Stephanie Misa

An altar for the fleshy tongue

I.

In my work *An altar for the fleshy tongue* (2023), a question is posed: Can languages be held within the body across generations? And if so, what tools do we need to reawaken this dormant knowledge? This proposition examines my own linguistic inheritance as it relates to other peoples, and as it relates to my son's own inherited language-worlds. It inevitably leads me to look at the languages that grow in community and are in danger of erasure, and those that are gone but have left traces. The artwork is an installation composed of two 4:3 ratio screens facing each other, on one screen is myself, on the other, my son. I am sounding out words of various body parts in my mother tongue, and he repeats them back to me. The videos loop in unison after seven minutes. Scattered around the room are various altars—sites of gratitude, grief, and remembrance. An altar of chicken's feet cast as wax candles

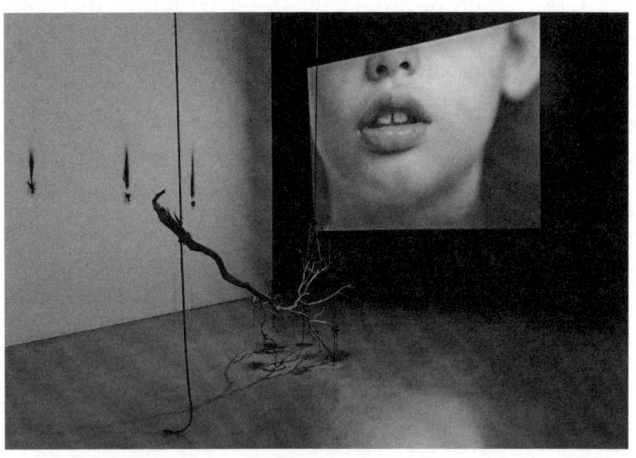

Fig. 9 Stephanie Misa, *An altar for the fleshy tongue*, installation view,
RMIT Gallery, Naarm (Melbourne), 2023

is set along the smoke-stained rear wall—a spectral residue evoking the summoning of powerful immaterial forces and a bridging of the past and present. The main altar, a tree branch affixed to the floor by delicate pillars of wax, is the heart of the installation. It hovers in the room, as tenuous and fragile as the mother tongue of a colonized people.[1]

The installation grew from the artistic research practice of listening to articulations of oralities (languages that are mostly expressed verbally) and determining their persistence, circulation, and continuation as unsung methods of colonial resistance. As a speaker of an informal, casual, and community-based language called Cebuano, colloquially known as Bisaya (I will refer to the language as Bisaya in this essay), from the Central Region of the Philippines, I've seen the exclusionary structural violence that languages considered outside the formal read-write frameworks are often subjected to—unvalued, undermined, and in some cases erased.

> *Written words are residue. Oral tradition has no such residue or deposit. When an often-told oral story is not actually being told, all that exists of it is the potential in certain human beings to tell it.*[2]

To counter the idea of a pervasive outsider tongue kept strong by a community that engaged it as a survival (decolonial) strategy, I wanted to survey a language that was erased by similar violent colonial structures. I was introduced to the archive of Fanny Cochrane Smith through the website of the National Film and Sound Archive of Australia (NFSA). The archive had released a clip from a series of recordings made in 1899 and 1903, which was accompanied by a note

Fig. 10 Fanny Cochrane Smith and Horace Watson, Hobart, Tasmania, 1903. The square is a placeholder. We were unable to obtain permission for the image use at this time.

1 "Stephanie Misa: An altar for the fleshy tongue," RMIT Gallery, Naarm (Melbourne), September 5–30, 2023.
2 Walter J. Ong, *Orality and Literacy: The Technologizing of the Word* (New York: Routledge, 1982), 11.

from the curator Sophia Sambono that read: "The quality of the recording is rather scratchy, but it is still amazingly clear. Fanny Cochrane Smith sang into the bell of the gramophone to record these songs on wax cylinders."[3] And the image that accompanies this clip is fantastic: A small woman is standing next to a gigantic contraption. The horn of the gramophone is almost as large as she is, and as she leans precariously toward it, it looks about to swallow her. She is out of focus. The other person in the image, behind the recorder, is a tall man, polished, with well-groomed hair and a neat moustache. He daintily holds a brush in his hand as he looks down at the recorder. He is in focus. This black-and-white image held me. What is going on? Who is she, and who is he?

The photo was taken on October 10, 1903, at Barton Hall in Sandy Bay, a suburb of Hobart, the capital of Tasmania. The man is Horace Watson and the woman, of course, Fanny Cochrane Smith. I would later learn that Smith is the only recorded speaker of a Tasmanian Indigenous language.

In 1899 and 1903, Smith, with Watson, made the only recordings of her First Nation's Tasmanian language. Her songs, encoded in wax, are today almost inaccessible owing to the impermanence of the medium. Yet Smith's songs do exist— they are kept within the archival holdings of the NFSA and managed by the Tasmanian Museum and Art Gallery.

I am telling you many stories. I will tell you the story of my mother tongue, of what I have come to know of Fanny and her songs, and of what it means for the body, voice, sound, and tongue to endure even in the face of evisceration. Where the tongue as the site where language leaves the body and enters the world becomes the focus, as I seek to understand what secrets potentially lie embedded in this fleshy transmitter.

Rain dreamed from sounds.
The pauses. Exhalation.
Affirmations. All the affirmations.

Little by little

Not possible to distinguish the speech
Exhaled. Affirmed in exhalation.
Exclaimed in inhalation.
To distinguish no more the rain from dreams
or from breaths.

Tongue inside the mouth inside
the throat inside
the lung organ alone. The only organ.
All assembled as one. Just one.[4]

II.

"Mother, my first sound. The first utter. The first concept."[5] It starts with an impulse, a fascination. I was drawn to the mouth, and to the ways we describe parts held within it: mother tongue, milk teeth, roof of the mouth, etc. Though as heartwarming and fuzzy as the term "mother tongue" is, conceptually it does suggest a singular starting point (and human being) for the coming into language: the mother, as if *mother*, too, was singular in origin and meaning. The idea becomes fraught when it doesn't necessarily hold for many contemporary, transnational, bilingual, or multilingual speaking

3 Sophia Sambono, curator's notes for "Fanny Cochrane Smith's Tasmanian Aboriginal Songs (1899)," Australian Screen, accessed December 8, 2024, https://aso.gov.au/titles/music/fanny-cochrane-smith-songs/clip1/.

4 Theresa Hak Kyung Cha, *Dictee* (Berkeley: University of California Press, 2001), 67.

5 Cha, 50.

identities. In my own experience of learning languages, and watching my son take on his (language), it all seemed a messier affair than the clear-cut clinical clarity of the emergence of *a* language. Rather, convoluted starting points and more complex, more plural possibilities of beginnings seemed the case—a process acknowledging that the language of enculturation can come from many different sites, and nine months in a mother's womb does not guarantee eloquence in her tongue.

The focal point for this artistic research investigation was always: How does the idea of "multitudes," of being one yet composed of many, generate new ways of positioning oneself to break with monolithic, essentialist representations within language? In a chapter of *Borderlands / La Frontera* (1987) aptly called "How to Tame a Wild Tongue," Gloria Anzaldúa writes about how language can straddle worlds. Anzaldúa conjures this in-betweenness and the shame (but also defiance) that often comes with being made to feel as if your language were illicit: "Chicano Spanish is considered by the purists and by most Latinos deficient, a mutilation of Spanish. But Chicano Spanish is a border tongue which developed naturally. Change, *evolución, enriquecimiento de palabras nuevas por invención o adopción* have created variants of Chicano Spanish, *un nuevo lenguaje. Un lenguaje que corresponde a un modo de vivir*. Chicano Spanish is not incorrect, it is a living language."[6]

This question engages the idea of an *outside language*, a language that has been relegated to an orality yet still finds itself persisting and alive through a community of speakers. I'm defining orality quite broadly here. In Walter Ong's *Orality and Literacy* (1982), orality is seen as *potentiality* rather than the written and material residue of language.[7] As it pertains to this artistic research endeavor, orality refers to

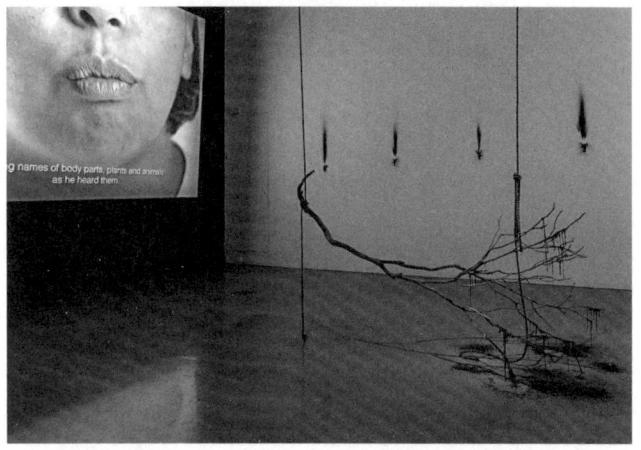

Fig. 11 Stephanie Misa, *An altar for the fleshy tongue*, installation view, RMIT Gallery, Naarm (Melbourne), 2023

6 Gloria Anzaldúa, *Borderlands / La Frontera: The New Mestiza*, 4th ed. (San Francisco: Aunt Lute Books, 2007), 76.
7 Ong, *Orality and Literacy*, 11.

languages that are cut from their written and read forms (be it in immigrant, Indigenous, or creolized and colonized communities) but remain vibrantly spoken within their communities and continue to be passed on intergenerationally. The tenacity of this outside tongue attests not only to its longevity but also to the resilience of the disenfranchised body that carries the orality. I see it as a living language, one that is tied to a people and not a structure.

What I find compelling about oralities are how they inhabit a speaker's body, the performativity they produce, the agency they carry as an embodied substantiation of something that would otherwise *not* have a medium of articulation. In this sense (with orality), I am engaging with the body that expresses it, and how it expresses it. I am especially wrapped up in the body caught in the middle—the body that molds the words and *sounds out* this in-betweenness.[8] I see orality as way to access an intersectionality, one that ruptures the idea of bound cultures and instead proposes that culture—and by extension, language—is in a perpetual flux marked by creative becomings. As Ong proclaims: "But, in all the wonderful worlds that writing opens, the spoken word still resides and lives. Written texts all have to be related somehow, directly or indirectly, to the world of sound, the natural habitat of language, to yield their meanings. 'Reading' a text means converting it to sound, aloud or in the imagination, syllable-by-syllable in slow reading or sketchily in the rapid reading common to high-technology cultures. Writing can never dispense with orality. […] Oral expression can exist and mostly has existed without any writing at all, writing never without orality."[9]

"You speak very softly, you speak in a whisper. In the dark, in secret. Mother tongue is your refuge."[10] This is how I often feel when I wrap my tongue around Bisaya after a long period of not speaking it, as if my mouth has rusted shut and only a whispery trace of rounded vowel sounds can emerge, gently. Bisaya is the language of Cebu, one of the many islands of the Philippine archipelago and my hometown. I was born in Cebu and spent my formative years in the city. My mother's large family was also from Cebu, so there was an endless number of cousins, uncles, aunties, and friends that formed my extended family. The language of my childhood is Bisaya, and it seeps through the pores of all my memories as much as the smell of mango blossoms.

There was a *thereness* to the language, a presence that just promptly disappeared once I moved to Manila for university. I picked up Tagalog then, though it was as foreign to me as learning German. This thereness is what is tangible when I open my mouth to speak Bisaya in conversation; it is in communion, appearing only when there is someone who can respond in kind, in community. Often, we forget the strength of community when it comes to keeping a language alive. Especially in Western education, where formalized school systems are seen as the only source and method for remembering and passing on: teaching and learning through reading and writing. We forget the power of the spoken and embodied word, the language of songs, of poems, and of stories that always lead us back and point to our return.

It always haunted me, my inability to read or write in "proper" (un-creolized) Bisaya. I soon learned there were two operative *me*s—the me that could speak in Bisaya to my friends and family outside of a classroom, and the one that

<hr>

8 A line quoted from the script of my lecture-performance *Filipinos, Cannibalism and Mothers Dancing on Tongues* (2022), most recently performed at the RMIT Gallery in Naarm (Melbourne) on September 5, 2023.

9 Ong, *Orality and Literacy*, 8.

10 Cha, *Dictee*, 45.

had to use proper (again this word) and useful language in school. These two *me*s could never mix: my Bisaya self was not welcome within the sacred halls of learning, enforcing a delineation between formal and informal language from very early on. I felt I had no mastery over the language except through verbal interactions. There was a disjunction between me and my mother tongue, where I felt it was paradoxically as *foreign* as it was close. But this foreignness was never uncomfortable. I was taught not to write in my mother tongue, so it took over my senses in a different way, through affect and joy and unseriousness. "Language is one of the sites through which social hierarchies are revealed and reinforced. It is a site where cultures undergo marginalization or erasure."[11]

I am one of 15.9 million "native" Bisaya speakers in an archipelagic country with a population of more than 109,035,343 million people.[12] Almost a fifth of the Philippines speaks Bisaya; it is not a language group in risk of obliteration anytime soon, but it has been a language largely relegated to oral use. Most modes of communication within the country—the medium of instruction in higher education, politics, government, and popular culture (books, television, magazines, films, formal documents)—are either in Filipino or English, the two official languages of the country. Filipino (Tagalog), the language of the country's capital, Manila, is inflated to the level of "national language" and imposed on all the other language groups. It was painful to register that the language of my laughter, of how I view the world and am situated in it, was considered less significant than the language I learned from books. Embedded within this way of seeing was, of course, the age-old colonial and classist stratification between those who could afford to be educated and learn a formal language (Spanish, then English, and of course Filipino) and those who could not. As the scholar Helen Ngo dissects in her essay on bilingual dwelling, the racialized erasure of cultures and languages in settler-colonial societies provides the critical framework to understand the specific experience of living between languages and of language loss. Ngo mentions a critical difference from a more generalized experience of bilingualism: "While bilinguals of all stripes might share experiences of switching, translation, and straddling language-worlds, these are not experienced in the same way by colonized or racialized subjects. Not only are languages differently valued along racialized lines (consider the traditional prestige accorded to French, German, and Latin) but so too are their speakers. Whereas the bilingualism of whites is often taken as a sign of one's status as educated, cultured, and open-minded, the bilingualism of non-whites is often viewed as suspicious, antisocial, and a sign of poor societal integration."[13]

The Philippines is an especially interesting lens through which to view the turning point of orality to literacy—the process from sound to pen (to paper) is so thoroughly marked

11 Lori Gallegos, "The Interpreter's Dilemma: On the Moral Burden of Consensual Heteronomy," in *Latin American Immigration Ethics*, ed. Amy Reed-Sandoval and Luis Rubén Díaz Cepeda (Tucson: University of Arizona Press, 2022), 258.

12 The source of this estimate of Bisaya speakers is Jeconiah Louis Dreisbach and Feorillo Petronilo Demeterio, "Intergenerational Language Preference Shift among Cebuanos on the Cebuano, Filipino, and English Languages," *LLT Journal* 23, no. 2 (June 2020), doi.org/10.24071/llt.2020.230203. A more current estimate could not be found. The population of the Philippines cited here is taken from the Philippine Statistics Authority's 2020 Census of Population and Housing—the last official census predating this writing. See "2020 Census of Population and Housing (2020 CPH) Population Counts Declared Official by the President," Philippine Statistics Authority, July 7, 2021, https://psa.gov.ph/content/2020 -census-population-and-housing-2020-cph-population-counts-declared-official -president.

13 Helen Ngo, "Her Mother's Tongue: Bilingual Dwelling, Being In-Between, and Intergenerational Co-creation of Language-Worlds," *Critical Philosophy of Race* 12, no. 1 (2024): 155–56.

by colonial conquest. The Philippines is home to 183 living languages, including a wide range of native languages mainly from the Malayo-Polynesian language family. In addition to the country's Indigenous tongues, Spanish was the official language for over three centuries. It arrived as Spanish colonizers took the Philippines, officially conquering it in 1565 as part of the Spanish Empire. Spanish became the language not only of government but also of elite universities, religion, and trade, and it spread with the introduction of public education in 1863. But there was a span of 298 years between the arrival of the Spanish and the implementation of the language in schools, which made it accessible to all. These 298 years were crucial for the development of native languages in the Philippines alongside the colonial lingua franca, making it harder to eradicate them. This rupture into literacy also came via Antonio Pigafetta, a Venetian scribe accompanying Ferdinand Magellan on his infamous quest to circumnavigate the globe. He transcribed as many words as he could during the voyage to the Philippines in the early 1520s, and was one of only eighteen sailors to complete the journey and return to Spain. Pigafetta's diaries were turned into a manuscript titled *Relazione del primo viaggio intorno al mondo* (Report on the First Voyage around the World), which became one of the most cited documents by historians studying the precolonial Philippines. He wrote down 160 words from the Bisaya language, listing names of body parts, plants, and animals. This was in 1521, but these words were there long before him.

Dila, he wrote—*Ala linga, la lengua*, the tongue.

Akong bâbâ nasayod gihapon niining mga tingog
(My mouth still knows these sounds).[14]

Pigafetta's list is regarded as the first European record of the Bisayan languages—the first time a white man took Bisaya words to paper. But he couldn't trap them there. It is but a small miracle that our language persisted; with a twist of fate, our bodies could have been easily cut from our sounds, replaced by a lingua franca, as what happened to other colonies, left with traces of archived words to read but not to hear, not to touch, not to taste.

Our ancestors run through our tongue as well, imbibed, embedded in the sounds that curl around our mouth and in the breath that hisses through our teeth. We make these sounds ours by passing them through us, through the list of places in our bodies that keep them:

Mouth, ears, eyes, palm.

Bâbâ, dalunggan, mata, palad.[15]

What is especially poignant about creating work on orality is that I am reminded time and again of my own positionality and the outsider tongue I carry with me. Bisaya was always, and probably always will be, an outsider language: the other, the unofficial, the *bastard* tongue. Yet in this inexplicable way, it is when I am speaking Bisaya that I feel to the tips of my hair how this language invades every nook of my body: I speak louder, I laugh wider, my cadence, my inflection all change, my body language is looser—more hand motions, more movement. How is it that the mere act of rolling different sounds in your mouth can move an entire body to speak differently? This is the question I grapple with as I try to ask: What is the embodied agency of an orality? I am speculating

14 From the video in the installation *An altar for the fleshy tongue* (2023).
15 From the video in *An altar for the fleshy tongue.*

that the embodiment of an orality, its containment in a colonized, disenfranchised, diasporic body, is exactly what gives it power—one that cannot be divorced from the body that carries it.

> There. Later, uncertain, if it was
> the rain, the speech, memory.
> Re membered from dream.
> How it diminishes itself. How to Dim
> inish itself. As
> it dims.

> To bite the tongue.
> Swallow. Deep. Deeper.
> Swallow. Again even more.
> Just until there would be no more of organ.
> Organ no more.
> *Cries.*[16]

III.

The simple act of retelling a story, especially one canonized in an archive, can bring about an unexpected tremor, a sudden instability caused by laying out the details once more, an act of subversion that points to the fluidity of history, and a permeability of positions. *Slowness* as an alternative archival temporality is an important methodology adapted within this project. As an archive produces knowledge that presumes a linear understanding of time, a critical methodology when viewing archival material requires a strategy that combats this notion of the temporal and "instead opens up to the multiple times of cultures and civilizations upon

Fig. 12 The wax-cylinder historical recordings of Fanny Cochrane Smith. The rectangle is a placeholder. We were unable to obtain permission for the image use at this time.

16 Cha, *Dictee*, 69.

which Western Civilizations impose its conceptualization of time."[17] What is offered in a *slowing* of time is a theory of imbrication: an overlapping of edges and patterns, in which there are intervals and open spaces alternating with connections that bridge and touch. These alternating patterns can be seen as engendering a form of productive time and space articulated in a rhythm almost akin to breathing (an in and out), a beat, a cadence—yet also a kind of friction that arises at the places where things rub together. It is important, in these rhythmic cycles, to think of what happens in the in-between. *Slow down*, suggest the scholars Kimberly Christen and Jane Anderson. "In this change of pace, slow archives do not presume one course of action, nor are they held in a binary temporal opposition to 'fastness.' In fact, what slow archives allow is for changing course, for shifts, and for unexpected endings. Slow archives pivot around the register of decolonization as a processual move."[18]

To consider that things may *refuse* to unfold before you is another aspect to this encounter with the slowing down of time.[19] In my years as an artistic researcher, being a woman—and a woman of color—has often worked in my favor. It is a privilege, within the framework of the narratives I am interested in, to be able to come closer with a commonality. Not only in the sense of an empathy that goes beyond a conceptual understanding of what it is to be *other*, but to offer a felt and lived conviviality of the margins (this space we have all been pushed toward and now congregate in). I understand it as a place from which I can access stories that are beyond my own lived experiences, but also from which I can offer solidarity.

With Fanny Cochrane Smith's story, I came to the research knowing that I was outside of it. A friend's (admittedly glib) affirmation that "we are all Indigenous somewhere," which I've taken on, maybe did not and could not contain the expansiveness needed to fully understand the Tasmanian Aboriginal experience. During my research trip to Australia from July to September 2023, I was hoping to talk to the institutions around the Smith archive—the NFSA, the Tasmanian Museum and Gallery, and most important, the Tasmanian Aboriginal Center (TAC), the sole agency in charge of the language program to revitalize *palawa kani* ("Tasmanian Aborigines speak"). I was hoping to get to know the people who run TAC as well as the community they engage with through the language program. A lot of the questions in my research—on orality and the mother tongue, and the dispossession of it from the body—hinged on being able to ask these questions to persons relearning a tongue that was stripped from them. Unfortunately, the TAC did not want to entertain my efforts to reach out, or to engage in my attempts to speak to them. I was refused.

Perhaps one could say it was the political climate of the moment. The constitutional referendum vote for "the Voice" was about to take place. This referendum proposed an amendment to the Australian Constitution that would allow for an Aboriginal and Torres Strait Islander Voice that, through a political body, could speak to the parliament on matters relating to Aboriginal and Torres Strait Islander peoples. The no vote for the referendum was using the same right-wing and ultra-nationalist tactics that were witnessed in the UK's Brexit referendum. Everyone was on edge as the settler-colonial origins of Australia were laid bare once again

17 Alvina Hoffman, "Interview – Walter Mignolo/Part 2: Key Concepts," *E-International Relations*, January 21, 2017, https://www.e-ir.info/2017/01/21/interview-walter-mignolopart-2-key-concepts/.
18 Kimberly Christen and Jane Anderson, "Toward Slow Archives," *Archival Science*, no. 19 (2019): 90.

and challenged in a land that was never ceded. The opacity that cloaked this moment refused entry to anyone who could not sit with the stories, the complex colonial history, and the community to give it the time needed to establish a relationship with the one asking questions. I realized early on that while slowness was imperative to the project, the practicalities of my stay in Australia as a short-term visitor would not allow it. I was on a three-month artist residency and had to produce a solo show in my second month there; time was not my friend. I could not, if I respected the community, rush them to consider me a worthy trustee of their stories under these circumstances. Who was I to insist on conviviality under time pressure? I've bemoaned hurried research in the Philippines enough to know that I could not, under these circumstances, produce work that merited approaching the personhood of Fanny Cochrane Smith or an understanding of the worlds she straddled. I can only speculate, but these speculations may not be welcome, as it is perhaps not my story to tell.

What the slowing of time also does is open a space that is necessary for emphasizing how knowledge is produced, circulated, and exchanged through a series of relationships that may not emerge in quick visits and consultations with people, community, or material. It asks you to *settle with*, to allow for time or for yourself to slowly unravel the complex set of relations before you. Slowing down is about focusing differently, listening carefully, and acting ethically. Slowness in this context is imagined and enacted in terms of relationality. What I can pose are questions I would have liked to ask, in the hope that perhaps one day, in the unfolding of all things, the answers may become clear. Could we read Smith's "displacement" in contemporary terms, as in Alzaldúa's "*nosotros los* Chicanos straddle the borderlands"?[20] Would a retelling of her story through the fragments left in the archive generate a new perspective that lends a better understanding of her personhood, her discomfort, and her "alienness"?

As Anzaldúa writes: "I am a border woman. […] I have been straddling that *tejas*-Mexican border, and others, all my life. It's not a comfortable territory to live in, this place of contradictions. Hatred, anger and exploitation are prominent features of this landscape. However, there have been compensations for this *mestiza*, and certain joys. Living on borders and in margins, keeping intact one's shifting and multiple identity and integrity, is like trying to swim in a new element, an 'alien' element." She continues, "The alien element has become familiar—*never comfortable*, not with society's clamor to uphold the old, to rejoin the flock, to go with the herd. No, not comfortable but home."[21]

The wax-cylinder recordings of Fanny Cochrane Smith remain the only recorded trace of a First Nations Tasmanian language. It is a testament to resistance and a gesture against erasure. These recordings are in the archival holdings of the NSFA and overseen by the curator of the Indigenous collections of the Tasmanian Museum and Art Gallery.

Smith lived on an Aboriginal settlement called Wybalenna, and when it closed, its forty-seven survivors were transported from Flinders Island to Oyster Cove, an ex-convict station near Hobart. This included Fanny, her mother Tanganutura, the man she called Father, whose name was

19 My discussion of refusal and "opacity" here draws from Édouard Glissant, "For Opacity," in *Poetics of Relation*, trans. Betsy Wing (Ann Arbor: University of Michigan Press, 1997), 189–94. I also see opacity as a strategy of resistance, an active "no" as an effective method of negotiating ways of being seen. In Glissant, opacity overcomes the risk of reduction and assimilation by being beyond comprehension.

20 Anzaldúa, *Borderlands / La Frontera*, 62.

21 Anzaldúa, preface to *Borderlands / La Frontera*, n.p. (last italics added).

Nicermenic, her half sister, her half brother, and Truganini, who was widely considered the "last full-blood" Tasmanian Aboriginal, as evidenced by a letter sent to the colonial secretary by the secretary of the Royal Society of Tasmania requesting possession of her corpse as a valuable scientific specimen.[22]

As mentioned in a 2022 broadcast of Nicole Steinke and Nick Baker's "The History Listen" on ABC Radio National, at age nineteen Fanny married a white settler named William Smith. On the occasion of their marriage, the government of the colony gave her a land grant of one hundred acres at the nearby Nicholls Rivulet—in recognition of her people's dispossession—and a pension of twenty-four pounds a year.[23] They had eleven children, and her marriage allowed her to escape the Oyster Cove settlement. In 1884, Parliament passed another resolution granting Fanny two hundred more acres in addition to the hundred she already owned, the reason being that she was the "last survivor of the aboriginal race," a title she fought hard for and claimed after Truganini's death.[24]

This decision to claim the title may have been contentious for Fanny. When she passed at the age of seventy-four on February 24, 1905, the Pakana people and their language (palawa kani) were recorded as "extinct." Her children and other Aboriginal descendants were simply erased. What few traces remain have become an invaluable carrier of culture.

Since the early 1990s, TAC has been recognized both within the Aboriginal community and beyond as the organization responsible for the meticulous work of restoring original languages. This involves reviving words and phrases and utilizing multiple historical languages to construct a single "official" Tasmanian Aboriginal language, palawa kani. Greatly contributing to this revitalization, the recordings of Smith

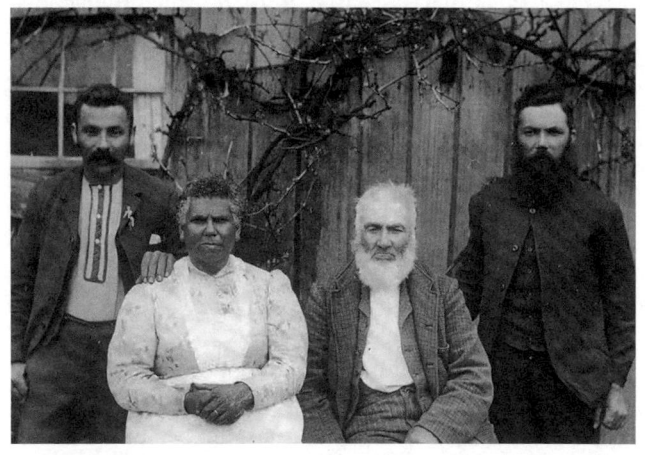

Fig. 13 Fanny Cochrane Smith with William and two of their sons, ca. 1885–99

22 Lyndall Ryan, *Tasmanian Aborigines: A History since 1803* (Sydney: Allan & Unwin, 2012), 169.

23 Nicole Steinke and Nick Baker, "Fanny Smith: The 'Genocide Survivor' Whose Voice Will Echo through the Ages," ABC Radio National, The History Listen, July 26, 2022, https://www.abc.net.au/news/2022-07-27/fanny-smith-last -aboriginal-tasmanian/101250498.

24 Murray J. Longman, "Songs of the Tasmanian Aborigines as Recorded by Mrs. Fanny Cochrane Smith," *Paper and Proceedings of the Royal Society of Tasmania* 94 (1960): 79–86.

are the only source of a spoken Tasmanian Indigenous language. The palawa kani program was run almost exclusively through the TAC.[25] The program was among the first in the country where the First Nations community learned the necessary linguistic methods for retrieving the only Aboriginal language in Lutruwita (Tasmania) today. "Not being a common vehicle for communication, palawa kani is a consciously created artifact that looks to a future in which Indigenous articulations increasingly foreground claim over content, and in which groups strive to come to terms with dispossession and loss by organizing around disjuncture itself."[26]

As Helen Ngo eloquently points out, "Although little discussed in the philosophical accounts of language, what the lived experiences of bilingualism and language's loss show us is that language and its maintenance (and/or recovery) can demand a certain labor. This labor can take many different forms and span different scales, ranging from collective action to intimate personal reorientations. […] The variety and extent of community initiative and support required for the task of language revitalization, where language is just not a result of personal migratory circumstances but a deliberate and integrated part of the British colonial project," a total erasure, is massive. She continues, "Language serves as an 'important … site of potential resistance,' and language revitalization projects thus play a critical role in efforts of decolonial reclamation, even if some have problematized the usual framing of such projects."[27]

There were two recording sessions with Watson and Smith: the first at the Royal Society of Tasmania in 1899 and the second at Barton Hall in 1903. The phonograph was cutting-edge technology at the time, and Watson might have been one of the earliest to use this recording equipment for documentary purposes. The wax cylinders of the phono-graph are cut by a needle attached directly to the brass horn that receives the sound. At the National Film and Sound Archive in Canberra, I had a long conversation with Gerard O'Neill, a senior film-sound and audio-disc specialist. I was fascinated with not only *how* the sound was recorded through the phonograph, the physicality of it, but also the quality of recordings the process produced, and how this was then digitized.

It turns out that creating a three-minute recording was a physical strain. One had to shout into the horn of the pho-nograph to move the needle and make an impression on the wax cylinder. It was not a coincidence that the best-quality wax-cylinder recordings were of brass-band sessions, as the wind coming from the instruments naturally forced the needle down. O'Neill led me through the process of record-ing such a cylinder. I wanted to be in Smith's shoes as she put sound to wax. The NFSA had an Edison Phonograph on hand, as well as a half-used wax-cylinder record that we could try out. A slowness and patience were necessary when dealing with such testy technology. As in all cases where the body of technology is entirely mechanical, the right settings need to be fully in place: the right needle length, the right horn, the way the cylinder sits on the cradle, the distance you had to be for the sound to travel precisely, the volume level you had to reach for the needle to move. The question that led my research then refocused on the materiality of the object before me. How could the archive's ability to occupy different temporalities be made or rendered audible and

25 Christopher D. Berk, "Palawi Kani and the Value of Language in Aboriginal Tasmania," *Oceania* 87, no. 1 (2017): 2.
26 Berk, 3; James Clifford, *The Predicament of Culture: Twentieth-Century Ethnography, Literature, and Art* (Cambridge, MA: Harvard University Press, 1988).
27 Ngo, "Her Mother's Tongue," 160–61.

visible through decolonial methods of artistic research, such as that of slowness? If I could not access Smith through the community, then perhaps understanding the circumstances of the recording and wax as a material could help me uncover aspects of her legacy as voice, as an orality.

> *In the case of language loss, there is a certain labor in trying to reacquaint oneself with it; to rediscover its music, to find its fluidity, to fill the void left of a tongue cut out.*[28]

The strain endured by Smith in singing loudly and in a sustained manner into this horn was likely considerable. In the recording, she sounds as if she's calling from very far away, projecting her voice over a distance. The scratchiness of the sound is an inherent factor of the recording—wax cylinders were made of a relatively soft wax formulation and would wear out the more they were played. For the language of an entire people to be held in such a delicate, self-destructing medium seemed to me the epitome of precarity. The wonderous thing about the Smith wax-cylinder recordings is that they have survived.

O'Neill set up the phonograph for me and marked the spot where I should stand. "Can you sing?" he asked. "I can try," I replied. And then with all my strength, stanzas of "Usahay" came ringing through the bell of the gramophone:

Usahay nagadamgo ako
Nga ikaw ug ako nagkahigugmaay
Nganong damguhon ko ikaw
Damguhon sa kanunay sa akong kamingaw

Usahay magamahay ako

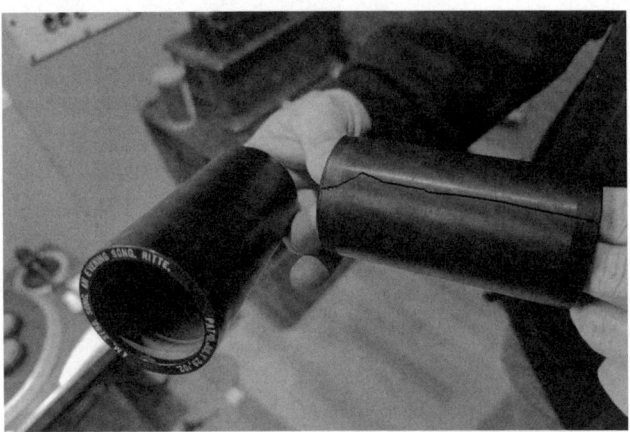

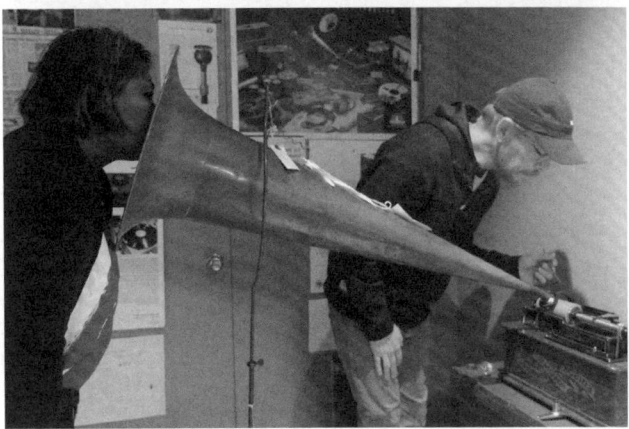

Fig. 14 Gerard O'Neill holding a copy of a working wax-cylinder record and an irreparable cracked one at the recording studio of the National Film and Sound Archive of Australia, Canberra, 2023
Fig. 15 Creating our own wax-cylinder recording at the recording studio of the National Film and Sound Archive of Australia, Canberra,

28 Ngo, 161.

Nganong nabuhi pa ning kalibutan
Nganong gitiaw-tiawan
Ang gugma ko kanimo kanimo day

(Sometimes, I dream
you and I are in love.
Why do I dream of you
So often in my loneliness?

Sometimes, I regret
Why I was born into this world
Why, do you jest
At my love for you,
for you my dear)[29]

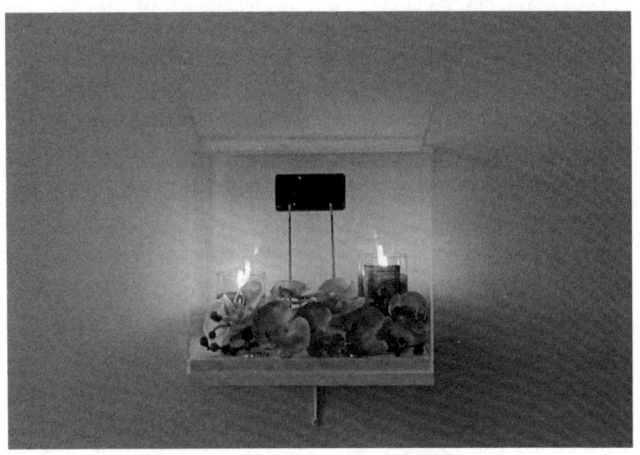

Fig. 16 Vitrine containing a wax-cylinder record, electric candles, orchids, gumnuts, and various religious paraphernalia. Stephanie Misa, *An altar for the fleshy tongue*, installation view, RMIT Gallery, Naarm (Melbourne), 2023.

29 The popular love song "Usahay" is considered a *kundiman*, a genre of Filipino serenades whose first renditions were in Tagalog. Incorporating Spanish musical styles during colonization brought about a cross-fertilization (and new genre) called the kundiman folk song, the first known version being the "Kundiman ng 1800" (Kundiman of 1800) in 1800. While kundiman songs are largely about love and courtship, they also contain strong undertones of nationalism and a yearning for liberty. Typical themes of unrequited love and suffering soon became metaphors for Spanish oppression. This modern version of the kundiman, "Usahay," was written in Bisaya by Gregorio Labjan in 1950.

Literature

Anderson, Quiliano Niñeza. "Kundiman Love Songs from the Philippines: Their Development from Folksong to Art Song and an Examination of Representative Repertoire." PhD diss., University of Iowa, 2015. https://doi.org/10.17077/etd.hivytk5h.

Anzaldúa, Gloria. *Borderlands / La Frontera: The New Mestiza*. 4th ed. San Francisco: Aunt Lute Books: 2007.

Berk, Christopher D. "Palawa Kani and the Value of Language in Aboriginal Tasmania." *Oceania* 87, no. 1 (2017): 2–20. https://doi.org/10.1002/ocea.5148.

Cha, Theresa Hak Kyung. *Dictee*. Berkeley: University of California Press, 2001.

Christen, Kimberly, and Jane Anderson. "Toward Slow Archives." *Archival Science*, no. 19 (2019): 87–116. https://doi.org/10.1007/s10502-019-09307-x.

Clifford, James. *The Predicament of Culture: Twentieth-Century Ethnography, Literature, and Art*. Cambridge, MA: Harvard University Press, 1988.

Dreisbach, Jeconiah Louis, and Feorillo Petronilo Demeterio. "Intergenerational Language Preference Shift among Cebuanos on the Cebuano, Filipino, and English Languages." *LLT Journal* 23, no. 2 (June 2020). doi.org/10.24071/llt.2020.230203.

Gallegos, Lori. "The Interpreter's Dilemma: On the Moral Burden of Consensual Heteronomy." In *Latin American Immigration Ethics*, edited by Amy Reed-Sandoval and Luis Rubén Díaz Cepeda, 243–64. Tucson: University of Arizona Press, 2022.

Glissant, Édouard. *Poetics of Relation*. Translated by Betsy Wing. Ann Arbor: University of Michigan Press, 1997.

Hoffman, Alvina. "Interview – Walter Mignolo/Part 2: Key Concepts." *E-International Relations*, January 21, 2017. https://www.e-ir.info/2017/01/21/interview-walter-mignolopart-2-key-concepts/.

Longman, Murray J. "Songs of the Tasmanian Aborigines as Recorded by Mrs. Fanny Cochrane Smith." *Paper and Proceedings of the Royal Society of Tasmania* 94 (1960): 79–86.

Ngo, Helen. "Her Mother's Tongue: Bilingual Dwelling, Being In-Between, and Intergenerational Co-creation of Language-Worlds." *Critical Philosophy of Race* 12, no. 1 (2024): 145–81.

Ong, Walter J. *Orality and Literacy: The Technologizing of the Word*. New York: Routledge, 1982.

Ryan, Lyndall. *Tasmanian Aborigines: A History since 1803*. Sydney: Allan & Unwin, 2012.

Steinke, Nicole, and Nick Baker. "Fanny Smith: The 'Genocide Survivor' Whose Voice Will Echo through the Ages." ABC Radio National, July 26, 2022. The History Listen. https://www.abc.net.au/news/2022-07-27/fanny-smith-last-aboriginal-tasmanian/101250498.

andrea ancira

Unlearning the Archive
A River as Trace

> An archive gives you a kind of valley in which your
> thoughts can bounce back to you, transformed.
> You whisper intuitions and thoughts into
> the emptiness, hoping to hear something back.
>
> Valeria Luiselli, *Lost Children Archive*, 2019

For more than ten years, I've been assembling a family archive. When I started this endeavor, I thought that through the archiving process, I'd be able to unpack my family's experiences of migration, exile, clandestinity, and forced disappearance during the Guatemalan civil war, which lasted from 1960 to 1996—one of the longest in Latin America. While this is still part of its raison d'être, what guides my work with/in this archive today is a communizing drive, a methodology that understands this collection as a space to explore collective mourning and what Tina Campt calls adjacency, a mode of working that refuses to participate in imperial Othering.[1] Despite its intimate manifestations, this collection of texts, photographs, films, drawings, and newspapers reinscribes me and these objects in a topography where what might be thought as belonging to the most fundamentally personal is nonetheless planted in a collective history. Rather than a registry that confirms the history of my family, this archive acts as a junction in which different experiences and narratives of the war intersect and are put in relation and conflict—after all, despite the impossibility of comparing histories of violence, these can be connected, whether historically, politically, or structurally. It is only if we think of these violent histories alongside and in connection to one another that we can be open to resonances and entanglements among them.[2] Within different timelines and histories, the objects of this archive participate in collective mourning and generate potential histories through stories and geographies that allow "for the appearance of events and for our appearance as their narrators."[3] As an individual and collective mode of remembering, these rehearsals of memory with the archive, rather than attempting to represent the objective and complete truth of an event, seek to document, co-construct, and poetically negotiate a narrative with multiple voices, perspectives, truths, and meanings in order to offer a nuanced understanding of situated and transitional accounts of social and personal histories.

1 Tina Campt's use of this term derives from her analysis of artworks by Luke Willis Thompson and wider practices of Black refusal. In Willis Thompson's work, the viewer is asked to find their position in relation to the ongoing oppression of Black bodies, and to feel how they are complicit in this violence and the structures that sustain it. According to Campt, through the "affective labor of adjacency" one can find a proximity to another's situation, and in recognizing this distance, work toward addressing it. Tina Campt, "Black Visuality and the Practice of Refusal," *Women in Performance* 29, no. 1 (2019): 79–87.

2 Michael Rothberg, *Multidirectional Memory: Remembering the Holocaust in the Age of Decolonization* (Stanford, CA: Stanford University Press, 2009), 1–29.

3 Ariella Aïsha Azoulay, "Potential History: Thinking Through Violence," *Critical Inquiry*, no. 39 (2013): 565.

Either/Or: Incomplete Mournings and Infinite Archives

"I used to call it the tunnel," I said, pointing to the entrance of my grandparents' basement.

"But why? It looks more like bunker," she replied, looking at the small entrance.

"Because as I would start descending the concrete stairs, I knew that a long, narrow, deep, dark passageway awaited me at the bottom. After walking half-blindly, groping along the walls, each time my hand would locate the right switch, the light would welcome me to a whole new portal."

This was one of my favorite playgrounds in my childhood. The darkness, the humidity, and the isolation of this room without windows could open a portal to another world in which life, as I knew it, could be interrupted. Before the end of the war, this room was almost empty, so my sisters, my cousins, and I gave it all kinds of shapes and functions. However, this portal was later cluttered with files and boxes that my mom stored there when we moved from Mexico to Guatemala. I still remember visiting this place occasionally, no longer to play but to dive into those dusty boxes that seemed to shelter another life that I had once had and that no longer seemed to be mine. I was thirteen.

Twenty-five years later, after my grandfather passed away, my grandmother began the daunting task of organizing his books, files, notes, and correspondence. Inadvertently, by dismantling my grandfather's archive, she became an archivist. In the process, she began to separate, categorize, and gather materials I might be interested in, which she gave me every time I visited. She knew that, for years, I had been trying to put together the pieces of a puzzle full of gaps and silences. However, as time passed, this generous way of opening up and distributing the materials began to extend to other people and institutions.

Archival work can be closely bound up with experiences of grief and bereavement.[4] Making and keeping records, following leads, deciphering materials, categorizing, connecting loose ends, opening up new routes, making new records, organizing—all these procedures play an important role in the grieving process as a means to continue a relationship with loss and what has been lost. Watching how my grandmother reassembled my grandfather's archive—and, in a way, being part of this operation—made me revisit my own archival endeavor and the way I had approached the archive until that moment. This experience gave me clues to approach the archive not with the aim of gluing together its fragments, bridging its gaps, or filling its silences; rather, it prompted me to work with its absences, with the connections it could afford, with its biases and its echoing silences.

I'm interested in the relationship to loss that archives forge. Can different procedures in the archive make room for forms of mourning and being-together *otherwise*? Or put differently, can the mourning process take different forms depending on how memory is mobilized through the making or reassembling of an archive? The acknowledgment of grief as a driving force of the collection I've assembled has brought to the forefront a recurring question that has to do with memory and mourning. Can an archive be a site that can

4 Jennifer Douglas, Alexandra Alisauskas, and Devon Mordell, "Treat Them with the Reverence of Archivists: Records Work, Grief Work, and Relationship Work in the Archives," *Archivaria*, no. 88 (2019): 84–120.

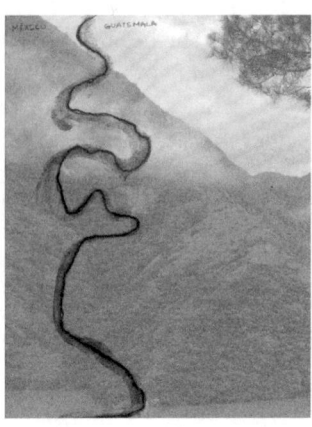

Fig. 17 andrea ancira, *The River Writhed Like a Wounded Snake 1*, 2023.
Photograph and watercolor.

hold collective memory practices? Can an archive become a
site to explore a grieving that aims not to overcome but to
work through collective trauma and conflicting relations to
the past? Can this grieving process through the archive make
room for shared vulnerabilities and resistance?

At first, when I resorted to the archive to elaborate this
personal as well as collective history of loss and trauma, I
wondered if it could be an appropriate memory device for
mourning or whether it could only afford to draw a melancholic relationship with the past. At that point, I was still
thinking within a Freudian binary scheme. Freud addresses
mourning and melancholia as mutually exclusive responses
to loss.[5] According to him, while both begin with the denial
of a loss and an unwillingness to recognize it, in the case of
mourning, the object is introjected and therefore openly declared lost or dead, whereas in melancholia, the loss remains
pathologically unacknowledged.

Some say that a clear-cut distinction between mourning and melancholia can actually betray the grieving process. For example, Jacques Derrida argues that when a lost object is assimilated, mourning is marked by an "unfaithful fidelity" that actually denies or betrays the infinite alterity of that which has been lost: "Mourning is an unfaithful fidelity if it succeeds in interiorizing the other ideally in me, that is, in not respecting his or her infinite exteriority."[6] In other words, a mourning that remains faithful to the infinite alterity of what has been lost must fail in Freudian terms, and if it is never completed successfully, it cannot be fully distinct from melancholy and its aporias.[7] Melancholy welcomes failure and the refusal of introjection. It makes room for a mourning that never quite allows us to forget that "to keep the other within oneself, as oneself, is already to forget the other," because "forgetting begins there."[8] This suggests that mourning must remain unsuccessful to some extent, and thus melancholic.

During one visit, my grandmother told me she had been hearing voices in the garden for weeks but had not mentioned it to anyone so as not to raise any concern. Her intuition drove her to the basement, where she found some boxes she did not recognize. Opening them, she found a series of reports from the Forensic Anthropology Foundation of Guatemala (Fundación de Antropología Forense de Guatemala, FAFG) with information about clandestine cemeteries in the Quiché region and a typed testimony of a person who survived one of the massacres that took place in the town of Río Negro.

5 Sigmund Freud, "Mourning and Melancholia," in *General Psychological Theory* (New York: Macmillan Publishing Company, 1963), 164–80.

6 Jacques Derrida, *Points …: Interviews, 1974–1994*, ed. Elisabeth Weber (Stanford, CA: Stanford University Press, 1995), 321.

7 Jacques Derrida and Elisabeth Roudinesco, *For What Tomorrow… A Dialogue*, trans. Jeff Fort (Stanford, CA: Stanford University Press, 2004), 159–60.

8 Jacques Derrida, "Rams," in *Sovereignties in Question: The Poetics of Paul Celan* (New York: Fordham University Press, 2005). 160.

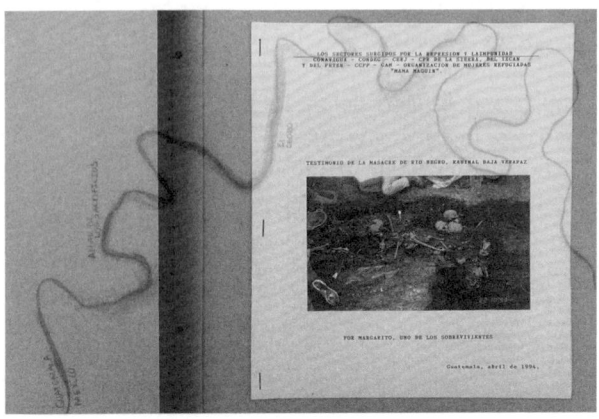

Fig. 18 andrea ancira, *The River Writhed Like a Wounded Snake 2*, 2023.
Photograph and watercolor.

In the early 1990s, survivors of the civil war began to report clandestine graves in their communities that contained peasants massacred during the scorched-earth policy pursued by the government a decade earlier. Since the government failed to pursue the investigations, local human-rights organizations requested the support of forensic teams that worked in the aftermath of the military dictatorships in Chile and Argentina.[9] These teams trained those who later formed FAFG. Since its creation in 1992, FAFG has investigated, documented, and provided expert assessments of human-rights violations, particularly unresolved murders, that occurred during the civil war, as well as cases derived from the violence that currently afflicts Guatemala. My grandmother speculated that these documents were part of the files transferred to the house after my grandfather finished his term at the Human Rights Office in the late nineties, when my mom, sisters, and I moved back to Guatemala.

She took the boxes out of the basement and placed them with the rest of the materials to give me on my next visit. After I took them, she told me that the voices quieted down. I was not sure what to do with these documents. Where or to whom do they belong? To the FAFG? To the communities that are mentioned and photographed in the reports? To the survivor who shared his testimony? I decided to go to Río Negro. I had read that the community was running a museum of historical memory in the town.

According to Ariella Azoulay, long before the archive was promoted as a form of salvation to overcome the frailty and vulnerability of memory, it was a technology used to organize masses of people, mainly slaves, and for looting.[10] Along with other thinkers, she argues that the archive, with its apparently neutral procedures, has contributed to organizing and dividing the world through exclusionary categories that undermine other forms of organization and relationships beyond the imperial imagination.[11] Following this critique, Azoulay suggests that one needs to unlearn the archive as an institution to unveil how its violence renders obsolete other forms of being-together. This unlearning process entails refusing the spatial and temporal regimes that the archive institutes, disregarding the boundaries set by its guardians, and contending with/in the archive, accompanied by those whom it excludes.[12]

Archives shelter memory, and shelter themselves from this memory. They hide their absences, and by doing so they also forget. It is only from their structure and their

9 Alma Nydia Vásquez Almazán, *Aporte de la antropología forense en la investigación de casos de violencia común en Guatemala: Fundación de Antropología Forense de Guatemala* (Guatemala City: USAC, 2007), 11.

10 Ariella Aïsha Azoulay, "Archives: The Commons, Not the Past," in *Potential History: Unlearning Imperialism* (London: Verso, 2019), 122–202.

11 Azoulay, 42–43.

12 Azoulay, 123.

procedures that it becomes possible to decipher what archives repress.[13] Every archive is haunted by its absences and its traces. This haunting triggers and mobilizes questions that transcend what the archive can or wants to narrate. Working with my family's archive beyond the fantasy of it being a "direct registry" of the past has allowed me to follow its absences and traces as well as to critically approach its "constitutive exclusion."[14] The repressive, unconscious, anti-archival force contained within any archive points to its incompleteness, its openness, and its infiniteness.[15]

The scholar Ann Cvetkovich elaborates on a different kind of exclusion or incompleteness in the archive—that which characterizes archives of trauma. According to her, the objects that compose this specific kind of archive and their psychic life are always arbitrary.[16] This is so because trauma can only make itself present outside the field of representation. It is an encryption, a ghost—it is defined by its compulsive returning, given that it fails to inscribe itself symbolically. Since the absence of trauma remains hidden, archives of trauma are always, by their very nature, partial and infinite.

An archive of trauma is an archive of memory gaps, of absent presences. It's a place to hold the unbearable nature of an event and the unbearable nature of its survival. It's a site to mourn collectively an event that has not yet come to an end. An archive of this kind is a space to co-witness and preserve traumatic histories in ways that challenge the meaning of the archive and memorials. It's an archive driven not by accumulation but by gestures of care. It's an archive that aims for affective power rather than factual truth. An archive that understands "the quest for history as a psychic need rather than a science."[17]

The River Writhed Like a Wounded Snake

Exile and migration are experiences that raise the question of belonging, not only for those who experience it firsthand but also for the generations that follow. My grandparents' exile in Mexico as well as our eventual "return" to Guatemala in the nineties were transitions that shaped my porous and oscillating identity between the two countries. The Usumacinta River is a body of water that flows through an in-between space that speaks to the question of belonging to one country or another. Originating in the highlands of Quiché and Totonicapán in Guatemala, this river draws a line that defines part of the border with Mexico, and continues all the way to the Gulf of Mexico. An arm of the Usumacinta, the Chixoy River, or Río Negro, is the third longest river in Guatemala, located in a "strategic" region, because of its abundant natural resources, and home to the community of Río Negro. In 1970, during the civil war, the dictator Carlos Arana had the state and army displace communities that inhabited an area they wanted to use for the construction of the hydroelectric Chixoy Dam, today the country's main electric power plant. The

13 Jacques Derrida, *Archive Fever: A Freudian Impression* (Chicago: University of Chicago Press, 1998), 2.

14 For Chantal Mouffe and Ernesto Laclau, exclusion is an essential ontological feature of all political systems. Exclusion is the logic that grounds the existence of political bodies and political agency, particularly under existing regimes of white supremacy, heteronormativity, patriarchy, and ableism. This notion troubles the idea of the democratization of the archive (or any political apparatus) in terms of inclusion because the marking of a "constitutive outside" will always require a political "inside." The eagerness to democratize the archive promises to include everyone; however, this move toward inclusion continues to be based on certain assumptions about who is included, therefore failing to overcome the constitutive exclusion that determines the idea of inclusion in each case. Chantal Mouffe and Ernesto Lacalu, *Hegemony and Socialist Strategy* (London: Verso, 1986).

15 Derrida, *Archive Fever*, 68.

16 Ann Cvetkovich, *An Archive of Feelings: Trauma, Sexuality, and Lesbian Public Cultures* (Durham, NC: Duke University Press, 2003), 268.

17 Cvetkovich, 268.

people who refused to resettle were kidnapped, tortured, and murdered on the false claim that they were part of guerrilla groups.[18] This became a common state alibi to justify massacres on the land and noncompliance with the compensation agreements, neglecting the people affected by the project.

The construction of the dam was approved in 1975 as part of the government's development program, with financial support from international institutions such as the Inter-American Development Bank and the World Bank.[19] Since its construction, the village of Río Negro was left with only two entry points, one via the river and the other by land. You can only access the first through the dam facility and a twenty-minute boat ride. Walking to the community through the second entry point takes around eight hours from the last bus stop. While the Chixoy Dam is deemed one of the government's most ambitious projects, there was no comprehensive census of affected peoples conducted, and the land was not acquired legally. Moreover, they did not provide proper compensation, resettlement, or alternative livelihoods for the 3,500 (mostly Mayan) residents who were displaced or for the thousands in the surrounding communities confronted with the flooding of their land and property.[20] The international institutions involved in the project were aware of these problems; nonetheless, they continued to loan money in the name of so-called development.

When the construction of the dam was complete and the reservoir waters rose in January 1983, military and civil forced the remaining population to leave at gunpoint. In this village, more than half of the population was killed; ten communities in the river basin had already been either massacred or forcibly displaced. Ten years after these events, Guatemala's Commission for Historical Clarification declared that this state-sponsored violence constituted genocide.

The state's creation of the Northern Transversal Strip (NTS) through the implementation of an agrarian development law is an example of how the reconfiguration of territory in Guatemala is tied to a combination of war and extractivist policies that have historically driven multiple processes of accumulation by dispossession.[21] Río Negro's case is one of many that show how extractivism has been predicated in Guatemala on a legacy of appropriation and exploitation of nature by convenient alliances forged at different historical moments between transnational or regional elites and the political class. As the sociologist Diego Padilla Vassaux suggests, "The formation of the Nation-State has always included violent extractive operations that facilitate the exploitation of territories in favor of transnational and corporate processes of the accumulation of capital."[22]

18 International Rivers Network / Witness for Peace, "NGOs Demand World Bank Investigation into 1980s Massacres at Guatemalan Dam: Report Reveals 376 Murdered after Resisting Eviction," press release, May 9, 1996, http://www.hartford-hwp.com/archives/47/158.html.

19 Nathan Einbinder, *Dams, Displacement and Development: Perspectives from Río Negro, Guatemala* (Berlin: Springer, 2017).

20 In 2012, the Interamerican Court of Justice ruled in favor of the Río Negro community and ordered the state to make a series of reparations, which has not yet happened. Regina Pérez, "Comunidades afectadas por represa Chixoy en Guatemala, a la espera de que el Estado cumpla medidas de reparación," *Desinformémonos*, November 12, 2022, https://desinformemonos.org/comunidades-afectadas-por-represa-chixoy-en-guatemala-a-la-espera-de-que-el-estado-cumpla-medidas-de-reparacion/.

21 Negli Gallardo Alvarado, "Accumulation by Dispossession and Its Restrictions on the Citizen Exercise of Indigenous People's Rights in Guatemala: The Marlin Mine Case, San Miguel Ixtahuacán, San Marcos," *Estudios Interétnicos*, no. 31 (2020): 43–65; Santiago Bastos Amigo, "Introduction: Community, Dispossession, and Ethnic Rearticulation in Mexico and Guatemala," *Latin American and Caribbean Ethnic Studies* 16, no. 1 (2020): 1–21; David Harvey, *The New Imperialism* (Oxford: Oxford University Press, 2003), 143–44.

22 Diego A. Padilla Vassaux, "El extractivismo neoliberal en Guatemala: Una mirada histórica crítica a la formación del Estado y la explotación del agua," in *Aguas turbias: Extractivismo (neo)liberal, acción jurídica indígena y la transformación del Estado en Guatemala*, ed. Lieselotte Viaene and María Jacinta Xón Riquiac (Madrid: ERC RIVERS Project – Universidad Carlos III de Madrid, 2022), 16. Translations by the author unless noted otherwise.

I began to engage in a conversation with the Usumacinta River, navigating its passages, its furies, and its stillness. I drew closer to it with the same empathy with which I have grown closer to the archive of objects that I have assembled. As I visited the river, I began to listen to the questions and thoughts that run in its waters. Each visit involved, at its core, an active and timeless listening. A kind of listening in nonlinear time, in which knowledge, experiences, and imaginations intersect. A listening that has indeed marked my continuous but impermanent relationship with this body of water. Through repeated visits, the river revealed itself as a line of times, "a place to be with the histories and futures that are buried in the dominant storying of land as white, as nation-state, as Christian, as resource."[23] A place to trace memory, belonging, and grief within water's plural and indivisible flows and layers.

I arrived at the Chixoy Dam early in the morning. Once again, S had gotten permission from the authorities to enter the facility. S would pick me up with his boat. Every time I visit, S drives the boat as close to the gates of the dam as possible. It's hard to say what motivates this ritual. Respect for the river? Contempt for the dam? A gesture of accepting the inevitable? We are both in the boat, standing still, right before the gates. The same gates that flooded twenty-three villages, cropland, and forty-five archaeological sites in 1982. The same gates that keep 2,500 years of history underwater.

When we arrived at Río Negro, I left my things in a multi-purpose room set up for lodging and workshops. This house is part of the History and Education Center Riij Ib'ooy, which is managed by the community. Since its construction in 2008, this center seeks to hold the memory of the times, both glorious and gruesome, of this community's long history. The

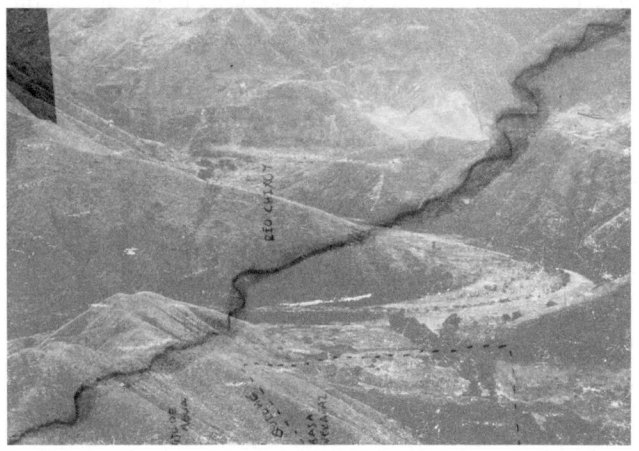

Fig. 19 andrea ancira, *The River Writhed Like a Wounded Snake 3*, 2023.
Photograph and watercolor.

23 Eve Tuck, Haliehana Stepetin, Rebecca Beaulne-Stuebing, and Jo Billows,
"Visiting as an Indigenous Feminist Practice," *Gender and Education* 35, no. 2
(2023): 144.

historical museum that brought me to Río Negro is part of this center, and goes by the name Casa de la Memoria. In the one-room building made of stone with two wood-frame windows is a permanent exhibition with testimonies about the massacres of the community during the war, as well as the names and portraits of those who were killed. It also displays broken Mayan ceramic vessels and other remains from the sites flooded by the dam's reservoir.

I met J and S the first time I went to Río Negro to offer the documents from my grandfather's archive to Casa de la Memoria. J and S are the only survivors of the massacres who still live in the community. Perhaps this explains their strong commitment to the community's social center, to the memorial at the Pacoxom hill, where a Mayan ceremony is conducted on March 13 every year to remember the women, men, and children who were murdered, and to the Coordinadora de Comunidades Afectadas por la Construcción de la Hidroeléctrica Chixoy.[24]

S asked if I had brought the printed map, and I nodded. This rehearsal of memory was suggested by J and S. It involved locating on a map the different towns and mountains that run along the middle basin of the river and marking them with their Maya Achí names. These names have been transmitted orally from generation to generation, and they do not appear on any official map of Guatemala. In this rehearsal, naming and mapping became a way to remember and honor the past within the present. To retrace, to walk within the traces and to make new ones—a palimpsest of eras. The rehearsal was a way to acknowledge how the river's flows have shaped and keep shaping our shared history. But it also revealed the river as a disquieted trace of an impossible archive composed of infinite traces without an inventory.

Find the river

Feel its scars
Trace the wounds

What remains?

Objects evoke conversations
Conversations evoke memories
Memories evoke landscapes
Landscapes evoke prophetic visions of the past

You know nothing.
You are the subject of an infinite rehearsal.

24 The COCAHICH is a political platform that articulates the demands
of the communities affected by the construction of the hydroelectric dam
and follows up on the fulfillment of the reparation plan they signed with the
government in September 2006.

Literature

Vásquez Almazán, Alma Nydia. *Aporte de la antropología forense en la investigación de casos de violencia común en Guatemala: Fundación de Antropología Forense de Guatemala.* Guatemala City: USAC, 2007.

Azoulay, Ariella Aïsha. "Potential History: Thinking Through Violence." *Critical Inquiry*, no. 39 (2013): 548–74.

Azoulay, Ariella Aïsha. *Potential History: Unlearning Imperialism.* London: Verso, 2019.

Bastos Amigo, Santiago. "Introduction: Community, Dispossession, and Ethnic Rearticulation in Mexico and Guatemala." *Latin American and Caribbean Ethnic Studies* 16, no. 1 (2020): 1–21.

Campt, Tina. "Black Visuality and the Practice of Refusal." *Women in Performance* 29, no. 1 (2019): 79–87.

Cvetkovich, Ann. *An Archive of Feelings: Trauma, Sexuality, and Lesbian Public Cultures.* Durham, NC: Duke University Press, 2003.

Derrida, Jacques. *Archive Fever: A Freudian Impression.* Chicago: University of Chicago Press, 1998.

Derrida, Jacques. *Sovereignties in Question: The Poetics of Paul Celan.* New York: Fordham University Press, 2005.

Derrida, Jacques, and Elisabeth Roudinesco. *For What Tomorrow… A Dialogue.* Stanford, CA: Stanford University Press, 2004.

Derrida, Jacques, and Elisabeth Weber. *Points: Interviews, 1974–1994.* Stanford, CA: Stanford University Press, 1995.

Douglas, Jennifer, Alexandra Alisauskas, and Devon Mordell. "Treat Them with the Reverence of Archivists: Records Work, Grief Work, and Relationship Work in the Archives." *Archivaria*, no. 88 (2019): 84–120.

Einbinder, Nathan. *Dams, Displacement and Development: Perspectives from Río Negro, Guatemala.* Berlin: Springer, 2017.

Freud, Sigmund. "Mourning and Melancholia." In *General Psychological Theory*, 164–80. New York: Macmillan Publishing Company, 1963.

Gallardo Alvarado, Negli. "Accumulation by Dispossession and Its Restrictions on the Citizen Exercise of Indigenous People's Rights in Guatemala: The Marlin Mine Case, San Miguel Ixtahuacán, San Marcos." *Estudios Interétnicos*, no. 31 (2020): 43–65.

Harvey, David. *The New Imperialism.* Oxford: Oxford University Press, 2003.

Mouffe, Chantal, and Ernesto Lacalu. *Hegemony and Socialist Strategy.* London: Verso, 1986.

Padilla Vassaux, Diego A. "El extractivismo neoliberal en Guatemala: Una mirada histórica crítica a la formación del Estado y la explotación del agua." in *Aguas turbias: Extractivismo (neo)liberal, acción jurídica indígena y la transformación del Estado en Guatemala*, ed. Lieselotte Viaene and María Jacinta Xón Riquiac, 15–52. Madrid: ERC RIVERS Project – Universidad Carlos III de Madrid, 2022.

Rothberg, Michael. *Multidirectional Memory: Remembering the Holocaust in the Age of Decolonization.* Stanford, CA: Stanford University Press, 2009.

Tuck, Eve, Haliehana Stepetin, Rebecca Beaulne-Stuebing, and Jo Billows. "Visiting as an Indigenous Feminist Practice." *Gender and Education* 35, no. 2 (2023): 144–55.

Nina Hoechtl

A Visual Glossary, Expanded
Delirio güero (White Delusion)

In this essay, after a short prologue to introduce the word *güero/a/x* (whitey)—predominantly used in Mexican and Chicano Spanish—I add three more entries to the visual glossary I first published in 2020.[1] Building on my film *DELIRIO GÜERO WHITE DELUSION. 2211, 2018, 1825 and Back* (2018), these new entries enable a necessarily incomplete dialogue around a concept I coined, *delirio güero* (White delusion)—a dialogue that engages in a complex practice of entanglement and entitlement, implication and aspiration, innocence and ignorance, denial and delusion. The film chews over various delirio güero acts in Mexico carried out by the monarchs Maximilian of Habsburg and Charlotte of Belgium, the self-appointed explorer-artist Jean-Friedrich Waldeck, the architect-researcher-photographer Teobert Maler and Anton "Toni" Mayr—both followers of Maximilian—and a relative of Mayr, the artist who made *DELIRIO GÜERO*.

This essay is divided into sections: (1) "The White Savior vs. 'Politics of Location,'" which divests the figure of the White savior insinuated in the film's closing words; (2) "Autohistoria-teoría Practices to Unlearn Privileges," which challenges the internal and external güero by collaboratively writing a song (which plays over the credits of *DELIRIO GÜERO*); and (3) "A Hauntological (Auto)Biography: White Genetic Essentialism," which focuses on a brief, seemingly innocent statement to contemplate a hauntological approach to inheritance and heritage (as dark they might be and in any form they might take—personal, biological, cultural, visual, or epistemological).

Prologue: A Spoiled Egg

"In 1611, Sebastián de Covarrubias, a Spanish cleric, lexicographer, Romanist and Hispanist, declared 'Díxose güero el güevo del que no pollo, y corrompido es de muy mal olor.' 'The egg that does not hatch is called güero, and if it rots, it smells bad,'" the film's host, La Güera, says as she opens her show.[2] Emitting a strong sulfurous smell, the spoiled egg looms over the whole film and the different kinds of delirio güero it tackles. La Güera explains further: "Women, whose only child was sick, pale, discolored, and with small chances to survive, sometimes said, 'Dióme dios un güevo, i diómele güero.' 'God gave me an egg (*güevo*), I gave him a güero.' From this proverb comes the expression 'salió güero,' hence it 'worked out güero' means 'it failed.' Güero was thus associated with pale, sickly, doomed people."

1 Nina Hoechtl, "A Visual Glossary: *Delirio güero* (White Delusion)," in *Sharpening the Haze: Visual Essays on Imperial History and Memory*, ed. Giulia Carabelli et al. (London: Ubiquity Press, 2020), 159–74.

2 Nina Hoechtl, *DELIRIO GÜERO WHITE DELUSION. 2211, 2018, 1825 and Back, 2018*. 53 min. 33 sec., https://vimeo.com/511236180 (Spanish with English subtitles), https://vimeo.com/291412548 (German with English subtitles).

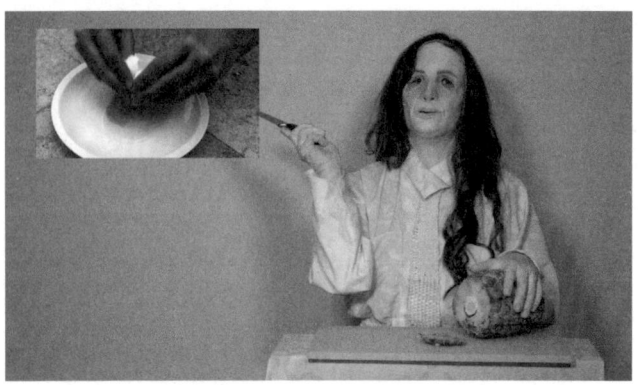

Fig. 20 Nina Hoechtl, *DELIRIO GÜERO WHITE DELUSION. 2211, 2018, 1825 and Back*, 2018. Video still.

DELIRIO GÜERO can be viewed on Vimeo in German or Spanish with English subtitles. Watching this film or reading the first three entries of the visual glossary is not required to comprehend the following three entries. These chapters work independently from each other, although they are united by a shared concern for the delirio güero as a process that masks devastating implications and impacts.

The White Savior vs. "Politics of Location"

Whatever the issue, they [Natives] are entrapped
in a circular dance where they always find themselves
a pace behind the white saviors.

Trinh T. Minh-ha, *Woman, Native, Other*, 1989

Internalized anti-Blackness is real,
and it will have you on the frontlines reinforcing
a system of white supremacy and upholding

racist policies and practices
that legitimize your own suffering and demise.

April Baker-Bell, *Linguistic Justice*, 2020

Let's dwell on the final scene of *DELIRIO GÜERO*, in which a mysterious know-it-all figure from the early years of the twenty-third century—a ghost from the future—asks the audience what they would like to hear about La Güera, the host. The ghost spills the beans:

> She thought that the system was discriminatory, exploitative, corrupt, and malicious? That she thought. That she was sorry? That she was. That she wasn't like the rest? If you had seen her at an art opening she would have told you exactly that. She would have said that only she and perhaps a few others of her tribe had eyes that could see, and that she was appalled by what she saw and that it motivated her to resist. She would have purported to be without prejudice, to love disadvantaged and Indigenous peoples, to listen to them, to support them and to work with them. And probably you would have believed her. She almost believed herself.

It becomes clear that La Güera is yet another who easily assumes one of the preferred and reflexive positions of White people: the White savior.[3] In the case of La Güera, she is a

---

3 If not lowercased in citations or terms coined by theorists, the term "White" is capitalized in this text following Nell Irvin Painter's proposal: "Being racialized makes white people squirm, so let's racialize them with that capital W." Nell Irvin Painter, "Why 'White' Should Be Capitalized, Too," *West Central Tribune*, July 23, 2020, https://www.wctrib.com/opinion/nell-irvin-painter-why-white-should -be-capitalized-too. Sonita Sarker has suggested capitalizing the term to indicate a collective racialization and the responsibilities that this collectivity carries, and to counteract the ways in which individualization is promoted through the lowercase *w*. Sonita Sarker, "The Whiteness Problem," *Modernism/modernity* 7, cycle 3, June 12, 2023, https://doi.org/10.26597/mod.0258.

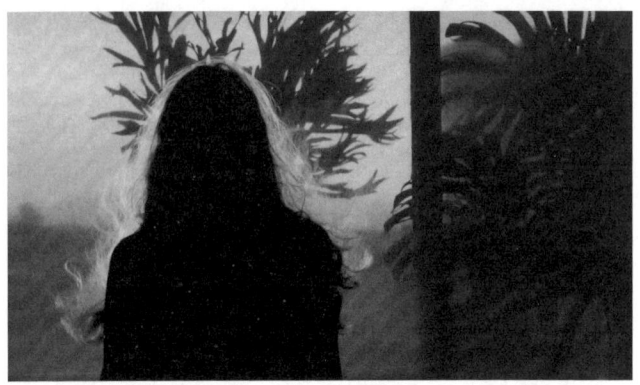

Fig. 21 Nina Hoechtl, *DELIRIO GÜERO WHITE DELUSION. 2211, 2018,*
1825 and Back, 2018. Video still.

supposed rescuer of disadvantaged and Indigenous peoples,
even working with them in the arts. What better field than
the arts—with its unregulated market riddled with unethi-
cal practices, "free labor and rampant exploitation,"[4] insider
trading, gender, racial, class, and cultural imbalances, which
all stem from colonial-imperial legacies!

Gayatri Chakravorty Spivak astutely comments that the
"most frightening thing about imperialism, its long-term toxic
effect, what secures it, what cements it, is the benevolent
self-representation of the imperialist as savior."[5] Driven by
good intentions, La Güera defects from "her tribe," conveniently setting herself apart as a savior while riding on imperialism. Although she seeks to position herself through a
savior narrative, she is neither outside the system nor neutral
or innocent. Quite the opposite! La Güera is well-meaning
and complicit in this system. A system that La Güera, as an
individual, did not create but benefits from. A system that,
in today's Mexico, is predominantly defined by *mestizaje*

(mixture). Resulting from a history of conquest and colonization, this racial and/or cultural mixing is a critical part of nation-building and cultural identity for Mexico in particular, and across Latin America in general.[6]

In her empirical research on anti-Indigenous and anti-Black racism in Mexico, Mónica Moreno Figueroa has opened up a space within the complex interconnections between mestizaje and *blanquitud* (Whiteyness).[7] While Bolívar Echeverría conceptualizes blanquitud as an ethical or civilizational form of racism demanded by capitalist modernity, Moreno Figueroa brings to the fore how the mestizo/a/x category is the referent that orders all identities asymmetrically in a racist logic. "Mestizaje operates as complex form of whiteness, that is, as a normative privileged location of identity that is normalized and ambiguous," she explains.

4 Hito Steyerl, "Politics of Art: Contemporary Art and the Transition to Post-democracy," in *The Wretched of the Screen* (Berlin: Sternberg Press, 2012), 96.

5 Gayatri Chakravorty Spivak, "Acting Bits/Identity Talk," in *An Aesthetic Education in the Era of Globalization* (Cambridge, MA: Harvard University Press, 2013), 166.

6 Edward Telles and his colleagues at the Project of Race and Ethnicity in Latin America (PERLA) show the ideology of mestizaje as the foundation of nation-states across Latin America. For example, strong mestizo ideologies took hold in Mexico and Brazil, and to some degree in Peru; in contrast, mestizaje had little resonance in nation-states of the Southern Cone (Argentina, Uruguay, and, to some degree, Chile and Costa Rica). These different conceptions of state, race, and mestizaje have sociopolitical consequences. See Edward E. Telles and the Project on Ethnicity and Race in Latina America (PERLA), *Pigmentocracies: Ethnicity, Race, and Color in Latin America* (Chapel Hill: University of North Carolina Press, 2014).

7 Bolívar Echeverría coined the term "blanquitud" and its translation, "whiteyness," in reference to the title figure of Rainer Werner Fassbinder's movie *Whity* (1971), the obedient butler who is the illegitimate son of a White rancher and his Black cook. Bolívar Echeverría, "'Blanquitud': Considerations on Racism as a Specifically Modern Phenomenon," *Revista Nueva Realidad*, no. 1 (July/August 2020): 9. Echeverría marks an important distinction between *blancura* (whiteness)—as a racial category based on the biological and cultural marking of the skin—and blanquitud. See Bolívar Echeverría, *Racismo y blanquitud* (Mexico City: Zineditorial, 2018), 26; and the English translation, *Modernity and "Whiteness,"* trans. Rodrigo Ferreira (Cambridge: Polity Press, 2019). Ferreira puts "whiteness" in quotation marks to capture Echeverría's distinction. Throughout this text, I use blanquitud when referring to the context in Mexico.

"When mestizaje became 'the national', its characterization as historically racialized and national became blurred and the national prevailed, dominated, pervaded and consolidated a shift towards racelessness."[8] Mestizaje maintains blanquitud as its main reference, whether through movements that approach the imaginary of blanquitud or establish a certain distance to it. In Mexico, the mestizaje system could thus be seen as denying Indigenous and Black identities as much as Indigenous and African descent.[9] Researchers from the Project of Ethnicity and Race in Latin America (PERLA) have compared the correlation of social status and skin pigmentation in Latin American societies, as well as the privileges generally assigned to blanquitud in the region's "pigmentocracies."[10]

La Güera operates within this system but considers herself part of it only because she "loves" and "cares." Don't be fooled by La Güera's gender! Care as labor has been feminized, while its racialized aspect has been conveniently overlooked (likewise how it has been unequally distributed across geographical zones).[11] The desire of La Güera to uphold her position, however precarious and complicit, under the disguise of doing and being good, produces a "mere benevolence" that keeps asymmetrical relations of power, such as gender, racialization, ethnicity, and class, in place—or, to use Spivak's wording, "in cement."[12] It is the delirio güero of ignorance and innocence that shields the "discriminatory, exploitative, corrupt and malicious" system from interrogation and the transformation of the cement.[13]

This delirio güero is simultaneously informed by Charles Mill's concept of "the epistemology of white ignorance" and "white innocence," a syndrome and paradox that Gloria Wekker explores in relation to the Netherlands today.[14] The epistemology of white ignorance, as Mills argues, involves systemically supported and socially induced patterns of (mis) understanding that function to sustain redundant oppression and privilege. Such ignorance conceals the consequences of the cemented exploitative system so that those who benefit from it, as La Güera does, do not have to consider their complicity in perpetuating it. Wekker has shown how white innocence lies at the heart of the passionate denial of racial discrimination alongside aggressive racism and xenophobia in the Netherlands. Although the systems of locally dominant ways of (not) dealing with histories of racialization and racist logics are different in the Netherlands and Mexico, there is a similarity insofar as "Mexicans do not recognize themselves as racial subjects, but as national subjects and citizens" alongside what Moreno Figueroa spells out as "the

8 Mónica Moreno Figueroa, "Distributed Intensities: Whiteness, Mestizaje and the Logics of Mexican Racism," *Ethnicities*, no. 10 (2010): 399.

9 María Josefina Saldaña-Portillo, *The Revolutionary Imagination in the Americas and the Age of Development* (Durham, NC: Duke University Press, 2003).

10 In PERLA's study, respondents were asked to self-identify rather than select a categorization created by others, as has become the international standard for racial or other kinds of classification in national censuses. See Edward Telles and René Flores, "Not Just Color: Whiteness, Nation and Status in Latin America," *Hispanic American Historical Review* 93, no. 3 (2013): 411–49, https://doi .org/10.1215/00182168-2210858; Telles and PERLA, *Pigmentocracies*; and PERLA, accessed January 17, 2024, https://perla.princeton.edu/.

11 The decolonial feminist scholar and activist Françoise Vergès has unpacked how the Global North constructs a "clean"/"dirty" dichotomy between different geographical zones. Their image of "cleanliness" is maintained by the present-day colonial practice of shipping waste to the Global South. Françoise Vergès, "Capitalocene, Waste, Race, and Gender," *e-flux journal*, no. 100, May 2019, https://www.e-flux.com/journal/100/269165/capitalocene-waste-race -and-gender/.

12 Spivak, "Acting Bits/Identity Talk," 166.

13 Hoechtl, *DELIRIO GÜERO*.

14 Charles W. Mills, "White Ignorance," in *Race and Epistemologies of Ignorance*, ed. Shannon Sullivan and Nancy Tuana (Albany: State University of New York Press, 2007); Gloria Wekker, *White Innocence: Paradoxes of Colonialism and Race* (Durham, NC: Duke University Press, 2016).

commonly spread idea that in Mexico there is no racism because 'we are all mixed.'"[15]

In a system that mystifies the güero through the mestizo/a/x category, the delirio güero plays neatly into the White savior role. "To a significant extent," Mills maintains, "white signatories [to the racial contract such as mestizaje and blanquitud] will live in an invented delusional world, a racial fantasyland, a 'consensual hallucination.'"[16] In Mexico, this space of ignorance and innocence generates specific types of delirio güero—delusional ways of perceiving and being in the world that are locally and socioculturally validated by dominant norms. The figure of the White savior is but one of many that involve the privilege of not needing to ask certain questions instead of just meaning well and doing and being good. While supporting the struggle of those they view to be more oppressed, "the preservation of that precious innocent sense of self," "loving, knowing ignorance," and "mere benevolence" may be exercised.[17] There is a fine line between acting with respect in solidarity or in thoughtless and delusional ways that simply reproduce the figure of the White savior. Consequently, the difference between acting with respect in solidarity and acting from La Güera's "own tribe" is not a minor issue. Exhorting White feminists to examine "thoughtlessly white" assumptions underpinning a wide range of approaches—such as the White savior figure—Adrienne Rich directs the focus to "the meaning of whiteness as a point of location."[18] As opposed to an ahistorical "lofty and privileged" abstract theorizing, Rich demands to recognize the location and "name the ground we are coming from and the conditions we have taken for granted."[19] This politics of location does not take locality as the site of foundational knowledge; rather, it understands location as the place of experienced and intersectional connections. Rich advocates not for transcending the body but for reconnecting the act of thinking/speaking/creating with situated experiences, particular geographies, and living bodies. Although La Güera does not transcend the body—if we are to believe the ghost from the future—delirio güero conveniently prevents her from seeing how she asserts her privilege time and again, even as she, supposedly, seeks to challenge it. In Mexico, blanquitud is an ongoing everyday social construct that is conveyed not only as a discourse but also through the practice or performance of power in the modern capitalist system—or, as I have argued in the "Whitey Masking Blanquitud" entry of my visual glossary, the employment of Whitey masks in order "to become *homo capitalisticus*."[20] Masking and enacting blanquitud becomes a way in which gendered, racial, and class hierarchies of belonging are materialized to achieve a higher status in an asymmetrical society. Consequently, Moreno Figueroa succinctly points out that it makes a difference to think about blanquitud in a context that has had mestizaje at the core of its colonial-modern nation-state, which is the case in Mexico, as Whiteness in the United States, "South Africa, and maybe some similarities with Europe have to do with logics of segregation."[21]

15 Mónica Moreno Figueroa, "Naming Ourselves: Recognising Racism and Mestizaje in Mexico," in *Contesting Recognition*, ed. Janice McLaughlin, Peter Phillimore, and Diane Richardson (Basingstoke: Palgrave, 2011), 123.

16 Charles W. Mills, *The Racial Contract* (Ithaca, NY: Cornell University Press, 1997), 18.

17 Wekker, *White Innocence*, 166; Mariana Ortega, "Being Lovingly, Knowingly Ignorant: White Feminism and Women of Color," *Hypatia* 21, no. 3 (Summer 2006): 56–74; Spivak, "Acting Bits/Identity Talk," 166.

18 Adrienne Rich, "Notes toward a Politics of Location" (1984), in *Blood, Bread, Poetry: Selected Prose, 1979–1984* (New York: Norton, 1986), 219.

19 Rich, 219.

20 Hoechtl, "A Visual Glossary," 162.

21 Mónica Moreno Figueroa, "Mestizaje: When the Shades Dissimulate Whiteness," *The Funambulist*, June 22, 2023, https://thefunambulist.net/magazine /fifty-shades-of-whiteness/mestizaje-when-the-shades-dissimulate-whiteness.

In her book *Playing in the Dark: Whiteness and the Literary Imagination* (1993), Toni Morrison points out that much energy has been invested in analyzing "the origin and fabrication of racism itself" rather than "the impact of racism on those who perpetuate it"—for example, those who benefit from the "*racist logic* that distributes privilege and exclusion within everyday life."[22] Despite the centrality of race in de(s)-colonial theory from Latin America, Breny Mendoza notes that "there is no elaborate mestizaje analysis, nor is there adequate self-reflection on the writer's place of enunciation in the system of race."[23] Mendoza calls for "a hard look at intersectionality [... to] examine our own involvement in the coloniality of power, [...] and our presence on the land we inhabit," in order to scrutinize social categories that maintain relative privileges within racist structures and dynamics, and to grapple with that which falls between these categories.[24]

Patriarchy, Rich points out, does not exist in a "pure state"; neither does Whiteness or blanquitud.[25] A politics of location thus addresses when, where, and under which conditions Whiteness and blanquitud operate in specific and different sociocultural contexts. In other words, a politics of location leads to a series of questions that reveal the contingency of meaning/making/creating processes: For whom am I writing/speaking/creating? Toward what end am I writing/speaking/creating this? Given the particularities of my location, what are the limitations of the knowledge I am participating in and creating? From when and where am I writing/speaking/creating? A politics of location constructs a potentially different kind of knowledge, one that centers difference rather than universality, maintaining a degree of accountability for its claims, which are understood as partial and situated. Hereafter, our task involves identifying, denouncing, and undoing the elements that reproduce multiple asymmetries of gender, sexuality, class, processes of racialization, and racist logics as part of the modern capitalist order, including and especially within the güero/a/x and the mestizo/a/x categories themselves. It starts with recognizing that the figure of the White savior predominately satisfies the savior's own emotional needs rather than prompting them to think intersectionally and constellationally to consistently work on structural and systemic changes. That is, a politics of location would see the structures and systems in place, the patterns in cement, and would reason out the need to "save" as much as the need for the need itself.

Autohistoria-teoría Practices to Unlearn Privileges (In Collaborative Formations, Willingly)

Personal experiences—revised and in other ways redrawn—become a lens with which to reread and rewrite the cultural stories into which we are born.

AnaLouise Keating, *Entre mundos / Among Worlds*, 2005

The major project for me is to unlearn our privilege as our loss; however personally disadvantaged we might be.

Gayatri Chakravorty Spivak, *The Post-colonial Critic*, 1990

22 Toni Morrison, *Playing in the Dark: Whiteness and the Literary Imagination* (New York: Vintage Books, 1993), 11; Moreno Figueroa, "Distributed Intensities," 388.

23 Instead of "decolonial," I use "de(s)colonial" to emphasize that Mendoza's theories are critically informed by *feminismos descoloniales* that emerged in Latin America and are mainly written and practiced in Spanish.

24 Breny Mendoza, "Decolonial Theories in Comparison," *Journal of World Philosophies*, no. 5 (Summer 2020): 57.

25 Rich, "Politics of Location," 218.

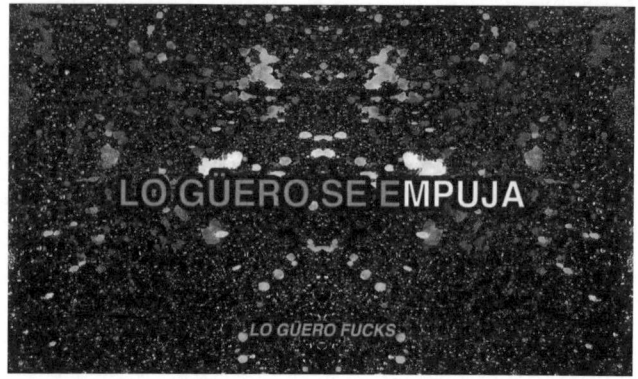

Fig. 22 INVASORIX, *ME DUELE LA CARA DE SER TAN GÜERA*, 2019.
Video still.

In the music video for the reggaeton song "ME DUELE LA
CARA DE SER TAN GÜERA" (My Face Hurts from Being
So Güero, 2019) by INVASORIX, bleach is dripped onto
black fabric, whitening its surface. Is it a play on the work of
Jackson Pollock, the Abstract Expressionist widely noted for
his dripping technique?[26] Similar to how the song's title plays
off the 1988 hit by the all-men rock group Los Inhumanos
from Valencia, Spain, "Me duele la cara de ser tan guapo" (My
Face Hurts from Being So Handsome)?

Since 2013, in different constellations of three to ten
members, INVASORIX has stationed their spaceship in
Mexico City. During a residency they held in 2019, I—a
privileged güerx migrant from Austria—joined them in
writing this song. The reggaeton track, featuring the feminist
rapper and self-defense trainer Dayra Fyah, builds on the
desire to challenge the internal and external güero—in
INVASORIX's earthling incarnations and the group itself and
their surroundings—as well as to upend reggaeton, a genre

of music that "mixes Spanish reggae, dancehall, and hip-hop in a sound whose cadence, sexually charged lyrics, violence, and symbolic excess have granted access to widespread internationalization."[27]

♪ LO GÜERO TAN OMNIPRESENTE
♪ LO GÜERO INSTALADO EN TU MENTE
♪ LO GÜERO INTERNO Y FREGADO
♪ LO GÜERO SIN MÉRITO TAN PRIVILEGIADO

♪ LO GÜERO SO UBIQUITOUS
♪ LO GÜERO SETTLED IN YOUR MIND
♪ LO GÜERO INTERNAL AND TRICKY
♪ LO GÜERO WITHOUT MERIT SO PRIVILEGED[28]

Gloria Anzaldúa's notions of *autohistoria* and *autohistoria-teoría* have actively informed INVASORIX and my own artistic research and practice. A key aspect of autohistoria-teoría is theorizing through narrative forms such as *autohistoria* (autohistory or autostory)—in other words, to make *teoría* (theory) of one's sociocultural contexts to understand them. The scholar AnaLouise Keating points out that Anzaldúa does not comprehensively elaborate on the theoretical scope of her notions of autohistoria and autohistoria-teoría, but their practice is demonstrated throughout her writings,

26 In her presentation "Métale la mano: Taches, rimas y otros gestos feministas" (2021), the art historian and curator Rían Lozano calls this gesture in the music video a "feminist and anti-racist version of Jackson Pollock's dripping." See "FORO Grrrr: Género, ritmo, rabia, rima y ruido," posted May 28, 2021, by CIEG UNAM, YouTube video, https://www.youtube.com /watch?v=SOwpCCmyzQw. Translations are by the author unless noted otherwise.

27 Alfredo Nieves Moreno, "A Man Lives Here: Reggaeton's Hypermasculine Resident," in *Reggaeton*, ed. Raquel Z. Rivera, Wayne Marshall, and Deborah Pacini Hernandez (Durham, NC: Duke University Press, 2009), 252.

28 INVASORIX, *ME DUELE LA CARA DE SER TAN GÜERA*, 2019, 5 min., 37 sec., https://vimeo.com/338390523 (with English subtitles). Subsequent lyrics are also from this source.

interviews, conversations, and lectures.[29] The breadth of materials contained in Anzaldúa's archives at the University of Texas at Austin, in particular unpublished essays and drafts, are an ideal resource to dive deeper into her articulations on these notions and grasp their distinctions and multilayered dimensions.[30] Anzaldúa explains: "In the autohistorias-teoría the self-reflective theorizing and analysis takes precedence over the anecdotal, personal narrative. It theorizes about the autobiographical essay and its process in an attempt to determine or explore identity and other issues."[31] Among her published works, one brief discussion of autohistoria-teoría appears in a footnote: "Autohistoria is a term I use to describe the genre of writing about one's personal and collective history using fictive elements, a sort of fictionalized autobiography or memoir; and autohistoria-teoría is a personal essay that theorizes."[32] Anzaldúa argues that autohistoria and autohistoria-teoría are effective meaning-, knowledge-, and identity-making methods that combine personal reflections with theorizing about sociocultural contexts, and that have the explicit task of developing theories from one's self-history.[33] "More than writing self into existence," Kakali Bhattacharya and AnaLouise Keating comment, "autohistoria-teoría represents a hybridized space of creativity and bridge-building, in which we use our life stories to develop deep critical, spiritual, and analytical insights, to boldly theorize experiences and insights against the broader landscape of specific sociocultural discourses."[34] In this sense, narrating yourself can extend toward others in ways that can be conducive to further actions and collaborative forms of meaning-making. As INVASORIX has disclosed, at least half of the group has been read and addressed as güerx in their earthling incarnations, and, without a doubt I am the most güerx of them all.[35]

the word [güerx] can refer to people with blond hair and/or light skin and/or European ancestry and/or supposedly "superior" social and cultural status. Therefore, acts of "güerear" could be used as a strategy to take advantage of those who are not. In some contexts, "güerear" is an action in which in parallel, one takes advantage of someone for responding to or representing the status of güerx. [Cherríe] Moraga further shared the following: "It is frightening to acknowledge that I have internalized a racism and classism, where the object of oppression is not only someone outside of my skin, but the someone inside

29 AnaLouise Keating, *Entre mundos / Among Worlds: New Perspectives on Gloria Anzaldúa* (New York: Palgrave Macmillan, 2008), 5–6.

30 In an unpublished 1989 paper, Anzaldúa offers her first formal articulation of autohistoria-teoría, in which she delves into different forms of autobiography and gives her own theory. Gloria Anzaldúa, "Autohistoria-teorías," manuscript drafts and notes, box 91, folder 30, Gloria Evangelina Anzaldúa Papers, Nettie Lee Benson Latin American Collection, University of Texas, Austin. For more on autohistoria-teoría, see box 92, folders 16–21, Anzaldúa Papers.

31 Gloria Anzaldúa, "*Autohistorias-teorías – Mujeres que cuentan vidas*: Personal and Collective Narratives That Challenge Genre Conventions," manuscript drafts with readers' comments, box 94, folder 4, Anzaldúa Papers.

32 Gloria E. Anzaldúa, "now let us shift … the path of conocimiento … inner work, public acts," in *This Bridge We Call Home: Radical Visions for Transformation*, ed. Gloria E. Anzaldúa and AnaLouise Keating (New York: Routledge, 2002), 238. This text is a rich demonstration of autohistoria-teoría, outlining the path of *conocimiento* (knowledge) via reflection on Anzaldúa's personal experiences (the Loma Prieta earthquake that struck California in 1989, receiving a diagnosis of type 1 diabetes in 1992, and the hysterectomy she underwent in 1980, among other events in her life).

33 Gloria E. Anzaldúa, preface to *Light in the Dark / Luz en lo oscuro: Rewriting Identity, Spirituality, Reality* (Durham, NC: Duke University Press, 2015), 6.

34 Kakali Bhattacharya and AnaLouise Keating, "Expanding beyond Public and Private Realities: Evoking Anzaldúan Autohistoria-teoría in Two Voices," *Qualitative Inquiry* 24, no. 5 (2018): 345.

35 INVASORIX play with the idea that they are aliens and that, on their planet, social categories such as gender, sexuality, race, and ethnicity do not exit. They are only confronted with these categories and their associated discriminations in their earthling incarnations.

my skin. In fact, to a large degree, the real battle with such oppression, for all of us, begins under the skin."

INVASORIX clarify that this "someone inside my skin," of which the feminist Chicana writer, activist, poet, essayist, and playwright Cherríe Moraga speaks, "is also found inside our skins, in our group."[36]

♪ ¿DE VERAS LES DUELE LA PIEL?
♪ MÉTALE LA MANO A SU PUESTO VIP

♪ SERIOUSLY, YOUR SKIN HURTS?
♪ COP A FEEL OF YOUR VIP POSITION

Published in the 1981 anthology *This Bridge Called My Back: Writings by Radical Women of Color*, Moraga's essay "La Güera" is another demonstration of autohistoria-teoría. Moraga writes: "I was 'la güera': fair-skinned. Born with the features of my Chicana mother, but the skin of my Anglo father, I had it made."[37] Being fair-skinned, Moraga could pass as White, and consequently enjoyed a less troubled childhood than a person with darker skin. By contrast, in "La Prieta," published in the same collection, Anzaldúa describes the difficulties of being a dark-skinned child in a family where everybody else had fairer skin. Anzaldúa elaborates on an intricate process that connects self-exploration and reflection in the inner world with sociocultural transformation in the external world: "I believe that by changing ourselves we change the world, that traveling El Mundo Zurdo path is the path of a two-way movement—a going deep into the self and an expanding out into the world, a simultaneous recreation of the self and a reconstruction of society. And yet, I am confused as to how to accomplish this."[38] By affirming that self-change and sociocultural transformation are interdependent, Anzaldúa lays out her strong belief that transformative processes of the self and the collective must evolve together while acknowledging that these transformations are difficult, complicated endeavors, filled with doubts and open questions.

While in "La Prieta" Anzaldúa "comes to realize that it is through her body that she also learns how to resist conventions while transforming how she perceives the world around her […] and how to navigate in white space," as the scholar Tara Conley writes, Moraga recognizes her privilege by realizing she "had it made" by being able to comfortably access White environments.[39] Moraga writes of feeling "both bleached and beached": "I feel angry about this—the years when I refused to recognize privilege, both when it worked against me, and when I worked it, ignorantly, at the expense of others. These are not settled issues."[40] Indeed, more than forty years later, these are still unresolved issues in Mexico City and elsewhere.

In an attempt to "unlearn our privileges as our loss," INVASORIX considers their reggaeton track "an invitation

36 INVASORIX, "Me duele la cara de ser tan güerx," *iMex: México Interdisciplinario / Interdisciplinary Mexico* 9, no. 17 (2020/21): 157, https://www.imex-revista.com/xvii-invasorix-guerx/.

37 Cherríe Moraga, "La Güera," in *This Bridge Called My Back: Writings by Radical Women of Color*, ed. Cherríe Moraga and Gloria Anzaldúa (London: Persephone Press, 1981), 28.

38 Gloria E. Anzaldúa, "La Prieta," in Moraga and Anzaldúa, *This Bridge Called My Back*, 232.

39 Tara L. Conley, "Black Women and Girls Trending: A New(er) Autohistoria-teoría," in *This Bridge We Call Communication: Anzaldúan Approaches to Theory, Method, and Praxis*, ed. Leandra Hinojosa Hernandez and Robert Gutierrez-Perez (Lanham, MD: Lexington Books, 2019), 245; Moraga, "La Güera," 28.

40 Moraga, "La Güera," 34.

to what Gayatri Spivak calls 'doing [y]our homework.'"[41] In a discussion with the postcolonial and feminist theorist Sneja Gunew, Spivak gives the example of a politically correct White male student who retreats to the position that he can't speak since he is White and male, "basing everything on skin color [...] and genitalism." Spivak calls this "somewhat derisively, chromatism," and advocates for both investigating what silences you and "doing your homework." Instead of taking up such a "deterministic position—since my skin color is this, since my sex is this," Spivak calls for undertaking the challenge to "learn what is going on there through language [...] but also at the same time through a *historical* critique of your position as the investigating person."[42]

While doing their homework and pondering their positions as collaborating artists, INVASORIX took on the task of identifying "the geopolitical and institutional coordinates of power relations where our practices are situated."[43] Alongside the reggaeton video, they designed a workshop to reflect on White(y)ness and whitewashing processes by whitening color T-shirts. For the workshop, people were invited to bring "T-shirts of color" from their closets to develop a critical message derived from reading and discussing quotations on White(y)ness, from Anzaldúa and Moraga to Echeverría, Ruth Frankenberg, bell hooks, and Chandra Talpade Mohanty, among other writers. Equipped with bleach and brushes, these messages were applied to the T-shirts to make not only the whitening process evident but also to materialize eye-catching messages. Feel free to adapt this workshop by adding quotes from your own context.

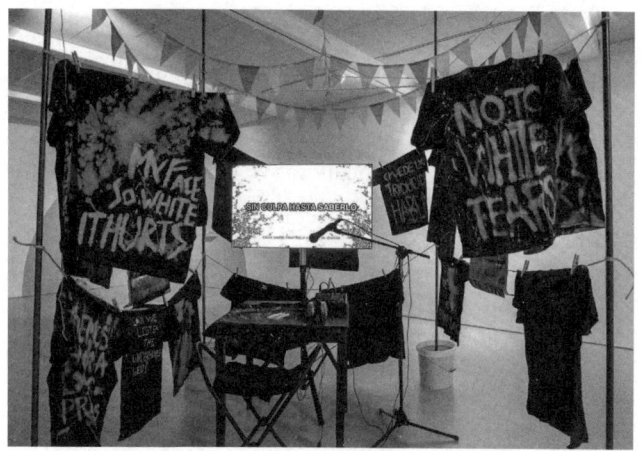

Fig. 23 INVASORIX, *Me duele la cara de ser tan güera*, 2019.
Installation view, Kunstraum Innsbruck, 2021.

41 Gayatri Chakravorty Spivak, "Criticism, Feminism, and the Institution,"
in *The Post-colonial Critic: Interviews, Strategies, Dialogues*, ed. Sarah Harasym
(London: Routledge, 1990), 10; INVASORIX, "Me duele la cara de ser tan güerx,"
158.

42 Spivak, "Questions of Multi-culturalism," in Harasym, *The Post-colonial
Critic*, 62 (italics in the original).

43 INVASORIX, "Me duele la cara de ser tan güerx," 158.

♪ LEER DE RACISMO NO TE HACE SUDAR
♪ NUESTRA BLANCA ACADEMIA
   DISECA MELANINA

♪ TO READ ABOUT RACISM DOESN'T
   MAKE YOU SWEAT
♪ OUR WHITE ACADEMY DISSECTS MELANIN

When INVASORIX wrote the reggaeton track and conceptualized the workshop, they had already been collaborating for more than six years. Their working exchange allowed them to incorporate perspectives and experiences sometimes at odds with the collaborative formation. Caring for these complex personal stories and experiences is at the heart of what INVASORIX seeks while being stationed on earth. While working on the reggaeton track, borders were crossed, fixed positions within the collaborative formation were destabilized, which led to shifts in dynamics and perspectives concerning preestablished roles and approaches, particularly through humorously imagining themselves as aliens and seeing the world through their eyes, if only for the length of writing, singing, recording, filming, karaoke-style subtitling, installing, and workshopping.[44]

"To write autohistorias-teorías is to participate in two or more literary genres, registers, separate temporalities, historical periods, some belonging to the dominant culture and some to the colonized," Anzaldúa explains. "Characteristic 'moves' in autohistorias-teorías from close-up to long shots and back to zoom-in for middle shots makes them self-reflective, meta-discursive in approach."[45] The reggaeton lyrics and video do not fall neatly into what Anzaldúa describes as autohistorias-teorías or what she defines as *border arte*: "an art that supersedes the pictorial. It depicts both the soul del artista y el alma del pueblo. It deals with who tells the stories and what stories and histories are told." Anzaldúa calls "this form of visual narrative 'autohistorias.'" Nonetheless, the reggaeton video converges with autohistoria-teorías and border arte insofar as it "goes beyond the traditional self-portrait or autobiography." In sharing their stories in relation to lo güero in reggaeton style, INVASORIX participates in several genres and registers that commix separate temporalities belonging to dominant and colonized cultures simultaneously. Concurrently, their work "also includes the artist's cultural history" told through a collaborative voice sung in Spanish with different accents, sprinkled with words and expressions from other places, which also transverses their collaborative becoming.[46]

♪ ¡HEY MONIX, AGUANTEN Y ESCUCHEN!

♪ HEY MONIX, SUCK IT UP AND LISTEN!

For example, *mono/a/ix* is a word used in Colombia for güero/a/x, and it shows how lo mono and lo güero cross autohistorias in and from different geographies. Anzaldúa emphasizes that autohistoria, as a form of visual narrative, is "a kind of making history, of inventing our history from our experience and perspective through our art rather than

44 INVASORIX's installation was included in the MexiCali Biennial "CALAFIA: Manifesting the Terrestrial Paradise," curated by Ed Gomez, Luis G. Hernandez, and Daniela Lieja Quintanar in 2019, which took place on the US–Mexico border in both California and Baja California, and the 2021 exhibitions "A Haunting from the Future," curated by Ivana Marjanovic at Kunstraum Innsbruck, and "Tiempo Compartido" at the Museo de Arte Carrillo Gil in Mexico City.
45 Gloria Anzaldúa, "Autohistorias-teorías – Mujeres que cuentan vidas," manuscript draft with readers' comments, box 92, folder 2, Anzaldúa Papers.
46 Gloria E. Anzaldúa, "Border Arte," in *Light in the Dark*, 62.

accepting our history by the dominant culture."[47] Rather than accepting lo güero as an external determination perpetuated by the dominant culture, and ignoring the internal(ized) güero, INVASORIX build on the necessity of listening to the multitude of histories that comprise their daily lives. This gives way to not only interrogating their collaboration formation and each of their own positions in the larger net of asymmetries and oppressions but also understanding INVASORIX, and each individual member, as layered. What's more, INVASORIX never forgets humor in regarding themselves as aliens or the potential to poke fun at themselves in their earthling incarnations by telling us: don't be "afraid of losing material and psychological privilege," and—in Anzaldúa's phrasing—don't let yourself be drowned by and don't drown others with "white noise"![48] As the end-credit song of *DELIRIO GÜERO*, "ME DUELE LA CARA DE SER TAN GÜERA" reminds everyone to move their bodies, and to

♪ ¡PÓNGALE LA CARA AL SABROSO PODEROSO!
♪ ¡PÓNGALE LA CARA AL SABROSO PODEROSO!

♪ FACE YOUR TASTY PRIVILEGES!
♪ FACE YOUR TASTY PRIVILEGES!

A Hauntological (Auto)Biography:
~~White Genetic Essentialism~~

Whiteness could be described as an ongoing and unfinished history, which orientates bodies in specific directions, affecting how they "take up" space.
Sara Ahmed, "A Phenomenology of Whiteness," 2007

As *DELIRIO GÜERO* unravels, viewers learn that the host, La Güera, is haunted, but not by the fore-people whom Spivak would like to be haunted by. Responding to a conference on memoir writing, Spivak made the fascinating declaration: "I want to be haunted." She reflected on what it means to be part of a genealogy of women, of "big-boned" fore-mothers who have no institutional education. Understanding her task as a teacher as one of rearranging desires, Spivak shared that her desire was to write in such a way that her fore-people "find the questions answerable." She ended her commentary with: "It's a hauntological autobiography."[49]

DELIRIO GÜERO could be considered a hauntological (auto)biography—necessarily fragmentary, it answers some questions while other uncomfortable, unsettling challenges arise. In the film, La Güera is haunted by those who, like her, came to what today is called Mexico: all "*güerxs* and, somehow, related to the contemporary Republic of Austria."[50] La Güera is a body with a heritage: in Mexico, a body with a güero heritage in general, and a delirio güero heritage in particular. Anton "Toni" Mayr is the great-great-great-uncle of the artist and filmmaker of *DELIRIO GÜERO*—me, the author of this article. My direct and indirect ancestors are part of a genealogy of güeros occupying the space of privilege, of blanquitud in Mexico. This privilege has had, as *DELIRIO GÜERO* shows, devastating consequences for anyone who failed or refused to "employ a [W]hitey mask to become *homo capitalisticus*."[51] My güero heritage plays

47 Anzaldúa, 62.

48 Anzaldúa, "now let us shift," 145–46.

49 Gayatri Chakravorty Spivak, "If Only," in "Writing a Feminist's Life: The Legacy of Carolyn G. Heilbrun," ed. Nancy K. Miller and Victoria Rosner, special issue, *Scholar and Feminist Online* 4, no. 2 (2006), https://sfonline.barnard.edu/heilbrun/spivak_01.htm.

50 Hoechtl, "A Visual Glossary," 166.

51 Hoechtl, 162.

out differently in Mexico, with mestizaje as the foundation of national identity, than my White heritage in Austria, a post–National Socialist society that exemplifies a kind of "colonialism without colonies."[52] Although Austria is not part of the classical colonial powers (France, Great Britain, Spain, and Portugal), and understands itself outside the realm of colonialism, it nevertheless engaged in and has benefited from imperial operations and relations in a variety of ways. This complex position is epitomized in the case of a cultural object, the *penacho* (*quetzalapanecáyotl* in Nahuatl), which is entangled with my güero heritage in Mexico and my White heritage in Austria.[53]

The headdress of more than twelve thousand feathers was first and inaccurately listed in Europe in 1596 as "a Moorish hat," part of the inventory of Archduke Ferdinand II. The quetzalapanecáyotl ended up in the collection of the Weltmuseum in Vienna because of colonial-imperial relations. Part of the museum's collection since the beginning of the nineteenth century, over the last forty years it has faced conflicting desires, divergent readings, discussions, and intensifying demands for restitution.[54] In 2020, Beatriz Gutiérrez Müller, a writer, researcher, and the wife of the president of Mexico at the time, visited Vienna to once again request the restitution of the quetzalapanecáyotl, or at least a loan. It goes without saying that she left without the headdress in her luggage. Shortly thereafter, Sabine Haag, then director of the Kunsthistorische Museum in Vienna, which the Weltmuseum is part of, argued that today the quetzalapanecáyotl is "part of the DNA of Austrians."[55] There is a lot to chew on here. Let's follow Spivak's call to "learn what is going on there through language." Sara Ahmed's invocation to think through Whiteness "as a form of inheritance" and Sarah

Franklin's "genetic essentialism" are useful for unpacking the delusional and grim implications of Haag's argumentation.[56]

Drawing on Karl Marx's conceptualization of history as heritage and Frantz Fanon's theorizing of a world that colonialism has made White, Ahmed argues that Whiteness "becomes a social and bodily orientation" to a world that is "'ready' for certain kinds of bodies," a world that "puts certain objects within their reach."[57] The way Whiteness works, in Ahmed's account, is by creating an environment that is amenable to and comfortably "reachable" by the bodies inhabiting Whiteness, a space that is welcoming to Whiteness. In the context of disputed objects such as the quetzalapanecáyotl and the built environment of a museum, there is a directive to adjust to the needs and habits of a Whiteness that requires reorientation on the part of those who do not fit it. "The corporeal schema," in Fanon's wording, is already racialized; that is, race does not just interrupt such a schema but structures its mode of operation. If the world is made White,

52 Patricia Purtschert, Francesca Falk, and Barbara Luethi, "Switzerland and 'Colonialism without Colonies': Reflections on the Status of Colonial Outsiders," *Interventions* 18, no. 2 (2016): 286–303.

53 Since 2011, I have sought to question and set in motion, or better, start wrestling with, the quetzalapanecáyotl and the complex, differentiated, changing relations of power and desires that go along with it. Each of the four editions of the long-term project *PENACHO VS PENACHO* (2011–ongoing)—the last two currently in process—point toward a different aspect and speculate about what else restitution could entail.

54 See Khadija von Zinnenburg Carroll, *The Contested Crown: Repatriation Politics between Europe and Mexico* (Chicago: University of Chicago Press, 2022); and https://repatriates.org/.

55 Constanza Lambertucci, "'El penacho de Moctezuma también es parte del ADN de los austriacos,'" *El País*, October 21, 2020, https://elpais.com /mexico/2020-10-21/sabine-haag-el-penacho-tambien-es-parte-del-patrimonio -cultural-de-los-austriacos.html.

56 Sara Ahmed, "The Orient and the Other Others," in *Queer Phenomenology: Orientations, Objects, Others* (Durham, NC: Duke University Press, 2006), 155; Sarah Franklin, "Essentialism, Which Essentialism? Some Implications of Reproductive and Genetic Technoscience," *Journal of Homosexuality* 24, nos. 3–4 (1993): 27–40, https://doi.org/10.1300/J082v24n03_02.

57 Ahmed, "Orient and the Other Others," 138.

then the body-at-home is one that can inhabit Whiteness. "Such an inheritance" of Whiteness, Ahmed proposes, "can be rethought in terms of orientations: *we inherit the reachability of some objects*, those that are 'given' to us, or at least made available to us, within the 'what' that is around. I am not suggesting here that 'whiteness' is one such 'reachable object,' but that whiteness is an orientation that puts certain things within reach."[58]

Doubtlessly, the quetzalapanecáyotl is reachable for Haag "at home," at the Weltmuseum, under her directorship. It has been reachable there for more than 425 years. In Austria, the Whiteness of the logics of museums and possession put the headdress "within their reach." As an Austrian citizen and a museum director, Haag inherited the object; here, "the word inheritance includes two meanings: to receive and to possess." Ahmed continues, "In a way, we convert what we receive into possessions, a conversion that often 'hides' the conditions of having received, as if the possession is too simply 'already there.'" Along with material possessions, Ahmed adds other kinds of objects, "such as a shared belief or even a shared love for the ego ideal of the [museum], which reproduces the [museum] as that which we wish to reproduce."[59] From 2010 to 2012, the Weltmuseum, as an institution dedicated "to the cultural diversity of humankind [that] strives to document the diverse historical ties between Austria and the world in its collections from all around the globe,"[60] embarked on a restoration and research project for the headdress in conjunction with Mexico's National Institute of Anthropology and History and the National Autonomous University of Mexico. The researchers from Austria and Mexico concluded that, for the time being, transporting the quetzalapanecáyotl would be too risky for its fragile feathers. By arguing that the artifact is "part of the DNA of Austrians," Haag enhances the "hidden" conditions of the headdress as "the possession [that] is too simply 'already there,'" and as such simply has to stay in proximity, "at home."[61]

Haag gave her statement to *El País*, the most widely read Spanish-language newspaper online. Even if her words were intended innocently, they deliberately foreground genetic essentialism, playing to a media eager to pick up on genetics-related subjects.[62] Since genetic essentialism is deeply entrenched in eugenics politics, this is the moment where innocence turns into White delusion in the name of maintaining the White privilege of having the quetzala-panecáyotl "within reach." Simultaneously, Haag willfully produced particular kinds of knowledge of the headdress, such as the notion that it is "part of the DNA of Austrians." Sarah Franklin, who coined the term "genetic essentialism" in 1993, duly points out that this idea of "'it's all in your genes' [had] flourished under the name of eugenics before WWII and has reappeared under various guises since."[63] In Europe, particularly in Austria and Germany, eugenics is associated primarily with National Socialist ideology. The Nazis enforced restrictions on marriage, implemented sterilization

58 Ahmed, 126.

59 Ahmed, 126.

60 "Weltmuseum Wien: It's All about People," Weltmuseum Wien, accessed November 21, 2023, https://www.weltmuseumwien.at/en/press/weltmuseum -wien-general-information/.

61 Ahmed, "Orient and the Other Others," 126.

62 Peter Conrad, "Genetics and Behavior in the News: Dilemmas of a Rising Paradigm," in *The Double-Edged Helix: Social Implications of Genetics in a Diverse Society*, ed. Joseph S. Alper et al. (Baltimore: Johns Hopkins University Press, 2002), 58–79; Dorothy Nelkin and M. Susan Lindee, *The DNA Mystique: The Gene as a Cultural Icon* (New York: Freeman, 1995).

63 During the twentieth century, for example, genetic ideas were distorted and misused to give scientific credence to White supremacy. Franklin calls genetic essentialism "a scientific discourse [...] with the potential to establish social categories based on an essential truth about the body." Franklin, "Essentialism, Which Essentialism?," 34.

programs, and enacted the systemic extermination of Jews, Roma, and Sinti, persons with disabilities, homosexuals, and other "undesirable elements." Over the last thirty years, genetic essentialism has not lost its appeal. Recent research has revealed that people "tend to think of genetic attributions as being immutable, of a specific etiology, natural, and dividing people into homogenous and discrete groups."[64] Although there are hardly any cases where such a tendency is appropriate, this limited understanding of genetics has led to harmful consequences in the form of racism, sexism, homophobia, transphobia, and the support of eugenics, among other discriminations. In brief, genetic essentialism erases ambiguity and complexity, leading people to view information and statements informed by DNA as predetermined.

Of course, neither ethnicity nor nationality can be detected by DNA. Living and working in a post–National Socialist society such as Austria, Haag dangerously relies on genetic essentialism in her argumentation. To make her position even more delusional, Haag adds that the quetzalapanecáyotl will not travel to Mexico until there is "teleportation, like in *Star Trek*."[65] With a punch line catapulting us to the universe of *Star Trek*'s science fiction, which differs from INVASORIX's proposal as it ultimately legitimizes colonial and patriarchal logics, any further speculation of restitution, let alone going beyond restitution, is shut down. In *Star Trek*, teleportation is but one of the colonial-imperial fictions that reinforce a clear dichotomy between the technological inferiority and superiority of planets.[66] Contrary to Haag's deployment of genetic essentialism to divert inquiries that are critical of quetzalapanecáyotl's residence in Vienna, her words on teleportation appeal to a common understanding that considers the beaming technology unlikely for another 425 years. For the length of *El País* interview, Haag's words serve as a delirious straightening device of Whiteness that shifts the orientation and keeps the quetzalapanecáyotl in place.

As a güerx in Mexico and a White person in Austria, I am faced with the constant call and challenge to "make it [my] task," as Spivak demands, "not only to learn what is going on there through language, through specific programmes of study, but also at the same time through a *historical* critique of your position as the investigating person."[67] I am the investigating practitioner of *DELIRIO GÜERO* with a specific interest in critical heritage and hauntological (auto)biographies, which allow for rethinking our relationships to the past and future while constantly weaving together what has gone before and lingers in the present.[68] A form of hauntological

64 Steven J. Heine, Ilan Dar-Nimrod, Benjamin Y. Cheung, and Travis Proulx, "Essentially Biased: Why People Are Fatalistic about Genes," in *Advances in Experimental Social Psychology*, vol. 55., ed. James Olson (Cambridge, MA: Academic Press, 2017), 137.

65 Lambertucci, "El penacho de Moctezuma."

66 *Star Trek*'s premise of space exploration is commonly read as a thinly disguised metaphor for colonial expansion. See Daniel Leonard Bernardi, *Star Trek and History: Racing Toward a White Future* (New Brunswick: Rutgers University Press, 1998); Amelie Hastie, "A Fabricated Space: Assimilating the Individual on *Star Trek: The Next Generation*," in *Enterprise Zones: Critical Positions on Star Trek*, ed. Taylor Harrison, Sarah Projansky, Kent A. Ono, and Elyce R. Helford (New York: Westview Press, 1996), 115–36; Kent Ono, "Domesticating Terrorism: A Neo-colonial Economy of Difference," in *Enterprise Zones: Critical Positions on Star Trek*, ed. Taylor Harrison, Sarah Projansky, Kent A. Ono, and Elyce R. Helford (New York: Westview Press, 1996), 157–88.

67 Spivak, "Questions of Multi-culturalism," 62.

68 Over the past two decades, critical heritage studies has emerged as a distinct yet varied subfield that questions traditional approaches to heritage theory and practice. While there are many strands, the core issues involve the democratization and decolonization of heritage concepts, the centering of peoples instead of things in the management of heritage sites, and a turn to historically marginalized narratives, communities, and cultures in defining what heritage is and what it does. Founded in 2010, the Association of Critical Heritage Studies (ACHS) currently has thousands of members from over eighty countries, consisting of heritage scholars, educators, policymakers, activists, community members, and practitioners. See Laurajane Smith, "2012 Manifesto," Association of Critical Heritage Studies, accessed January 25, 2024, https://www .criticalheritagestudies.org/history.

(auto)biography such as *DELIRIO GÜERO* seeks a commitment to acting in the presence of those who no longer exist in a way that acknowledges their reverberations. Like Spivak, I want to be haunted by my direct and indirect ancestors while being attentive to the fact that I cannot simply embrace what I am haunted with and by. It is a contradictory position, a discomforting one. I want to be haunted by violent historical deeds—continuing contemporaneously in all forms of violence, exploitation, extractivism, mining, and environmental degradation—that I am unable to change alone, that urgently need a pulling together of diverse voices and forces. To be haunted by the peoples that have no access to areas that I can occupy, those whom I can never reach, given our incommensurable difference. To be haunted by the task of looking carefully and sustaining one's listening to voices in the fissures and discontinuities of the present, and to faint echoes from the past and sounds of futures not yet imagined.

> You see these examples where one is privileged so that all you have is division—people can't work together anyway; whereas, on the other side, what wins is precisely people pulling together. That's my last word. Thank you.
> Gayatri Chakravorty Spivak, "Practical Politics of the Open End," 1987

Research for this text was supported by the Research Residency Fellowship Program at the Nettie Lee Benson Latin American Collection of the University of Texas at Austin 2023–24 granted by the Coordinación de Humanidades at the National Autonomous University of Mexico (UNAM). Thanks to the participants of the Permanent Seminar of Research and Gender at the Center of Gender Research and Studies at UNAM for providing feedback on the first three entries of my visual glossary. A special thanks to Isaura Castelao Huerta and Axel Rivera Osorio. Thanks to the participants of the writer's workshop "Standpoint Autotheory: Experiences and Relational Artistic Practice," organized by Ana de Almeida and Mariel Rodríguez, which took place on Zoom in January 2024, for commenting on this essay. And thanks to Serena Lee for correcting my English.

Literature

Ahmed, Sara. "The Orient and the Other Others." In *Queer Phenomenology: Orientations, Objects, Others*. Durham, NC: Duke University Press, 2006.

Ahmed, Sara. "A Phenomenology of Whiteness." *Feminist Theory* 8, no. 2 (2007): 149–68.

Anzaldúa, Gloria E. "Border Art." In *Light in the Dark / Luz en lo oscuro: Rewriting Identity, Spirituality, Reality*. Durham, NC: Duke University Press, 2015.

Anzaldúa, Gloria E. "now let us shift … the path of conocimiento … inner work, public acts." In *This Bridge We Call Home: Radical Visions for Transformation*, edited by Gloria E. Anzaldúa and AnaLouise Keating, 540–78. London: Routledge, 2002.

Anzaldúa, Gloria Evangelina. Papers. Nettie Lee Benson Latin American Collection, University of Texas, Austin. https://txarchives.org /utlac/finding_aids/00189.xml.

Anzaldúa, Gloria E. Preface to *Light in the Dark / Luz en lo oscuro: Rewriting Identity, Spirituality, Reality*. Durham, NC: Duke University Press, 2015.

Anzaldúa, Gloria E. "La Prieta." In *This Bridge Called My Back: Writings by Radical Women of Color*, edited by Cherríe Moraga and Gloria Anzaldúa, 220–33. London: Persephone Press, 1981.

Bernardi, Daniel Leonard. *Star Trek and History: Racing Toward a White Future*. New Brunswick, NJ: Rutgers University Press, 1998.

Bhattacharya, Kakali and AnaLouise Keating, "Expanding beyond Public and Private Realities: Evoking Anzaldúan Autohistoria-teoría in Two Voices." *Qualitative Inquiry* 24, no. 5 (2018): 345–54.

Carroll, Khadija von Zinnenburg. *The Contested Crown: Repatriation Politics between Europe and Mexico*. Chicago: University of Chicago Press, 2022.

Conley, Tara L. "Black Women and Girls Trending: A New(er) Autohistoria-teoría." In *This Bridge We Call Communication: Anzaldúan Approaches to Theory, Method, and Praxis*, edited by Leandra Hinojosa Hernandez and Robert Gutierrez-Perez, 231–56. Lanham, MD: Lexington Books, 2019.

Conrad, Peter. "Genetics and Behavior in the News: Dilemmas of a Rising Paradigm." In *The Double-Edged Helix: Social Implications of Genetics in a Diverse Society*, edited by Joseph S. Alper, Catherine Ard, Adrienne Asch, Jon Beckwith, Peter Conrad, and Lisa N. Geller, 58–79. Baltimore: Johns Hopkins University Press, 2002.

Echeverría, Bolívar. "'Blanquitud': Considerations on Racism as a Specifically Modern Phenomenon." *Revista Nueva Realidad*, no. 1 (July/ August 2020): 4–10.

Echeverría, Bolívar. *Modernidad y blanquitud*. Mexico City: Ediciones Era, 2010.

Echeverría, Bolívar. *Modernity and "Whiteness."* Translated by Rodrigo Ferreira. Cambridge: Polity Press, 2019.

Echeverría, Bolívar. *Racismo y blanquitud*. Mexico City: Zineditorial, 2018.

Franklin, Sarah. "Essentialism, Which Essentialism?" *Journal of Homosexuality* 24, nos. 3–4 (1993): 27–40. https://doi.org/10.1300 /J082v24n03_02.

Hastie, Amelie. "A Fabricated Space: Assimilating the Individual on *Star Trek: The Next Generation*." In *Enterprise Zones: Critical Positions on Star Trek*, edited by Taylor Harrison, Sarah Projansky, Kent A. Ono, and Elyce R. Helford, 115–36. New York: Westview Press, 1996.

Heine, Steven J., Ilan Dar-Nimrod, Benjamin Y. Cheung, and Travis Proulx. "Essentially Biased: Why People Are Fatalistic about Genes." In *Advances in Experimental Social Psychology*, vol. 55, edited by James Olson, 137–92. Cambridge, MA: Academic Press, 2017.

Hoechtl, Nina. "A Visual Glossary: *Delirio güero* (White Delusion)." In *Sharpening the Haze: Visual Essays on Imperial History and Memory*, edited by Giulia Carabelli, Miloš Jovanović, Annika Kirbis, and Jeremy F. Walton, 159–74. London: Ubiquity Press, 2020. https://doi.org/10.5334/bcd.j.

Hoechtl, Nina. *DELIRIO GÜERO WHITE DELUSION. 2211, 2018, 1825 and Back.* Filmed 2018. Vimeo video, 53:33, https://vimeo.com/511236180 (Spanish with English subtitles), https://vimeo.com/291412548 (German with English subtitles).

INVASORIX. *Me duele la cara de ser tan güera.* Filmed 2019. Vimeo video, 5:37, https://vimeo.com/338390523 (Spanish with English subtitles), https://vimeo.com/521944678 (Spanish with German subtitles).

INVASORIX. "Me duele la cara de ser tan güerx." *iMex: México Interdisciplinario / Interdisciplinary Mexico* 9, no. 17 (2020/21): 156–65. https://www.imex-revista.com/xvii-invasorix-guerx/.

Keating, AnaLouise. *Entre mundos / Among Worlds: New Perspectives on Gloria Anzaldúa.* New York: Palgrave Macmillan, 2005.

Lambertucci, Constanza. "El penacho de Moctezuma también es parte del de los austriacos." *El País*, October 21, 2020. https://elpais.com/mexico/2020-10-21/sabine-haag-el-penacho-tambien-es-parte-del-patrimonio-cultural-de-los-austriacos.html.

Mendoza, Breny. "Decolonial Theories in Comparison." *Journal of World Philosophies*, no. 5 (Summer 2020): 43–60.

Mills, Charles W. *The Racial Contract.* Ithaca, NY: Cornell University Press, 1997.

Mills, Charles W. "White Ignorance." In *Race and Epistemologies of Ignorance*, edited by Shannon Sullivan and Nancy Tuana, 11–38. Albany: State University of New York Press, 2007.

Moraga, Cherríe. "La Güera." In *This Bridge Called My Back: Writings by Radical Women of Color*, edited by Cherríe Moraga and Gloria Anzaldúa, 27–34. London: Persephone Press, 1981.

Moreno Figueroa, Mónica. "Distributed Intensities: Whiteness, Mestizaje and the Logics of Mexican Racism." *Ethnicities*, no. 10 (2010): 387–401. https://doi.org/10.1177/1468796810372

Moreno Figueroa, Mónica. "Mestizaje: When the Shades Dissimulate Whiteness," *The Funambulist*, June 22, 2023. https://thefunambulist.net/magazine/fifty-shades-of-whiteness/mestizaje-when-the-shades-dissimulate-whiteness.

Moreno Figueroa, Mónica. "Naming Ourselves: Recognising Racism and Mestizaje in Mexico." In *Contesting Recognition*, edited by Janice McLaughlin, Peter Phillimore, and Diane Richardson, 122–43. Basingstoke: Palgrave, 2011.

Morrison, Toni. *Playing in the Dark: Whiteness and the Literary Imagination.* New York: Vintage Books, 1993.

Nelkin, Dorothy, and M. Susan Lindee. *The DNA Mystique: The Gene as a Cultural Icon.* New York: Freeman, 1995.

Nieves Moreno, Alfredo. "A Man Lives Here: Reggaeton's Hypermasculine Resident." In *Reggaeton*, edited by Raquel Z. Rivera, Wayne Marshall, and Deborah Pacini Hernandez, 252–79. Durham, NC: Duke University Press, 2009.

Ono, Kent. "Domesticating Terrorism: A Neocolonial Economy of Difference." In *Enterprise Zones: Critical Positions on Star Trek*, edited by Taylor Harrison, Sarah Projansky, Kent A. Ono, and Elyce R. Helford, 157–88. New York: Westview Press, 1996.

Ortega, Mariana. "Being Lovingly, Knowingly Ignorant: White Feminism and Women of Color." *Hypatia* 21, no. 3 (Summer 2006): 56–74.

Painter, Nell Irvin. "Why 'White' Should Be Capitalized, Too." *West Central Tribune*, July 23, 2020. https://www.wctrib.com/opinion/nell-irvin-painter-why-white-should-be-capitalized-too.

Purtschert, Patricia, Francesca Falk, and Barbara Luethi. "Switzerland and 'Colonialism without Colonies': Reflections on the Status of Colonial Outsiders." *Interventions* 18, no. 2 (2016): 286–303. https://doi.org/10.1080/1369801X.2015.1042395.

Rich, Adrienne. "Notes toward a Politics of Location." In *Blood, Bread, Poetry: Selected Prose, 1979–1984*, 210–31. New York: Norton, 1986.

Saldaña-Portillo, María Josefina. *The Revolutionary Imagination in the Americas and the Age of Development.* Durham, NC: Duke University Press, 2003.

Sarker, Sonita. "The Whiteness Problem." *Modernism/modernity* 7, cycle 3, June 12, 2023. https://doi.org/10.26597/mod.0258.

Smith, Laurajane. "2012 Manifesto." Association of Critical Heritage Studies. Accessed January 25, 2024. https://www.criticalheritagestudies.org/history.

Spivak, Gayatri Chakravorty. "Acting Bits/Identity Talk." In *An Aesthetic Education in the Era of Globalization*. Cambridge, MA: Harvard University Press, 2013.

Spivak, Gayatri Chakravorty. "Criticism, Feminism, and the Institution." In *The Post-colonial Critic: Interviews, Strategies, Dialogues*, edited by Sarah Harasym, 1–16. London: Routledge, 1990.

Spivak, Gayatri Chakravorty. "If Only." In "Writing a Feminist's Life: The Legacy of Carolyn G. Heilbrun," edited by Nancy K. Miller and Victoria Rosner. Special issue of *Scholar and Feminist Online* 4, no. 2 (2006). https://sfonline.barnard.edu/heilbrun/spivak_01.htm.

Spivak, Gayatri Chakravorty. "Questions of Multi-culturalism." In *The Post-colonial Critic: Interviews, Strategies, Dialogues*, edited by Sarah Harasym, 59–66. London: Routledge, 1990.

Steyerl, Hito. "Politics of Art: Contemporary Art and the Transition to Post-democracy." In *The Wretched of the Screen*, 92–101. Berlin: Sternberg Press, 2012.

Telles, Edward, and René Flores. "Not Just Color: Whiteness, Nation and Status in Latin America." *Hispanic American Historical Review* 93, no. 3 (2013): 411–49. https://doi.org/10.1215/00182168-2210858.

Telles, Edward E., and the Project on Ethnicity and Race in Latina America (PERLA). *Pigmentocracies: Ethnicity, Race, and Color in Latin America.* Chapel Hill: University of North Carolina Press, 2014.

Vergès, Françoise. "Capitalocene, Waste, Race, and Gender." *e-flux journal*, no. 100, May 2019. https://www.e-flux.com/journal/100/269165/capitalocene-waste-race-and-gender/.

Wekker, Gloria. *White Innocence: Paradoxes of Colonialism and Race.* Durham, NC: Duke University Press, 2016.

Verena Melgarejo Weinandt

A Deep Dive into the (Collective) Self
Creating Autohistoria-teoría with the Performative Alter Ego Pocahunter

I will start with names. When I was about nine or ten, a friend's grandmother, whom I liked very much, used to call me *Indianer-Kind*.[1] I remember the loving sound of her voice when she called me that, and that I didn't mind the nickname at all. When I was a teenager, a group of friends from my sports team gave me a completely new name, Wanowa, based on a North American Indigenous name one of them had once read in a book. For years, this was my nickname, and I also identified with it. To have been given a new name gave me the sense of a special bond with the group. Although they weren't my real names, they were also more than just fiction. The projections bound to the names became part of my identity, my history, my experience, and my self-perception. The way we are named and how we name ourselves is a powerful act.

One of my names of choice is Pocahunter, which I first used in 2011.[2] When the animated Disney film *Pocahontas* premiered in German cinemas in 1995, people started saying to me—at the bus stop, on the subway, on the street—"Has anyone ever told you that you look just like Pocahontas?" Whereas before people did not know which ethnic stereotype to attribute to me, because I was apparently an "unclear" case, the Disney character provided a way to categorize my appearance based on Indigenous stereotypes.[3] The comparison with Pocahontas has taken on absurd proportions over the course of my life, and Pocahunter became an expression of the transformative potential that new names can have on us. It is a way to appropriate the names given to me and projections related to them, and to open up new spaces to deal with what sometimes seems ungraspable. It has become hard to detect the single strands of a tightly woven cord—the way projections and fictions are braided into my biography and experience and form my creative practice and knowledge production. This text is an attempt to express how fiction creates reality, and how, through my art, I aim to transform these projections into something that contests those collectively shared and historically cultivated imaginations.

Anzaldúa's Path

The way my own biography influences my artistic work is strongly related to the writing of Gloria E. Anzaldúa

---

1 When I use the German words *Indianer* or *Indianerin*, I am not referring to Indigenous people (like the English synonyms, male Indian and female Indian). Rather, I use the words explicitly as a reference to a fictitious identity that reflects its own history of appropriation and definition in the German-speaking world.

2 My artistic research on Pocahunter is part of the research project Repatriates (https://repatriates.org/), which has received funding from the European Research Council under the European Union's Horizon 2020 research and innovation program (grant agreement No. 101001407 – Repatriates).

3 My mother is German and my father is from Bolivia and has Quechua descendants.

(1942–2004), especially her theory of *autohistoria-teoría*.[4] Anzaldúa, who described herself as a "chicana dyke-feminist, tejana patlache poet, writer, and cultural theorist," has strongly influenced my work and my life since 2016, the year I first curated an exhibition around her drawings.[5] The methods and processes through which Anzaldúa's reflections, concepts, and texts emerged are a central element of her work. By describing them, she explains how political, spiritual, and identity-forming moments of her life became the ground for her knowledge creation.[6] It is therefore striking that, in contrast to her other methods and concepts, Anzaldúa does not completely explain what autohistoria-teoría is, although she uses it as a central tool in her work. As Andrea J. Pitts notes, "Anzaldúa does not fully articulate the theoretical scope of the concept of *autohistoria-teoría*, but the practice of *autohistoria-teoría* is performatively demonstrated throughout her writings."[7] The term combines three elements. *Auto* stands for the self and *historia* is used in Spanish for historical as well as fictional narratives; through this twofold meaning, Anzaldúa signals the creation of a narrative or story based on one's own history and one's own experiences, one's autobiography. The extension of this concept to the third element, *teoría* (theory), points to the broadening of this narrative toward a positioning within social, historical, political, or other collective situatedness and structures.

The current text has two aims. On the one hand, I deal with the significance of my own biography in the work of my performative alter ego Pocahunter to explain how Anzaldúa's method of autohistoria-teoría unfolds within my work. On the other hand, I explain how autohistoria-teoría can function, in turn, as an analytic tool for the work of Pocahunter. I see this essay not only as a description of my work and method but also as a way to influence how I think about my own artistic practice. I explore how Pocahunter came into being and how she has developed, and various influences that led to the character's existence and shaped the way she acts, how she decides where she positions herself, and why she keeps articulating what troubles her.

Feminist researchers have placed their own experience at the center of their research to expose the so-called neutrality of academic research, which hides a mostly white, male

---

4 Anzaldúa's output has played a central role in my curatorial and artistic research over the last ten years. I am currently working on the German translation of her 1987 book *Borderlands / La Frontera: The New Mestiza*. Through my curatorial projects, I have had the privilege to create connections among artists inspired by Anzaldúa's work through several exhibitions and workshops. An excerpt of these artists' work will be published in the forthcoming volume *Wissen über Brücken / Saberes sobre Puentes: Gloria E. Anzaldúa as Method in Decolonial Artistic Research and Art Education*. Both books are being published by Archive Books. See "Wissen über Brücken – Conocimiento sobre puentes," District * School without Center, accessed May 1, 2024, http://www.district-berlin.com/de /wissen-ueber-bruecken-conocimiento-sobre-puentes-2/.

5 AnaLouise Keating, ed., *Entre Mundos / Among Worlds: New Perspectives on Gloria Anzaldúa* (New York: Palgrave Macmillan, 2008), 2.

6 Anzaldúa's use of different forms of knowledge has been deeply influential for my artistic work in questioning not only the kinds of knowledge that can reproduce epistemic violence but also how we can unlearn and challenge our modes of gaining, accessing, and producing knowledge. The decolonial study group "coloniality/modernity," which mainly consists of authors from Latin America, has looked in detail at how knowledge is part of our modern capitalist structure of violence, calling this approach "coloniality of knowledge." See Ramón Grosfoguel, "The Structure of Knowledge in Westernized Universities: Epistemic Racism/Sexism and the Four Genocides/Epistemicides of the Long 16th Century," *Human Architecture: Journal of the Sociology of Self-Knowledge* 11, no. 1 (2013): 73–90; Edgardo Lander, "Ciencas sociales: Saberes coloniales y eurocéntricos," in *La colonialidad del saber: Eurocentrismo y ciencas sociales; Perspectivas latinoamericanas*, ed. Edgardo Lander (Buenos Aires: CLACSO, 1993), 11–40; Walter Mignolo, *Local Histories / Global Designs: Coloniality, Subaltern Knowledges, and Border Thinking* (Princeton, NJ: Princeton University Press, 2000); Aníbal Quijano, "Die Paradoxien der eurozentrierten Moderne," *PROKLA: Zeitschrift für kritische Sozialwissenschaft* 40, no. 158 (2010): 29–47; and, for a comparative study with other theories of epistemic violence, Claudia Brunner, *Epistemische Gewalt: Wissen und Herrschaft in der kolonialen Moderne* (Bielefeld: transcript, 2020).

7 Andrea J. Pitts, "Gloria E. Anzaldúa's *Autohistoria-teoría* as an Epistemology of Self-Knowledge/Ignorance," *Hypatia* 31, no. 2 (Spring 2016): 358.

heteronormativity that pretends to be the voice of a universal subject.[8] Anzaldúa is of special interest for my artistic practice, and those of many others, because she always articulated her methodological approach in relation to art and its capacity to generate social and spiritual change and healing. The relevance of Anzaldúa's concepts, analyses, and methods for artists has not had the prominence and dissemination in artistic-academic discourses that they deserve, given her influence on artists articulating marginalized identities within their artworks.

In relation to a genealogy of academic feminist standpoint theory in the United States, Anzaldúa identified with the Third World women's movement in the United States. Chela Sandoval situates Anzaldúa's knowledge production in the political context of the civil rights movement, the women's movement, and the ethnic, race, and gender liberation movements of the 1960s.[9] Sandoval's concept of "differential consciousness" describes "nothing more and nothing less than the modes the subordinated of the United States (of any gender, race, or class) claim as politicized and oppositional stances in resistance to domination."[10] Sandoval differentiates between US Third World feminism and other forms of social resistance, whose agency and negotiation she understands as flexible, moving between different forms of resistance (a typology she divides into four categories). She uses the symbolism of a clutch to describe the possibility of switching and choosing between these different forms of resistance, describing the coalition building and solidarity within the US Third World women's movement as a reaction to the violence women of color are facing and as a survival strategy.[11] The anthology *This Bridge Called My Back* (1981), edited by Anzaldúa and Cherríe Moraga, can be seen as the founding document of this collective movement.[12]

Anzaldúa's concept of autohistoria-teoría articulates a methodological approach that allows me to understand my performative practice in relation to its embeddedness within and intersections with my life, my experiences, my body, my cultural situatedness. I see her methods less as a guide than a grounding, a path whose destination I do not know but whose trajectory feels right, a path that I do not walk alone and that others have cleared. I see Anzaldúa as one of my most important mentors.

Who Is Pocahunter?

My approach to Pocahunter was based on rewriting the Disney story *Pocahontas*, which erased the violence experienced by Matoaka, the woman whose real-life biography was used for the fictional story. A member of the Powhatan, Matoaka was abducted by English colonialists in what is now the state of Virginia, married to the tobacco farmer John Rolfe, and taken to England. She died on the way back to Virginia and was buried in the English coastal town of Gravesend in 1617. John Smith, Pocahontas's love interest in the Disney film, was a real historical figure, a colonizer of Virginia who, twelve years after she died, spread a tale that Matoaka had saved his life.

For my first performance of Pocahunter, in 2014, I created a version of Matoaka as a zombielike fighter who rises from her grave to take revenge not only on John Smith but also on

8 Sandra Harding, ed., *The Feminist Standpoint Theory Reader: Intellectual and Political Controversies* (New York: Routledge, 2004).

9 Chela Sandoval, "US Third World Feminism: The Theory and Method of Differential Oppositional Consciousness," in Harding, *Feminist Standpoint Theory Reader*, 196.

10 Sandoval, 200.

11 Sandoval, 203.

12 Ruth Sonderegger, *Vom Leben der Kritik: Kritische Praktiken – und die Notwendigkeit ihrer geopolitischen Situierung* (Vienna: Zaglossus, 2019), 300.

all the colonial, racist, and sexist imagery and narratives that have used and continue to use her. With the skull of Smith hanging from her belt, she sets off into people's dreams and imaginaries to fight against the violent images and fictional stories of Matoaka.

The shifting of boundaries between reality and fiction, as AnaLouise Keating writes, carries a special potential in Anzaldúa's work: "Fictionalizing our stories activates imagination; this activation, when approached with integrity and the desire to create new knowledge, gives access into the imaginal, opening the way for additional wisdom and information about reality—information that cannot be accessed via rational thought."[13] According to Anzaldúa, rational thought, language, and text become tools for conveying, transferring, developing, and connecting the knowledge gained.

The fictional retelling of Matoaka's story with Pocahunter attempted to counter the overwhelming reproduction of her fictional story over centuries. I wanted to express how this tale propagates clichés and violent narratives, affecting the perception of my identity. By appropriating and transforming this story, I found a way to articulate the entanglements between fiction and reality, past and present. Through Pocahunter, I am able to create new connections between the past and the present. I can change how time is conceived and how we can express connections not comprehensible through our linear understanding of time, where the past is something always behind us, and the present is the only thing we can exist in, and the future is something we are unable to reach. Pocahunter, through her existence in the present, her real but unreal identity, allows me to explore and express different notions of time, where I can, for example, revisit the past and create my presence in an already existing future.

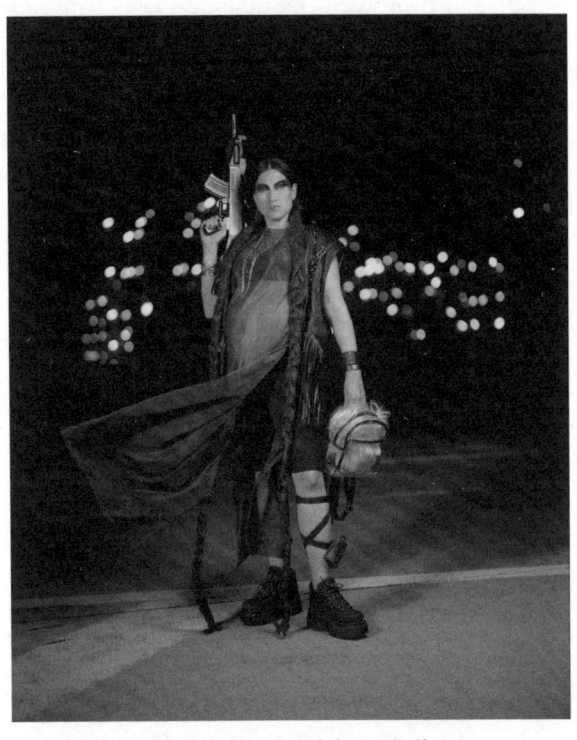

Fig. 24 Verena Melgarejo Weinandt, *Pocahunter (Re)born*, 2020

13 AnaLouise Keating, *The Anzaldúan Theory Handbook* (Durham, NC: Duke University Press, 2022), 85.

Pocahunter also deals with the fact that, since there is no firsthand account from Matoaka herself, I cannot access her perspective or own words. Pocahunter bears witness to a constant denial of Matoaka's agency, a vacuum in place of a voice, a silence that could not be louder, inscribed over centuries in books, plays, comics, films, and infinite images.

In the poem I whisper in my video *Invocation. Connecting in Darkness* (2022), I search for words to express my relation with this alter ego, who she is, and where she exists:

Pocahunter,

I am your body, your soul, your mind
we are one, and also not

now you are here
you were always

what can I call you?
zombie – Pocahunter
nightmare – Pocahunter
wandering ancestor
with wandering names

you haven't found rest in the underworld
are haunting people in their dreams
the head of John Smith is dangling on your belt

you wander through all times
not belonging to the past, to the present, nor the future
still you inhabit all of them at once

wandering the in-between, the liminal space
where all contradictions concur
you move in constant transformation

you're neither death nor life
continue to die
and awaken

it was 1995
Disney's Pocahontas was released
gazes and questions full of violence
renewed
made you
pierced through me

in your first life, your name was Matoaka, daughter of the
Powhatan
they kidnapped you, abducted you, changed your name
I don't know which atrocities you had to live through
Don't know what your resistance was like

zombie – Pocahunter
nightmare – Pocahunter
wandering ancestor
with wandering names

I am your body, your soul, your mind
we are one, and also not

now you are here
you were always.

Collective Connectedness

Indeed, a key element of Anzaldúa's autohistoria-teoría is using the exploration and expression of the self to create connections and relate this self to others. This is beautifully expressed when she writes: "We don't want to be / Stars but parts / of constellations."[14] Autohistoria-teoría is based on the understanding that one's own experiences and identity are always interwoven with the stories of others in historically evolved structures, dimensions, and subjectivities. Keating writes, "Unlike mainstream western autobiography, autohistoria is never conceived of, enacted as, or interpreted to be the story of an entirely unique, self-enclosed individual; autohistoria and autohistoria-teoría always intentionally, overtly include communal, collective components."[15]

Anzaldúa inscribes the self into collective structures through a variety of different configurations.[16] She thus creates a collective method of knowledge production within which the articulation of the self acts as a bridge to create further action and meaning production.[17] This epistemic approach reveals Anzaldúa's understanding of an interconnectedness with the world and all that exists in it, which she recognizes as participants in her knowledge production. She does not believe in the individual process of knowledge production, but rather, as Pitts writes, "the epistemic and affective content of written and spoken works is considered 'a collaborative affair' that develops in situ."[18]

How did Pocahunter emerge via these collaborative affairs? Collective formations have not only influenced the character, but she has also developed within and through them. She first appeared as an image that was created with my friend and colleague, my *compañera de la vida*, the Peruvian

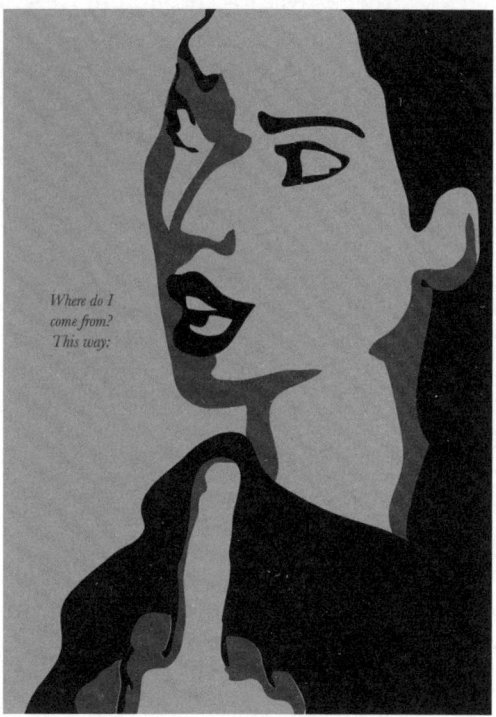

Where do I
come from?
This way:

Fig. 25 Imayna Caceres and Verena Melgarejo Weinandt,
Where Do I Come From?, 2011. Silk print.

14 Gloria E. Anzaldúa, "The New Speakers," in *The Gloria Anzaldúa Reader*, ed. AnaLouise Keating (Durham, NC: Duke University Press, 2009), 25.

15 Keating, *Anzaldúan Theory Handbook*, 87.

16 The "conversational partners" through and with whom Anzaldúa collectively produces her knowledge are her "surroundings, consensual reality, life events, sister theories, readers." Keating, 69–73.

17 Pitts, "Anzaldúa's *Autohistoria-teoría*," 358.

18 Pitts, 359. Anja Bandau's linguistic analyses of Anzaldúa's use of autobiographical, historiographical, and discursive text forms also shows the relation between the I (ego/protagonist) and the we. Bandau describes a movement of integration that is constantly interrupted by distancing oneself from the collective at the same time. Anja Bandau, *Strategien der Autorisierung: Projektionen der Chicana bei Gloria Anzaldúa und Cherríe Moraga* (Hildesheim: Georg Olms, 2004), 80ff.

artist and researcher Imayna Caceres, in 2011. We were both studying at the Academy of Fine Arts Vienna, and time and again we were mistaken for each other. I remember one evening when we sat together in the small kitchen of my shared flat. We laughed about the absurdity of the inability to differentiate between us. A collaborative creative process began in which we conceptualized Pocahunter and produced the first visuals together as a screen print.

Pocahunter's first live performance took place during a collective artistic intervention in Linz on March 8, 2014, organized by MAIZ, an association founded by migrants from Abya Yala that was already an important reference for me in terms of merging political and activist work with art and research.[19] Other alter egos took part in this performance as well, each articulating different experiences of marginalization in Austria. Madame Kloé, a figure dressed in a medieval-looking costume made of toilet paper, referenced the precarious employment and working conditions of migrants in Austria's cleaning industry, and the figure of Superputa, by the Black Brazilian artist Marissa Lôbo, addressed sex work. Here, Pocahunter was embedded in a collective network of different performance figures and alter egos, all of whom were formed according to their own specific sociocultural situations and experiences. This collective performance in public space enabled a common agency, an interweaving of our experiences and histories that also pointed conceptually to considering these experiences and situations in their entirety. I remember the intensity with which people looked at me. I wore red contact lenses and held a dream catcher made of metal chains in front of my face, through which my blood-filled eyes met the gaze of passersby. During the performance, we shared the experience of receiving different reactions,

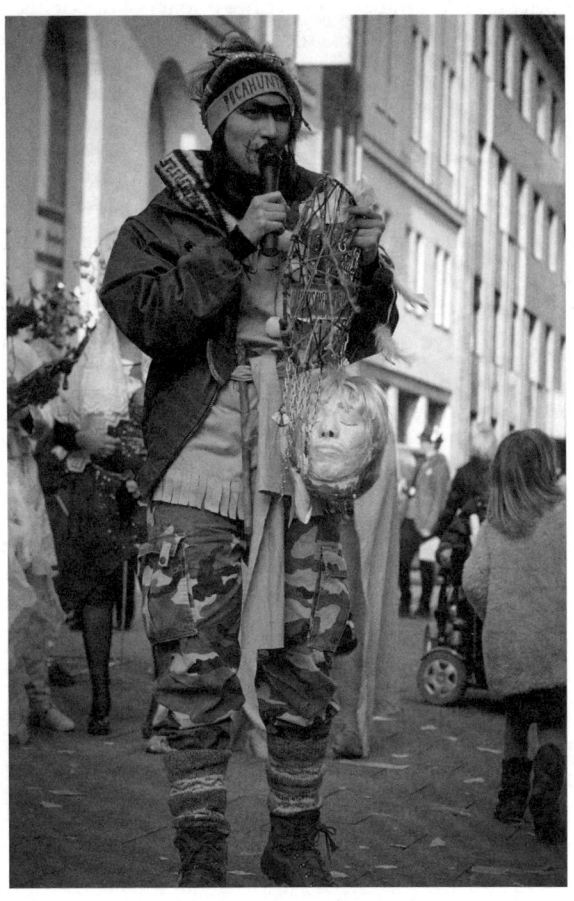

Fig. 26 zoe*fotografie, *Feminismus und Krawall*, 2014

19 MAIZ, Autonomes Zentrum von & für Migrantinnen, accessed
February 20, 2024, https://www.maiz.at/en. Abya Yala is a term from the Kuna
language, meaning "living land" or "land that flourishes," and is used by
decolonial activists and academics instead of Latin America, the name given
by the invaders.

and the group offered me a form of protection in the public sphere. I was aware of the strong impact of our collective presence, which made this first Pocahunter performance an empowering experience.

Years later, Pocahunter experienced a revival. The Berlin-based curator and artist Suza Husse invited me and the Israeli artist Oreet Ashery to create videos for Manifesta 14 in 2022.[20] Because of the COVID-19 pandemic, we couldn't meet in person, so we held several meetings online to discuss our works and their progress. We transcribed and published these conversations in a zine. The invitation and collaborative process gave me the possibility to reflect on and reconnect to Pocahunter, whom I hadn't performed in over five years. In our discussion, I considered the process:

> For the work for re.act.feminism #3, I thought of a performance in form of a ritual that would give her [Pocahunter] strength for becoming what she is, a recapturing of the elements that brought her into existence, the elements that give her power. To bring them together and honour that, use that as a point to look back and reflect on what she actually is about and what it is that gives her strength. But it also is a search for a way to reconnect with her, calling her into presence yet again. This work is also a mirror of my current state: I am taking care of my very young child in my queer family. I do all this creative work while doing a lot of care work and redefining and changing as a person, too. I am in a moment where I feel quite sensitive in general as a being.[21]

The collective reflection made me conscious of the distant relationship I had with my own artistic practice and the need to define what elements were important in order to revitalize the process and my artistic expression of Pocahunter. But it also made me aware of how my artistic production is informed, or formed, not only by artistic processes but also by the way I am connected to others. Childcare was strongly and inherently defining and changing my life and the way I produced art. I remember the shooting of the video *Invocation. Connecting in Darkness*. We had to film when it was dark, and since it was summer, sunset came late. The camerawoman and I each had a toddler at that time, so we were very sleep-deprived. We shot for one and a half hours until we became too tired to continue.

Autohistoria-teoría creates an awareness and sensitivity to how Pocahunter's work and knowledge is not only based on my individual process but is part of a network and connected in different ways to other collective structures, subjectivities, entities, and dimensions. This conscious approach enables me to explicitly seek out these collective settings, to actively shape them and find forms of expression for how I can make the collective influences visible in my work, how they can be named, and how they can be reflected within it. I understand these connections as threads woven throughout the whole work. They are sometimes obvious and provide the general structure, give shape and stability. Sometimes they are hardly visible, but they certainly question the understanding that creating art is an individual and isolated process.

20 "Launch of re.act.feminism #3," Manifesta 14, accessed October 28, 2024, https://manifesta14.org/event/9633/.

21 Verena Melgarejo Weinandt, "Revenge Is like Time Travel," in *She Creates Nightmares against Colonial Desires*, ed. Suza Husse (re.act.feminism #3, 2022), https://test.linarta.com/react/pdf/Revenge%20Zine%20print.pdf.

The Self as a Bridge

Situating myself within my work allows me to weave elements of my history, my body, my feelings, and my experiences into Pocahunter and to understand them within the larger context. To approach the relationship between autobiographical elements and the analysis of socially effective structures, I ask about the historical and social structures in which Pocahunter is embedded. I relate to autohistoria-teoría because it is not my own biography or my specific, singular experiences that I want to retell through Pocahunter; rather, I want to use her as contextualization, to "make sense" of these experiences in a larger context and create movement and change around these issues.

In her book *The Anzaldúa Theory Handbook* (2022), AnaLouise Keating draws attention to the fact that, within autohistoria-teoría, the actual biographical narrative recedes into the background and the theoretical reflection associated with it becomes the dominant narrative component.[22] When I think about how I have embedded my biography into my artistic practice, and how that has served as a starting point for my research and understanding of a historical, social, and cultural complex, I think of my first performance character, La Bolita Berlinesa, which I developed while I was living and studying in Buenos Aires in 2013.

Being German-Bolivian in Argentina meant being confronted with very different and contradictory reactions. I was regularly assigned to the structurally discriminated minority of immigrants from the neighboring countries of Bolivia or Paraguay because of my appearance—being addressed as a saleswoman in stores, for example. However, the encounters were full of respect and interest when I was identified as

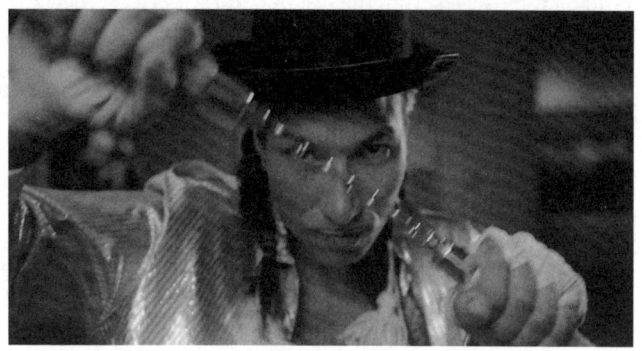

Fig. 27 Verena Melgarejo Weinandt, *La vuelta de la malona*, 2014. Video still.

22 Keating, *Anzaldúan Theory Handbook*, 83. Keating is the editor of a volume of interviews with Anzaldúa and has published three books with texts by and about her: *The Gloria Anzaldúa Reader* (2009), *Light in the Dark / Luz en lo oscuro* (2019), and *The Anzaldúan Theory Handbook* (2022).

German.[23] To understand this experience, I had to engage with Argentinean history and see how the racist assumptions about me as a Bolivian and my idealized status as a German had historically grown out of Argentina's colonial history and national politics, which have failed to critically deal with and confront Argentina's violent history toward Indigenous communities. Argentines' identification with Europeans, based on their migration history from Europe, is expressed by distancing themselves from the rest of Latin America, especially the Indigenous population. This distancing still shapes anti-immigration policies and racial discrimination today.

This experience led me to develop the character La Bolita Berlinesa. *Bolita*, which means small ball in Spanish, is a derogatory term used for Bolivians; *berlinesa* is the Spanish name of a type of German dessert and refers to my upbringing in Berlin.

I shaped my experiences in Buenos Aires into the performative alter ego of La Bolita Berlinesa, leading to the production of a poster series, a video-performance at the Museo de Bellas Artes in Buenos Aires, and several workshops.[24] Most importantly, I got in touch with different artists and political activists I supported, learning from them through exchanges and conversations about the similar social issues we wanted to impact. A collective of Bolivian migrants that advocates for workers in the illegal textile industry invited me to show my work at their events, and the artistic collective Serigrafistas Queer asked me to translate La Bolita Berlinesa into a stencil and participate in their public stencil actions.

Reflecting on the significance of being read and addressed as an Indigenous woman in a German-speaking context has revealed the deep roots of these experiences in German history. Although in contemporary activist and academic debates

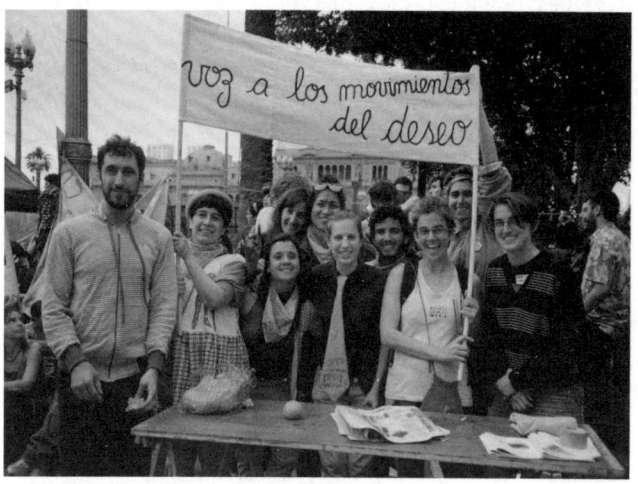

Fig. 28 La Bolita Berlinesa participating in a Serigrafistas Queer public
stencil action at the Pride parade in Buenos Aires, 2013

23 Bolivians and Paraguayans make up the biggest migrant groups in
Argentina and provide most of the labor force in fruit and vegetable shops, the
domestic and care-work sector, and the mostly illegal textile industry.

24 Verena Melgarejo Weinandt, *La vuelta de la malona*, 2014, https://
www.youtube.com/watch?v=gDJ5mFgR48U. In this work, La Bolita Berlinesa
"confronts" Ángel Della Valle's 1892 painting *La vuelta del malón* (The Return
of the Indian Raid). When I use the term "video-performance," I refer to a
performance created to be filmed and thus shaped by that process, versus a
filmed performance, which means that while a performance took place it was
documented on film. Of course, the distinction between the two can be blurry,
because a documented performance is influenced by being filmed and a filmed
performance may also include unscripted performance acts.

there is a greater sensitivity toward and engagement with Indigenous communities as well as their cosmovision and activism, an understanding of Germany's role and colonial history is mostly absent in these discussions.[25] Pocahunter points out this void, speaks to it, examines it, wants to express it, make it tangible—she *is* this void.

A contradiction also becomes clear at the level of visual representation. While racist, exoticizing, and sexualized stereotypes of Indigenous people in the German-speaking context are visibly present, there is an almost complete absence of representations of real Indigenous people. Books, films, plays, all forms of images and stories that circulate among a wide audience play a formative role in maintaining these images as part of the collective imagination. The absence of real representation is reinforced by the recurring misconception that Indigenous people did not survive colonialism and other genocides. The survivors are again stereotyped in their identities and ways of life. In the German perspective, Indigenous people are not recognized as participants in a globally interconnected world.

Pocahunter emerged partly through my research into the historical formation of these clichés. One of the most widely read German writers, Karl May (1842–1912), played a vital role in the creation of specifically German stereotypes and their popularity. Sales of his adventure novels exceed those of J. K. Rowling's *Harry Potter* series (keep in mind that May's were written over 100 years ago). His best-known work is a series of books about Winnetou, a fictional Apache character first introduced in 1893. Winnetou's adventures are described from the perspective of his white friend Old Shatterhand. May claimed that the tales were inspired by his journeys through the Wild West; in fact, he was over sixty when he left Europe for the first time. The character of Winnetou has shaped clichés of Indigenous people in German-speaking countries like no other. Successful film adaptations, particularly from the 1960s, have popularized these stories.[26] In 2020, a modified version of his Winnetou stories was released in cinemas. After massive criticism on social media about the stereotypical portrayal of the title character, the publisher removed two children's books based on the film from its catalogue. This led to intense debates about cancel culture and cultural appropriation, which, in my view, often fail to address the historical significance of these stereotypes.[27] Adaptations of May's books and this character are continually passed on to new generations, especially in the visual universes created for children and young people growing up in Germany, becoming part of the childhood imprint that many May enthusiasts hold on to throughout their lives.[28]

25 There is not enough space for a detailed discussion here, but regarding Indigenous activism, especially from North America, I am thinking of the presence of Indigenous movements in social media such as the Standing Rock protests, which have generated a lot of visibility in German-speaking countries through their articulation in English. In an academic context, there is an increased reception of Indigenous knowledge in general. In addition to Indigenous theorists such as Linda Tuhiwai Smith or Eve Tuck, non-Indigenous theorists who employ Indigenous knowledge are receiving attention in German-speaking academia—for example, Donna Haraway's *Staying with the Trouble: Making Kin in the Chthulucene* (2016), which was translated into German in 2018.

26 *The Treasure in Silver Lake* (1962) was the first of eleven film adaptations of May's Winnetou books. The French actor Pierre Brice became famous for his role as the title character.

27 Peter Jungblut, "'Gefühle anderer verletzt': Verlag zieht Winnetou-Bücher zurück," NDR Kultur, August 23, 2022, https://www.ndr.de/kultur /buch/Ravensburger-zieht-Winnetou-Buecher-zurueck-Gefuehle-anderer -verletzt,winnetou178.html; "Ravensburger-Verlag nimmt Winnetou-Kinderbücher aus dem Programm," *Frankfurter Allgemeine Zeitung*, August 22, 2022, https://www.faz.net/aktuell/feuilleton/debatten/ravensburger-verlag -nimmt-winnetou-kinderbuecher-vom-markt-18260927.html.

28 In the podcast *Winnetou ist kein Apache* (Winnetou is no Apache), the journalist Ben Hänchen critically reflects on his own active involvement in Karl May's mythologies since his childhood, and interviews various fans of the author as well as critical voices. Ben Hänchen, host, *Winnetou ist kein Apache*, six episodes, 2022, MDR Kultur, https://www.mdr.de/kultur/podcast/winnetou/index.html.

The question of an overall social correlation, and the links between my experiences and those of others, led Pocahunter to investigate the historical and cultural events that have formed Indigenous stereotypes in the German-speaking context. It became clear that there is a specificity to Indigenous stereotypes here that differs from other Indigenous stereotypes around the globe, and that the identification with this stereotype is historically relevant for Germany and the creation of a national identity. The scholar Hartmut Lutz established the concept of "Indianthusiasm" to describe Germans' fascination with Indigenous people. Lutz indicates that this is much more than a "yearning for all things Indian, a fascination with American Indians, a romanticizing about a supposed Indian essence," but rather an identification with the idea and stereotypes of an Indigenous identity from North America, which in the nineteenth century played an important role in the creation of a still unformed German national identity.[29] Among the foundational stories of German identity was Tacticus's *Germania*, written around 58–120 AD, which was taken up by the German Renaissance in the fifteenth and sixteenth centuries to establish the Teutons as the historical ancestors of the Germans. Lutz shows how the characteristics attributed to Germanness corresponded to those of the "noble savage": "In short, centuries before Rousseau's *bon sauvage*, Tacitus assigned to the Germanic tribesmen the dual stereotype of the noble yet bloodthirsty savage, a cliché that was consistently reapplied to ethnic groups outside Hellenism or Christianity."[30] This constructed similarity made the stereotype of Indigenous people a useful counterpart to confirm a German national identity "created in a cultural context that constructed ethnicity as blood based, that is interested in escapist folk traditions, and favors genetic-essentialist approaches toward nation-building." During the Nazi period, Indianthusiam was also instrumentalized for its racist politics. Hitler himself declared Winnetou the perfect example of a German military officer. In this period, the "idealized" Indigenous stereotype represented by Winnetou was the compatriot who confirmed German identity and was used to create "compensatory self-aggrandizement."[31] The American-studies scholar Frank Usbeck has analyzed the use of this identification by the National Socialists and shown how these identifications are still used today as part of far-right imagery.[32]

Pocahunter interrogates the manifestations of Indianthusiasm today. Which of these appearances reveal the need for Indigenous stereotypes to enforce a German national identity and history? How are they expressed, what forms and formats do they take, and how are they passed on? In which places and in which ways can Pocahunter address them? Which gestures, which words, which language, which sounds, which images can she counter them with?

The Boomerang Effect

Anzaldúa describes reading her texts, in which she interweaves her own positionality, as an experience that can produce collectivity. Calling this a "boomerang effect," she writes how people who recognize their own or familiar experiences in her writings also see meaning in these experiences

29 Hartmut Lutz, "German Indianthusiasm: A Socially Constructed German National(ist) Myth," in *Germans & Indians: Fantasies, Encounters, Projections*, ed. Colin G. Calloway, Gerd Gemünden, and Susanne Zantop (Lincoln: University of Nebraska Press, 2002), 168, 170–71.

30 Lutz, 173.

31 Lutz, 179.

32 Frank Usbeck, *Fellow Tribesmen: The Image of Native Americans, National Identity, and Nazi Ideology in Germany* (New York: Berghahn, 2015).

and can articulate them for themselves.[33] The empathy triggered by her texts encourages readers to reflect on their own positionality, enabling self-reflection to become part of the reading experience.

Pocahunter creates this boomerang effect by mirroring collective imaginaries back to the audience. "Confronting" the audience by making fictional ideas "real," I hope to foster a relation to their own projections or need for self-representation when it comes to people who identify with parts of what I articulate. The images I select are meant to create a dialogue with the viewer. I try to amplify my presence through sound and voice, seeing the video format as a way to create intimacy with the viewer. For example, I can whisper something, I can provide glimpses of the smallest details through close-ups, I can create and share visual worlds that don't necessarily correspond to reality but that reflect my personal perspective. However, since I cannot determine the way these aspects affect the viewer, my work is always created anew depending on how it is received.

I perceive Pocahunter as a being with whom I can enter into dialogue. This exchange allows me the feeling of coexisting with her—a form of collectivization of my own voice.

Transforming the Self

Anzaldúa's theory and method are based on her own biography and are deeply connected to her childhood and its cultural, political, historical, and social circumstances and settings. Her knowledge production is connected to her identity and experiences. She was born in 1942 in South Texas, a child of farmworkers. Raised as a Chicana, she grew up within this structurally marginalized minority and initially became politically active within various Chicano organizations, whose dominant masculinity she criticized. She was the first in her family to pursue a career in academia, earning an MA in English and education and working as a teacher for the children of farmworkers. She began her PhD work at the University of California, Santa Cruz, and taught at various universities. As a woman of color, she criticized the structural ignorance regarding racism within activist, lesbian, and feminist circles. According to Anzaldúa, an identity subject to constant transformation is formed through navigating difficulties and contradictions, which became the starting point for her theories. Art, creativity, and self-reflection are central tools to develop new strategies, perspectives, and insights.

Although autohistoria-teoría as a method takes one's biography as foundational, it differs considerably from the established genre of autobiography. Identity-forming experiences are not only retold here; rather, what is addressed is identity itself, its formation and transformation processes, which is the starting point for many of Anzaldúa's concepts. The central components of autohistoria-teoría are therefore the handling and processing of experiences and the self-perception that develops from them. Keating describes the examination of one's own history within this method as "reflective self-awareness," which implies "self-reflection, imagination, analysis, and intuition."[34] A range of processes can be involved, from academic analysis to spiritual practices. Keating points out that autohistoria-teoría refers to a process through which one's perception of the self changes, and thus

33 Gloria E. Anzaldúa, *Interviews/Entrevistas*, ed. AnaLouise Keating (New York: Routledge, 2000), 243.
34 Keating, *Anzaldúan Theory Handbook*, 84.

the self is re-explored and reconfigured.[35] Revisiting these experiences becomes the starting point for gaining new insights: "As the writer intentionally revisits earlier events in their life, seeking clarity, they discover and create new insights."[36] The aim is not an exact and realistic recapitulation of what has happened but rather a reprocessing that expresses a changed attitude and perspective on what has happened, which can lead to multiple results and insights.

My video-performance *Braiding Renewal* (2023) expresses the ability to heal through transformation.[37] I was invited by the curators Katia Sepúlveda and Yuderkys Espinosa Miñoso to participate in a collective research process—leading to an exhibition at La Virreina Centre de la Imatge in Barcelona in autumn 2023—to think about the question of what the world would look like if Europe as a trope never existed or wouldn't exist in the future. My response was a process, method, and ritual I believe artists can contribute to, which is the capacity to imagine things, worlds, and all beings—in short, reality in a different way. By expressing that imagination, we transform these fictive visions into something real.[38]

For *Braiding Renewal*, I used braids as a symbol for transformation and the process of braiding as a symbol for the work this transformation entails. Braids are a recurring theme in my artistic production. In 2017, the artist Maque Pereyra and I created the video-performance *Trenzación*, where we collectively explored processes of identity formation and transformation through hair and braids, connecting to our Indigenous ancestors. Cutting off one's own braids is a powerful gesture—one our ancestors enacted at some point in their lives—that represents how Indigenous women in Bolivia disconnect from their Indigenous identity in order to better access the labor market and experience less discrimination and racism. In the work, Pereyra and I used our hair and the process of braiding to connect to our ancestors as well as to ourselves and each other, creating community and a collective aesthetics of transformation.[39]

Trenzación is continued from Pocahunter's perspective in *Braiding Renewal*. She braids a garment for herself, an armor of sorts, using all the different histories as threads woven into her identity. This garment, which contains her history, is used to create connections, tensions. It holds, pushes, stretches, bends her, creates experiences, shapes life, causes pain and release. All this accumulated energy braided within the garment is then released by entering a body of water and washing the braids, letting the accumulated energy continue its path, transforming it, giving it back, releasing what is not mine but what I have experienced and held on to. It is a letting go. This performance expresses the end and the beginning of a process, a cyclic understanding of time, where the ability to change is understood as the fundamental tool of inner power and healing.

My performance practice often continues resonating within me, creating a transformation, sometimes in unexpected ways. I understand only retrospectively how my performances have influenced me, how they relate to my life at the moment I perform them. Usually, I am aware

35 This is closely related to Anzaldúa's concept of the Coyolxauhqui process or imperative, which articulates constant reconfiguration and transformation of one's identity based on the influence of profound life experiences that Anzaldúa calls "sustos" (a term she uses for experiences that have a shock element to them and lead to the alteration and transformation of one's path in life).

36 Keating, *Anzaldúan Theory Handbook*, 85.

37 Verena Melgarejo Weinandt, "Transformation. Braiding Renewal (Pocahunter Part II)," Repatriates, April 15, 2024, https://repatriates.org/transformation-braiding-renewal-pocahunter-part-ii/.

38 See "The Future Is Gone: Cimarrón Anti-Futurism Seminar-Laboratory," La Virreina Centre de la Imatge, October 16, 2021–October 15, 2022, https://ajuntament.barcelona.cat/lavirreina/en/research/future-gone-cimarron-anti-futurism/550.

that I cannot yet fully understand and articulate this impact through rational reflection. Autohistoria-teoría, as a concept and method, is an attempt to find access to repressed knowledge, including painful experiences, that has become embedded in our bodies without us being aware of it. It describes a "deep diving" into our self, a turning toward our "Shadow Beast," as Anzaldúa conceptualizes it.[40] In this critical self-analysis, inner resistance, one's own refusal, and painful feelings are also decisive. Pitts writes: "The pain that [Anzaldúa] describes with every step highlights forms of resistance that allow or disallow one from learning about oneself or from others."[41] Recapitulating my experiences and their impact on my self-perception can be a painful process that impacts my artistic work, even if not always visibly or clearly expressed in the outcome. Dedicating myself to these different manifestations of painful memories and expressing them in a transformed manner through Pocahunter is a form of processing them. Keating describes working with the self as a bridge or translation tool for knowledge production: "Anzaldúa's deep dive into the embodied personal leads her into transpersonal avenues of knowledge creation; as she relives scenes from her life, she works with the emotions that these deep dives unleash, viewing them almost like little bridges or translational devices leading her into images and, eventually, into words."[42]

These bridges or translation devices are not always clear to me. In addition to my rational reflections, many developments are difficult to put into words—I'm not always aware of them, or I can only name their influence after the actual performance has occurred. I'm thinking of a photo performance that took place three weeks before the birth of my child. As Pocahunter, I wore a leather jacket, platform shoes to make me taller, and lots of heavy jewelry all over my body. I held a plastic machine gun and a backpack with a plaster head smeared with red paint to represent the chopped-off head of John Smith (see fig. 24). The photo shoot went late into the night. All the while, I stood in the dark in front of the illuminated, smoking towers of a refinery. Pocahunter gives me an awareness of my own strength. Even though the photo shoot was staged, the feeling was very real, immediate, and lasting. This performance was extremely helpful when I was giving birth three weeks later. I was able to draw on the awareness of my own strength more easily.

With Pocahunter, I have translated elements of my biography into different outputs; through the process of translation, these elements themselves have been transformed. My personal history and experiences become visible parts of new formations where new perspectives and meanings are created. Revisiting my story—transforming, abstracting, and connecting it with other stories—also enables me to distance myself from my history, to process it and thus open up a different perspective to find its interconnectedness with collective dimensions.

Autohistoria-teoría has anchored my own experience as a methodological approach for Pocahunter. I am repeatedly moved by Anzaldúa's ability to include vulnerability, painful experiences, and knowledge that is otherwise discarded as emotional or invalid as tools and starting points for her work. She articulates the wound and the (creative) process as a remedy, not only for the individual but for collective impact and transformation, and therefore healing: "We are

39 Verena Melgarejo Weinandt and Maque Pereyra, *Trenzación*, 2017, https://vimeo.com/280176028.

40 Keating, *Anzaldúan Theory Handbook*, 86.

41 Pitts, "Anzaldúa's *Autohistoria-teoría*," 363.

42 Keating, *Anzaldúan Theory Handbook*, 69.

all wounded, but we can connect through the wound that's alienated us from others. When the wound forms a cicatrix, the scar can become a bridge linking people split apart. What happened may not have been in our individual control, but how we react to it and what we do about it is. Let's use art and imagination to discover how we feel and think and help us respond to the world."[43]

43 Gloria E. Anzaldúa, *Light in the Dark / Luz en lo oscuro: Rewriting Identity, Spirituality, Reality*, ed. AnaLouise Keating (Durham, NC: Duke University Press, 2015), 21.

Literature

Anzaldúa, Gloria E. *Borderlands / La Frontera: The New Mestiza*. San Francisco: Aunt Lute Books, 2012.

Anzaldúa, Gloria E. *Interviews/ Entrevistas*. Edited by AnaLouise Keating. New York: Routledge, 2000.

Anzaldúa, Gloria E. *Light in the Dark / Luz en lo oscuro: Rewriting Identity, Spirituality, Reality*. Edited by AnaLouise Keating. Durham, NC: Duke University Press, 2015.

Bandau, Anja. *Strategien der Autorisierung: Projektionen der Chicana bei Gloria Anzaldúa und Cherríe Moraga*. Hildesheim: Georg Olms, 2004.

Brunner, Claudia. *Epistemische Gewalt: Wissen und Herrschaft in der kolonialen Moderne*. Bielefeld: transcript, 2020.

Grosfoguel, Ramón. "The Structure of Knowledge in Westernized Universities: Epistemic Racism/Sexism and the Four Genocides/Epistemicides of the Long 16th Century." *Human Architecture: Journal of the Sociology of Self-Knowledge* 11, no. 1 (2013): 73–90.

Harding, Sandra, ed. *The Feminist Standpoint Theory Reader: Intellectual and Political Controversies*. New York: Routledge, 2004.

Keating, AnaLouise. *The Anzaldúan Theory Handbook*. Durham, NC: Duke University Press, 2022.

Keating, AnaLouise, ed. *Entre Mundos / Among Worlds. New Perspectives on Gloria Anzaldúa*. New York: Palgrave Macmillan, 2008.

Keating, AnaLouise, ed. *The Gloria Anzaldúa Reader*. Durham, NC: Duke University Press, 2009.

Lander, Edgardo. "Ciencas sociales: Saberes coloniales y eurocéntricos." In *La colonialidad del saber: Eurocentrismo y ciencas sociales; Perspectivas latinoamericanas*, edited by Edgardo Lander, 11–40. Buenos Aires: CLACSO, 1993.

Lugones, María. "Heterosexualism and the Colonial/Modern Gender System." *Hypatia* 22, no. 1 (2007): 186–209.

Lutz, Hartmut. "German Indianthusiasm: A Socially Constructed German National(ist) Myth." In *Germans & Indians: Fantasies, Encounters, Projections*, edited by Colin G. Calloway, Gerd Gemünden, and Susanne Zantop, 167–84. Lincoln: University of Nebraska Press, 2002

Lutz, Hartmut, Florentine Strzelczyk, and Renae Watchman. *Indianthusiasm: Indigenous Responses*. Waterloo: Wilfrid Laurier University Press, 2020.

Mignolo, Walter. *Local Histories / Global Designs: Coloniality, Subaltern Knowledges, and Border Thinking*. Princeton, NJ: Princeton University Press, 2000.

Pitts, Andrea J. "Gloria E. Anzaldúa's *Autohistoria-teoría* as an Epistemology of Self-Knowledge/ Ignorance." *Hypatia* 31, no. 2 (Spring 2016): 352–68.

Quijano, Aníbal. "Die Paradoxien der eurozentrierten Moderne." *PROKLA: Zeitschrift für kritische Sozialwissenschaft* 40, no. 158 (2010): 29–47.

Sandoval, Chela. "US Third World Feminism: The Theory and Method of Differential Oppositional Consciousness." In Harding, *Feminist Standpoint Theory Reader*, 195–209.

Sonderegger, Ruth. *Vom Leben der Kritik: Kritische Praktiken – und die Notwendigkeit ihrer geopolitischen Situierung*. Vienna: Zaglossus, 2019.

Usbeck, Frank. *Fellow Tribesmen: The Image of Native Americans, National Identity, and Nazi Ideology in Germany*. New York: Berghahn, 2015.

Who Is Mai Ling?
Challenges of Anonymity and
the Practice of Care

Mai Ling is an anonymous artist collective and association whose members work mainly in the field of culture. Based in Vienna, we specifically center the voices and experiences of FLINTA* (a German acronym for women, lesbian, intersex, nonbinary, trans, and agender people) of Asian diasporas and migrant communities from queer-feminist and anti-racist perspectives.[1] The members work "anonymously" as a strategy for multilayered, nonrepresentational voices. We do not hide our faces or bodies; instead, we use anonymity as a strategy to embrace differences within the collective. All activities and works are signed under the name Mai Ling.[2] The number of members and their profiles are never disclosed publicly, and the group's dynamic changes depending on the activities and context in which these activities unfold. Since its founding in 2019, Mai Ling has been creating and organizing various forms of art and activism, ranging from public interventions to video and audio works, installations, cooking performances, and community gatherings, mainly in Austria and German-speaking contexts, while building broader networks with other collectives, groups, and organizations that resonate with Mai Ling's voices to deal with intersectional discrimination in the West and beyond.

As an anonymous and collective being, Mai Ling uses the plural pronoun "we" to reflect myriad voices, experiences, and strategies shaped by numerous activities, discussions, conversations, feedbacks, conflicts, and failures within the collective. We are Mai Ling, and we speak and write as Mai Ling; "we" become the embodiment of Mai Ling. However, the collective has always had an ambiguous feeling about using the plural pronoun. Who is included in the "we"? Who is/are Mai Ling?

Our collective's name comes from an eponymous 1979 sketch on German TV by the Bavarian comedian Gerhard Polt, in which an Asian woman named Mai Ling represents a strange mixture of Western stereotypes and fantasies about exotic, submissive Asian women.[3] She is a mail-order bride from Bangkok who has straight black hair, wears a Japanese kimono, and cooks Chinese food. The sketch demonstrates a racist, patriarchal attitude, remarking how she is "clean [...] as the Asian as such doesn't get dirty at all," "a little too yellow,"

1 The current membership and extended Mai Ling community include not only FLINTA* but also diverse genders who relate to and understand the intersectional and structural discrimination caused by the heterosexual patriarchy that Mai Ling is fighting against. We also have diverse cultural backgrounds. Some belong to the second or third generation of Asian diasporas, having grown up inside and/or outside Austria, while others have migrated to Austria for various purposes. We all met in Vienna. Although we primarily identify as cultural workers, many of us are involved in diverse fields.

2 According to our current communication guidelines for press relations: "Use the name 'Mai Ling' when referring to the artist collective or an individual within the collective. Mai Ling could refer to one individual (singular) or in plural form (many Mai Lings)." The style of credits for Mai Ling's work has changed as the collective has developed, and there has been ongoing discussion about how to acknowledge the people involved.

3 This thirty-minute sketch was broadcast in the evening program *Da schau her*. In 2010, the sketch was reenacted live on stage without any changes to the script, with Polt and the same woman, whose actual name and occupation remain unknown. Gerhard Polt, "Auf der Bühne: Mai Ling," accessed February 23, 2024, https://polt.de/polt-auf-der-buehne-mai-ling/#gs.4st981.

and good in bed because of her "enormous exotism."[4] As she is introduced by her White chauvinist husband, played by Polt, she does not open her mouth but sits next to him silently. Despite its overtly misogynistic, sexist, and racist portrayal of an Asian wife, the sketch is one of Polt's most famous works. A well-known figure in southern Germany, Polt is believed to have intended the piece as satire with a clear and cynical purpose.[5] Today, the generation who grew up with his brand of comedy still defends him when we talk about how brutal the sketch is, arguing that it critically and politically mirrored the German society of the time, which condoned systematized human trafficking and sex slavery, though several articles have mentioned that Polt's humor was flatly racist and xenophobic.[6]

In 2018, we discovered a video of this sketch while coming up with ideas for our collective name. The skit stirred feelings of anger and disgust while reopening unspoken wounds and trauma, as each of us could relate to this character to a different extent. We have embodied this fictional figure in our daily lives, and have been treated like her no matter how diverse our bodies, backgrounds, experiences, conditions, or histories. The stereotypical image of the Asian woman with a White husband and over-sexualized Asian femininity is so persistent that it is relentlessly projected onto different female-appearing Asian bodies, reproducing the same violence and microaggressions in universities, art institutions, public transportation, the streets, supermarkets, and domestic spheres.[7] While tackling such assumptions and prejudices, we also noticed the potential of using this character as a subversive strategy for the collective, which consists of different transnational Asian migrants and diaspora members. The character of Mai Ling ironically represents the Asian hybrid that can accommodate different Asian cultural and geopolitical narratives while unveiling the structurally gendered, sexualized, and racialized conditions of living and working. We decided to appropriate the character as and within the collective. With this Asian hybridity, we aim to reclaim our own individual and collective agency as and through Mai Ling. Establishing the collective can be attributed to this pivotal impetus to fight against racist stereotypes that produce discrimination and the desire to foster an intricate array of voices, creating discourses and building communities through the lens of shared experiences as Asian FLINTA* in a predominantly White society, especially in a German-speaking context such as Austria.[8]

4 Translated from the original German script.

5 Korbinian Eisenberger, "Gute Miene zu Mai-Ling," *Süddeutsche Zeitung*, April 13, 2018, https://www.sueddeutsche.de/muenchen/ebersberg/kritik-gute -miene-zu-mai-ling-1.3943608.

6 Today there is still an industry that organizes marriages between German men and Southeast Asian women with rhetoric that describes an Asian wife as submissive, loyal, and sexual. For a critique of Polt's work, see Patrick Guyton, "Gerhard Polt wird 80: Wia im richtigen Leben," *Frankfurter Rundschau*, May 6, 2022, https://www.fr.de/panorama/gerhard-polt-geburtstagw-wia-im -richtigen-leben-91524660.html. Polt counters that his provocation is not about bigotry or cultural appropriation but rather the risk of getting himself into the "shitstorm" he exposes himself to when testing the limits of satirizing other cultures. Doris Priesching and Gerhard Polt, "Gerhard Polt: 'Ich kenne kein Diktat, ich kenne auch keinen Diktator,'" *Der Standard*, April 18, 2022, https://www.derstandard.de/story/2000134939687/gerhard-polt-ich-kenne-kein -diktat-ich-kenne-auch-keinen.

7 These everyday intersectional discriminations were collected and articulated in some of Mai Ling's early installations and interventions, such as *Who Is Mai Ling?* (2019–20) and *My Name Is Mai Ling* (2019).

8 Following Nell Irvin Painter, we capitalize White to challenge and unmask "Whiteness" as a racial identity. Our use of the term "White society" has been greatly influenced by Sara Ahmed's approach to Whiteness through the lens of queer phenomenology. White society centralizes Whiteness in an ongoing process by orientating certain bodies in specific directions, affecting how they take up space and what they can do. Following this usage, we capitalize Brown and Yellow when referring to racialized subjects. Nell Irvin Painter, "Why 'White' Should Be Capitalized, Too," *West Central Tribune*, July 23, 2020, https://www.wctrib.com/opinion/nell-irvin-painter-why-white-should-be -capitalized-too; Sara Ahmed, *Queer Phenomenology: Orientations, Objects, Others* (Durham, NC: Duke University Press, 2006).

We consider Mai Ling a platform for sharing and exchanging experiences of discrimination—experiences often overlooked, self-censored, and self-blamed. We question the invisibility and lack of space for Asian voices within institutional narratives and politics, as the conditions, struggles, challenges, and embodied experiences of Asian diasporic and migrant FLINTA* are structurally dismissed in mainstream discourse of the politics of race and gender, especially in combination with the "model minority myth." This myth stereotypes Asians as diligent and economically and socially successful, thus incapable of experiencing racism.[9] The Korean American writer and poet Cathy Park Hong surmises that the model minority myth is often internalized within Asian diasporic and migrant consciousness, as a result leaving individuals with feelings of shame and melancholy rather than anger when encountering racism. Consequently, it continues to ignore systemic racial oppression against Asians. Influenced by Sianne Ngai's examination of the affective states of "ugly feelings," Hong describes the disfiguring sense caused by the denial of the experience of everyday racism as a "minor feeling." It is the "racialized range of emotions that are negative, dysphoric, and therefore untelegenic, built from the sediments of everyday racial experience and the irritant of having one's perception of reality constantly questioned or dismissed."[10] The American scholar Anne Anlin Cheng unveils this symptom as a blind spot, since both gender studies and race studies have overlooked Asian women, keeping them mute and absent, while the analysis and voices of "Women of Color" typically center on Black and Brown women, who are often seen as resistant and angry, protesting categories of "injury." In contrast, the Asian woman, or "Yellow woman," exemplified by the figure of Mai Ling, is portrayed as lacking feelings, not angry, and not experiencing forms of injury and violence in the same way as other Women of Color. In using the term "Yellow," we do not mean to essentialize Yellow femininity or specify a single reading of Asian femininity. The color yellow, as Cheng argues, reveals the ambivalence in using such a racialized term, highlighting a condition of denigration and violence that is expressed through the language of aesthetics in the context of Asiatic femininity.[11] As Cheng suggests, answering a perplexing yet constantly recurring question that makes the Asian FLINTA* an exception within Women of Color—"Is the yellow woman injured—or is she injured enough?"—requires focusing on the very real formation of her figure in Euro-American culture and society.[12]

In her book *Ornamentalism* (2019), Cheng tracks the "incarnation of Asiatic femininity and Asian female representation in Western modernity and its expansive embroilment with the ornamental and the Orient."[13] Employing Edward Said's critical perspectives on Orientalism, she points out that the existing discourse of ornamentalism only considers

9 In the US context, the term was used as a racial wedge to divide Asian and Black communities, portraying Asians as well-integrated, silent, and White-adjacent. This oversimplified and homogenous perception of a racial group has been used to pit communities of Color against one another while ignoring the complexities of social, cultural, and historical differences, which in turn perpetuates systemic racism.

10 Cathy Park Hong, *Minor Feelings: An Asian American Reckoning* (New York: One World, 2020), 55; Sianne Ngai, *Ugly Feelings* (Cambridge, MA: Harvard University Press, 2005).

11 Anne Anlin Cheng, *Ornamentalism* (New York: Oxford University Press, 2019), xi. Cheng specifically uses the term "Asiatic" in her book.

12 Cheng uses the term "Yellow woman" rather than "Asian woman in the West" to highlight the discomfort associated with an inescapably racialized and gendered figure that has been overlooked. However, focusing solely on Yellowness might create another blind spot—for instance, excluding Brown Asian women. In the history of Mai Ling, this has been one of the biggest issues in terms of how the category of "Asia" is understood and imagined in the West, which is inseparable from the colonial power dynamics within Asia itself. This aspect will be discussed later in this essay.

13 Cheng, 3.

gender and class analysis and has ignored the process of race-making. Cheng argues that Asian femininity has been narrated in ornamental languages and gestures as well as constructed as a hybrid being—human/object, present/absent, organic/synthetic, a figure of civilizational value and a disposable object of decadence. Asian women are portrayed in various ways, often rendered abstract, objectified, and sexualized, yet excluded from sexuality as the aesthetic project of "a phantasmic corporeal syntax that is artificial and layered."[14] They have been caught in a constant cycle of being shaped and reshaped by aesthetic and ornamental undertakings. Ornamentalism, as the theoretical frame, unpacks the processes of racialization and the structure of Yellow femininity: the conditions and consequences of living as an aesthetic being. It is a conceptual framework for approaching a history of racialized person-making and aesthetics with a critical analysis beyond the limits of race and historical periodization carried by Orientalism, primitivism, and modernism.

This abstracted submissive Asiatic femininity—as an aesthetic, decorative person/object—has given rise to the invisible and overlooked wounds that affect how actual Asian-looking feminized bodies are perceived and treated. Here, the injury caused by the exposure to such race-making is often denied by the fact that their experience and existence are being framed and obscured as an aesthetic that is deemed irrelevant to racism. Furthermore, their bodies are materially reduced to an ornamental object that also serves as decoration for the institutional rhetoric of "diversity."[15] Sara Ahmed analyzes how diversity policies within institutions are ultimately structured around Whiteness although ostensibly including bodies that look different and thus can embody nonwhite otherness. They entail the involvement and creation of a body that is perceived and appreciated as a palatable difference, providing a flavor and sweetness to the institutional surface.[16]

Cheng's theory intrigues us. The ornamentalization of Asian women in the domestic sphere precisely describes the original Mai Ling in Polt's sketch, and in Vienna the Jugendstil movement flourished by incorporating shapes of female bodies into their ornamental languages while being inspired by an "Asian" aesthetic. Against this backdrop, ornamentalism opens up the possibility of dealing with and deviating from the construction of dehumanized subjects such as the exotic Oriental Other that do not embody the personhood of the modern West.

Accordingly, in Austria, where racism and sexism against Asians and the construction of Asian femininity are hardly recognized compared to the established discourse in English, Mai Ling's early works emphasized calling out intersectional discrimination against Asian FLINTA* by asking the question "Who is Mai Ling?" and reclaiming it with, "My name is Mai Ling." *The Beautiful Alien Girl* (2019), Mai Ling's first artistic manifestation, reveals the reality of the objectification and commodification of oversexualized Asian women in the heteronormative Eurocentric imagination. By using Polt's original sketch, with its clichés of an Asian woman as a submissive and silent wife or loyal pet who serves to please her master in a domestic setting, the work unveils the commodification and exoticization of Asian female-looking bodies that still linger today. Even though the work functions as a collective statement against racism and sexism, it leaves

14 Cheng, 5–6.
15 Mika Maruyama, "Aesthetic Project of Ornament and Racially Gendered and Sexualised Synthetic Experience," in *Notes for Mitsouko & Mitsuko*, ed. Miwa Negoro and Matsune Michikazu (Vienna: Studio Matsune, 2021).
16 Sara Ahmed, *On Being Included: Racism and Diversity in Institutional Life* (Durham, NC: Duke University Press, 2012).

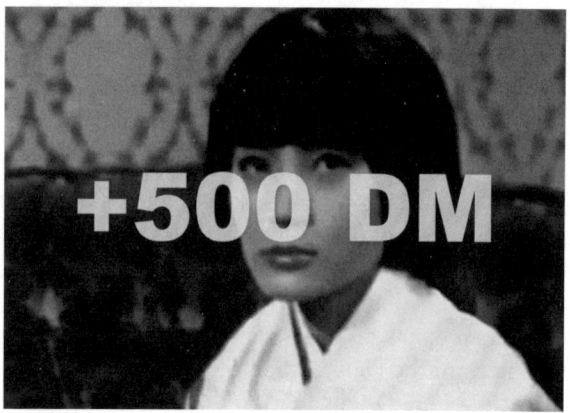

Fig. 29 Mai Ling, *The Beautiful Alien Girl*, 2019

us with an ambivalent feeling. On the one hand, it provocatively addresses a White audience who is ignorant of how the Western imagination has constructed, racialized, and sexualized Asian female-looking bodies. On the other hand, showing the problematic scene reproduces the same violence as the original. It is necessary to critique a racist and sexist society and bring the issues to the table, but we have realized that the act of restaging the original scene is unbearably hurtful for the affected communities, as it is our and their reality and shared experiences.[17]

The Challenge and Conflict of Anonymity and Collectivity

From the beginning, the anonymity of the collective has played an important role in creating non-individualized voices to fight against intersectional discrimination and protect members from the unintended consequences of activism. As the collective grew, anonymity became a two-fold strategy as an attempt to embrace differences that could not be reduced. On the one hand, it is a strategy of obfuscation, the "right to opacity," in the words of Édouard Glissant.[18] It is a recognition of not being able to gain access to the full story of Mai Ling and the individuals in the collective. We use this opacity as an active refusal against reduction, compartmentalization, labeling, normalization, and assimilation of cultural differences into a singular identity and absolute truth, instead allowing for gaps, absences, and complexities to be present within Mai Ling as a fictional character and an embodiment of the character. On a practical level, different Mai Ling members with different bodies and voices appear at various public events and projects, which disorients the audience as to "who Mai Ling is/are."[19] Precisely, being opaque—not being graspable as a single Mai Ling—has the subversive potential of deconstructing the migratory narratives that do not fall into the "reaction to Whiteness" or the single story of the Asian female expected by the Eurocentric Orientalist lens.[20]

On the other hand, anonymity allows for "fluidity" within the collective setting and structure—each project is produced by different formations of group members from various backgrounds, practices, disciplines, and fields. Thus, the agency and voices of Mai Ling are destabilized, morphing, shape-shifting, and embracing the differences in various settings. Again, it is an open question: "Who is Mai Ling?"

17 Some of our colleagues from the Asian diasporic community in Vienna told us that they could not continue watching *The Beautiful Alien Girl* for this very reason.
18 Édouard Glissant, *Poetics of Relation*, trans. Betsy Wing (Ann Arbor: University of Michigan Press, 1997), 189–94.
19 This anonymity has resulted in communication problems with institutions that have been confused by Mai Ling's structure as a group of individuals.
20 Hong, *Minor Feelings*, 104.

This aspect of anonymity also challenges the category of "Asia," which needs to be approached from a critical viewpoint. Mai Ling's inception is rooted in the belief that an intersectional and multilayered approach serves as a counterforce to essentialist identity politics and the perpetuation of discrimination based on stereotypes that have been created by White-supremacist patriarchy. This approach conscientiously attends to the nuanced dynamics of class, gender, sex, sexuality, age, ethnicity, and religion within Asia. Our aim is to initiate a discourse on Asia as a contested paradigm, encompassing its diasporas, migrant populations, and resident communities. At the same time, we also acknowledge the danger of categorizing Asia and the many differences and complexities in the racialization, gendering, and sexualization of subjects of Asian descent. The geopolitical positionalities from West, Central, South, Southeast, and East Asia cannot be captured as a single narrative. The hybrid figure of Mai Ling challenges, with multiple voices, precisely such complexity, whose representation is constantly in flux, being re- and undefined. Anonymity appears here as a tool to embrace these impossibilities, to fix them as a collective, allowing space to grow, change, and transform together.

Aside from this, it is worth acknowledging that struggles, conflicts, and challenges constantly emerge from the concept and practice of an anonymous, fluid collective that have to be navigated differently depending on the context (e.g., institutional or noninstitutional), format (e.g., video work or gathering that can be exposed to the public with or without our presence), and need (e.g., activist urgencies). This is critical especially because Mai Ling is not just a collective but an "artist" collective. First and foremost, Mai Ling is against social injustice, for discourse-making, for sharing voices, and not driven to promote individual institutional careers.[21] Yet a conflict between artistic egos and collective efforts is one of the fundamental challenges in a group and association like Mai Ling. For instance, when we make decisions collectively, without a hierarchical structure or strong directorship, we often need to negotiate artistic individuality and aesthetics within our anonymous, collective identity. While clashes between different artistic methods, aesthetics, and egos create tension like in any other collective, anonymity adds another aspect to the group dynamic. It requires each of us to accommodate collective being over individual effort since none of us is supposed to publicly claim the resulting work as an individual achievement.

At the same time, we are confronted with the difficulty of balancing the strict control of anonymity in the age of social media and the importance of individual credits and ways of expression that were achieved through Mai Ling. In other words, anonymity and collectivity in a neoliberal market-driven art world can unwittingly become exploitative, diminishing and erasing individual efforts by not crediting them the way a single artist is usually credited. Because of both the precarious condition of freelancers in the arts and our nonestablished working methods, we have experienced ugly feelings, injuries, and failure within the collective in the past. Therefore, we always need to reflect, as individuals and as a collective, on how we envision collectivities to decentralize voices, experiences, values, knowledge, resources, labor, and temporalities. Decentralization involves individual dedication built on trust and vulnerabilities that should

21 In 2021, the members of Mai Ling wrote out the principles of the practice, which state the basic understanding of working together as an anonymous collective. The shared values include collective decision-making, transparency, and open communication, as well as the equal commitment of each member in both institutional and noninstitutional settings. The members continually discuss this way of working, and the document is updated whenever necessary.

be mutually acceptable under such conditions, not only conceptually but also at the organizational and structural levels. We follow the path of the anonymous Mai Ling, driven by the shared passion and hope for a collective spirit, and our work is built on efforts that defy description within a neoliberal framework. Yet we inevitably find ourselves confronted with the frustration arising from the reality of a capitalist and discriminatory society that prioritizes individualism and competition.

Eating as Pleasure and Provocation

While embracing the challenges of a collective and anonymous being, Mai Ling's work is not tied to the condition in which the original Mai Ling character was invented but rather aims to articulate the matrix of power and resist constructed Asian femininity. Our works express the anger, shame, and frustration of marginalized communities of Color and migrants from the non-West. Whenever we see a connection with the context of Mai Ling, we make a public statement about racism and tokenism, as this was a primary reason we formed as a collective: not to keep silent about the injustice we witness. For instance, the online collective protest *Not Funny!* (2020) was made in reaction to the late-night show *Gute Nacht Österreich* (Good Night Austria) on national television, which in March 2020 aired a racist parody of a Chinese correspondent reporting on the COVID-19 crisis that ridiculed Chinese cuisine and eating habits.[22] In February 2023, another open statement was published, followed by an on-site protest, to denounce the production of *Der goldene Drache* (The Golden Dragon, 2014) at the Musik Theatre an der Wien, an opera whose stereotypical, racist

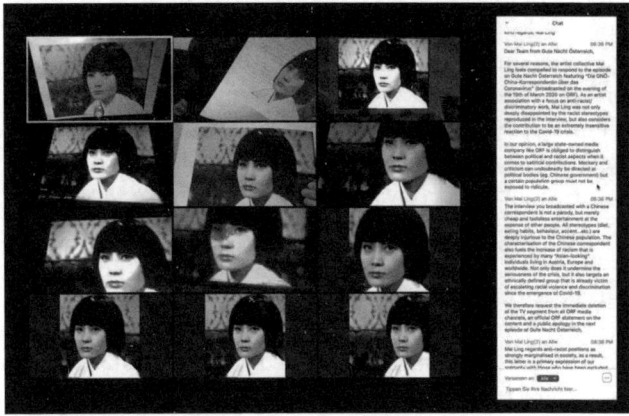

Fig. 30 Mai Ling, *Not Funny!*, 2020. Documentation of the online collective protest.

22 With *Not Funny!*, Mai Ling addressed an open letter to the TV show with the request for an apology and the deletion of the content. Mai Ling, "An Open Letter from Mai Ling to *Gute Nacht Österreich*," April 6, 2020, https://files.cargocollective.com/c2168277/2020Statement_ORF_EN.pdf.

depictions stigmatize migrants of Asian descent in the gastronomy industry.[23]

As these cases indicate, Asian stereotypes are often associated with culinary habits that are seen as uncivilized and exotic, associated with the consumption of "unusual" animals, while Asian cuisines and restaurants are generally popular and have been appropriated by Western capitalist society. Food, at its root, is a medium to nurture a sense of community and kinship, a gesture of care, survival, and healing, especially for diaspora and migrant communities. Examining culinary politics from a South Asian diasporic perspective, the scholar Anita Mannur analyzes how the affective value of food functions in creating a memory of home and the past in order to maintain a sense of belonging as immigrant subjects, even if those attachments and images of a homeland are imaginary or fictional.[24]

Therefore, food has been a central theme in Mai Ling's activities. Addressing the entangled sociopolitical narratives connected to migration histories and diasporic food culture, *Mai Ling Kocht* (Mai Ling Cooks, 2020–ongoing) was conceived as a series of oral, auditory, and haptic performances. The series involves sharing various recipes and communal eating as a gesture to resist the racist and sexist gaze, challenging how culinary culture gets exoticized and ridiculed. For example, inspired by popular social-media genres such as mukbang and ASMR, the second episode, *Mai Ling Kocht 2: Eating as Pleasure and Protest* (2021), addresses the pleasure and comfort in food culture and the exoticization of Asian eating habits through the phenomenon of eating alone while staying connected in the virtual realm, especially during COVID-19. In doing so, the work deals with the food systems and industries that perpetuate social injustices, economic

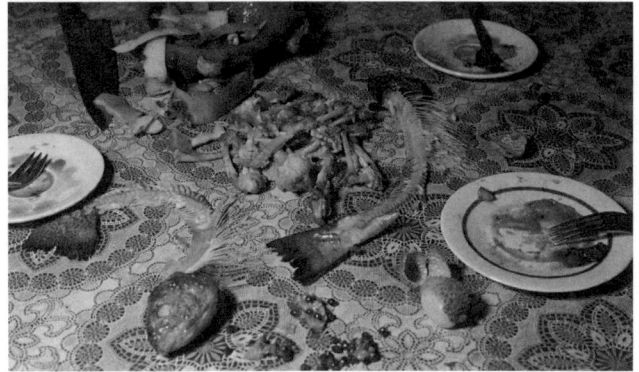

Fig. 31 Mai Ling, *Mai Ling Kocht 2: Eating as Pleasure and Protest*, 2021

23 *Der goldene Drache* was composed by the Hungarian composer Peter Eötvös with a libretto by the German playwright Roland Schimmelpfennig. Set in the kitchen of a Thai-Chinese-Vietnamese restaurant in Germany, it tells a "tragic" story of illegal Chinese immigrants. The opera stereotypically portrays Asians as illegal migrants working in "miserable," "unhealthy," and "precarious" (human trafficking) conditions without access to health care. The protest was organized in front of the opera on the day of its last performance and published as an open statement. In both cases, Mai Ling did not receive a response. Mai Ling, "Public Statement on 'Der goldene Drache (The Golden Dragon)' at Musiktheater an der Wien," February 16, 2023, https://mai-ling.org/STATEMENT.

24 Anita Mannur, *Culinary Fictions: Food in South Asian Diasporic Culture* (Philadelphia: Temple University Press, 2010), 28.

disparities, and precarious labor conditions, which are all intertwined with gender, race, and class struggles.

The third episode, *Mai Ling Kocht: We All Eat Dirt* (2021), examines stinky fermented foods from East Asia, which often elicit disgust from Western palates, in contrast to popularized "authentic" Asian food. These pickled and fermented foods are the staple of the working class and migrants due to their low cost and accessibility, and their preservation over centuries is symbolic of their resilience and resistance against oppression, aggression, and alienation. Touching on childhood memory, national policy, labor migration, and recent health-food trends and beauty products, the work unravels the complex interplay of consumption, desire, and disgust related to fermented food, and its entanglement with racialized and gendered representation.

At the end of the performance, the audience is invited to eat these foods, thereby confronted with "consuming" the story of the Others, of oppression. By doing so, we literally embody Otherness, confronting the White Orientalist gaze and its desire with the provocative remark "When you eat our food, you are eating us." Embodying the Other becomes an act of recognition to reclaim our narratives. The consumption of exoticized Asian bodies as decorative commodities in the context of our collective is juxtaposed with the condition of the global capitalist society that appropriates, consumes, and markets Asian foods.

In some cases, the commodification of our artistic labor directly affects the conditions in which we produce and perform. In 2022, we initiated a public intervention to call out racist and sexist behavior at the Donaufestival in Krems. Mai Ling was invited to perform a new edition of *Mai Ling Kocht: We All Eat Dirt* under the festival's theme, "Stealing the Stolen," which discusses the politics of cultural appropriation and the possibility of re- or counter-appropriation. During the final performance, instead of serving food we held a public intervention to confront the actual "dirtiness" of the racist and sexist condition of the arts demonstrated in the festival. It was a joint effort with WILTS Press; a group of students in the Master in Critical Studies program at the Academy of Fine Arts Vienna; the artist Nomcebisi Moyikwa, who was also participating in the festival; and other BIPOC (Black, Indigenous, and People of Color), migrant, and diaspora organizations in Austria.[25] Our statement was not only directed at this particular festival but came from the daily struggles of BIPOC FLINTA* communities that are often tokenized by Austrian institutions and festivals. In fact, it was incredible to witness how a coalition of participants formed in less than a day. At the same time, to continually point out institutional violence and microaggressions is emotionally labor-intensive. When we fight against discriminatory structures that overtly tokenize us and then are hounded by inquiries from journalists and activists (some of whom are quite racist and disdainful themselves), coupled with the high expectations from our communities, we can't help but feel exhausted, injured, and even retraumatized. Not knowing how to handle these emotionally charged situations, and not having the time to digest the emotions shared within the collective, we often become frustrated with one another, which leaves another layer of emotional scars. We often ask why it

25 The Donaufestival is an annual festival of music and performance that takes place in the state of Lower Austria. Following an intervention by WILTS Press, who pointed out a racist and sexist text in the festival reader—which the festival refused to acknowledge—the public intervention was held within Mai Ling's performance to bring public awareness to the matter and question institutional accountability and care. After the intervention, Mai Ling had an hour-long meeting with a festival director. However, no accountability was offered, and instead the situation exposed the festival's patriarchal structure.

is so difficult to care for each other, especially since we are protesting for our collective well-being. This was a moment to reflect on our own injuries and think more about self-care and recuperation from individual and collective wounds and their aftermath.

In this situation, it was natural to want a space where wounds could be shared by gathering in order to heal together. The question of how to create and experience our own pleasure in our activities became critical, which raised the issue of who is allowed to seek pleasure instead of serving others. In some cases, Asian women are still expected to sacrifice their own happiness and joy for the family. The subordinated Asian woman, just like the original Mai Ling, was a product of strong patriarchal structures and is the source of many Asian conventions. To seek our own pleasure individually and collectively became a healing process to "reclaim our whole, happy, and satisfiable selves from the impacts, delusions, and limitations of oppression and/or supremacy," as the writer and activist adrienne maree brown encourages in *Pleasure Activism*.[26]

Toward Collective Healing

The need for joy brought Mai Ling to a new chapter: addressing ways of collective survival by focusing on the healing aspect of creativity instead of always being confrontational to Whiteness. Following bell hooks's examination of how White people's desire for the racial other functions as a "technology for the reproduction of Whiteness" and as "eating the other," Sara Ahmed analyzes how otherness might become an "orientation device" for extending the reach of Whiteness.[27] Therefore, disorienting and reorienting our approach—once centered "around" White society, which produces intersectional discrimination—became essential to not reinforce such Whiteness but rather expand and amplify alternative and decentralized voices.[28]

In 2022, Mai Ling was invited to participate in the festival "Vivências," held in Vienna that year. The festival featured a series of performances and workshops for migrant and BIPOC communities whose positionality and lived experiences resonated with those of the collective.[29] We wanted to try new approaches to food, so the participatory performance *Mai Ling Soup Bath* (2022–ongoing) was conceptualized as a meditative cooking ritual to seek collective pleasure through food as a medium: a gathering with a meditation session followed by the collective cooking of a soup with Asian ingredients. Each participant was invited to share stories and memories related to food while the others chopped vegetables and stirred pots. We wanted to share pleasurable moments with the audience instead of antagonistic feelings, and enjoy a bowl of warm soup together. Many of the stories were personal—sometimes heartwarming, nostalgic, and touching—bringing smiles and tears of joy into the space. The gathering was pleasurable and empowering, suffused with various emotions, memories, and smells. Anita Mannur discusses how cooking and eating together forms a sense of kinship, intimacy, and sociopolitical belonging for marginalized communities, and how radical spaces of belonging and unbelonging emerge for nonnormative subjects in the public

26 adrienne maree brown, *Pleasure Activism: The Politics of Feeling Good* (Chico, CA: AK Press, 2019).

27 Ahmed, *Queer Phenomenology*, 128.

28 Ahmed employs words to describe directionality and orientation such as "around" and "toward" to articulate how bodies are temporally and spatially shaped by positioning Whiteness as the center of normativity.

29 "Vivências" was curated by Denise Palmieri and Marissa Lôbo and organized by kültür gemma! at Kulturhaus Brotfabrik Wien.

realm while producing different narratives of intimacy. She argues that it is not possible to imagine sociality without the existence of publics, and that these publics are also formed "by those who function as strangers," unfamiliar and foreign agents. This notion of the public is central to her inquiry into what happens when marginalized bodies eat in the realm of the public.[30] The emotionally intense experience of a ritual involving the sharing of food made us reorient Mai Ling's positionality as the artist and activist collective as we navigated our practice. We realized the necessity of holding a space where we can embrace and share both our struggles and our pleasures as forms of communal care.

More recently, Mai Ling further expanded the potential of collective healing through a somatic practice of exploring "stickiness" as an agency of resistance and pleasure. Stickiness, often associated with disgust, is a chain of effects that affects how certain bodies are (re)shaped. Connecting things in both metaphorical and material senses, it unfolds an attachment of ugly, uncomfortable, and confrontational feelings as the "aesthetics of negative emotions."[31] It also shows "how emotions 'stick' to certain bodies, such as how the negative affects of racism stick to the racialized subject," while implying the dirty and sticky entanglements of migration, coloniality, and imagination.[32] At the same time, the call to stick together has an emancipatory potential for collective empowerment. In the two-channel video installation *Becoming Stickiness* (2023), the concept of stickiness is used to counter Viennese ornamentalism through ornamental and invasive migratory humans and plants intermingling. Multiple Mai Ling bodies ultimately become one, embracing transformative, sticky, pleasurable, and resilient qualities.

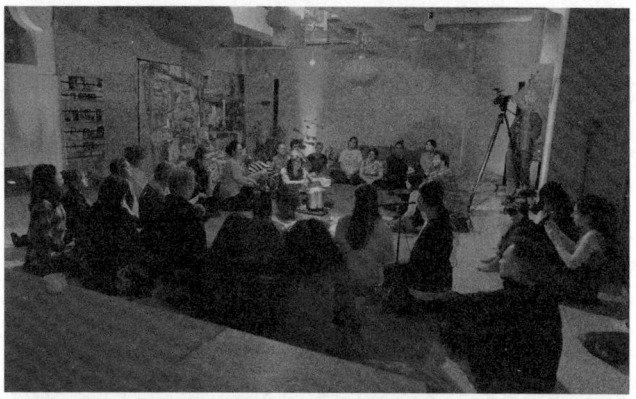

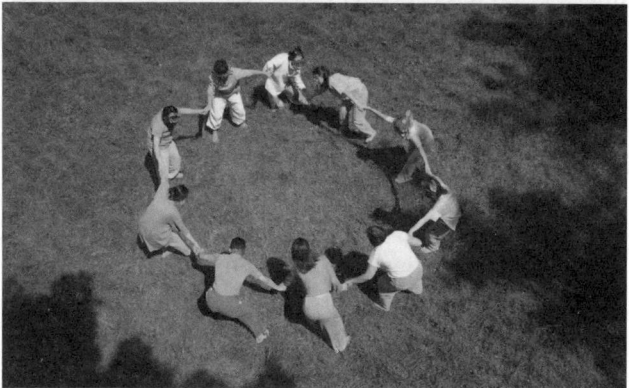

Fig. 32 Mai Ling, *Mai Ling Soup Bath*, 2022–ongoing
Fig. 33 Mai Ling, *Becoming Stickiness*, 2023

30 Anita Mannur, *Intimate Eating: Racialized Spaces and Radical Futures* (Durham, NC: Duke University Press, 2022).

31 Ngai, *Ugly Feelings*, 1.

32 Carlos Kong, "Anti-Asian and the Art Institution," *The Public Review*, October 20, 2023, https://www.thepublicreview.org/read/Carlos-Kong-Anti -Asian-and-the-Art-Institution-Mai-Ling. Kong's review of Mai Ling's solo exhibition "Not Your Ornament" (Secession, Vienna, 2023) refers to Ahmed's concept of "stickiness." See Sara Ahmed, *The Cultural Politics of Emotion* (Edinburgh: Edinburgh University Press, 2014), 4.

Care and Responsibility

With Mai Ling's clear shift from provocation aimed at White society to collective healing of our own, the care and responsibility within the collective naturally became the center of discussion and activities under our name. In collective practices, nonhierarchical relationships and democratized processes are often easily idealized, and when it comes to feminist collective practice, the discourse around the need for care is unconditionally normalized. Concepts of "the collective" and "care" have been instrumentalized and institutionalized in recent years in both academia and art, which sheds light on both labor issues in the cultural sector and individualism.

Within Mai Ling, where most activities are formed and guided by the members' individual—yet collective—interests, passions, and motivations, without any directorship, we do not aim to implement any hierarchy in decision-making or production in order to maintain our various voices. Naturally, we require a longer time for decision-making to best employ individual skills and ideas and encourage creativity, embracing different ways of artistic expression, communication, and paces of working. We see, for instance, the tendency to prioritize verbal skills over other forms of expressions. Being a collective often entails additional, sometimes inefficient, work for communication, negotiation, and (dis)agreement. On the other hand, there is no one way to collectively practice care on structural and production levels, as the framework for distributing artistic and organizational labor inherently produces invisible hierarchies among art, activism, and administration. At some point, we realized that we were close to burnout. Different aesthetics and disciplines, as well as various ways of working, become obstacles in the collective, especially when it comes to the production of an "artwork."

We also have witnessed the potential misuse of "care" and "collectivity," concepts that can be easily abused to excuse the irresponsible behavior of individuals, which contributes to eroding trust and burdening others. Because we are anonymous, the commitment of each member is not visualized as an individual achievement; in this situation, even a basic level of responsibility might be ignored. In the end, such an idealized structure was impossible to sustain. We realized that collective work is only possible if every individual takes responsibility with the "radical honesty" of openness to accept critical feedback and share vulnerability with others, no matter how various disagreements and conflicts occur within the collective. As the anthropologist Bianca C. Williams writes, radical honesty values "personal experience and narratives as important tools for learning," providing "space for vocalizing these truths and us[ing] them to connect the dots between individual and group experiences of (dis)empowerment to institutional and systemic analyses of racism and sexism." At the same time, honesty toward others within the collective "emphasizes a critical eye toward analysis, intention, and authenticity, where multiple truths may be taken together to figure out beneficial and effective practices."[33] Building collective trust in other members and their practices in order to commit to a shared value is a gradual process that needs time.

How do we care for ourselves within an anonymous collective in a healthy and sustainable manner while sharing and envisioning a collective direction? We always ask ourselves

33 Bianca C. Williams, "Radical Honesty: Truth-Telling as Pedagogy for Working Through Shame in Academic Spaces," in *Race, Equity, and the Learning Environment: The Global Relevance of Critical and Inclusive Pedagogies in Higher Education*, ed. Frank Tuitt, Chayla Haynes, and Saran Stewart (New York: Routledge, 2016), 73.

this question. Within the undefined structure of Mai Ling, whose working methods and group dynamics need to function differently depending on each project and the members and collaborators involved, we want to seek a form of responsibility—what Donna Haraway calls "response-ability"—an ability to respond to worlding, which opens up possible dialogues and mutual growth.[34] This notion of response-ability can be understood as an ethics of care to respond to one another's feelings, needs, skills, strengths, and vulnerabilities. Responsibility also extends to how we understand group dynamics and approach mutual care in our collective practices.

At the same time, when it comes to the practice of community-building, another difficulty lies in distancing ourselves from the identity politics that reinforce the normalization of social categories such as "Asian," "migrant," and "FLINTA*," escalating the divisions, and even hostility, between marginalized communities. We do not form a collective just because we are Asian FLINTA*s; instead, we nurture a thriving community by sharing the same agenda against racist, essentialist, heteronormative patriarchy. We have developed and tried out various methodologies for a decentralized Mai Ling, and we have learned from numerous failures. These methodologies are not established and never will be, as they are continuously evolving as the multilayered locus of decentralization grows and mutates. Navigating the ever-shifting situatedness of Mai Ling, we keep practicing the emancipatory potential of the anonymous and fluid artist collective with care, responsibility, and radical honesty to seek alternative ways of being and becoming as a hybrid.

34 Donna J. Haraway, *Staying with the Trouble: Making Kin in the Chthulucene* (Durham, NC: Duke University Press, 2016), 105.

Literature

Ahmed, Sara. *The Cultural Politics of Emotion*. Edinburgh: Edinburgh University Press, 2014.

Ahmed, Sara. *On Being Included: Racism and Diversity in Institutional Life*. Durham, NC: Duke University Press, 2012.

Ahmed, Sara. *Queer Phenomenology: Orientations, Objects, Others*. Durham, NC: Duke University Press, 2006.

brown, adrienne maree. *Pleasure Activism: The Politics of Feeling Good*. Chico, CA: AK Press, 2019.

Cheng, Anne Anlin. *Ornamentalism*. New York: Oxford University Press, 2019.

Eisenberger, Korbinian. "Gute Miene zu Mai-Ling." *Süddeutsche Zeitung*, April 13, 2018. https://www .sueddeutsche.de/muenchen/ebersberg /kritik-gute-miene-zu-mai-ling -1.3943608.

Glissant, Édouard. *Poetics of Relation*. Translated by Betsy Wing. Ann Arbor: University of Michigan Press, 1997.

Guyton, Patrick. "Gerhard Polt wird 80: Wia im richtigen Leben." *Frankfurter Rundschau*, May 6, 2022. https://www.fr.de/panorama/gerhard -polt-geburtstag-wia-im-richtigen -leben-91524660.html.

Haraway, Donna J. *Staying with the Trouble: Making Kin in the Chthulucene*. Durham, NC: Duke University Press, 2016.

Hong, Cathy Park. *Minor Feelings: An Asian American Reckoning*. New York: One World, 2020.

Kong, Carlos. "Anti-Asian and the Art Institution." *The Public Review*, October 20, 2023. https://www .thepublicreview.org/read/Carlos-Kong -Anti-Asian-and-the-Art-Institution -Mai-Ling.

Mannur, Anita. *Culinary Fictions: Food in South Asian Diasporic Culture*. Philadelphia: Temple University Press, 2010.

Mannur, Anita. *Intimate Eating: Racialized Spaces and Radical Futures*. Durham, NC: Duke University Press, 2022.

Maruyama, Mika. "Aesthetic Project of Ornament and Racially Gendered and Sexualised Synthetic Experience." In *Notes for Mitsouko & Mitsuko*, edited by Miwa Negoro and Matsune Michikazu. Vienna: Studio Matsune, 2021.

Ngai, Sianne. *Ugly Feelings*. Cambridge, MA: Harvard University Press, 2005.

Painter, Nell Irvin. "Why 'White' Should Be Capitalized, Too." *West Central Tribune*, July 23, 2020. https://www.wctrib.com/opinion/nell -irvin-painter-why-white-should-be -capitalized-too.

Priesching, Doris, and Gerhard Polt. "Gerhard Polt: 'Ich kenne kein Diktat, ich kenne auch keinen Diktator.'" *Der Standard*, April 18, 2022. https://www .derstandard.de/story/2000134939687 /gerhard-polt-ich-kenne-kein-diktat -ich-kenne-auch-keinen.

Williams, Bianca C. "Radical Honesty: Truth-Telling as Pedagogy for Working Through Shame in Academic Spaces." In *Race, Equity, and the Learning Environment: The Global Relevance of Critical and Inclusive Pedagogies in Higher Education*, edited by Frank Tuitt, Chayla Haynes, and Saran Stewart, 71–82. New York: Routledge, 2016.

Elif Süsler-Rohringer

The Persistence of Patterns
From Strong Subjectivity to Local and Global Sartorial Exchanges

I have worked as an artist and freelance designer since my undergraduate years. After studying visual arts and visual communication design in Istanbul, I was accepted into the textile art and design graduate program at the University of Arts Linz, based on my textile-focused portfolio—which is just one of many. I have a collection of portfolios, motivation letters, biographies, and rejection letters, each performing a different part of my life.

Creativity is difficult to categorize when it is attached to the criteria necessary to cross borders. The procedure to apply for a student visa was quite time-consuming and financially demanding, even with an official acceptance letter. As part of my work on the intersection of migration and textile history, I began researching the institutional dimension of creativity, looking at my collection of rejection letters in a new way. There are many reasons for such rejections, and institutional unfamiliarity is a big one. Sometimes you might have to employ unfamiliar language when applying for a creative job or a grant. If it's a more research-based application, then the curriculum vitae has to connect with the creative part of your life or it won't look complete and coherent. Hence the multiple portfolios and CVs. In my research, I look at the migration of creative textile work, focusing on the subjective histories of the actors involved. I work on sartorial knowledge transfers to make visible the neglected creative interventions into fashion and migration history undertaken by migrants from Turkey. Thinking about the multiple identities I wear and strategically employ has led me to search for a history of creativity that is either lost among the different identities labor migrants might have adopted or boosted by them.

The Creativity of the Work

My work is about the institutional organs that define and regulate skilled work and creative labor in a transnational context. The recruitment of "guest workers" was accelerated through an official labor agreement between Turkey and Austria enacted in 1964. At that time, businesses were not just compensating for a labor shortage but actively looking to hire skilled workers from Turkey. In the creative fields, this demand was focused on the textile industry. However, it has remained invisible since academic research and media attention on integration policies and citizenship mostly focuses on the labor of caretaking and cleaning, while critical fashion studies oriented toward Turkey mainly centers on the veil.[1] Both perspectives leave a lacuna: the qualified

1 Linda Bosniak, "Citizenship, Noncitizenship, and the Transnationalization of Domestic Work," in *Migrations and Mobilities: Citizenship, Borders, and Gender*, ed. Seyla Benhabib and Judith Resnik (New York: New York University Press, 2009), 127–56; Gülay Toksöz, "Irregular Migration and Migrants' Informal Employment: A Discussion Theme in International Migration Governance," *Globalizations* 15, no. 6 (2018): 779–94; Nilüfer Göle, "The Voluntary Adoption of Islamic Stigma Symbols," *Social Research* 70, no. 3 (2003): 809–28; Anna C. Korteweg and Gökçe Yurdakul, *The Headscarf Debates: Conflicts of National Belonging* (Stanford, CA: Stanford University Press, 2014).

and creative dimension of labor migration. Men and women from migrant backgrounds have contributed to the textile industry and taken part in tailoring practices. Bridging design history, textile history, and migration studies connects literature from disparate fields that has yet to be brought into dialogue. I found inspiration in research projects that deal with the changing meanings of home and homemaking in migrant communities, and that engage with both material-culture studies and personal stories.[2] However, these projects mainly focus on practices of collecting, consuming, and decorating, and not the dimension of creating these objects. My research examines the creative adaptations of design in conjunction with the transnational migrant fashion experience from the perspective of tailors and dressmakers. How is this perspective reflected (or not) in the archives through the official mechanisms of recruitment and education?

The anthropologist James Clifford argues that routes and travels enrich encounters and cultural transfers.[3] Travels are what define culture; the point of departure is just the beginning. Here, I am building on Clifford's discussion of "roots" and "routes": roots can precede routes, but displacement is a fundamental component of cultural meaning and knowledge. I argue that creativity is also work but translated differently, through routes in which the results can overshadow the process. It is in this process where knowledge production happens and where gaps become visible, since migration history is made of discontinuities as much as continuities. Creativity can also refer to the methods that lead to production independent from spatial context. Creativity entails not only the artistic design work defined by cultural norms but also the domestic production of clothes through the many stages of production. We see the beginning and the end, but research can illuminate the process. In textile history, the material presences of this process are just as pivotal, if not more, than the final apparel. This process is not abstract but dynamic—a *vehicle* for creativity.

Mobilizing Traces: Archives, Nostalgia, and Memory

During this dynamic process, I wonder how my personal standpoint affects my research. This standpoint has nostalgic beginnings. My grandmother was a home dressmaker and made our clothes—I grew up between fabrics, fashion, and style magazines. This personal connection influenced my decision to study art and design. My work was about fabrics but used the skills and creativity differently. This was only possible with the support of my family and the political and economic conditions in Turkey and abroad. My family encouraged my decision to study art and design, while bilateral agreements between countries offered artists opportunities for mobility through international exchange programs and artist residencies. Although these opportunities supported artists financially and gave them a global identity and a chance to network, they were not independent of national cultural

2 Sanja Bahun and Bojana Petric, eds., *Thinking Home: Interdisciplinary Dialogues* (New York: Routledge, 2018); Özlem Savaş, "Taste Diaspora: The Aesthetic and Material Practice of Belonging" (PhD diss., University of Applied Arts, Vienna, 2008); Daniel Miller, *The Comfort of Things* (Cambridge: Polity, 2008); Alison J. Clarke, "Taste Wars and Design Dilemmas: Aesthetic Practice in the Home," in *Contemporary Art and the Home*, ed. Colin Painter (London: Routledge, 2002), 131–51.

3 James Clifford, *Routes: Travel and Translation in the Late Twentieth Century* (Cambridge, MA: Harvard University Press, 1997).

4 For a critical reading on art's instrumentalization of globalism and cosmopolitanism, see Peggy Levitt, *Artifacts and Allegiances: How Museums Put the Nation and the World on Display* (Berkeley: University of California Press, 2015); and Nikos Papastergiadis and Daniella Trimboli, "From Global Turbulences to Spaces of Conviviality: The Potentialities of Art in Mobile Worlds," in *Handbook of Art and Global Migration: Theories, Practices, and Challenges*, ed. Burcu Doğramacı and Birgit Mersmann (Berlin: De Gruyter, 2019), 38–53.

agendas.[4] The artist, fashion designer, historian, and curator Christine Checinska situates her African-Caribbean heritage in England through the histories of global fashion. She argues that "what we see are borrowings and translations," as she observes textile arts, crafts, and design across multiple generations.[5] Similarly, how does labor migration as an ongoing historical process change these borrowings and translations? This journey is about displacement—not just across national borders but from the personal to the local and the global.

The indirect and informal effects that home dressmaking and domestic design work have on fashion are a focus of my research, and in my childhood as well. For me, dressmaking is linked to memories of the family being together and wearing clothes made from the same fabrics, even wearing identical skirts, dresses, shorts, and blouses, which created a sense of belonging. This might seem unimportant in an everyday context, but it is connected to how identities are reshaped again and again. This personal nostalgia is also closely tied to material-culture history, as certain fabrics, cuts, and magazines function as a reminder of the past. In my research, I follow traces of people, materials, objects, and images, assembling a narrative through archival practices in which these elements are present or absent, or both. The literary scholar Marianne Hirsch uses the word "mobilizing" in place of "activating" when she talks about the contributions in the anthology *Women Mobilizing Memory*.[6] This term, which is usually reserved for military or political contexts, becomes a call for action. Similarly, my projects about the archive aim to mobilize the records of memory and create another narrative based on the subjectivities of minorities.

The immigration of sartorial workers was concentrated in Vorarlberg, home to Austria's embroidery and textile industry, and Vienna, where the organization that regulated the recruitment of "guest workers" was situated. My archival research in these regions has shown that textile companies there hired skilled textile workers from Turkey.[7] Although clothes and artifacts of visual arts and design can transcend borders without the need for translation, there are still organizations that regulate their meaning, since these skills can also be a means for people to physically change places. (I remember how worried a classmate from China and I were while waiting for our oral exam in the corridors of the University of Arts. We didn't speak much German, and we were not sure if the images in our portfolio would translate on their own.)

To research the official recruitment process of Turkish migrants to Austria, I relied on two different but intertwined methodologies: oral history and archival research. Oral history interviews led me to revisit the archives and became a source for the questions asked in this essay, starting with: How to connect personal departures to global histories?

My archival research shows how the professions of tailoring and textile work became part of a bureaucratic process through intermediary bodies. How are these occupations defined? How does gender become a factor in acknowledging skilled work? I researched the official recruitment documents of labor migration to understand the definitions, categorizations, translations, obstacles, and catalysts for assessing creativity. Through emails exchanged with Siegfried

5 Christine Checinska, "Spinning a Yarn of One's Own," in *A Companion to Textile Culture*, ed. Jennifer Harris (Hoboken, NJ: Wiley-Blackwell, 2020), 42; Christine Checinska, "'Cut & Mix': Collage, Creolisation and African Diaspora Aesthetics," *Mobilities*, no. 9 (2020): 46–60.

6 Marianne Hirsch, "Introduction: Practicing Feminism, Practicing Memory," in *Women Mobilizing Memory*, ed. Ayşe Gül Altınay et al. (New York: Columbia University Press, 2019), 2.

7 Erich Brüstle, interview by Rupert Tiefenthaler and Annette Bleyle, 2001, Wirtschaftsarchiv Vorarlberg, Feldkirch.

Pflegerl, head of the Austrian Recruitment Commission in Istanbul from 1964 until its closure in 1993, I learned that he donated many relevant documents from the 1970s onward to the archives of the Wirschaftskammer Österreich (Economic Chamber of Austria). In these documents, there is a section, revised almost annually, that contains codes for each profession in Turkey. The İş ve İşci Bulma Kurumu (Turkish Labor Market Administration) created this list and sent it to Pflegerl to be translated. There are documents handwritten by Pflegerl explaining the professions, including an additional page under the heading "Professions where it is not clear what work is being done."[8] Officials created categories for jobs based on these lists, having to invent new labels for the ones that had no equivalents in Austria. Fortunately, tailoring was a universal job, though men and women were put in separate categories. Was it necessary to implement gendered categories? This was the only officially gendered profession in the recruitment files. Clothmaking was always translated correctly from the Turkish, but instead of *terzi* (*Schneider*, tailor), the gender-neutral name of the profession in Turkey, the files include the terms *erkek terzisi* (*Herrenschneider*, tailor of men's clothing) and *kadın terzisi* (*Damenschneider*, tailor of women's clothing). In a later document, the same profession is written as *terzi* (*erkek*) and *terzi* (*kadın*).[9] Nonetheless, the examination criteria were the same for both genders. Using sewing machines, they had to trace certain repetitive drawings of very basic patterns to evaluate the applicant's technical skill and familiarity with the trade (fig. 34).

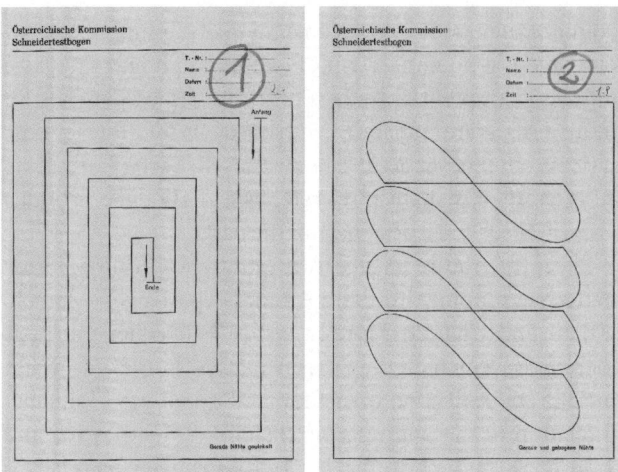

Fig. 34 Tailors' test sheets for the examination of professional suitability, 1977

8 "Ne iş yapıldığı anlaşılamayan meslekler." Quotations have been translated by the author unless indicated otherwise.

9 This can be translated as "tailor (man)" and "tailor (woman)" or "tailor (male)" and "tailor (female)." It probably referenced the gender the clothes were meant for and not the gender of the person making the clothes.

Patterns Performing as
Betweener Image Vehicles

Kaat Debo, curator of the 2003 exhibition "Patterns" at MoMu – Fashion Museum Antwerp, emphasizes the connection with the body in the design process: "Technically speaking, the pattern is the 2-dimensional transition between the 3-dimensional body and the final item of clothing. Each pattern carries a potential item of clothing in it and therefore, indirectly, a potential body too."[10] These past patterns for future designs are embedded with nostalgia for a former time that was often never actually experienced. Each time cutting patterns are reused, there is a reference to a body (or a bodily performance) and a design from the past.

Recent literature engages with migration from a performative standpoint through personal experiences. Marcelo Diversi and Claudio Moreira write "betweener" autoethnographies, in which they perform along borders as academicians and reflect on their firsthand experiences "situated in relation to the politics of exclusion of everyday life and knowledge production."[11] They self-reflectively merge their personal experience with writing as academics. Cami Rowe, a researcher in international politics with a performance and theater studies background, responds to the theatricality of border security with a performance of another scripted role "played" by herself.[12] This interconnectedness of theory and methodology resonates with my artistic and research practice, which revolves around collecting archival material. I often reenact the design and production process as a performative act to understand the material, historical, and technical connotations of the textile medium. As opposed to theater studies and academia, my artistic research involves subtle performances between patternmaking and designing in the context of labor migration. Cutting fabrics based on patterns, for example, was done by machines in factories, but regulating the orders and controlling these stages was carried out by skilled migrants, most of whom were professional tailors coming from and trained in Turkey. These performances might seem too technical and therefore invisible in the context of creativity, or might not be visible enough because the processes of production are not always transparent, contrary to the creative labor of actors.

In principle, patterns enable the designs to resurface in the future. As suggested by the fashion historian and theorist Gertrud Lehnert, garments can be analyzed as *imagines agentes*—images that act.[13] Imagines agentes refer to a sequence of images that appear in one's mind and are the basis for remembering. Since they appear in specific historical contexts, Paisley shawls can be approached as imagines agentes. On the other hand, they are not just images but things with material presences embedded in social encounters. The art historian Aby Warburg used the concept of *Bilderfahrzeuge* (image vehicles) to analyze migrating images, motifs, and archetypes across space and time in his unfinished project *Bilderatlas Mnemosyne*, which he began in 1927. He grounds his theory on the repetition of images through transformation and circulation to reveal the continuity between antiquity and early Renaissance. This theoretical approach can also be applied to the migration of concepts, objects, and

10 Kaat Debo, "Patterns," in *Patronen/Patterns: Modemuseum Antwerpen*, ed. Kaat Debo, Linda Loppa, and Bob Verhelst (Ghent: Ludion, 2003), 9.

11 Marcelo Diversi and Claudio Moreira, *Betweener Autoethnographies: A Path towards Social Justice* (New York: Routledge, 2018), 17.

12 Cami Rowe, "Seized: Performance Autoethnography in the UK Border Force National Museum," *Millennium* 50, no. 2 (2022): 379–404.

13 Gertrud Lehnert, *Mode: Theorie, Geschichte und Ästhetik einer kulturellen Praxis* (Bielefeld: transcript, 2013), 144–45.

people: as they migrate, they transform and create various converging paths through appropriation, repetition, and transformation, filling in the gaps left by one another. The theorist and artist Mieke Bal argues that concepts such as narrative can be used for interdisciplinary work.[14] Concepts are mobile, which gives more freedom to work among various disciplines. Combining fashion and design history with migration studies and material-culture studies, I attempt to employ patterns not just as objects of research but also as a concept and methodology to analyze the material, cultural, and social experience of creative labor migration.

To research converging paths requires a perspective that also entails the inclusion of (high) fashion in everyday life. Patterns as design models have roles between everyday clothing and fashion on a performative level. In the 1970s, retail companies employed designers to attend fashion shows and "get inspired" by the latest items for their own line—for instance, the British fashion designer and skilled pattern cutter Sylvia Ayton working for the Wallis Fashion Group.[15] Fashion shows in the 1970s were very different from those today, which use multimedia, multisensorial performances, and augmented reality in collaboration with artists, architects, and stage designers to give an overall experience. Back then, it was forbidden to make sketches during the shows, so the designers had to take notes for companies to later copy the new high-fashion garments and make them internationally accessible in stores. After Aenne Burda, founder of the German magazine *Burda Moden*, would attend fashion shows in Paris and Milan, she and her coworkers translated the designs into an everyday clothing language (through the reworking of designs, photographs, and texts) to be published and distributed globally. The interviews I conducted at tailor shops in Vienna—small businesses owned by immigrants from Turkey—revealed that "high fashion" designers today employ tailors (*Maßschneider*) to execute their designs. These relationships between designers and tailors/seamstresses during production is an example of the transformation of a concept into something wearable and executable. Often, the designs could not be translated into existing patterns and fabrics, so the designers had to change them by consulting the expertise of these tailors. The patterns allowed the designers to produce the clothes more than once and made the garments accessible to the public, at least for those who can afford pricey items made in limited quantities. These aspects show the strong link between high-fashion items and everyday clothing.

We don't perceive fashion as a pure construction of clothes; we rather encounter it through people, media, texts, scenography, and categorizations. About the technologies that determine medium of the magazine, the scholar Dagmar Venohr writes: "The devices are, so to speak, the carriers of fashion and the conditions of the devices determine the possibilities of fashion."[16] Likewise, archival research and interviews create these possibilities in different forms of media, showing entanglements and disjunctures. Archival research is part of my methodological toolbox to reveal reoccurrences, gaps, and migrating concepts alongside migrating people. It also shows the institutional dimension of creativity through the documents produced by the factories, which accelerated

14 Mieke Bal, *Narratology: Introduction to the Theory of Narrative* (Toronto: University of Toronto Press, 1985); Mieke Bal, *Travelling Concepts in the Humanities: A Rough Guide* (Toronto: University of Toronto Press, 2002).

15 Kevin Almond, "Eliminating the Bust Dart: The Role of Pattern Cutting in the 1960–2002 Career of British Fashion Designer, Sylvia Ayton," *Journal of Dress History* 3, no. 2 (2019): 19.

16 Dagmar Venohr, *Medium macht Mode: Zur Ikonotextualität der Modezeitschrift* (Bielefeld: transcript, 2010), 149.

labor migration through the official recruitment agreements. Which institutions played a role in creating a network of shared knowledge, leading to creative familiarity between the individuals and the official organizations? How was this familiarity displayed in the visual material within the portfolios of the individuals and the factories?

Patterns as Moving Vehicle and Migrating Concept: Wirtschaftsarchiv Vorarlberg & Türkenmuster

I conducted research at the Wirtschaftsarchiv Vorarlberg in Feldkirch, where most of the textile history of the region is collected. The archival record, however, is fragmented. The institutional interests are in the economic and social history of the region—here, migrants only appear as a (temporary) labor force. Vocational training is archived through official reports. Although relevant, the creative labor of students has not been archived. The textile industry, migration, and creativity remain disconnected in institutional knowledge.

Although the archive has extensive records on graphic design, textile history is mainly conveyed through the factory records. The only visual record of student work is the graduation portfolio of Rita Bertolini, a second-generation Italian immigrant who became well known in Vorarlberg. After her graduation from Textilschule Dornbirn, she worked as a textile and graphic designer at the Franz M. Rhomberg Textile Company (in operation from 1832 to 1994), a factory famous both regionally and nationally, whose records are stored in the archive. Bertolini's classmates in a 1980–81 sewing course at the Textilschule included two Turkish women in their third year in the Fachschule für Bekleidungsindustrie Fachrichtung Damenbekleidung (Technical College for

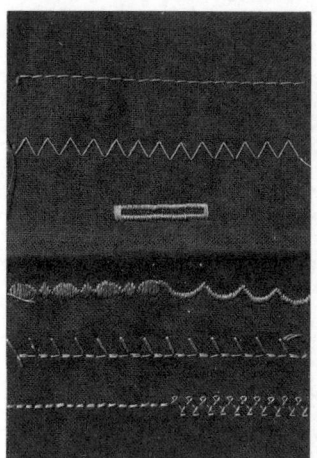
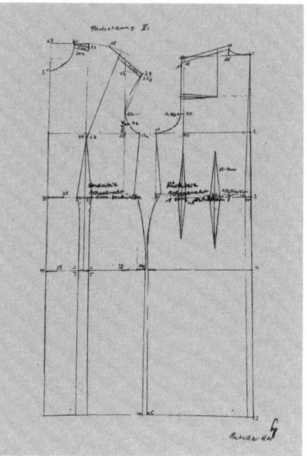

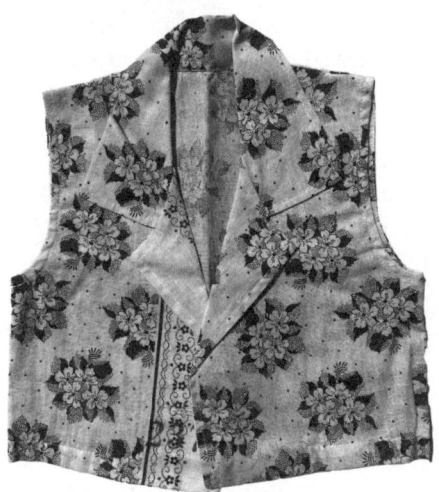

Fig. 35 Three examples from Rita Bertolini's graduation portfolio
from the sewing class at Textilschule Dornbirn, 1980–81

the Clothing Industry Specializing in Women's Clothing). Although there aren't any documents in the archive regarding the studies of these two women, Bertolini's portfolio gives us some insight into the expectations of the design process. Along with her final designs, there are sketches of sewing and stitching styles that she tried on a piece of cloth, and technical and artistic drawings of the conceived designs (fig. 35). Unfortunately, these fragmented pieces do not include any information about their relation to the rest of the designs.

In addition to Franz M. Rhomberg, there were many other textile companies based in Vorarlberg, often family businesses such as Herrburger und Rhomberg (1795–1983), F. M. Hämmerle (1836–2016), Getzner (1818–), Ganahl (1833–87), and Benedikt Mäser (first as Elastisana, 1884–95). Founded in 1889, the Textilschule Dornbirn provided both creative and technical skills for employment in these factories. The archival documents show that several members of the directing and educational staff were also from the families that ran the factories. Furthermore, they also reveal that the children of these families attended different specialized technical colleges (*Fachschulen*) within the Textilschule. The school was embedded in the Vorarlberg clothing industry. As part of the official knowledge transfers in the context of creative labor migration, vocational schools are significant. They were one of the best means to provide official familiarity if one wanted to be employed in the region's textile industry.

But how accessible was this educational body to the (second-generation) immigrant? In the archive, the Textilschule's annual reports from the 1970s and 1980s provide an overview of the study plans and regional and international student exchanges. These reports show the quantitative dimension of migration in the number of Turkish students and the training

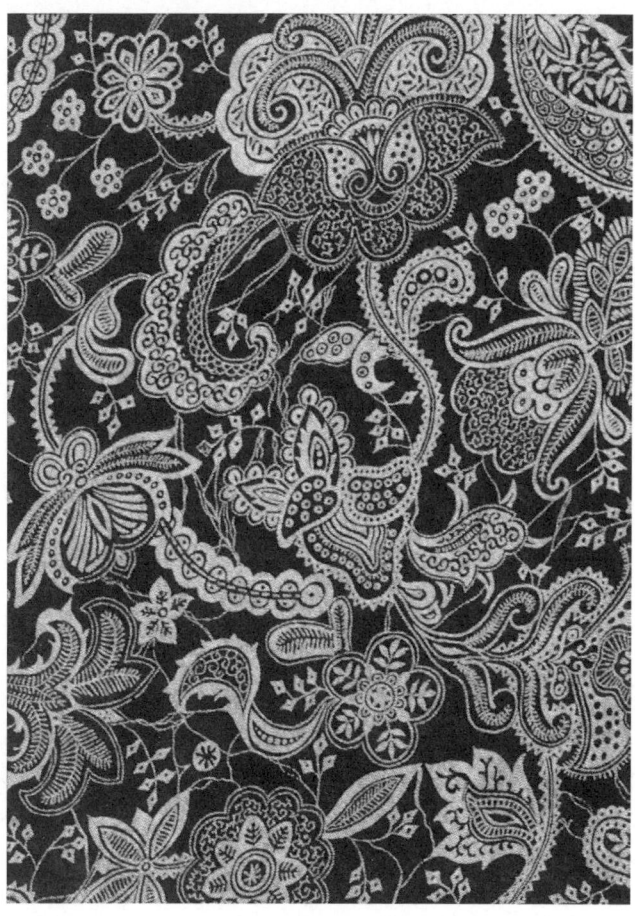

Fig. 36 Textile pattern designed by Rita Bertolini for the Franz M. Rhomberg Textile Company, 1990. Silk-screen print on fabric, 42 × 29 cm.

they sought. For instance, we learn that most of them attended the college specialized in weaving and spinning, but that proportionally there weren't many students with a migration background from Turkey.

In the archive, there are many documents showing a particular pattern design from Bertolini's career portfolio. In 1990, she worked on a design for the Rhomberg company inspired by the so-called *Türkenmuster* (Turkish pattern) (fig. 36).[17] This pattern acts as an image vehicle throughout the archive. Can we follow it to create a new structure based on migrating concepts, things, and people? Can it forge a path of the institutional dimension of creativity between personal and global histories?

I'm considering the pattern as a concept, structure, and object. The Türkenmuster is a recurring pattern design of the Franz M. Rhomberg Textile Company (figs. 37 and 38). It is composed mainly of hard-edged stylized floral motifs reminiscent of both central Anatolian designs and Ottoman illustrations. Unfortunately, the descriptions attached to these visuals don't explain the exact characteristics of the design or why they were called Türkenmuster. The paper accompanying figure 4 reads: "The two dresses from the successful product line MARINA by Franz M. Rhomberg have a sophisticated design but are simply finished. A fashionable variation of the Türkenmuster draws its charm from the unusual color combination of ocher/lilac and bilious green." When bigger versions of the motifs were used, a similarity to the Paisley pattern appears in a teardrop shape with an elongated and pointed tip (fig. 38). Other descriptions emphasize that the sophistication and simplicity of the Türkenmuster is due to the designs. Thus, the motif needs to be tamed by the design to be categorized as elegant and fashionable.

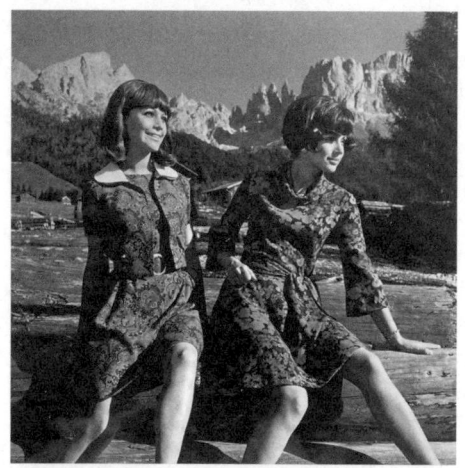

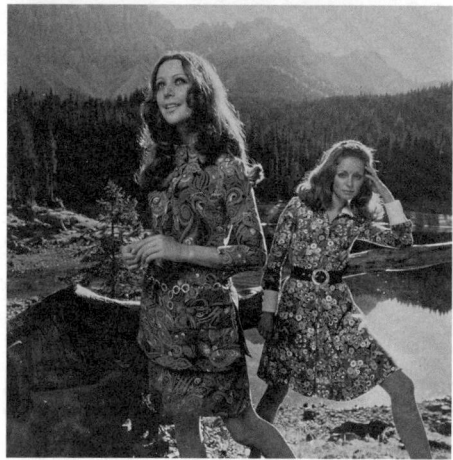

Figs. 37, 38 Winter 1969–70 collection, Franz M. Rhomberg Textile Company

17 Although it can be translated as "Turkish pattern," there is no English-language equivalent of this textile pattern.

The background scenery of the photographs—the South Tyrolean Dolomite mountains—shows the local appropriation of the design motif.

In the archive, this pattern experiences many revivals, as seen in figures 3 to 5. Owing to the interest in floral motifs and "Eastern" design ideas, including Paisley motifs, which made a mark on global fashion in the 1970s, these patterns resurfaced on dresses and tailored jackets. The patterns were reintroduced as part of a retro movement, a revival of Art Nouveau and Jugendstil that reinterpreted the floral designs and eroticism of the turn of the century through a new self-reflection on the topics of nature and freedom.

The Türkenmuster has a long history that precedes these revivals. In the eighteenth and nineteenth centuries, these patterns were described as "oriental" and became the preferred design for the *Wiener Schal* (Viennese shawl), a cashmere scarf that was worn to accompany a *Tracht*.[18] Handwoven cashmere shawls were first produced in the Kashmir region of today's India and Pakistan. The earliest exports were made to Persia and the Ottoman Empire in the eighteenth century. They were later exported to Europe and became luxury products, like other items appropriated from the East.[19] They were first worn by nobility, but became available to a wider public once they were produced by new weaving technologies. At the beginning of the twentieth century, production of these shawls started in Vienna. The Türkenmuster possibly relates to the Viennese shawls and nineteenth-century trade routes of the cashmere shawls between India, the Ottoman Empire, and Europe, which might be the reason for the similar visual properties in the Paisley designs. Shawls produced in Vienna were both a product of appropriation and a hybrid responding to market demand. "Hybridity is the celebratory sign of diversity and mixedness," as Homi Bhabha puts it, the "third space" where the reference to the original fades away.[20] Tied to the global market economy, this third space must be approached critically. The scholar Kien Nghi Ha views hybrid representations as "a new mode of production in a globalized economy that is increasingly obsessed with the consumption of cultural signs and meanings."[21] These scarves from Vienna were, in turn, exported to the Ottoman Empire, and their patterns also included floral motifs with gold and silver, which sold well in the imperial lands. Therefore, while the names Türkenmuster and Wiener Schal suggest a specific ethnic or geographic origin, the objects in fact have various origins—they are appropriated, transformed, and hybridized. Or in this case, they might have been invented to be something Turkish and oriental just to meet market demands.

As this example shows, clothing and textile items ascribed to a single national identity often represent, or suggest, a reductionist and exclusive history. Subjectivities and traces, on the other hand, have a persistence that can be followed through patterns that become image and object vehicles. How often and in which contexts do they appear and reappear? How do they relate to the (local and global) history and archives of individuals? These connections show that fashion

18 The term *Tracht* loosely refers to the traditional national costume, which must conform to certain standards defined differently by each district and region. It is mostly associated with Austria and Bavaria in Germany. This attire usually consists of embroidered leather shorts (*Lederhosen*) for men and colorful flowy dresses (*Dirndl*) with aprons for women. They can be also worn with matching structured jackets made of natural fabrics like wool.

19 Gertrud Lehnert, "Zum Luxus fremder Dinge: Der Kaschmirschal," in *Präsenz und Evidenz fremder Dinge im Europa des 18. Jahrhunderts*, ed. Birgit Neumann (Göttingen: Wallstein, 2015), 302–22.

20 Homi K. Bhabha, foreword to *Debating Cultural Hybridity: Multicultural Identities and the Politics of Anti-racism*, ed. Pnina Werbner and Tariq Modood (London: Zed Books, 2015), x.

21 Kien Nghi Ha, "Crossing the Border? Hybridity as Late-Capitalistic Logic of Cultural Translation and National Modernisation," *transversal texts*, 2006, https://transversal.at/transversal/1206/ha/en.

is not a linear history of developments but a circulation through time and displacement of both people and design concepts. People might bring back these designs nostalgically, but this circulation is also ruled by the financial and historical conditions of the time. While the Türkenmuster designs of the 1970s might, at first glance, look like a local development, they also reflect global textile history in motion. The Türkenmuster design shows how a local or regional history can be recontextualized in a history of global textiles and clothing.

Material-Based Research and Understanding the Principles of Patternmaking

With a background in the visual arts, graphic design, and textile design, I seek to understand the material specificities of textiles and clothing. Alongside my insider identity as a migrant with a background in a creative field, researching the gaps and connections among archival material led me to work on the plurality of voices in the archive and their relation to institutional structures. To develop an artistic research strategy, it is crucial to understand design through material presence. How can I translate this into the field of fashion design and migration? Patterns carry multiple meanings and functions in the practice of designing and making clothes. On the one hand, they can refer to the repeating motifs in textile design, as in the case of the Türkenmuster. On the other, they can refer to sewing patterns, cutting patterns, or paper patterns (terms used interchangeably in fashion). Pattern is a term that bridges designing clothes and textiles. In this section, it refers to sewing, cutting, or paper patterns, while proposing a joint theory that connects textile and clothing design. I am linking patterns' material characteristics, their role in production and reproduction, to a theoretical background encompassing archival practices.

How does one make patterns, and why do we need them? One way of constructing garments is to sew pieces of fabric together, which is duplicated through customized patterns, reflecting the individual size, shape, and posture of a human figure. These patterns are customized by making changes from a foundation called a block pattern, which is usually made of a stiff material like cardboard that can be easily traced to transfer the shape to a thinner paper, which is then pinned to the fabric. This method of production involves several stages of copying and allows the designer's ideas to be reproduced, usually with the help of assistants and seamstresses. These patterns hold the knowledge of the specific design in pieces.

The "agency" of patterns became readable in 1590, when they first appeared in published form in the Spanish tailor and mathematician Juan de Alcega's *Libro de geometría práctica y traça* (Book of the Practice of Tailoring, Measuring, and Marking Out).[22] His main motive was to guide tailors to use fabrics in an economical way owing to the high cost of the materials. However, it was only after tailors began to publish pattern books in the early nineteenth century that their methods and the "merits of different systems" of transforming body measurements into templates for clothing became available to a wider public.[23] Even this early appearance provides an insight into what I argue is the

22 According to actor-network theory, objects have the capacity to actively be part of a network of relationships. An agent is "anything that does modify a state of affairs by making a difference." Bruno Latour, *Reassembling the Social: An Introduction to Actor-Network-Theory* (Oxford: Oxford University Press, 2005), 71.

23 Winifred Aldrich, "History of Sizing Systems and Ready-to-Wear Garments," in *Sizing in Clothing: Developing Effective Sizing Systems for Ready-to-Wear Clothing*, ed. S. P. Ashdown (Cambridge: Woodhead Publishing, 2007), 6.

specific agency of this technical innovation: it facilitated the understanding of design for nonspecialists while avoiding unnecessary fabric purchases and also enabled cultural exchange long before modern migration, since mass-printed and transnationally available magazines created a platform for sharing designs.

Knowledge not only travels with and through people but also circulates in the form of fashion magazines, which publish patterns, photographs of fashion items, and accompanying text. For instance, every design in *Burda Moden*, a German fashion and style magazine distributed globally, was accompanied with a pattern that could be cut out (fig. 39). Although the magazine has been distributed in Turkey since the 1960s, it was first translated into Turkish in the 1990s. Paper patterns serve as social agents that facilitated the understanding of design for nonspecialists and enabled cultural exchange by sharing the steps of dressmaking. These patterns were created by anonymous designers and had a life of their own through repetition and modification across various publications.

Mass-produced commercial patterns acquire individual characteristics when transferred onto another paper or fabric, as well as over the course of fittings. As seen in figure 39, the design can be transferred onto tracing paper and can be adjusted based on measurements taken during the fitting. The pieces have to be pinned onto the fabric to transfer the pattern with chalk or a fabric pen. Later, the pieces can be cut out and sewn together. The design is involved in different processes of construction and deconstruction, as these pattern forms come together and are taken apart by the maker according to the measurements and demands of the person whom the clothing is being made for. Throughout the

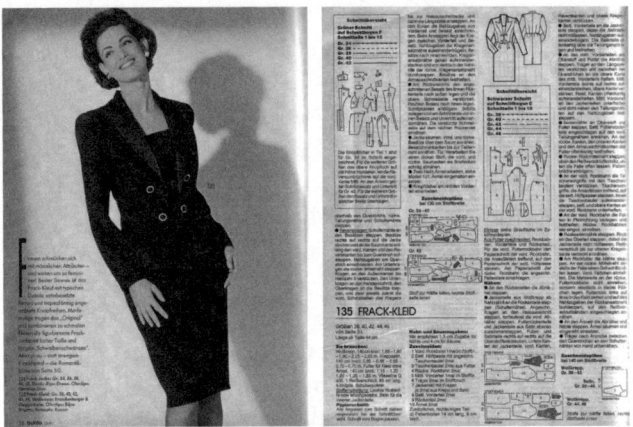

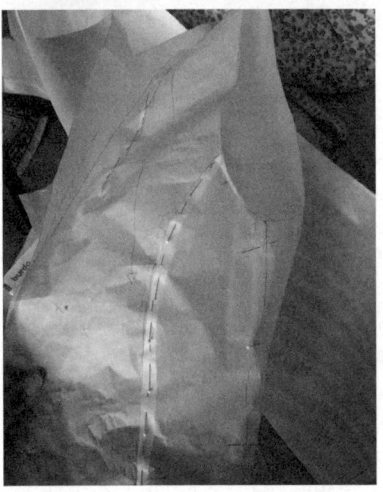

Fig. 39 *Burda Moden*, German edition, December 1993.
Photograph and explanatory text of one of the designs: dress coat and
dress (*top left*). Instructions to make the dress with the patterns and
technical detail (*top right*). Pattern transferred by pen onto tracing paper
and pinned to create a model for the design (*bottom*).

process, the measurements can change, as can aesthetic choices. From the perspective of the design process, there are many gaps in the descriptions of how to connect the pieces, allowing the maker to improvise their own interpretations in the overall design. There are also "designer patterns," which claim to be unique although they are created to make reproductions commercially available. Patterns, as mobile social agents, bring a more democratic perspective to the research on creative adaptations in fashion in the context of labor migration. My research on patterns and design models within the context of sartorial labor migration from Turkey to Austria also focuses on the social performances embedded in the design, drawing on both institutional and vernacular archives during the research process.

Bringing the Home into the Archive

Patternmaking from magazines represented an intervention into making clothes, a skill that was typically a privilege acquired in vocational and fashion schools that, as in the example of Vorarlberg, are closely tied to the design and textile industry. The intervention was to include the home, the most familiar of structures, as a space to create garments. The patterns and their creators democratized dressmaking by sharing design knowledge with home dressmakers who could not always formally and officially contribute to design history. This study shares the same intentions by questioning the heroic stance attributed to designers and designer clothes and showing the knowledge exchanges that take place through people and materials. This process is entangled with (labor) migration and traveling design ideas, motifs, and patterns as they are transferred, repeated, and appropriated.

Institutional archives hold this information of exchanges, but the aspect of creativity is very much tied to individual experiences. Designing and creating are socially embedded processes. To establish connections and construct a more accurate narrative, this project requires personal accounts from the creators of these clothes and designs, as well as patterns that serve as "betweener" or "process" objects. These elements highlight interconnectedness and provide a framework to integrate official reports with the oral and material testimonies of migration. They historicize and theorize the unseen actors and subtle performances of migration in the creative field of fashion, extending its meaning into the context of everyday life. In that sense, they act as both image vehicles and the agents driving them.

Literature

Aldrich, Winifred. "History of Sizing Systems and Ready-to-Wear Garments." In *Sizing in Clothing*, edited by S. P. Ashdown, 1–56. Cambridge: Woodhead Publishing, 2007.

Almond, Kevin. "Eliminating the Bust Dart: The Role of Pattern Cutting in the 1960–2002 Career of British Fashion Designer, Sylvia Ayton." *Journal of Dress History* 3, no. 2 (2019): 6–46.

Bahun, Sanja, and Bojana Petric, eds. *Thinking Home: Interdisciplinary Dialogues*. New York: Routledge, 2018.

Bal, Mieke. *Narratology: Introduction to the Theory of Narrative*. Toronto: University of Toronto Press, 1985.

Bal, Mieke. *Travelling Concepts in the Humanities: A Rough Guide*. Toronto: University of Toronto Press, 2002.

Bhabha, Homi K. Foreword to *Debating Cultural Hybridity: Multicultural Identities and the Politics of Anti-Racism*, edited by Pnina Werbner and Tariq Modood, ix–xiii. London: Zed Books, 2015.

Bosniak, Linda. "Citizenship, Noncitizenship, and the Trans-nationalization of Domestic Work." In *Migrations and Mobilities: Citizenship, Borders, and Gender*, edited by Seyla Benhabib and Judith Resnik, 127–56. New York: New York University Press, 2009.

Brüstle, Erich. Interview by Rupert Tiefenthaler and Annette Bleyle. 2001. Wirtschaftsarchiv Vorarlberg, Feldkirch.

Checinska, Christine. "'Cut & Mix': Collage, Creolisation and African Diaspora Aesthetics." *Mobilities*, no. 9 (2020): 46–60.

Checinska, Christine. "Spinning a Yarn of One's Own." In *A Companion to Textile Culture*, edited by Jennifer Harris, 235–55. Hoboken, NJ: Wiley-Blackwell, 2020.

Clarke, Alison J. "Taste Wars and Design Dilemmas: Aesthetic Practice in the Home." In *Contemporary Art and the Home*, edited by Colin Painter, 131–51. London: Routledge, 2002.

Clifford, James. *Routes: Travel and Translation in the Late Twentieth Century*. Cambridge, MA: Harvard University Press, 1997.

Debo, Kaat. "Patterns." In *Patronen/Patterns: Modemuseum Antwerpen*, edited by Kaat Debo, Linda Loppa, and Bob Verhelst, 9–19. Ghent: Ludion, 2003.

Diversi, Marcelo, and Claudio Moreira. *Betweener Autoethnographies: A Path towards Social Justice*. New York: Routledge, 2018.

Göle, Nilüfer. "The Voluntary Adoption of Islamic Stigma Symbols." *Social Research* 70, no. 3 (2003): 809–28.

Ha, Kien Nghi. "Crossing the Border? Hybridity as Late-Capitalistic Logic of Cultural Translation and National Modernisation." *transversal texts*, 2006. https://transversal.at /transversal/1206/ha/en.

Hirsch, Marianne. "Introduction: Practicing Feminism, Practicing Memory." In *Women Mobilizing Memory*, edited by Ayşe Gül Altınay, María José Contreras, Marianne Hirsch, Jean Howard, Banu Karaca, and Alisa Solomon, 1–23. New York: Columbia University Press, 2019.

Korteweg, Anna C., and Gökçe Yurdakul. *The Headscarf Debates: Conflicts of National Belonging*. Stanford, CA: Stanford University Press, 2014.

Latour, Bruno. *Reassembling the Social: An Introduction to Actor-Network-Theory*. Oxford: Oxford University Press, 2005.

Lehnert, Gertrud. *Mode: Theorie, Geschichte und Ästhetik einer kulturellen Praxis*. Bielefeld: transcript, 2013.

Lehnert, Gertrud. "Zum Luxus fremder Dinge: Der Kaschmirschal." In *Präsenz und Evidenz fremder Dinge im*

Europa des 18. Jahrhunderts, edited by
Birgit Neumann, 302–22. Göttingen:
Wallstein, 2015.

Levitt, Peggy. *Artifacts and
Allegiances: How Museums Put the
Nation and the World on Display*.
Berkeley: University of California Press,
2015.

Miller, Daniel. *The Comfort of
Things*. Cambridge: Polity, 2008.

Papastergiadis, Nikos, and
Daniella Trimboli. "From Global
Turbulences to Spaces of Conviviality:
The Potentialities of Art in Mobile
Worlds." In *Handbook of Art and Global
Migration: Theories, Practices, and
Challenges*, edited by Burcu Doğramacı
and Birgit Mersmann, 38–53. Berlin:
De Gruyter, 2019.

Rowe, Cami. "Seized: Performance
Autoethnography in the UK Border
Force National Museum." *Millennium*
50, no. 2 (2022): 379–404.

Savaş, Özlem. "Taste Diaspora:
The Aesthetic and Material Practice
of Belonging." PhD diss., University of
Applied Arts, Vienna, 2008.

Toksöz, Gülay. "Irregular Migration
and Migrants' Informal Employment:
A Discussion Theme in International
Migration Governance." *Globalizations*
15, no. 6 (2018): 779–94.

Venohr, Dagmar. *Medium macht
Mode: Zur Ikonotextualität der
Modezeitschrift*. Bielefeld: transcript,
2010.

Ruth Sonderegger

Writing Together through Institutions II
No Epilogue

When Ana and Mariel asked me to write a foreword for this book, I felt uneasy. It was a strange reaction, as I also felt honored by their invitation. I realized that my ambivalence had to do with my background as a philosopher and with the roles that my discipline has always claimed for itself, as well as with the expectations that have been and continue to be placed on it—expectations of inventing, ordering, and specifying the concepts, theories, and methods that others, that is, nonphilosophers, are then supposed to put into practice. This seemed even more problematic to me since most of the contributions were developed from some combination of artistic, collective, and activist practices. Prefacing these contributions with a philosophical prelude seemed an irresponsible gesture in view of the role that Western philosophy has repeatedly claimed and continues to claim.

Ana and Mariel immediately understood my problem, and we agreed that I could write an epilogue instead of a foreword.

This position is also not without its problems, because claiming the last word can be just as arrogant or violent as claiming the first. The alternative I am searching for is likely a way of breaking out of the very linearity that ascribes a special value to the first and/or last word as well as out of the way of thinking that separates theory from its so-called application. In my view, what Adorno expects from philosophical texts should also apply to book chapters: "In a philosophical text, all the propositions ought to be equally close to the centre."[1]

Therefore, this text cannot be a summary of this book, and it is not intended to provide a conclusive statement.[2] Rather, I will try to pick up some of the threads from the contributions. This approach seemed obvious to me because I crossed paths with many of the authors at the Academy of Fine Arts Vienna. Reading their texts in *Standpoint Autotheory* was enlightening, not least because it made me realize how much my way of thinking and writing has changed since I came to the Academy. This likely has less to do with the institution itself than with the people and collaborations I have encountered here, even though many of these encounters originated in shared engagements with the Academy and its history, and often with academia in a much broader sense. These interactions were sometimes critical, frustrating, or disappointing, but led me to start again, full of hope. In any case, the first part of the subtitle of Ana and Mariel's introduction, "Writing Together through Institutions," immediately struck me as fitting for what I wanted to write about. After all, the conversations and collaborations I had at the Academy provided me with opportunities to write together that I would never have

---

1 Theodor W. Adorno, *Minima Moralia: Reflections on a Damaged Life*, trans. E. F. N. Jephcott (London: Verso, 2004), 71.

2 Considering the argumentation in the text as part of an ongoing dialogue, the editors decided a posteriori to place the text by Ruth Sonderegger in its current position in the book.—Eds.

dreamed of before. Moreover, it was Ana and Mariel's use of "through" that particularly appealed to me. These collaborations had everything to do with working our way through the institution, in the sense of a Freudian *durcharbeiten*, as well as in the sense of "struggling through."

At the beginning of their introduction, Ana and Mariel write that the ghosts of the "Uni brennt" (Uni Burns) movement were still palpable when they arrived in Vienna. I had arrived with the protests, which started on October 20, 2009, in the auditorium of the Academy, two weeks into the semester. I quickly got to know most of the students, teaching staff, and representatives of the nonacademic staff in plenary meetings. That was a huge privilege. Not only because of the sudden extensive amount of time together, but also because institutions in crisis reveal more about their apparent dis/functioning than in so-called normal operation.

In the beginning, the central demand of the strike was to refuse the introduction of the bachelor/master structure because it would transform universities into schools based on strictly modularized teaching content, which promised (or threatened) to lead students from the seemingly simple to the allegedly difficult—as if there were a clear hierarchy of different types of knowledge.[3] In other words, before you have completed an introduction to, for example, cultural studies, you are not allowed to attend a course on a specific topic in the field of cultural studies. However, this initially limited demand to refuse the introduction of the bachelor/master structure quickly grew into a force capable of disrupting the entire university system. For at least one semester, from what I remember, it was no longer clear and increasingly less important, who was a lecturer and who was a student, who belonged to the university and who did not. In addition, along with the people who joined us from outside the Academy, new knowledge emerged that had not been perceived as knowledge until then, and, at the same time, fundamental questions were raised regarding who had access to the Academy and tertiary education in general. There was a reason that one of Uni brennt's demands at demos and rallies was "Rich Parents for All."

Coming from a teaching position in the Netherlands, I felt like I had arrived in paradise during this first semester at the Academy. In the Netherlands, the bachelor/master of arts structure (as called for in the Bologna Declaration but still not legally binding today) had long since been implemented, and the universities had turned into business-minded corporations that intended to make as much profit as possible from the tuition fees of huge cohorts of undergraduate students. The MA graduate degree, on the other hand, had quickly become an elite affair for prospective doctoral students. It was precisely this development that led me to apply for a new position—hopefully in a place that was not so blatantly distorted by commodification as the University of Amsterdam. Initially, Uni brennt was a daily sign that I had done the right thing.[4] But this supposed paradise also showed its other side,

3 For reflections on the 2009 strikes, see Gerald Raunig, "Fabriken des Wissens," in *Maschinen Fabriken Industrien* (Vienna: transversal texts, 2019), 159–230; Lina Dokuzović and Eduard Freudmann, "Fortified Knowledge: From Supranational Governance to Translocal Resistance," *eipcp journal: knowledge production and its discontents*, July 2010, https://transversal.at/transversal/0809 /freudmann-dokuzovic/en; and Lina Dokuzović, *Struggles for Living Learning: Within Emergent Knowledge Economies and the Cognitivisation of Capital and Movement* (Vienna: transversal texts, 2016). Dokuzović's book was adapted from her PhD dissertation at the Academy of Fine Arts Vienna.

4 When the University of Amsterdam, where I had taught for ten years, went on strike in 2015, I was surprised and deeply impressed, especially as the movement quickly spread within and beyond the Netherlands. Moreover, it focused on agendas that hadn't played a role during the Uni brennt protests: the funding structure of supposedly autonomous universities, which made them completely dependent on national governments, and the colonial dimension of western European higher education.

without diminishing what fascinated me about it. Not surprisingly, the Academy was a place of resistance and at the same time a closed and exclusive space—even in times of strike.

I found two things particularly important for recognizing this ambivalence. First, the "applicants survey" that circulated in the first semester of the strike. Published in February 2010, this study spoke a completely different language than the resistant and politicizing one that characterized the strike plenums.[5] Conducted by the sociologist Barbara Rothmüller, the survey aimed to investigate the social backgrounds of the students admitted to the Academy in 2009. The results were sobering: the institution that I found so inspiring turned out to be Austria's most elitist educational institution in the tertiary sector. The exclusions that seem to be constitutive of art education and—as formal qualifications are ever more important in all parts of neoliberal societies—of the art field as such have since occupied me in new ways, above all in their different mutual entanglements depending on the location.[6] With regard to the Academy, for example, the survey revealed that it is primarily students affected by classism and racism who are underrepresented, while there is little to criticize in terms of gender diversity. A few years later, I wondered whether the very meager support for the refugees who occupied the Academy's auditorium as an act of protest in 2013 was connected to the social positionings that Rothmüller's survey had unearthed.[7]

Second, I had a somewhat opposite experience during one of my first lecture courses on the history of philosophical aesthetics—opposite in the sense that this experience catapulted me off course in a positive sense. Some of the participants challenged my overly general conception of aesthetics and art by, quite rightly, wanting to know what specific kind of art I had in mind when I invoked these terms as a collective noun. I had no answer ready. But this led me to a new point of research, one that continues to this day. I wanted to understand why talking about art and aesthetics in the collective singular form had become natural to me, and why I rarely thought of specific works of art and their social context.

During this exploration, I quickly realized that the collective nouns "art" and "aesthetics" are closely linked to the emergence of philosophical aesthetics in western Europe in the eighteenth century, and that they are therefore anything but universal and natural. This insight led me to question why philosophical aesthetics and its collective singulars emerged in eighteenth-century western Europe. What were the developments in the history of ideas, and even more so in society, at that time that need to be understood as part of the advent of philosophical aesthetics? It didn't take much research to be reminded of how closely the development of western Europe in the eighteenth century is connected with, if not identical to, the formation of the bourgeoisie and colonial capitalism.

5 Barbara Rothmüller, "BewerberInnen-Befragung am Institut für bildende Kunst 2009," Academy of Fine Arts Vienna, AG Antidiskriminierung, February 2010, https://www.akbild.ac.at/de/universitaet/arbeitskreis-fur -gleichbehandlungsfragen/aufgaben-und-tatigkeitsfelder/endbericht.pdf.

6 Barbara Rothmüller and Ruth Sonderegger, "Über die Grenzen der Kunst," *Migrazine*, no. 1, 2014, http://migrazine.at/artikel/ber-die-grenzen-der-kunst; Barbara Rothmüller, Philipp Saner, Ruth Sonderegger, and Sophie Vögele, "Kunst. Kritik. Bildungsgerechtigkeit: Überlegungen zum Feld der Kunstausbildung," in *Soziale Ungleichheiten, Milieus und Habitus im Hochschulstudium*, ed. Andrea Lange-Vester and Tobias Sander (Weinheim: Beltz Juventa, 2016), 89–105; Ruth Sonderegger, "Doing Class: Hochschulzugang, Kunst und das Gewürz-Andere," *Zeitschrift für Medienwissenschaft* 10, no. 19-2 (2018): 93–100.

7 For an in-depth reflection on the refugee protests and their dissonance within the Academy, see Gin Müller, "Refugee-Protest im Spannungsfeld von Aktivismus, Institution, Kunst und medialer Sichtbarkeit: Protokoll/Reportage eines Supporters über die Monate nach der Besetzung der Votivkirche," in *Kunst, Theorie, Aktivismus: Emanzipatorische Perspektiven auf Ungleichheit und Diskriminierung*, ed. Alexander Fleischmann and Doris Guth (Bielefeld: transcript, 2015), 147–74.

It became inconceivable to separate the emergence of aesthetic theory and the field of art from these developments.

Mediated by the examination of the social changes in western Europe during the eighteenth century, the question of colonialism became ever more central in my search, initially in the sense of the decisive motor for the development of industrial capitalism and the resulting supremacy of the region. This examination of colonial capitalism inevitably led to a further question: whether and how the (founding) history of philosophical aesthetics is involved in the colonial-capitalist enterprise that western Europe was at that time. Rereading the classic aesthetic texts of the eighteenth century—which I thought I knew well—through the lens of colonialism and the associated racialization of much of humanity was disturbing and shameful. I hadn't noticed myriad references to colonial violence in the founding texts of philosophical aesthetics in my decades of reading them. And in some respects, I still can't read all the violent implications properly.

My anger about the fact that no one taught me about the colonial dimension of the history of European aesthetics—and that this obvious complicity still hardly plays a role, especially in the German-speaking world—soon gave way to astonishment. Astonishment at the fact that elsewhere—and (not surprisingly) especially in the former colonies of Europe—there was a lively scholarly debate on the entanglement of aesthetics and coloniality.[8] However, German-speaking academia still has decisive self-critical debates ahead of it, and I am keen to contribute to them—in particular, by providing students with approaches to western European aesthetics that enable them to read its colonialist aspects and its entanglements with classism, sexism, and ableism. These approaches no longer leave the collective singular nouns of art and aesthetics unquestioned.

However, this endeavor is also part of my own self-understanding, indeed my self-care, in precisely the sense that the philosopher Paul C. Taylor captures, in a related and at the same time completely contrary context, with the wonderful term "retroactive self-provisioning." He explains it as follows: "I have tried to write the book that I'd wanted to read, back when the size of the gap between the work I was prepared to do and the work I wanted to do began to become apparent."[9]

My preoccupation with racial and colonial violence in the genesis and success of Western aesthetics is still ongoing. And it has opened, or rather necessitated, many new paths of thinking.[10] One of these is the engagement with questions

8 The following texts have been particularly important for me in this regard: Gloria Anzaldúa, *Borderlands / La Frontera: The New Mestiza* (San Francisco: Aunt Lute, 1999); Édouard Glissant, *Poetics of Relation*, trans. Betsy Wing (Ann Arbor: University of Michigan Press, 1997); Ngũgĩ wa Thiong'o, *Decolonising the Mind: The Politics of Language in African Literature* (Nairobi: East African Educational Publishers, 1986); Sylvia Wynter, "Rethinking 'Aesthetics': Notes towards a Deciphering Practice," in *Ex-iles: Essays on Caribbean Cinema*, ed. Mbye B. Cham (Trenton, NJ: Africa World Press, 1992), 237–79.

9 Paul C. Taylor, *Black Is Beautiful: A Philosophy of Black Aesthetics* (Malden, MA: Wiley Blackwell, 2016), x. My affirmative reference to Taylor is not intended to blur the differences between our positionalities. Taylor speaks for and from a sociocultural network whose aesthetic contributions have been negated for centuries, while I am speaking from a context that has profited from a variety of violent privileges for more than three hundred years.

10 While at the beginning I mainly dealt with the coloniality of the classics of philosophical aesthetics, I later found it indispensable to study the history of the emergence of racial capitalism. The concept of "useless," which is both an aesthetic and an economic category, played a pivotal role in this shift. See Ruth Sonderegger, "Kants Ästhetik im Kontext des kolonial gestützten Kapitalismus: Ein Fragment zur Entstehung der philosophischen Ästhetik als Sensibilisierungsprojekt," in "Sensibilität der Gegenwart: Wahrnehmung, Ethik und politische Sensibilisierung im Kontext westlicher Gewaltgeschichte," ed. Burkhard Liebsch, special issue 17, *Zeitschrift für Ästhetik und Allgemeine Kunstwissenschaft* (2018): 109–25; and Ruth Sonderegger, "Uselessness and Purposelessness: On Central Norms and Imperatives of Western Aesthetics," in *Uselessness: Humankind's Most Valuable Tool?*, ed. Michelle Howard and Luciano Parodi (Berlin: De Gruyter, 2020), 49–63. Currently I am part of a collaborative research project on the entangled roles of the regimes of law, property, and aesthetics in the emergence and potential end of racial capitalism. See the website Perception, Jurisdiction, and Valorisation in Colonial Modernity: On the Nexus of Accumulation, Race, and Aesthetics, accessed June 25, 2024, https://accumulation-race-aesthetics.org/.

around the situatedness of knowledge. For the collective nouns art and aesthetics are prime examples of a denied situatedness. This situatedness is perhaps not even conceivable by the protagonists of said terms, even though the provincialism of the European aesthetics that became hegemonic globally is based on nothing other than a particularism. Not only did the theories that emerged in eighteenth-century western Europe presume to formulate norms for all aesthetic practices, but they also had no problem devaluing most of the aesthetic practices that Europeans encountered outside of Europe, or that they fantasied about based on wildly embellished travel or magazine reports as inferior or completely unaesthetic.[11]

On the other hand, I kept asking myself how I could have read texts by Hume, Kant, Schiller, Hegel, Schlegel, and many others for years without noticing their Eurocentrism, racism, and often anti-Semitism, whereas their classism and sexism were much more obvious to me. My initial question of why I had not been adequately introduced to these texts at the university—which simply shifted responsibility—slowly turned into an examination of why my ignorance remained hidden from me for so long. Or to put it another way: I did not, as one might expect from a philosopher, come to theories of situated knowledge through an examination of questions of truth and knowledge or through debates about universalism and relativism, but because I wanted to understand the societal and individual ideological structures that resulted in my so blatantly ignorant misreadings of the foundations of aesthetic theory.

In view of this background, situatedness for me meant dealing with my own personal and more-than-personal ideological limitations, and by no means asserting any subjective position of which I could have been proud. Therefore,

I found the basic claim of feminist theorists of science instantly convincing—that situating oneself, in the sense of actively disclosing personal as well as scientific and institutional histories, methods, and epistemological interests, does not make knowledge weaker or relativistic, but rather strengthens it.[12] For it is precisely and only the disclosure of a researcher's background and epistemological interests that is an invitation to free and unrestricted exchange. Anyone who seeks to practice critical—and that always implies self-critical—science would not start a conversation by saying, "I know," but rather by disclosing: "My research originated from this and that place, debate, etc.; with this or that prior knowledge, experience, data; in the face of this or that ethical-political challenge."

In turn, studying feminist theorists of science also opened my eyes to the extent to which questions of situatedness—albeit under different names, such as "critical attitude"—played a central role in early critical theory; that is, in precisely the kind of theory that had aroused my interest, indeed my enthusiasm for philosophy, when, during my high-school years, I was part of a reading group that tried to understand Theodor W. Adorno and Max Horkheimer's *Dialectic of*

11 To give but one example: at the beginning of his aesthetic theory, Kant sees it as proven that the Iroquois are only interested in food and have no sense of artistic beauty. Immanuel Kant, *Critique of Judgement*, trans. James Creed Meredith, ed. Nicholas Walker (Oxford: Oxford University Press, 2008) § 2, 36–37.

12 When I first read Donna Haraway's essay "Situated Knowledges," I was just as thrilled as when, also around the same time, I first encountered analyses that focused on Kant's racism—namely, Charles Mills's *The Racial Contract* and Robert Bernasconi's "Will the Real Kant Please Stand Up"—which is why these three texts are wired together in my brain to this day. Donna Haraway, "Situated Knowledges: The Science Question in Feminism and the Privilege of Partial Perspective," *Feminist Studies* 14, no. 3 (1988): 575–99; Charles W. Mills, *The Racial Contract* (Ithaca, NY: Cornell University Press, 2022); Robert Bernasconi, "Will the Real Kant Please Stand Up: The Challenge of Enlightenment Racism to the Study of the History of Philosophy," *Radical Philosophy*, no. 117 (January/February 2003): 13–22.

Enlightenment (1944).[13] With the help of feminist accounts of situated knowledge, I was now able to understand in a different way, or perhaps for the first time, what Horkheimer meant, in his essay "Traditional and Critical Theory" (1937), by the term "critical attitude": on the one hand, the acknowledgment that all (scientific) concepts and questions are not neutral but the result of social struggles, and on the other, a commitment to the self-critical disclosure of one's research interests, which Horkheimer identified as putting an end to those conditions in which people are powerless and at the mercy of the (capitalist) superpowers that they themselves have created.[14]

Feminist theories of situated knowledges also helped me better understand why Walter Benjamin, in his "Theses on the Philosophy of History" (1940), demanded that every endeavor of knowledge production requires an ethical-political justification of its relevance—relevance in light of the political constellation of the present—and that such "politicization" of science is all but turning science into (concealed) propaganda.[15] Rather, Benjamin and Horkheimer are of the opinion that such disclosure, and only such disclosure, enables open disputes about the relevance of research and the question of whether knowledge invites criticism actively enough. Or more specifically: I am not writing here about the fact that I see myself in the footsteps of Benjamin, Horkheimer, and Haraway so that readers think, "Of course, she is a feminist critic of science and a historical materialist," but so that I can question myself and potential readers can question me. Working toward such an understanding of self-critical knowledge seems particularly necessary in view of current authoritarian tendencies. I am referring to authoritarian politicians (and scientists) who invoke academic freedom for excluding or banning certain questions or entire fields of study and research, and who dismiss everything that is not welcome to their agenda as ideology, politicization, or propaganda—without ever disclosing their own (epistemological) interests or inviting discussions about them.[16]

Furthermore, the (Benjaminian) ethics of situatedness implies that, together with the disclosure of (personal, historical, institutional, etc.) backgrounds, prehistories, and knowledge interests, everything comes into view that made one's seemingly individual research possible in the first place. This makes all research and knowledge polyphonic from the outset. And in the best-case scenario, such polyphony also leads to differences and conflicts, which can prevent researchers from jumping to hasty conclusions. But that is no guarantee, as my own path as a scholar makes abundantly clear. As personally enlightening as my renewed engagement with the early Frankfurt School from the perspective of feminist theories of knowledge was, it was even more frustrating that, against this background, my academic socialization had not protected me from an ignorant and (color-)blind engagement with Western aesthetic theory.

13 Max Horkheimer and Theodor W. Adorno, *Dialectic of Enlightenment: Philosophical Fragments*, ed. Gunzelin Schmid Noerr, trans. Edmund Jephcott (Stanford, CA: Stanford University Press, 2022).

14 Max Horkheimer, "Traditional and Critical Theory," in *Critical Theory: Selected Essays*, trans. Matthew J. O'Connell et al. (New York: Continuum, 2002), 188–252.

15 Walter Benjamin, "Über den Begriff der Geschichte," in *Gesammelte Schriften*, vol. I.2, ed. Rolf Tiedemann and Hermann Schweppenhäuser (Frankfurt am Main: Suhrkamp, 1980), 691–704; "On the Concept of History," trans. Dennis Redmond, accessed June 25, 2024, https://www.marxists.org /reference/archive/benjamin/1940/history.htm.

16 See, for example, Andrea Pető, "Angriffe gegen die Institutionen der Wissenschaft und ihre Instrumentalisierung im illiberalen Regime: Eine Anregung zum Überdenken der gesellschaftlichen Rolle der Wissenschaft und ihre Perspektiven," in *Anti-Genderismus in Europa: Allianzen von Rechtspopulismus und religiösem Fundamentalismus; Mobilisierung – Vernetzung – Transformation*, ed. Sonja A. Strube et al. (Bielefeld: transcript, 2021), 187–201.

A second result of my preoccupation with the coloniality of European philosophical aesthetics was the realization that the tasks involved in such an endeavor cannot be solved, or even begun, by anyone on their own. Not only because inter-disciplinarity and collaboration are indispensable prerequisites for this research agenda, but also because the challenge is so vast that one can only despair of tackling it alone. On the other hand, the realization of the necessity of polyphonic collaborations was certainly also inspired by the manifold artistic and practice-based research alliances that I encountered at the Academy. In hindsight, I assume that they were decisive in giving me confidence in collaboration. For the mere theoretical knowledge that a specific research project cannot be realized alone can easily lead to despair if there are no examples of successful transdisciplinary collaborations around you. By now—that is, after fourteen years of teaching at the Academy of Fine Arts—I feel it is safe to say that collaborations are much more common among art students than, for example, philosophy students. In other words: I don't think I would have found the courage to engage in collaborations, which at some point just seemed to happen on their own, if there hadn't been so many around me.[17]

These examples of collaboration were probably also in the background when I decided to write the book *Polyphone Ästhetik* (Polyphonic Aesthetics, 2019) with four scholar friends after we had each given talks on colonial violence in (the history of) aesthetics at a conference of the German Society for Aesthetics. We wanted to find an alternative to the usual conference proceedings.[18] In the course of writing the book, I was persuaded by Ines Kleesattel and Sofia Bempeza, whom I had supervised as doctoral students a few years earlier, that we should experiment with less argumentative formats and invent stories we missed in philosophy—for example, in relation to Kant, whose aesthetics we had worked on together—which often oscillated between anger and humor.[19]

Bempeza and I later started an email exchange about writing together and its potential for change.[20] The exchange lasted over a year, and it was a total gift. Which is why I would like to conclude this epilogue with an observation Sofia made during the exchange:

An einer anderen Stelle spricht Haraway über das Denken als Praxis bzw. über die materielle Tätigkeit des Denken-Schreibens im Austausch mit anderen Denker*innen. Denken ist nach Haraway nämlich auch *Storytelling* (Geschichtenerzählen) und es ist ihr wichtig, dass wir die Erzählungen bzw. auch die Geschichten verändern

---

17 One of the first activist and practice-based research collectives that I encountered at the Academy, and that continues to fascinate me, is Platform History Politics. See Eduard Freudmann, "'Swastikas? Ornaments!' as a Continuity of Repression: History-Political Conditions of a Public Art and Educational Institution," trans. Lisa Dokuzović, *an-academy*, October 2010, https://transversal.at/transversal/1210/freudmann/en. I later had the pleasure to supervise and learn from Laura Nitsch and Barbara Juch's jointly written MA thesis "GLAUBE, LIEBE, HOFFNUNG: soziale topologien neu verorten" (2019), in which they engage with Didier Eribon's *Returning to Reims* (2009) and its significance for art education in general and the Academy in particular. A recent example of a collaborative project that I happily had the chance to be involved in via the Academy is Kristina Dreit and Karolina Dreit's book *Working Class Daughters: Über Klasse sprechen* (Vienna: Mandelbaum, 2024). These are just a few glimpses of a much denser network of collaborations that—together with various reading groups that emerged from seminars, conflicts, and sheer curiosity—keeps giving me hope for the possibility and actuality of (self-)critical knowledge production.

18 Sofia Bempeza, Christoph Brunner, Katharina Hausladen, Ines Kleesattel, and Ruth Sonderegger, *Polyphone Ästhetik: Eine kritische Situierung* (Vienna: transversal texts, 2019).

19 Sofia Bempeza, Ines Kleesattel, and Ruth Sonderegger, "Es war einmal eine Ästhetik (die hatte sich selbst sehr lieb)," in Bempeza et al., *Polyphone Ästhetik*, 149–62, https://transversal.at/books/polyphone-aesthetik.

20 Sofia Bempeza and Ruth Sonderegger, "Zusammen schreiben: Ein Versuch über das gute Schreiben," *Theorie Kritik*, February 2018, http://www.theoriekritik.ch/?p=4112.

können. Mich interessiert genau die Art des Erzählens und wie das (akademische) Schreiben selber – mitsamt seinen Konventionen und Freiheiten – eine Art *Storytelling* sein kann, das erstens: vielfältigen Erzählungen einen Platz gibt, zweitens: gegen sich selbst denken kann und drittens: sich selber auch verändert.[21]

21 "At another point, Haraway talks about thinking as a practice, or about the material activity of thinking-writing in exchange with other thinkers. According to Haraway, thinking is also *storytelling*, and it is important to her that we can change the narratives or stories. I am interested precisely in the nature of storytelling and how (academic) writing itself—with all its conventions and freedoms—could be a kind of *storytelling* that, first, makes room for diverse narratives; second, is able to think against itself; and third, also changes itself." Sofia Bempeza, email to author, February 2018. Translation by the author.

Literature

Adorno, Theodor W. *Minima Moralia: Reflections on a Damaged Life*. Translated E. F. N. Jephcott. London: Verso, 2004.

Anzaldúa, Gloria. *Borderlands / La Frontera: The New Mestiza*. San Francisco: Aunt Lute, 1999.

Bempeza, Sofia, Christoph Brunner, Katharina Hausladen, Ines Kleesattel, and Ruth Sonderegger. *Polyphone Ästhetik: Eine kritische Situierung*. Vienna: transversal texts, 2019.

Bempeza, Sofia, Ines Kleesattel, and Ruth Sonderegger. "Es war einmal eine Ästhetik (die hatte sich selbst sehr lieb)." In Bempeza et al., *Polyphone Ästhetik*, 149–62.

Bempeza, Sofia, and Ruth Sonderegger. "Zusammen schreiben: Ein Versuch über das gute Schreiben." *Theorie Kritik*, February 2018. http://www.theoriekritik.ch/?p=4112.

Benjamin, Walter. "Über den Begriff der Geschichte." In *Gesammelte Schriften*, vol. I.2, edited by Rolf Tiedemann and Hermann Schweppenhäuser, 691–704. Frankfurt am Main: Suhrkamp, 1980. "On the Concept of History," translated by Dennis Redmond, accessed June 25, 2024, https://www.marxists.org/reference/archive/enjamin/1940/history.htm.

Bernasconi, Robert. "Will the Real Kant Please Stand Up: The Challenge of Enlightenment Racism to the Study of the History of Philosophy." *Radical Philosophy*, no. 117 (January/February 2003): 13–22.

Dokuzović, Lina. *Struggles for Living Learning: Within Emergent Knowledge Economies and the Cognitivisation of Capital and Movement*. Vienna: transversal texts, 2016.

Dokuzović, Lina, and Eduard Freudmann. "Fortified Knowledge: From Supranational Governance to Translocal Resistance." *eipcp journal: knowledge production and its discontents*, July 2010. https://transversal.at/transversal/0809/freudmann-dokuzovic/en.

Dreit, Kristina, and Karolina Dreit. *Working Class Daughters: Über Klasse sprechen*. Vienna: Mandelbaum, 2024.

Freudmann, Eduard. "'Swastikas? Ornaments!' as a Continuity of Repression: History-Political Conditions of a Public Art and Educational Institution." Translated by Lisa Dokuzović. *an-academy*, October 2010. https://transversal.at/transversal/1210/freudmann/en.

Glissant, Édouard. *Poetics of Relation*. Translated by Betsy Wing. Ann Arbor: University of Michigan Press, 1997.

Haraway, Donna. "Situated Knowledges: The Science Question in Feminism and the Privilege of Partial Perspective." *Feminist Studies* 14, no. 3 (1988): 575–99.

Horkheimer, Max. "Traditional and Critical Theory." In *Critical Theory: Selected Essays*, translated by Matthew J. O'Connell et al., 188–252. New York: Continuum, 2002.

Horkheimer, Max, and Theodor W. Adorno. *Dialectic of Enlightenment: Philosophical Fragments*. Edited by Gunzelin Schmid Noerr and translated by Edmund Jephcott. Stanford, CA: Stanford University Press, 2022.

Kant, Immanuel. *Critique of Judgement*. Edited by Nicholas Walker. Translated by James Creed Meredith. Oxford: Oxford University Press, 2008.

Mills, Charles W. *The Racial Contract*. Ithaca, NY: Cornell University Press, 2022.

Müller, Gin. "Refugee-Protest im Spannungsfeld von Aktivismus, Institution, Kunst und medialer Sichtbarkeit: Protokoll/Reportage eines Supporters über die Monate nach der Besetzung der Votivkirche." In *Kunst, Theorie, Aktivismus: Emanzipatorische Perspektiven auf Ungleichheit und*

Diskriminierung, edited by Alexander Fleischmann und Doris Guth, 147–74. Bielefeld: transcript, 2015.

Nitsch, Laura, and Barbara Juch. "GLAUBE, LIEBE, HOFFNUNG: soziale topologien neu verorten." MA thesis, Academy of Fine Arts Vienna, 2019.

Pető, Andrea. "Angriffe gegen die Institutionen der Wissenschaft und ihre Instrumentalisierung im illiberalen Regime: Eine Anregung zum Überdenken der gesellschaftlichen Rolle der Wissenschaft und ihre Perspektiven." In *Anti-Genderismus in Europa: Allianzen von Rechtspopulismus und religiösem Fundamentalismus. Mobilisierung – Vernetzung – Transformation*, edited by Sonja A. Strube, Rita Perintfalvi, Raphaela Hemet, Miriam Metze, and Cicek Sahbaz, 187–201. Bielefeld: transcript, 2021.

Raunig, Gerald. "Fabriken des Wissens." In *Maschinen Fabriken Industrien*, 159–230. Vienna: transversal texts, 2019.

Rothmüller, Barbara. "BewerberInnen-Befragung am Institut für bildende Kunst 2009." Academy of Fine Arts Vienna, AG Antidiskriminierung, February 2010. https://www.akbild.ac.at /de/universitaet/arbeitskreis-fur -gleichbehandlungsfragen/aufgaben -und-tatigkeitsfelder/endbericht.pdf.

Rothmüller, Barbara, Philipp Saner, Ruth Sonderegger, and Sophie Vögele. "Kunst. Kritik. Bildungsgerechtigkeit: Überlegungen zum Feld der Kunstausbildung." In *Soziale Ungleichheiten, Milieus und Habitus im Hochschulstudium*, ed. Andrea Lange-Vester and Tobias Sander, 89–105. Weinheim: Beltz Juventa, 2016.

Rothmüller, Barbara, and Ruth Sonderegger. "Über die Grenzen der Kunst." *Migrazine*, no. 1 (2014). http:// migrazine.at/artikel/ber-die-grenzen -der-kunst.

Sonderegger, Ruth. "Doing Class: Hochschulzugang, Kunst und das Gewürz-Andere." In *Zeitschrift für Medienwissenschaft* 10, no. 19-2 (2018): 93–100.

Sonderegger, Ruth. "Kants Ästhetik im Kontext des kolonial gestützten Kapitalismus: Ein Fragment zur Entstehung der philosophischen Ästhetik als Sensibilisierungsprojekt." In "Sensibilität der Gegenwart. Wahrnehmung, Ethik und politische Sensibilisierung im Kontext westlicher Gewaltgeschichte," edited by Burkhard Liebsch, 109–25. Special issue 17, *Zeitschrift für Ästhetik und Allgemeine Kunstwissenschaft* (2018).

Sonderegger, Ruth. "Uselessness and Purposelessness: On Central Norms and Imperatives of Western Aesthetics." In *Uselessness: Humankind's Most Valuable Tool?*, edited by Michelle Howard and Luciano Parodi, 49–63. Berlin: De Gruyter, 2020.

Taylor, Paul C. *Black Is Beautiful: A Philosophy of Black Aesthetics*. Malden, MA: Wiley Blackwell, 2016.

Thiong'o, Ngũgĩ wa. *Decolonising the Mind: The Politics of Language in African Literature*. Nairobi: East African Educational Publishers, 1986.

Wynter, Sylvia. "Rethinking 'Aesthetics': Notes towards a Deciphering Practice." In *Ex-iles: Essays on Caribbean Cinema*, edited by Mbye B. Cham, 237–79. Trenton, NJ: African World Press, 1992.

Attempt to Situate
Speak or Let Speak?

Participant in History

"What I hear you say is that I could make it more personal."

That was how I summarized the feedback on a text about my research project provided by the fellows and staff at the IFK International Research Center for Cultural Studies in Vienna, a group I was part of during the winter of 2022–23.

One response was: "It *has* to be!"

So here I am, thinking about what "making it more personal" could mean exactly, and if and how I want to follow that request.

The title of my artistic research project is *Chaosmos of the Personal*. It is based on the writings of two deceased female family members: my grandmother Camilla Nissen (née Conti, 1902–1993) and her mother, my great-grandmother Nanna Conti (née Pauli, 1881–1951). A staunch National Socialist, Camilla's memoir and diary include several anti-Semitic, eugenic, and racist statements. Nanna was also an enthusiastic supporter of Hitler. In 1933, she was appointed *Reichshebammenführerin*, the head midwife of the German Reich, thus becoming one of the most prominent female perpetrators of the time. The writings she published in a German midwifery magazine leave no doubt about her belief in Hitler's ideology. I will describe the texts and context later in more detail.

My personal involvement with the subjects of my research is clear. The project is about the historical entanglements of my family with National Socialism and the ways its history manifests within family memory. I investigate how intergenerational emotional legacies reveal themselves in the way perpetrators were or were not spoken about in my family. The often ambivalent feelings that members of perpetrator families have in relation to their family history are the focus of my inquiry. How can these emotions become visible, audible, or tangible through artistic research? I use the history of my family, including myself, as an example.

I approach my research material with a methodology based on group dialogue—the *interpretation workshop* formulated by Maya Nadig—that is, I invite others to look, read, see, feel, speak, describe, analyze, and reflect *with* me, and, as I argue later on, at times *for* me.[1] The interpretation workshop is a method that allows me to seemingly stay silent while reflecting on the writings of my family members. Later

1 Jochen Bonz and Katharina Eisch-Angus, "Sinn und Subjektivität: Tradition und Perspektiven des Methodeninstruments Ethnopsychoanalytische Deutungswerkstatt/Supervisionsgruppe für Forscher:innen," in *Ethnografie und Deutung: Gruppensupervision als Methode reflexiven Forschens*, ed. Jochen Bonz et al. (Wiesbaden: Springer VS, 2017), 27–58; Jochen Bonz and Maya Nadig, unpublished conversation, 2012 (available upon request from Jochen Bonz: j.bonz@katho-nrw.de); Maya Nadig, "Einführung in eine ethnopsychoanalytische Deutungswerkstatt" (2009), Ethnopsychoanalyse, accessed January 10, 2024, http://www.ethnopsychoanalyse.org/seiten/forschung/methoden /deutungswerkstatt_methode.htm.

in this text, I will explain how this muteness is a conceptual decision and part of the reasoning behind choosing to work with the interpretation workshop in the first place. Until now, I have not revealed much about my personal story, emotions, and ways of dealing with distance and closeness in the process of researching. The question is if it will stay this way.

The abovementioned call to share more from my personal perspective within my research can be understood from two perspectives. On the one hand, it expresses a wish to learn how working on this project affects me, the kinds of reactions it provokes in my family, and how I navigate these within my research. This wish sounds to me like a desire to relate to my research on an emotional level. On the other hand, I see it as a demand from the readers and viewers of my project to situate myself more explicitly in order to better understand my research. I use *situate* in the sense of Donna Haraway's *situated knowledge*: "only partial perspective promises objective vision."[2] So, the more the audience knows about me and my background, as well as my research experience, the easier it is for them to read the project and its different contexts. These complex perspectives raise the question of the extent to which I am choosing to be a representative of my family—or, more generally, the descendants of families of perpetrators—and to what extent this role is imposed on me from the outside. My project is an attempt to mediate between assuming and rejecting the position as speaker for my family or even the larger group of descendants. Can I speak only for me? Or am I always speaking for a group? And if so, which one? Who defines that group?

As the act of situating is derived from feminist thinkers such as Haraway, it implies the promise to shape more just, critical, self-reflective, and progressive projects. I wonder how we can ensure that this is the outcome. What kinds of methodologies of situating can we use to critically reflect on hegemonies of thought, our own privileges and biases, hierarchies of power that manifest within our research project, and possible marginalized positions on the subject matter? Especially when working on projects that directly draw from our own lived experience, the question is how to uncover blind spots. Is it precisely this partial perspective that makes it impossible for me to grasp some of my own entanglements with historical injustices? Is there a way out?

I do want to respond to those who ask me to situate myself and for my personal story; this essay will be a first step in trying to formulate answers. Here, I will outline my current artistic research project by describing my research material, introducing the methodology of the interpretation workshop, explaining how I adapted it for my inquiry, and thinking about how it comes into play within my research. Then I will reflect on how the research project is an attempt to situate myself through a shared communicative and creative process. This reflection draws from concepts such Haraway's *situated knowledge*, Sandra Harding's *strong objectivity*, Lauren Fournier's description of *autotheory*, and the field of *ethnopsychoanalysis*.[3] I borrow and expand on terminology from the art historian Griselda Pollock—*allo-auto-biography*—in order to introduce the concept of *allo-auto-processes* as one

2 Donna Haraway, "Situated Knowledges: The Science Question in Feminism and the Privilege of Partial Perspective," *Feminist Studies* 14, no. 3 (1988): 575–99.

3 Sandra Harding, " 'Strong Objectivity': A Response to the New Objectivity Question," *Synthese* 104, no. 3 (1995): 331–49; Sandra Harding, "After the Neutrality Ideal: Science, Politics, and 'Strong Objectivity,' " *Social Research* 59, no. 3 (1992): 583; Lauren Fournier, *Autotheory as Feminist Practice in Art, Writing, and Criticism* (Cambridge, MA: MIT Press, 2022); Mario Erdheim, *Psychoanalyse und die Unbewußtheit in der Kultur* (Frankfurt am Main: Suhrkamp, 1988); George Devereux, *From Anxiety to Method in the Behavioral Sciences* (The Hague: Mouton, 1967).

possible way for the act of *situating oneself critically* within the context of artistic research.[4]

Implicated Material

My research material consists of two collections of texts.

The writings of my grandmother Camilla Nissen are autobiographical. She left behind a memoir and a diary. As she notes in the text itself, the memoir was written between August 1969 and August 1971. It was originally intended only for the closest family circle. On the first page, the sentence "Für meine Kinder" (For my children) appears—one could even read it as the title of her memoir.[5] My father told me she made her children promise to never publish the text. I don't know her motivation in asking for this, but I assume she thought it could be of interest to historians at some point. Or she wanted to make sure her children wouldn't face any trouble because of their high-ranking Nazi family members. Moreover, she must have been aware that some of her statements and formulations about Jews, disabled people, and National Socialism would have caused great offense in the German political climate of the early 1970s, which was marked by the worldwide leftist protests of 1968.

The memoir gives an account of her entire life. She begins with a short history of her mother's life, then focuses on her own and that of her children. She ends by addressing her children again, asking them "to stick together and help each other wherever you can."[6]

The second text, her diary, is titled "Flucht aus Mellensee" (Flight from Mellensee). Camilla refers to the diary in her memoir: "My diary notes of our flight, our stay at Stocksee, in Schleswig-Holstein, beginning on 21 April, so I don't need

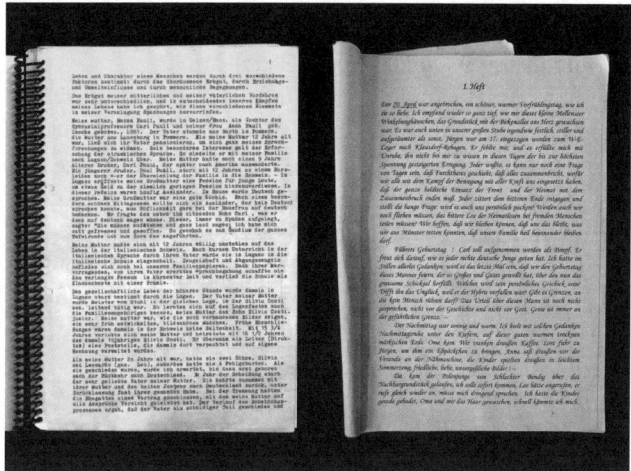

Fig. 40 First pages of Camilla Nissen's memoir (*left*) and diary,
as they were distributed to the author

4 Griselda Pollock, *Allo-thanatography or Allo-auto-biography: A Few
Thoughts on One Painting in Charlotte Salomon's "Leben? oder Theater?,"* 1941–42,
no. 28 of the series *100 Notes – 100 Thoughts* (Ostfildern: Hatje Cantz, 2011).
5 Camilla Nissen, "Für meine Kinder," 1969–71, 1 (unpublished memoir).
Translations are by the author unless noted otherwise.
6 Nissen, 140.

to write anything about it here. […] My flight diary ends at the time when Robert and I found each other again." Within the family this journal is referred to as the *Flucht-Tagebuch* (flight diary). Robert Nissen was Camilla's husband and my grandfather. But the version of the diary I possess does not end with the reunion of the two, which means that parts of the original diary must be missing. It originally consisted of a collection of handwritten sheets of paper that my grandmother had stored together until her death.

Both texts, the memoir and the diary, were transcribed from the original, which Camilla wrote in the old German Sütterlin script. Copies were then distributed within the family. These transcriptions, now easier to read, were made by the mother of the separated husband of one of my aunts. I don't know why she was chosen for this task, who initiated this process, and who was responsible for distributing the copies. I have never seen the original manuscript, so it is possible that some parts are different from the original, that things have been left out or additional information added. I'm not sure where the original Sütterlin versions of the two writings are kept. They must still be within the family.

The writings of my great-grandmother Nanna Conti are not private; on the contrary, they were intended to be read by an audience. As the head midwife of the Nazis, Conti centralized all local midwifery associations, managed the exclusion of all Jewish and politically dissenting midwives, and turned the magazine for professional midwives into a propaganda magazine. Furthermore, Nanna Conti was responsible for the implementation of population-policy measures. From 1939 on, midwives were obliged to report so-called unworthy life; they received an additional payment for these reports. Hence, Nanna Conti and the NS midwifery were complicit

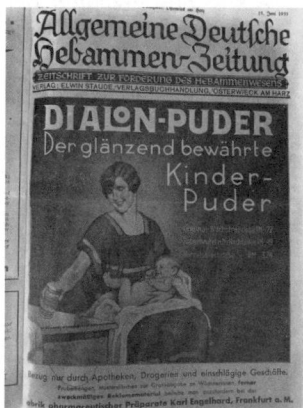
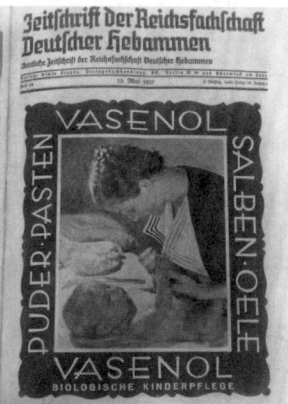
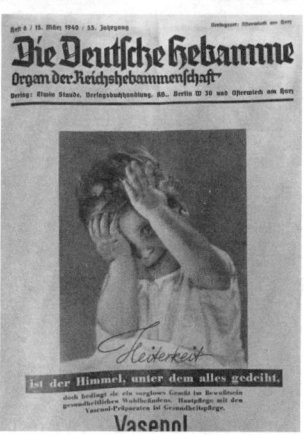

Fig. 41 Covers of the midwifery magazine with its different titles:
Allgemeine Deutsche Hebammen-Zeitung (1933), *Zeitschrift der
Reichsfachschaft Deutscher Hebammen* (1937), and *Die Deutsche
Hebamme* (1940)

in the systematic killing of children deemed "unworthy"—a practice known as *Kinder-Euthanasie* (child euthanasia). Nanna Conti also planned and conducted racial-ideology training courses for midwives at the Führerschule der Deutschen Ärzteschaft (Führer's School of the German Medical Profession).[7]

The midwifery magazine, of which she was the head editor, became her main publishing instrument. The magazine was established in 1886 under the title *Allgemeine Deutsche Hebammen-Zeitung*. From 1933 to 1939 it was published as *Zeitschrift der Reichsfachschaft Deutscher Hebammen*, and from 1939 to 1945 as *Die Deutsche Hebamme*. From 1949 until today it has been published as *Deutsche Hebammen Zeitschrift* by the Elwin Staude Verlag in Hannover, the same press that's published the magazine since its founding.[8]

The articles by Nanna Conti in the midwifery magazine are diverse: she describes current political decisions affecting midwifery, talks about international midwifery meetings abroad, writes book reviews, and comments on current political and social events. All these texts have one thing in common: they are infused with National Socialist ideology. Every single one of them leaves no doubt as to the author's political position. Nanna Conti also published in other contexts, such as a book on home birth called *Das ABC der Hausentbindung* (The ABCs of Home Delivery).[9] However, my research focuses on her writings in the midwifery magazine.

I call the material I am investigating *implicated* in the sense described by Michael Rothberg in *The Implicated Subject* (2019). Synonyms for this term include "entangled" or "involved." With the writing of Nanna Conti, the entanglement with National Socialist ideology and the violence of all members of the state apparatus is obvious, from both the texts themselves and the position of power from which she was writing. Although Camilla Nissen was not as prominent as her mother was, as a mother of five, a housewife, and a staunch National Socialist, she fulfilled the ideals of a Nazi woman.[10]

As a great-granddaughter of a Nazi perpetrator and the granddaughter of an active supporter of the Nazis, I am also implicated. For Rothberg, "an implicated subject is neither a victim nor a perpetrator, but rather a participant in histories and social formations that generate the positions of victim and perpetrator, and yet in which most people do not occupy such clear-cut roles. Less 'actively' involved than perpetrators, implicated subjects do not fit the mold of the 'passive' bystander, either. Although indirect or belated, their actions and inactions help produce and reproduce the positions of victims and perpetrators."[11] I am such a "belated implicated subject." For many years, my inaction—namely, continuing the family's silence about its historical entanglement with National Socialism—made me complicit in the violence perpetrated by Nanna Conti. Through the research project I describe in this essay, I hope to transgress this position, in

7 For information on the biography of Nanna Conti and her involvement in National Socialism, see Anja Peters, *Nanna Conti (1881–1951): Eine Biographie der Reichshebammenführerin* (Berlin: Lit, 2018); and Anja Peters, *Der Geist von Alt-Rehse: Die Hebammenkurse an der Reichsärzteschule, 1935–1941* (Frankfurt am Main: Mabuse-Verlag, 2005).

8 Most of the publications from the years 1933 to 1945 are accessible at the State Library in Berlin, and in the archive of the publishing house. For more information on the press and to access the online content of today's midwifery magazine, see *Deutsche Hebammen Zeitschrift*, https://www.dhz-online.de/.

9 Nanna Conti, *Das ABC der Hausentbindung* (Stuttgart: Hippokrates-Verlag, 1942).

10 From 1938 on, women with at least four children were awarded the Mutterkreuz (mother's cross). For more on the ideal of the mother in National Socialism, see Irmgard Weyrather, *Muttertag und Mutterkreuz: Der Kult um die "deutsche Mutter" im Nationalsozialismus* (Frankfurt am Main: Fischer, 1993).

11 Michael Rothberg, *The Implicated Subject: Beyond Victims and Perpetrators* (Stanford, CA: Stanford University Press, 2019), 1.

which my actions and inaction continue to reproduce historical violence. Not with the aim of reconciliation—the problematic of such an endeavor has strikingly been described by the writer and curator Max Czollek as the "theater of reconciliation"[12]—but with the unconditional desire to take both a personal stance and my family history as a starting point for discussions about recent history and current sociopolitical challenges. I hope these discussions will not stop at fact-checking and speaking about historical context, and will enable a confrontation with the continuation of historical patterns of thought and emotional heritage in a way that focuses on affect and feeling. The goal with this is to work toward a different, more relatable kind of remembrance work, one that speaks directly to its audience from the present.

Focusing on the psychosocial reverberations of having National Socialist perpetrators in one's own family, my research investigates if it is possible to uncover inherited feelings (*Gefühlserbschaften*). In this project, inherited feelings are understood as affects and emotions that have been passed on from former generations. These could be feelings of shame in the face of the violence perpetrated by family members or a sense of responsibility toward the family not to speak about the perpetrators in order to protect them from persecution. In the second step of my artistic research, I explore different aesthetic decisions regarding how to make the uncovered affective entanglements and historical patterns of thought perceptible, and how they can influence the interpretation of one's family's role in National Socialism, as well as the effects the inherited feelings might have on one's own life and behavior.

Although my research material is composed of different kinds of texts, such as memoir and diary and published articles and commentaries, I approach all of them with the method of the *Deutungswerkstatt*. The German verb *deuten* means "to interpret" or "to construe," so I have translated this term as "interpretation workshop." It originated in the field of ethnopsychoanalysis.

Interpretation Workshop

In 2014, during my studies at the Academy of Media Arts in Cologne, I was introduced to ethnopsychoanalysis by Marie-Luise Angerer.[13] I had created a number of experimental films with analogue footage I'd shot on travels. I think she pointed me to ethnopsychoanalysis to help me reflect on my position as an artist, as someone making images abroad. I made my way through the literature that Angerer suggested to me, which led me to the method that lies at the core of this project: the interpretation workshop. I had wanted to create a piece using this method for many years, and in 2020 I found the right project for it. I will first explain the method and then dive into how it plays out in my research.

Georges Devereux (1908–1985) was the first to think psychoanalysis and ethnography together. In his book *From Anxiety to Method in the Behavioral Sciences* (1967), he argues that an analysis of the ethnographic researcher's affects and

12 For more on Czollek's critique of German remembrance culture and the theater of reconciliation, see Max Czollek, *Gegenwartsbewältigung* (Munich: Carl Hanser, 2020); and Max Czollek, *Versöhnungstheater* (Munich: Carl Hanser, 2023).

13 Angerer sadly passed away in 2024, way too early. She was a great inspiration and had an immense influence on my education and those of many others at the Academy of Media Arts, where she was professor for media and cultural studies/gender.

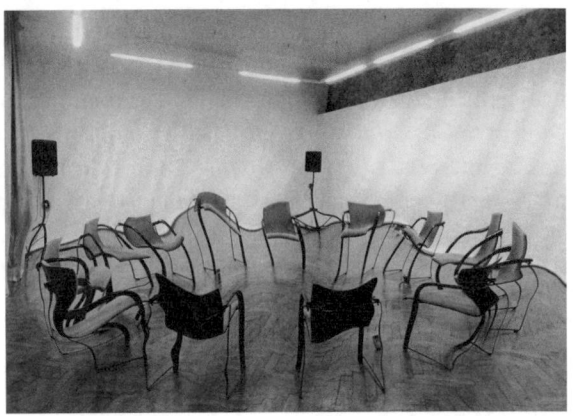

Fig. 42 Lena Ditte Nissen, *Deutungswerkstatt – fließend* (Interpretation Workshop – Flowing), 2020/23

countertransferences is an important source of knowledge production:[14]

> The data of behavioral science are, thus, threefold: 1. The behavior of the subject. 2. The "disturbances" produced by the existence and observational activities of the observer. 3. The behavior of the observer: His anxieties, his defensive maneuvers, his research strategies, his "decisions" (= his attribution of a meaning to his observations). Unfortunately, it is about the third type of behavior that we have the least information, because we have systematically refused to study reality on its own terms. […] An authentic behavioral science will come into being when its practitioners will realize that a realistic science of mankind can only be created by men most aware of their own humanity precisely when they implement it most completely in their scientific work.[15]

Informed by the work of Devereux and colleagues from the field of ethnopsychoanalysis such as Goldy Parin-Matthèy, Paul Parin, and Mario Erdheim, Maya Nadig systemically developed the interpretation workshop in the 1990s. In establishing its methodology, she also drew from her own experience as a practicing psychoanalyst. Nadig implemented the workshop to analyze text-based ethnographic research material—"thick descriptions" such as transcribed interviews, field notes, or excerpts from field diaries.[16] The method takes the form of exploratory group conversations that aim to work with the unconscious dynamics of the material provided. To uncover dynamics that materialize only implicitly in the *thick material*, the members of the interpretation group first focus on spontaneous affects, "images or feelings, even if they appear to be illogical, unscientific, or far removed in terms of content, or to contain inappropriate (i.e., politically incorrect) emotions." These "irritations" are then connected with the "social and emotional dynamics of the relationships" that can be observed in the material. And then: "Only in a subsequent step is it collectively considered how the object-related emotions, conflicts, fears, and forms of resistance in this specific situation are wrapped up in cultural behavior patterns. It is only here that a cautious interpretative link between the emotional and the cultural takes place: for example, between the cultural differences of the researcher and her

14 Devereux defines the Freudian term as such: "Countertransference is the sum total of those distortions in the psychoanalyst's perception of, and reaction to his patient which cause him to respond to his patient [...] in terms of his own [...] unconscious needs, wishes and fantasies." He uses both transference and countertransference and applies them respectively to the subject in fieldwork (instead of the analysand) and the researcher in their field (instead of the analyst). Devereux, *From Anxiety to Method*, 41–42.

15 Devereux, 19–20.

16 Clifford Geertz, "Thick Description: Toward an Interpretive Theory of Culture," in *The Interpretation of Cultures: Selected Essays* (New York: Basic Books, 1973), 3–30.

conversation partners, or between the conversation partners themselves, who are of different ages, status, gender, etc., and each represent different lines of conflict and perspectives."[17]

The concrete outcome of an interpretation workshop consists of the notes the researcher takes during the conversation. These may include affects, emotions, imaginations, and thoughts recorded as either short observations of or quotations from group members, as well as affects, emotions, imaginations, and thoughts experienced by the researcher during the workshop. The findings from an interpretation workshop include not only what is expressed verbally but also notions expressed implicitly. In the same way that the research material is not only analyzed as a concrete written text but also examined for its implicit content, the results from the group manifest not only in what is spoken but also in facial expressions, gestures, and group dynamics. What the researcher then does with the gathered material, how and whether they integrate it into their research process, is not defined by the method but depends on the researcher's subjective decisions. In the case of my project, this is where the creative process begins.

The workshops were part of my art and theory fellowship at the Künstler:innenhaus Büchsenhausen in Innsbruck, Austria.[18] They were led by Jochen Bonz, whose continuous interpretation workshop groups I had participated in as part of the preliminary research for my PhD project. I found the participants for the conversations through an open call that was distributed in Innsbruck and the Tyrol region with the help of the institution. Eleven people responded to the call, and all of them eventually took part in the workshops. The group consisted of ten women and one man, all between the ages of twenty-three and sixty-seven, nine of whom were students or had completed academic training and two of whom had attended art academies in Austria.[19] All were Caucasian and only one participant did not have Austrian roots—their parents were from Romania. The group was therefore relatively homogeneous. Before the first session, preparatory individual meetings were held either in person or by telephone, during which the participants could ask questions.

The group gathered on two weekends in 2020, the first at the end of January and the second in mid-September. Originally the workshops were planned to take place within a span of two months, but the COVID-19 pandemic and the restrictions on gatherings made that impossible. Four extracts of Camilla Nissen's diary and four passages of her memoir were interpreted. On each day, two interpretation workshops took place; in total, twelve hours of conversations were documented with several audio recorders. I transcribed the recordings afterward.

The main themes that emerged from analyzing the transcriptions and my notes were as follows: the generational differences of the participants in relation to the texts and how that affected the way they reacted emotionally; the role of women in National Socialism and its impact on the role of women in Austria and Germany today; and the question of the motivation of the diarist/memoirist. Another prominent aspect was how the group found it incomprehensible that my grandmother continued to be anti-Semitic and nationalist after 1945, which she clearly depicts in her memoir.

17 Nadig, "Einführung in eine ethnopsychoanalytische Deutungswerkstatt."
18 I want to thank Andrei Siclodi, director of Künstler:innenhaus Büchsenhausen, for giving me the opportunity to realize these interpretation workshops. The conversations I had with my fellow resident, the artist Anna Dasović, were also invaluable.
19 I am using "man" and "women" here in a binary way, as this is how gender manifested within the group.

The older participants seemed much more emotionally affected by the close reading of the texts. They were both angry and sad, and discussed memories of their own family members whom they had confronted about their National Socialist convictions. These stories were marked by the participants' disappointments in the family members owing to their lack of reflection and condemnation of the Nazis and their actions or lack thereof during the time of National Socialism. I did not have the chance to confront my grandmother, who died in 1994 at the age of ninety-two. I listened to the experiences of the older interpreters and felt they were a sort of substitute for the open conflicts I wish I'd had.

The group discussed their understanding that the role of women in National Socialism was limited to being a devoted housewife and having as many children as possible. They spoke about Camilla's fulfillment of these ideals, although as a teenager and young woman she was politically engaged. Together with her two older brothers, she was involved in the youth organization of the Deutschnationale Volkspartei (DNVP).[20] She briefly worked as a secretary for a nationalist magazine, and her memoir states that she published a piece in it, but I haven't been able to verify this yet. The group commented on how she ended her early political involvement when she married and had children. They spoke about how women were viewed as less political beings than men, and still are today. And that even if women are not active in a political party, they can still have strong political views that shape the way they educate their children.

My grandmother's motivation to write a memoir that clearly shows her continued belief in National Socialist ideas and ideals was another much-discussed topic. It seemed that the group could not or did not want to believe that she did not condemn National Socialism during the leftist protest movement that began in 1968 and reverberated into the next decade. They kept returning to this issue. As one of the participants pointed out, Camilla decided to write about her life at a moment when younger generations were posing questions to their parents and grandparents about what they did during National Socialism. The group wondered if this specific political environment had led her to write her memoirs, or if there had been direct inquiries from her children. This question remains unanswered.

In September 2020, I was invited by the curators Petra Poelzl and Pauline Doutreluingne to create a performative piece in an old Nazi military cemetery in Berlin. I decided to use the transcribed interpretation workshops to write a fictionalized script for two actresses: Almut Zilcher from Deutsches Theater in Berlin, who is Austrian, and Ruth Rosenfeld from the Schaubühne in Berlin, who is US-American and Jewish. Embodying the perspective of the descendants of perpetrators as well as that of the victims of National Socialism, Zilcher and Rosenfeld cited excerpts of the original writings of my grandmother, speaking as a choir. These excerpts were then discussed by Zilcher and Rosenfeld in a dialogue that was based on the interpretation workshops. The quotations and their reflections were complemented by biographies of different female perpetrators of National Socialism written and performed by the historian Sandra Franz, the director of the NS Documentation Center in Krefeld. These three layers of language—the original writing by my grandmother Camilla, reflective conversation, and historical perpetrator biographies—were interwoven in

20 The Deutschnationale Volkspartei was founded on November 24, 1918, and dissolved in June 1933. It was a national-conservative party in the Weimar Republic whose agenda encompassed nationalism, national liberalism, anti-Semitism, and imperial-monarchist conservatism.

a performative walk through the cemetery. The COVID-19 pandemic was still ongoing when I was invited to show the piece in an exhibition at Kunstpavillon Innsbruck in the winter of 2020/21. I re-created the script in a completely different manner to create an installation piece that could be visited without encountering other people. I decided for a minimalist approach, as I wanted the attention to be on the spoken words.

On the middle screen of a three-channel video installation, the excerpts of the original writing were spoken; Rosenfeld and Zilcher discussed them from the screens on either side. The screens were staged in such a way that the actors could see themselves speaking on the center screen. The concave wall behind the screens created a space for the viewers to enter the conversation. Wallpaper showed the image of the circle of chairs in which the interpretation workshops took place. Just like the method of the workshop itself creates a kind of feedback loop, I wanted to re-create the continuous oscillation between original writing, affect, and reflection within the setting of the installation.

One and the Other

In the introduction, I mentioned the title of my research project—*Chaosmos of the Personal*. I want to come back to it now. As defined by the *Duden* dictionary, *chaos* means "dissolution of all order" and *cosmos* refers to "the world as an organized whole." As a teenager, learning about my family's relationship to National Socialism created chaos inside of me. I had grown up with leftist parents, I went to demonstrations with them, and I identified with their political convictions. Suddenly, there was a different family story to

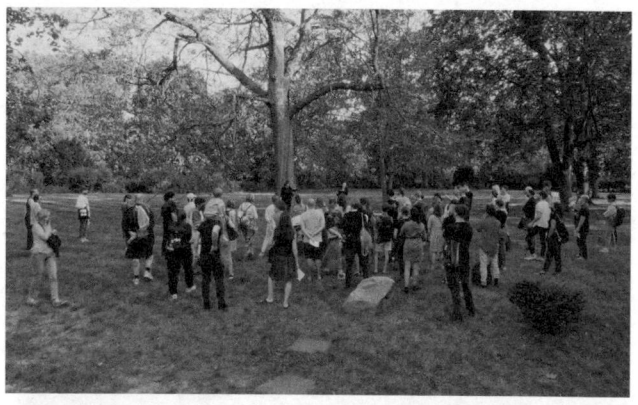

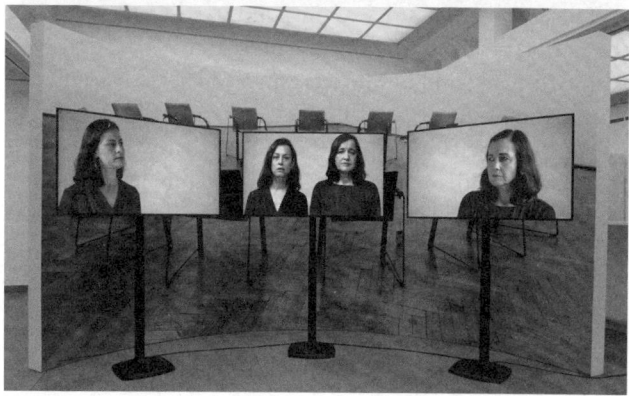

Fig. 43 Lena Ditte Nissen, *NEHMT ES WIE ES IST* (Take It as It Is), 2020.
Performance documentation.
Fig. 44 Lena Ditte Nissen, *NEHMT ES WIE ES IST* (Take It as It Is), 2021.
Installation view.

react to and position myself against. The cosmos in which I have since acted as a political citizen both in private and with my work as an artist and filmmaker has been framed by this history. For many years, I tried to separate the two realms of my life. Precisely because of my family's entanglement with Germany's violent history, I did not want to position myself as a political artist. Rather, through the choice of specific topics, materials, and ways of working, my guiding political principles implicitly entered my practice. Then in 2015, the year of the so-called refugee crisis and renewed rise of right-wing politics in Germany and Europe, I felt the need to reconsider this decision. I concluded that I wanted my practice to explicitly work with political topics for that very reason: my family history. It was a logical step to put that history at the core of my work.

I believe that the story of my family, especially regarding the notion of silence, is in part representative of the story of many German families who were involved in the Nazi regime. It was important for me to find a way to speak about it, to use it, to render it productive in a way that would make it relatable for a broader public without generalizing and losing important information. The history of my family is without a doubt specific, and the crimes committed by some of its members need to be specifically named as such. Yet, the individualization of stories of families with Nazi perpetrators makes it much easier for others to immediately distance themselves from them without considering possible points of connection with their own history. This is supported by numbers—for instance, 69.8 percent of Germans believe there were no Nazi perpetrators in their family.[21] By sharing the historical material related to perpetrators in my family with the participants of the interpretation workshop, I could engage with it on both a personal and a conceptual level by no longer reflecting on it alone.

The participants helped me overcome the obstacle of breaking the silence on the National Socialist convictions and crimes committed by some of my family members. I recognize them as allies in my wish to make public, to condemn, and to interpret my family history from a range of contemporary perspectives. In bringing to the table their specific affects and thoughts on the material, they also made visible how others can relate to this specific history. The participants of the interpretation workshop made it possible for me to oscillate between closeness and distance, individual history and the general dynamics of perpetrator families, without being overwhelmed by either.

Reflective Alliances

"Insofar as the spaces of interaction [of the researcher] in the field represent the specific reference for the interpretation group work, the method [the interpretation workshop] can only be used to a limited extent for analyzing historical documents," write Jochen Bonz and colleagues. "For although they address us […] in a variety of human ways, they do not react to the researcher, so no mutual relationship develops."[22] It is true that the material does not talk back to me; my grandmother's writings do not show me affects. Yet I would

21 Jonas Rees, Andreas Zick, Michael Papendick, and Franziska Wäschle, *Multidimensionaler Erinnerungsmonitor (MEMO) II/2019*, Forschungsbericht IKG (Bielefeld: Institut für interdisziplinäre Konflikt- und Gewaltforschung [IKG], Universität Bielefeld, 2019). For more on the history of perpetrators within families in often repressed, see by Harald Walzer, Sabine Moller, and Karoline Tschuggnall, *"Opa war kein Nazi": Nationalsozialismus und Holocaust im Familiengedächtnis* (Frankfurt am Main: Fischer, 2002).

22 Jochen Bonz, Katharina Eisch-Angus, Marion Hamm, and Almut Sülze, "Ethnografische Gruppensupervision als Methode reflexiven Forschens: Eine Einleitung," in Bonz et al., *Ethnografie und Deutung*, 15.

argue that it is possible to use the interpretation workshop in my specific research. Rather than solely writing about the concrete examples of the workshops, I will focus on how the method comes to work systematically within my project.

From my experience and notes, I argue that the members of the group engage in an intersubjective process of reflection on three levels within my project. Intersubjectivity is understood as an intentional reciprocal exchange between at least two subjects.[23] First, they relate their own personal history and intergenerational family culture of memory to the texts and their context; second, they connect the historical material to current sociopolitical issues through their specific lived experience; and third, they become a kind of distorted mirror for my affects, feelings, and thoughts about the writings. I will focus on the latter here, as I believe it is the most important mechanism of the method in relation to this publication.

The interpretation workshop aims at "restaging a liminal space of dialogue of field work: a threshold situation that opens up through the encounter of field and researcher with their different cultural imprints and expectations."[24] In the case of my project, this threshold situation as reference does not exist in the same way. One could say that what is restaged in the workshop is my relation to the text material as it manifested for many years: I did not speak about it, and neither did anyone in my family. This silence about family members who were perpetrators of National Socialism is a symptom that can be observed in many German families.[25] At times, this silence is expressed as a clear rule within families, or it is a tacit expectation. Within the setting of the interpretation workshop, I sit silently in the circle together with the group's participants. I see my silence during the conversation as representative of the silence of many. I embody and reinscribe it through my presence. The silence remains and, at the same time, it is structurally thematized through the method itself.

To understand what this restaging of silence means for the interpretation workshops in my project, I would like to examine two quotations. George Devereux writes about disturbances of data in behavioral research: "Since the existence of the observer, his observational activities and his anxieties (even in self observation) produce distortions which it is not only technically but also logically impossible to eliminate, […] any effective behavioral science methodology must treat these disturbances as the most significant and characteristic data of behavioral science research."[26]

Ethnopsychoanalysis theoretically aims to uncover disturbances that occur through the subjectivity of the researcher, and the interpretation workshop methodologically aims to unpack them. As Antje Krueger formulates it, the method manages to "correct the distortions of individual patterns of perception and action [of the researcher] (and thus possible manipulative and suggestive elements) and reveals internalized social norms and values."[27] One of the elements that support this process of correction is *restaging*. Bonz explains how it plays a role within the method:

23 Andrea Lailach-Hennrich, "Der Begriff 'Intersubjektivität': Ein Begriffsmerkmal" (conference paper, 22nd Deutscher Kongress für Philosophie, Ludwig-Maximilians-Universität Munich, September 11–15, 2011), 2.

24 Bonz et al., "Ethnografische Gruppensupervision als Methode reflexiven Forschens," 6.

25 For more on the silence in German families with Nazi perpetrators, see Alexandra Senfft, *Schweigen tut weh: Eine deutsche Familiengeschichte* (Berlin: List, 2008); and Alexandra Senfft, *Der lange Schatten der Täter: Nachkommen stellen sich ihrer NS-Familiengeschichte* (Munich: Piper, 2018).

26 Devereux, *From Anxiety to Method*, 17.

27 Antje Krueger, "Die ethnopsychoanalytische Deutungswerkstatt," in *Kritik mit Methode? Forschungsmethoden und Gesellschaftskritik*, ed. Ulrike Freikamp et al. (Berlin: Karl Dietz, 2008), 131.

The relationship [between the researcher and their field] in the group is then restaged; it can be named by the participants or by me as the group leader. But even without being explicitly named, this enables the researching subject to experience and perceive something that they could not experience and perceive otherwise, because the group shows how they experienced the situation themselves, in other words: how they actually were. You see the situation, and therefore yourself, as if from the outside, and yet you are emotionally connected to it. This intense, displaced perception leads to the fact that you yourself are somewhat displaced. The researching subject experiences a decentering. This shattering of one's own perceptual habits opens up another perspective on the field of investigation, which is the additional knowledge that arises for the field researcher because he has now gained a different access to his own experience.[28]

What is interesting here is that Bonz sees the correction of disturbances happening through *displacement*, *decentering*, and the *shattering of perceptual habits*. Thus, it is made possible through mechanisms that distort the researcher's usual subjective way of looking at, thinking of, and making meaning. In a different article, Bonz and colleagues describe this as "emancipatory realization," which again links the method back to psychoanalysis.[29] One step of the dynamic in the therapeutic process is based on the fact that parts of the unconscious become conscious and thus make changes of behavior possible. This *becoming conscious* cannot be reversed.

In the quote above, Devereux speaks of the effect of the "observational activities" and "anxieties" of the researcher in and toward their field.[30] When transferring this to my project, it becomes clear that the positions of the observer and the observed are not easily distinguished, like in the classical behavioral sciences. On the one hand, as the researcher, I look at the historical text material, which the group's participants do as well. Yet in the setting of the interpretation workshop, I observe the group, and they, while focusing on the analysis of the research material, also observe me. Thus, a complex system of reciprocal observation is at play, and with it the affects of all of those involved, alternating as observers and observants. As such, many different "distortions of individual patterns of perception and action" manifest through the different steps of the research process.[31]

From my experience of the setting and the methodology, my physical presence seemed to function as a reminder for the group to interpret the historical material in relation to me. This meant considering how the texts might make me feel, what I might think about them. At times this became explicit—when the group mentioned me in the third person or by name. Sometimes, however, it was implicit, as participants voiced reflections I've thought before—some of which I wouldn't dare to verbalize, as they would feel either too harsh or too kind toward the writer, in this case my grandmother. These ambivalent reactions, or rather, the ambivalence silently validating my feelings and thoughts, was perceived by the group as they spoke them out loud.

Thus, during the affective interpretation of the historical text material, the participants speak for themselves, of

28 Jochen Bonz, "Gruppenanalytische Supervision für ethnografisches Feldforschen," in *Gruppenpsychoanalyse: Theorie, Geschichte und Praxisfelder der gruppenanalytischen Methode*, ed. Günter Dietrich and Florian Fossel (Vienna: Facultas, 2022), 333.

29 Bonz et al., "Ethnografische Gruppensupervision als Methode reflexiven Forschens," 8.

30 Devereux, *From Anxiety to Method*, 17.

31 Krueger, "Die ethnopsychoanalytische Deutungswerkstatt," 131.

course, but also on behalf of me through a variety of transferences and countertransferences among the observers and observants. "However, one should be aware that the group's articulation of the latent remains an articulation; it is not a fixed truth about social reality," as Bonz and Katharina Eisch-Angus write.[32] I therefore argue that the participants function as a kind of distorting mirror. Some of their subjective observations, and mine, might align. Just as in a distorting mirror, some parts might be visible clearly and in the right proportions, while others appear warped. Staying with the metaphor of the distorting mirror, this *becoming visible* is equivalent to emancipatory realization.

Allo-auto-process

In *Autotheory as Feminist Practice in Art, Writing, and Criticism*, the curator and artist Lauren Fournier writes: "Most simply the term [autotheory] refers to the integration of theory and philosophy with autobiography, the body, and other so-called personal and explicitly subjective modes. It is a term that describes a self-conscious way of engaging with theory—as a discourse, frame, or mode of thinking and practice—alongside lived experience and subjective embodiment, something very much in the Zeitgeist of cultural production today. [...] Autotheory is the integration of the *auto* or 'self' with philosophy or theory, often in ways that are direct, performative, or self-aware."[33] The works she describes as manifestations of autotheory within creative productions are mostly conceived in *auto*nomous processes—that is, the artists/writers/critics engage with theory by and with themselves in subjective processes, not in collaborative, intersubjective processes with other human beings. This leads me to the question of whether *auto*theoretical work must be created in an *auto*nomous process, or if it could also be conceived in collaborative projects?

Earlier I argued how, as the researcher, I make my voice heard within the methodology of the interpretation workshop without speaking but by creating a space for others to speak. To describe this process of uncovering the subjective position of the researcher through the integration of other perspectives, I would like to introduce the term *allo-auto-process*.

A similar term, *allo-auto-biography*, was used by Griselda Pollock in a publication of hers about the work of the artist Charlotte Salomon (1917–1943). In the essay, she refers to the term with one sentence: "The person acquires a selfhood, *autós*, only because of a space or a relay with *allós*—another, the addressee."[34] Pollock does not explain how her neologism is to be read exactly, nor does she hint at how it might be used in other contexts. But there is already a lot to unpack in that sentence.

Pollock translates autós as *selfhood* rather than self. As defined by *Oxford Languages Dictionary*, selfhood is "the quality that gives a person or thing an individual identity and makes them different from others." Rather than using the word as a simple prefix, she gives it the position of an individual human subject. By referring to "a space or relay" with another (and here one might add another autós), she opens a realm to think the relation as one that unfolds spatially as well as through communication. The word *relay* refers to a transfer of information; *to relay* means, according to *Oxford*, to "receive and pass on (information or a message)," which puts both versions of autós in active positions. When Pollock defines one of the autós as "the addressee," the other

32 Bonz and Eisch-Angus, "Sinn und Subjektivität," 41.
33 Fournier, *Autotheory as Feminist Practice*, 7, 13.
34 Pollock, *Allo-thanatography or Allo-auto-biography*, 6.

must be the addresser. She writes about an artist who created a piece in an autonomous process that then ideally had and has an audience. I would like to expand this relation to make it applicable for my project, adding that during research an addressee can also be an addresser, or, as Donna Haraway writes, an *agent*: "Situated knowledges require that the object of knowledge be pictured as an actor and agent, not as a screen or a ground or a resource, never finally as slave to the master that closes off the dialectic in his unique agency and his authorship of 'objective' knowledge."[35]

The multitude of agents in my project—the different historical texts, the participants and me as the leader of the interpretation workshops, collaborators such as actresses and historians, the institutions in and through which I realize the artistic research, my family and friends—all bring their specific sensibilities and contexts to the project.[36] It is an undertaking in which I, as the researcher, work with those partial perspectives and specific agendas in order to gather information about my object of research, which, in a sense, is the sum of those subjectivities, including my own.

As previously acknowledged, the interpretation workshop does not manifest fixed truths. What's more, the situatedness of the researcher, made partially visible through the methodology as a distorted mirror, can never exactly describe where and how the researcher is situated. Yet it approximates the "real" situatedness—one that is always in movement. It does not stand still. With each renewed insight, it changes slightly. With the learning of historical facts that were unknown before, it becomes different. Through a new perspective, it is pushed in a different direction. A detail in a conversation adds yet another layer of understanding. A new contextualization makes visible an aspect that hadn't been seen before.

Thus, and in contrast to how *Oxford Languages Dictionary* defines *to situate* as an antonym of *to move*, the act of situating is exactly that: an action. An action driven by decisions taken by the one trying to situate oneself and by external circumstances, such as access to resources and knowledge, or deliberate and accidental communication with others. I would like to suggest that through allo-auto-processes, such as the interpretation workshop, that continuously oscillate between the speaking and the letting speak of autós (the researcher) and allós (the other agents in the research project), the researcher's situatedness is understood as always in process. It can be revised repeatedly, with earlier mistakes corrected, to make it "less false" in the sense of strong objectivity.[37]

In writing about the interpretation workshop, Maya Nadig indicates the importance of self-situating and critical reflection on the balance of power in research: "Methods are needed that can capture dynamic and complex cultural processes. It is now generally recognized that research undertakings and ethnological studies in particular can no longer be regarded as objective processes. The methodological consequence is the situating of the researcher in the research process as well as the consideration of power relations and self-reflection."[38]

35 Haraway, "Situated Knowledges," 592.
36 This research project has been funded and supported by the fellowship in Büchsenhausen, a grant by the local government of North Rhine-Westphalia, the cities of Cologne and Innsbruck, the Cultural Senate of Berlin, the Danish Arts Foundation, Stiftung Kunstfonds, Stiftung Erinnerung Verantwortung Zukunft, ver.di München, the Austrian Academy of the Sciences, the IFK International Research Center for Cultural Studies of the University of Arts Linz, and the Graduiertenkolleg für Medienanthropologie at Bauhaus University in Weimar. It is embedded in the PhD program of the University of Arts Linz. At each of these institutions I am in contact with people who have become agents in my project. Also, the Study Group on Intergenerational Consequences of the Holocaust and its members are an important support system for my undertaking.
37 Harding, "After the Neutrality Ideal," 586.
38 Nadig, "Einführung in eine ethnopsychoanalytische Deutungswerkstatt."

The interpretation workshop, with its emphasis on collaborative interpretation, can lead to achieving strong objectivity by incorporating diverse viewpoints and experiences into its analysis to situate the researcher in a (self-)reflective process. This method encourages the participation of individuals with varied backgrounds and experiences. By incorporating a variety of perspectives, including those from marginalized or underrepresented groups, it broadens the range of interpretations and insights into the material researched. The method thus aligns with the aim of strong objectivity to encompass multiple standpoints to consider historical, social, and cultural contexts, and to acknowledge power imbalances through those standpoints. Nadig writes, "If all observers share a particular value or interest, whether this arrives from the larger society or is developed in the group of legitimated observers, how is it meant to be revealed by the repetition of observations by these like-minded people?"[39]

Thus, I argue that autotheory does not have to be created within an autonomous process—developing knowledge through the self can benefit immensely from also including other voices. In the title of this paper, I ask, "Speak or let speak?" I would answer: "Both, at the same time, together, and in turns." This, for me, is the main strength of this method as an allo-auto-process. And I am curious to find, try out, and possibly develop others of its kind as well.

I want to add a short note on why the interpretation workshop is particularly suitable as a methodology for artistic research, which is linked to the notion of restaging described earlier. The exploratory nature of the method as conducting experimental arrangements—whose course is beyond the control of the researcher during the event—mirrors artistic works that are often created in consciously experimental processes that aren't controlled by the artist but develop in a certain way—for example, owing to the characteristic properties of a material, such as a specific type of paint. The processual condition of the interpretation workshop, which unfolds in the concrete passage of linear time and therefore has the character of a non-repeatable performance, corresponds with time-based artistic forms of expression such as film, performance, and video.

To come back to my project once more: One thing that became clear during the analysis of the first rounds of interpretation workshops with my grandmother's memoir and diary was that the participants could have been more diverse to foster an even more productive conversation with a broader variety of perspectives. The age range proved to be valuable to speak about the intergenerational differences in coping with National Socialist family history. The next step of my inquiry is to create a space for interpretation workshops about a selection of writings by my great-grandmother Nanna Conti, the leading Nazi midwife. For this, I will focus on bringing together a group of interpreters that represents a larger spectrum of the people living in the region of the former German Reich today.

With the above in mind, I have decided to provisionally split my project into two conceptually different parts: one is the application of the interpretation workshop and the use of its outcome within artistic work, and the other is the written reflection on this process. In the first, I will withdraw from sharing my personal story, affects, feelings, and thoughts throughout the research project, while in the second, I will use writing to convey these sentiments in thinking them together with theory. It might become autotheory.

39 Nadig, "Einführung in eine ethnopsychoanalytische Deutungswerkstatt."

Literature

Bonz, Jochen. "Gruppen-analytische Supervision für ethno-grafisches Feldforschen." In *Gruppen-psychoanalyse: Theorie, Geschichte und Praxisfelder der gruppenanalytischen Methode*, edited by Günter Dietrich and Florian Fossel, 328–46. Vienna: Facultas, 2022.

Bonz, Jochen, and Katharina Eisch-Angus. "Sinn und Subjektivität: Tradition und Perspektiven des Methodeninstruments Ethno-psychoanalytische Deutungswerk-statt/Supervisionsgruppe für Forscher:innen." In *Ethnografie und Deutung: Gruppensupervision als Methode reflexiven Forschens*, edited by Jochen Bonz, Katharina Eisch-Angus, Marion Hamm, and Almut Sülzle, 27–58. Wiesbaden: Springer VS, 2017.

Bonz, Jochen, Katharina Eisch-Angus, Marion Hamm, and Almut Sülze. "Ethnografische Gruppensupervision als Methode reflexiven Forschens: Eine Einleitung." In *Ethnografie und Deutung: Gruppensupervision als Methode reflexiven Forschens*, edited by Jochen Bonz, Katharina Eisch-Angus, Marion Hamm, and Almut Sülzle, 1–24. Wiesbaden: Springer VS, 2017.

Conti, Nanna. *Das ABC der Haus-entbindung.* Stuttgart: Hippokrates-Verlag, 1942.

Czollek, Max. *Gegenwartsbewäl-tigung.* Munich: Carl Hanser, 2020.

Czollek, Max. *Versöhnungstheater.* Munich: Carl Hanser, 2023.

Devereux, George. *From Anxiety to Method in the Behavioral Sciences.* The Hague: Mouton, 1967.

Erdheim, Mario. *Psychoanalyse und die Unbewußtheit in der Kultur.* Frankfurt am Main: Suhrkamp, 1988.

Haraway, Donna. "Situated Knowledges: The Science Question in Feminism and the Privilege of Partial Perspective." *Feminist Studies* 14, no. 3 (1988): 575–99.

Harding, Sandra. "After the Neutrality Ideal: Science, Politics, and 'Strong Objectivity.'" *Social Research* 59, no. 3 (Fall 1992): 567–87.

Harding, Sandra. "'Strong Objectivity': A Response to the New Objectivity Question." *Synthese* 104, no. 3 (1995): 331–49.

Krueger, Antje. "Die ethno-psychoanalytische Deutungswerkstatt." In *Kritik mit Methode? Forschungs-methoden und Gesellschaftskritik*, edited by Ulrike Freikamp, Matthias Leanza, Janne Mende, Stefan Müller, Peter Ullrich, and Heinz-Jürgen Voß, 127–45. Berlin: Karl Dietz, 2008.

Lailach-Hennrich, Andrea. "Der Begriff 'Intersubjektivität': Ein Begriffsmerkmal." Conference paper, 22nd Deutscher Kongress für Philosophie, Ludwig-Maximilians-Universität, Munich, September 11–15, 2011.

Nadig, Maya. "Einführung in eine ethnopsychoanalytische Deutungswerkstatt." Ethno-psychoanalyse, accessed January 10, 2024. http://www.ethnopsychoanalyse .org/seiten/forschung/methoden /deutungswerkstatt_methode.htm.

Nissen, Camilla. "Flucht aus Mellensee." Unpublished diary, 1945.

Nissen, Camilla. "Für meine Kinder." Unpublished memoir, 1969–71.

Peters, Anja. *Der Geist von Alt-Rehse: Die Hebammenkurse an der Reichsärzteschule, 1935–1941.* Frankfurt am Main: Mabuse-Verlag, 2005.

Peters, Anja. *Nanna Conti (1881–1951): Eine Biographie der Reichshebammenführerin.* Berlin: Lit, 2018.

Pollock, Griselda. *Allo-thanatography or Allo-auto-biography: A Few Thoughts on One Painting in Charlotte Salomon's "Leben? oder Theater?," 1941–42.* 100 Notes – 100 Thoughts, no. 28. Ostfildern: Hatje Cantz, 2012.

Rees, Jonas, Andreas Zick, Michael Papendick, and Franziska Wäschle. *Multidimensionaler Erinnerungsmonitor (MEMO) II/2019*. Forschungsbericht IKG. Bielefeld: Institut für interdisziplinäre Konflikt- und Gewaltforschung (IKG), Universität Bielefeld, 2019.

Rothberg, Michael. *The Implicated Subject: Beyond Victims and Perpetrators*. Stanford, CA: Stanford University Press, 2019.

Senfft, Alexandra. *Der lange Schatten der Täter: Nachkommen stellen sich ihrer NS-Familiengeschichte*. Munich: Piper, 2018.

Senfft, Alexandra. *Schweigen tut weh: Eine deutsche Familiengeschichte*. Berlin: List, 2008.

Welzer, Harald, Sabine Moller, and Karoline Tschuggnall. *"Opa war kein Nazi": Nationalsozialismus und Holocaust im Familiengedächtnis*. Frankfurt am Main: Fischer, 2002.

Weyrather, Irmgard. *Muttertag und Mutterkreuz: Der Kult um die "deutsche Mutter" im Nationalsozialismus*. Frankfurt am Main: Fischer, 1993.

Cana Bilir-Meier

Becoming a Storyteller
*Methodologies in Collaborative,
Activist, Artistic, and Archival Work
in Remembering*

My Name Is Foreigner

I work here,
I know how I work.
The Germans know it too.
My work is hard
My work is dirty
I say I don't like it.
"If you don't like it, go home," they say.
My work is hard
My work is dirty
"I also pay taxes," I say.
I'll say it again and again;
If I keep hearing
"Find yourself another job"
But the Germans aren't to blame.
Nor the Turks.
Turkey needed currency,
Germany workers.
My country sold us abroad,
Like stepchildren
Worthless people.
In spite of everything, it was needed for …
The currency, the calm …
My country sold me to a foreign state
My name has become FOREIGNER …

Semra Ertan, 1982

Benim Adım Yabancı

Burada çalışıyor,
Nasıl çalıştığımı biliyorum.
Almanlar da biliyorlar.
İşim ağır
İşim pis
Beğenmeyince söylüyorum.
"Beğenmezsen dön vatanına" diyorlar.
İşim ağır
İşim pis
Ben de vergi veriyorum diyorum.
Devam edeceğim demeye;
Hep böyle duyarsam
"Kendine başka iş ara"
Fakat kabahat Almanlarda değil.
Türklerde değil.
Türkiye'nin dövize ihtiyacı vardı,
Almanya'nın işçiye.
Türkiye bizi Avrupa'ya yolladı,
Evlatlık çocuk
Lüzumsuz insan gibi.
Her şeye rağmen İhtiyacı vardı, …
Dövize, sakinliğe …
Türkiye beni yabancı devlete yolladı
İsmim YABANCI oldu …

Semra Ertan, 1982

In 1982, the twenty-four-year-old poet, activist, and worker Semra Ertan, who was also my aunt, wrote the poem "Mein Name ist Ausländer" (My Name Is Foreigner) in German and Turkish in her notebook.[1] It is one of more than 350 poems she wrote in both languages. Almost thirty-eight years later, my mother and I edited a collection of her poems under the same title.

That same year, on May 26, a few days before her twenty-fifth birthday, Ertan died after setting herself on fire in Hamburg as a protest against racism. She had first called NDR, a northern German news agency, to announce her political protest and explain her motive: "Why these prejudices, I ask myself. The people who are prejudiced don't see us as human beings. I don't know where I belong, I can't live in Turkey or Germany. If I go to Turkey without an education, I will be treated like a second-class citizen. I want foreigners not only to have the right to live like human beings, but also to have the right to be treated like human beings. That's all. I want people to love and accept each other. And I want them to think about my death."[2] Ertan was taking a stand against racism in Germany. During this call, she made her intentions clear by reciting "Mein Name ist Ausländer."

For more than fifteen years, I have been working with and maintaining my aunt's archive, legacy, political work, and poetry to make her voice accessible for present and future generations. It began in 2009 with a box in my parents' cellar in Munich full of Ertan's belongings—photos, notes, poetry, newspapers, official documents, and other personal items. I began to wonder how, outside my family, Semra Ertan could be remembered as a poet, activist, and worker. I found myself

---

1 Semra Ertan, *Mein Name ist Ausländer – Benim Adım Yabancı* (Münster: edition assemblage, 2020), 176–77. Translations are by the author unless noted otherwise.
2 Ertan, 6.

in the role of not only a family member but also a collaborator, mediating between the personal and public perspectives on her legacy—a mediator who talks and cares for a person who is not alive anymore but still speaks to us, a person we can still understand through the knowledge she left us. In my new role, I saw myself responsible for sharing her poetry, her activism, and her knowledge—all of which were invisible to the public for almost forty years—to a broader audience.

Ertan drew from her working-class roots and a feminist and migrant perspective. Born in Mersin, Turkey, in 1957, she was part of the Arabic-speaking Alevi minority. In 1972, at the age of fourteen, she moved to Germany to join her parents, who were employed as *Gastarbeiter* (guest workers) in Kiel. In Germany, she worked as a technical draftswoman and began writing. Shortly before her death, she joined the German Writers' Association to connect with other writers and receive union support—a commitment that reflected the values driving her entire oeuvre. Her artistic practice was inseparable from the political circumstances of her time—a period when migrants were excluded from full participation in society. She reacted to this context in her writing and activism. During her lifetime, most of her poetry remained private and largely unknown. I learned about her biography, personality, and background through the stories shared by my family.

Tell Your Own Stories—Don't Let Others Tell Your Stories—Tell Your Stories by Amplifying Your Messages—Become a Storyteller

After her death, my family—primarily my mother and grandmother—collected Ertan's notes, poems, letters, certificates, photos, and newspaper articles as their own personal archive of remembrance. Along with her marriage license, I found a medical certificate; her poems were stored with a series of German-language exercises. Continuing my research outside of the family archive, I discovered a radio program, a music composition, and a television report that referred to Ertan. In a 1990 broadcast of a Bayerischer Runkfunk radio program that interviewed so-called experts on migration, Ertan's poems were read aloud in German and Turkish. The program, which lasted over an hour, was accompanied by Turkish folk music, imbuing the readings with a sense of melancholy, transporting the listeners far from Germany. At the end of the program, Ertan's name was briefly mentioned as the speaker and poet. She is not listed in the program's credits.

In 1962, the Federal Republic of Germany and Turkey signed an *Anwerbeabkommen* (recruitment agreement) to regulate the subsequent westward flow of migrant labor. That same year, my maternal grandfather, Gani Bilir, began work at an engine factory in Kiel. Ten years later, his wife and my maternal grandmother, Vehbiye Bilir, came to Germany and was employed as a hospital cleaner. They later brought over all six of their children. In 1973, Germany ended the recruitment agreement. My grandparents returned to Mersin in 1988.

During her lifetime, Ertan campaigned for equal rights and against racism, volunteering as an interpreter for dealing with authorities and protesting the far-right NDP (National Democratic Party of Germany) and the affiliated Hamburger Liste für Ausländerstopp (Hamburg's List to Stop Foreigners), which campaigned for parliament in 1982. As a working-class poet, she addressed social injustice through her writing. As a woman, she spoke out against gender inequality. As part of the Arabic-speaking Alevi minority, she experienced social rejection in Germany as well as marginalization and discrimination in Turkey.

The poetry and lessons of Ertan give me valuable tools for reflecting on my own biography as a woman, a German, and an Alevi from Turkey. My quest is not merely to find answers; rather, it is about creating spaces—both personal and public—that encourage remembrance, mourning, education, exchange, and unity. To understand our own biographies, we need to be in constant conversation with others. By sharing our experiences, we become our own storytellers. We can reshape how others perceive us. We can amplify the stories of a diverse community through our collective needs, imaginations, demands, similarities, and differences. It is by sharing our stories that we encourage others to share their own.

In 2013, I made the short film *Semra Ertan*, which features three of her poems: "Unheimlich Glücklich" (Unbelievably Happy), "Mein Name ist Ausländer," and "Begegnung" (Encounter). The film includes a recording of Ertan reciting "Mein Name ist Ausländer" and shows her handwriting, our family archives, and footage from the German television and radio shows that featured her in the late eighties and early nineties. The eight-minute-long work was one of the first films I made while studying at the Academy of Fine Arts Vienna.

In 2015, I completed my master's degree in art education with a thesis exploring ways of remembering Ertan. In Turkish and German, the title of my thesis includes a quote of hers: "Gazetelerde bir şiir karaladım tesadüfen. Güzel, oldu: Poetin, Schriftstellerin, Aktivistin, Arbeiterin. Wie erinnern an Semra Ertan? Eine fragmentarische Annäherung" (I Scribbled a Poem in the Newspapers and It Turned Out Well: Poet, Writer, Activist, Worker. How to Remember Semra Ertan? A Fragmentary Approach).

Tell Your Stories by Disrupting and Changing the Dominant Narrative

While making *Semra Ertan*, I realized I couldn't paint a full picture of a person in one short film, especially someone who is no longer living. I wondered about other approaches to counter the way she was depicted in German media so long ago. If a film became poetry, what could it achieve? Presenting fragments of a life became an important method within my art practice. The film is not a complete biography of Ertan, nor does it survey her overall work. Rather, it is about, and in dialogue with, her poetry and activism.

The film is also a depiction of my research process and the ways others communicate with Ertan—a type of biomythography. The concept—a portmanteau of "biography" and "myth"—was coined by the Black writer Audre Lorde in her book *Zami: A New Spelling of My Name* (1982). The dance-studies scholar Ted Warburton writes: "Biomythography is the weaving together of myth, history and biography in epic narrative form, a style of composition that represents all the ways in which we perceive the world."[3] I am interested in the process of constructing memory and biography together—a personal archive in continuous exchange with others.

In 2018, I founded the Initiative in Gedenken an Semra Ertan (Initiative in Remembrance of Semra Ertan) in Hamburg together with other activists and my mother, Zühal Bilir-Meier. In 2020, my mother and I edited *Mein Name ist Ausländer*, which includes eighty-two of Ertan's poems in German and Turkish. During my research, I discovered three German publications from the 1980s that include Ertan's poetry, each focused on migration and racist debates about

---

3 Quoted in "About Biomythography," BioMyth, accessed November 26, 2024, https://biomyth.wordpress.com/about/.

"foreigners." I find the subordination of her poetry to these themes another way of making her invisible; at the same time, these books are important documents of the era in which they were published.

The first book I came across was *Eine Fremde wie ich: Berichte, Erzählungen, Gedichte von Ausländerinnen* (Strangers like Me: Reports, Stories, Poems by Women Foreigners, 1985), which included "Mein Name ist Ausländer." The editors, Hülya Özkan and Andrea Wörle, write that "of the twenty-three women who contributed to this volume, six are from Turkey, four from other European countries, the others from Europe."[4] The second book I found was *Zu Hause in der Fremde: Ein bundesdeutsches Ausländer-Lesebuch* (At Home in a Foreign Land: A German Book for Foreigners, 1981), edited by Christian Schaffernicht, which includes Ertan's poems "Ich habe gesehen" (I Have Seen) and "Wofür lebe ich" (What Do I Live For).[5] The third book, *Täglich eine Reise von der Türkei nach Deutschland: Texte der zweiten türkischen Generation in der Bundesrepublik* (A Daily Journey from Turkey to Germany: Texts by the Second Turkish Generation in the Federal Republic, 1980), compiled texts and poems by second-generation immigrants. However, in a degrading move, the book only published the contributors' first names, omitting all surnames.[6]

In each of these books, Ertan is made visible as a "Turkish guest worker" and a "foreigner." This categorization creates a racial divide between her and the German population; she is labeled as "other." This perception, or rather representation, also constructs a stereotyped, borderline fetishized image of her. But subjects like Ertan are not self-contained—they cannot only be reduced to an unambiguous category like "guest worker." A person's biography is entangled in a web of diverse narratives—and these must also be recognized as heterogeneous. After fifteen years of working with my family's archive and connecting it with other collective stories, I still wonder how we can make these stories visible. As the education and colonialism scholar Linda Tuhiwai Smith asks: "Whose research is it? Who owns it? Whose interests does it serve? Who will benefit from it? Who has designed its questions and framed its scope? Who will carry it out? Who will write it up? How will its results be disseminated?"[7]

In this essay, I reflect on what I have learned over the last decade, and continue to learn, about remembrance, the experiences of victims of right-wing terrorism in Germany, and the way these experiences are expressed through the survivors' political, cultural, and educational work. As a relative of Ertan, as an activist, art educator, and art practitioner in institutional and political spaces, I will provide an overview of my experiences of the obstacles and achievements of grassroots organizing and activist community work in Germany.

Encountering Initiatives of Survivors in Germany

Racism, anti-Semitism, police violence, and right-wing terrorism have a long, interconnected history in Germany. In the dominant white society we live in, it takes tremendous effort to bring visibility to catalyzers like Semra Ertan and others who were murdered or committed suicide. The

4 Hülya Özkan and Andrea Wörle, eds., *Eine Fremde wie ich: Berichte, Erzählungen, Gedichte von Ausländerinnen* (Munich: Deutscher Taschenbuch, 1985), 81.

5 Christian Schaffernicht, ed., *Zu Hause in der Fremde: Ein bundesdeutsches Ausländer-Lesebuch* (Fischerhude: Atelier im Bauernhaus, 1981), 106.

6 Förderzentrum Jugend Schreibt e. V., ed., *Täglich eine Reise von der Türkei nach Deutschland: Texte der zweiten Generation in der Bundesrepublik* (Fischerhude: Atelier im Bauernhaus, 1980), 102.

7 Linda Tuhiwai Smith, *Decolonizing Methodologies: Research and Indigenous Peoples* (London: Zed Books, 1999), 10

recognition of initiatives led by survivors and family members who are speaking up and making demands is growing although not yet self-evident—the work is mainly carried out by those who have been directly affected and are fighting to be heard and remembered. In this section, I name survivors and victims of right-wing terrorism in Germany to acknowledge their struggles, activism, memories, and voices.

İbrahim Arslan

"Victims and survivors are the main witnesses to what happened—we are not extras."
İbrahim Arslan, 2016[8]

İbrahim Arslan survived a racially motivated arson attack in Mölln, near Hamburg, on November 23, 1992. He has since become an activist, educator, and leading public figure in anti-racist resistance to right-wing terrorism. Arslan emphasizes that the voices of key witnesses to racist and anti-Semitic violence—namely, the survivors—should not be ignored. He calls for a self-determined approach to commemoration, empowering survivors to reclaim their experiences by telling their own stories. Three of his family members, Ayşe Yılmaz and Yeliz and Bahide Arslan, were murdered in the 1992 attack.

I met Arslan in 2016 in Cologne, at a conference on the National Socialist Underground, a right-wing terrorist group. He encouraged me to pursue a self-determined remembrance of Ertan as a way to gain agency and a voice against the silencing and erasure that usually occurs in media reports and state-led commemorations. We have since participated in public panels, engaged with schools and universities, and conducted workshops on combatting anti-Semitism, anti-Muslim racism, police violence, and right-wing terror. I am grateful to have him as a long-term collaborator and friend. He motivated me and many others in Germany to raise our voices and gain confidence in our demands for a dignified remembrance of those we have lost.

Arslan recognizes that each individual desires to share their own experiences with their communities. Moreover, he emphasizes that survivors can be role models for those encountering racism. Throughout the years, I have seen how Arslan encourages those who have not been directly discriminated against to listen and empathize with those who have experienced discrimination. For instance, in 2022, to commemorate the thirtieth anniversary of the racist attacks in Mölln, the Arslan and Yılmaz families wrote:

To fight for remembrance—of those who are missing, of what happened, of what has been forgotten, of what has been silenced, of the causes and the consequences, of what came before and what followed. These demands remain as relevant as ever. [...] Solidarity means aligning ourselves with the survivors and those affected by this violence. There are many experiences and stories. Many wounds. Many desires and needs. Many perspectives. These must be heard, brought out of isolation, connected, amplified, brought to the forefront. In this way, we challenge the politics of remembrance—as a collective in diversity.[9]

8 "Opfer und Überlebende sind die Hauptzeugen des Geschehenen, wir sind keine Statisten," NSU Watch, November 19, 2016, https://www.nsu-watch .info/2016/11/opfer-und-ueberlebende-sind-die-hauptzeugen-des-geschehenen -wir-sind-keine-statisten/.

9 "30. Jahrestag des Gedenkens an die rassistischen Brandanschläge von Mölln," Gedenken Mölln 1992, November 7, 2022, https://gedenkenmoelln1992 .wordpress.com/2022/11/07/30-jahrestag-des-gedenkens-an-die-rassistischen -brandanschlage-von-molln/.

Since 2013, the city of Mölln has organized an annual commemoration of the 1992 attack, but without consulting the families. İbrahim Arslan, along with the initiative Freundeskreis im Gedenken an die rassistischen Brandanschläge in Mölln 1992 (Circle of Friends in Memory of the Racist Arson Attacks in Mölln in 1992), has pointed out that the city doesn't acknowledge their wishes. Arslan and the initiative organize their own commemoration, the Möllner Rede im Exil (Mölln Speech in Exile), which takes place in a different city each year. As Arslan explained in 2013: "I believe good speeches can also be given in exile. That's why we choose an appropriate venue in other cities, because Mölln is everywhere."[10]

The empowering aspect of the Möllner Rede lies in the fact that the Arslan and Yılmaz families decide on the form of the commemoration. Every year, they invite a special guest to give the keynote speech to share their personal story. In 2017, for example, they invited the Holocaust survivor and anti-fascist activist Esther Bejarano. "It's the survivors who have to fight for their own remembrance," Arslan said in 2013. "Remembrance cannot be shaped without taking into account the interests of the survivors. We are the main witnesses of what happened. Even twenty-one years after the racist arson attack in Mölln, we must fight to reclaim memory. Reclaim and remember. Now more than ever."[11]

Gamze Kubaşık

"We didn't want anything impossible. We wanted you to listen to us seriously, to us, who suspected before anyone else that Nazis were behind these murders. We are part of this country and we will continue to live here. I am fighting for full disclosure and justice, for my father, but also for all other families."

Gamze Kubaşık, 2006 [12]

Gamze Kubaşık is the daughter of Mehmet Kubaşık, who was murdered in 2006 by the National Socialist Underground (NSU). From 1993 to 2011, the NSU killed more than ten people, primarily men of color who ran local businesses, and carried out several bomb attacks and bank robberies. Their crimes only entered the public consciousness in 2011, after the group claimed responsibility for the attacks in a letter. Until that point, the media, law enforcement, public authorities, and a large part of German white society accused the victims' families of being the perpetrators, excluding racism as the motive. The families of nine victims—Mehmet Kubaşık, Enver Şimşek, Abdurrahim Özüdoğru, Süleyman Taşköprü, Habil Kılıç, Mehmet Turgut, İsmail Yaşar, Theodoros Boulgarides, and Halit Yozgat—had to draw attention to the role of right-wing terror in these murders on their own initiative. In 2006, five years before the self-disclosure of the NSU, the families organized a demonstration in Kassel

10 "Pressemitteilung: 21. Jahrestag der rassistischen Brandanschläge von Mölln," Gedenken Mölln 1992, October 21, 2013, https://gedenkenmoelln1992 .wordpress.com/2013/10/20/pressemitteilung-21-jahrestag-der-rassistischen -brandanschlage-von-molln-gedenken-kann-nicht-an-den-interessen-der -uberlebenden-vorbei-gestaltet-werden/.

11 "Pressemitteilung."

12 Initiative Bündnis Tag der Solidarität, accessed on May 20, 2024, https:// tagdersolidaritaet.wordpress.com/.

with the name "Kein 10. Opfer" (No Tenth Victim). (In 2011, the NSU committed their tenth murder, that of the police-woman Michèle Kiesewetter.) The demonstration was organized together with the Kurdish-Alevi community in Dortmund, to which the Kubaşık family belongs. Anti-Kurdish and anti-Alevi racism is prevalent both in Turkey and within Turkish communities in Germany and Austria.

Since the early 2010s, Gamze Kubaşık has been involved in numerous educational projects, visiting schools to teach students about victims' experiences of right-wing terror, including the case of her father's murder by the NSU. She founded the initiative Bündnis Tag der Solidarität (Day of Solidarity Alliance) and fights alongside other family members of NSU victims for dignified remembrance. For Kubaşık, remembrance means listening, remembrance means recognizing, remembrance means educating, remembrance means knowing, remembrance means joining forces, remembrance means encouraging, remembrance means changing. Remembrance means that German authorities must fully support the families' demands for justice and recognize the structural and institutional racism that allowed these murders to happen.

According to Kubaşık, Germany does not investigate right-wing violence or acknowledge it as part of its history. The case of the NSU cannot be closed until there is a full investigation into the web of their supporters and accomplices. In 2020, together with the Bündnis Tag der Solidarität, Kubaşık and Ali Şirin, a social scientist and social-justice and anti-racism educator, self-published the booklet *Trauer, Wut und Widerstand: Antirassistische Initiativen und Gedenkpolitik* (Grief, Anger, and Resistance: Antiracist Initiatives and Commemorative Politics).[13] The publication includes initiatives in Germany like İbrahim Arslan's and those of victims of police violence. It recounts cases of the death of the Kurdish refugee Amed Ahmad in 2018 during his wrongful imprisonment and the 1991 pogroms in Hoyerswerda, where residences of contract workers and refugees were attacked by more than five hundred right-wing fascists. The police offered no protection, and the residents were forced out of their apartments.[14] The booklet also highlights the resilience of those impacted by this violence, amplifying their voices and the demands of their families.

On the website of Bündnis Tag der Solidarität, Kubaşık writes: "With our educational work in schools, we ourselves are helping to ensure that our history is perceived as part of the history of this country. […] I am disappointed that we still have to fight, but I am also grateful that we are not fighting this battle alone. The solidarity of the other people affected gives us strength." In 2023, to build solidarity among those affected by racist and anti-Semitic violence, Kubaşık and Şirin invited me and my mother to give a reading of Ertan's poems at the Literaturhaus Dortmund. Here, too, I discovered the importance of Ertan's poetry for the families of the victims of the NSU and for everyone affected by ongoing right-wing terror.

13 Bündnis Tag der Solidarität, *Trauer, Wut und Widerstand: Antirassistische Initiativen und Gedenkpolitik*, 2020, https://tagdersolidaritaet.wordpress.com /trauer-wut-und-widerstand/.

14 Initiative "Pogrom 1991," last updated September 11, 2017, https:// pogrom91.tumblr.com/. See also the online documentation about the attacks, accessed May 20, 2024, https://www.hoyerswerda-1991.de/.

Talya Feldman and İsmet Tekin

"Listening is in itself a political act."
Talya Feldman, 2021[15]

"It's a wound that doesn't heal. The pain is there every day—for four years. Another person cannot know and say what those of us who are affected and bereaved need. Self-determination is important!"
İsmet Tekin, 2023[16]

Talya Feldman is an artist, activist, and survivor of the anti-Semitic, racist, and misogynistic attack in Halle on October 9, 2019, the Jewish holiday of Yom Kippur. The perpetrator tried to force his way into a synagogue, but the security door prevented his entry. He went on a rampage, shooting and killing Jana Lange on the street and Kevin Schwarze in a Turkish restaurant, while injuring others. In 2020, during the terrorist's trial, Max Privorozki, the head of the local Jewish community in Halle, said: "There have been two attacks on the two synagogues of the Jewish community. Each occurred on the 9th day of an autumn month. The first was in November 1938, during the November Pogrom [often called Kristallnacht in English]. The second was in October 2019, on the Jewish holiday of Yom Kippur. We are here today because of both of them."[17]

İsmet Tekin, the owner of the restaurant, was shot on the street during the attack and survived, later becoming an activist. However, he was not recognized as an official victim. He made a statement in the courthouse about the disappointing verdict, which refused to acknowledge racism as a motive or him as a victim. In an interview, he said, "I want to make

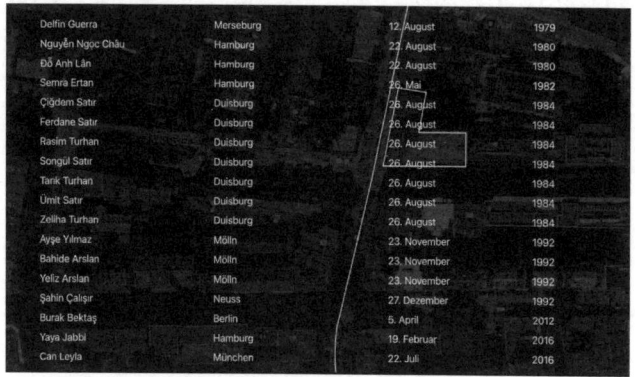

Fig. 45 Talya Feldman, *WIR SIND HIER*, 2024. Screenshot.

15 Quoted in Jennifer Schumacher, "Dortmund: Opfer rechtsextremer Gewalt gestalten Ausstellung," *WAZ*, June 20, 2024, https://www.waz.de/kultur /article406617223/dortmund-opfer-rechtsextremer-gewalt-gestalten-ausstellung .html.

16 Quoted in Ali Şirin, *Erinnern heißt Kämpfen: Kein Schlussstrich unter unseren Stimmen* (Münster: UNRAST, 2024), 224.

17 "Listen to the Survivors! Closing Statements of Survivors at the Halle Trial," NSU Watch, December 18, 2020, https://www.nsu-watch.info/2020/12 /listen-to-the-survivors-closing-statements-of-survivors-at-the-halle-trial/. Brackets in original quotation.

use of my right to be part of the investigation."[18] Finding strength and courage, sharing pain and desires, forming demands and exchanging experiences is necessary for survivors and people affected by right-wing terror.

In 2020, Feldman asked me to participate in her sound installation *The Violence We Have Witnessed Carries a Weight on Our Hearts* (2021), which investigates right-wing terror in Germany from 1979 to the present through voice recordings of survivors, victims' families, and grassroots initiatives. I contributed audio of Ertan's poetry and recordings of me and other family members speaking about our own activism and solidarity-building efforts. In 2021, Feldman received the DAGESH Art Prize from the Jewish Museum in Berlin and DAGESH: Jewish Art in Context for this project.

Feldman's *WIR SIND HIER* (We Are Here, 2022–ongoing) is a digital cartography project made in close collaboration with initiatives and individuals combating racism and anti-Semitism across Germany.[19] Like her sound installation, it demonstrates how survivors possess the language and tools to reclaim their own stories, free from stereotypes and mainstream media narratives. *WIR SIND HIER* exists as a digital space for individual and collective mourning and resistance. I also see it as an educational tool that emphasizes radical listening. During a recent phone call, Feldman and I discussed how creating art is a way to transform individual trauma into collective trauma—a powerful force for enacting real change. We also talked about how remembering the lives of the victims means keeping them alive. *WIR SIND HIER* asks users to imagine an alternative reality and future by remembering the victims through their families and bringing back their spirit and identities.

Feldman invited me and my mother to participate in *WIR SIND HIER*. In our contribution, you can read and hear a letter written by my mother to Ertan as well as two of my aunt's poems and our initiative's demands.[20] These kinds of collaborations, spaces, conversations, and projects are crucial for individuals to share their remembrances, knowledge, and activism with a broader audience, and to create and imagine spaces for grieving and hope. Feldman's digital maps and videos of city spaces are accompanied by audio recordings, songs, letters, and poems by the anguished families. Like the work of İbrahim Arslan, Feldman centers the families' voices, as they are the prime witnesses to what happened. Nobody should speak for us: we speak for ourselves.

Abu Jabbi

"I, Abu Jabbi, speaking as a brother. I would like to thank everyone for your effort and support. Sometimes I saw the efforts coming from everyone or every branch is it makes me so strong and make me believe that I am not alone. This type of effort is not something common in humans. […] I hope that this is the last incident we witness."

Abu Jabbi, 2019[21]

18 Rachel Spicker, "'Ich möchte mein Recht wahrnehmen, Teil der Aufklärung zu sein,'" *Belltower News*, September 14, 2020, https://www.belltower.news/halle-prozess-ich-moechte-mein-recht-wahrnehmen-teil-der-aufklaerung-zu-sein-104161/.

19 *WIR SIND HIER*, accessed May 20, 2024, https://wir-sind-hier.digital/en/memorials.

20 "Semra Ertan, Hamburg, May 26, 1982," *WIR SIND HIER*, accessed May 20, 2024, https://wir-sind-hier.digital/en/memorial/semra-ertan-en.

21 Quoted in "Yaya Jabbi, Hamburg, February 19, 2016," *WIR SIND HIER*, accessed November 26, 2024, https://wir-sind-hier.digital/en/memorial/yaya-jabbi-en.

On February 19, 2016, Yaya Jabbi was murdered in police custody in Hamburg. After being arrested for possessing a small amount of cannabis—part of a racist policy known as the "Hamburg Task Force on the War on Drugs"—he was taken to a juvenile detention center, where he died four days later under suspicious circumstances. His older brother Abu Jabbi and the initiative Remember Yaya call for a thorough investigation into his death and encourage active remembrance and public recognition of his violent passing. They also call for an immediate end to the racist police force that imprisoned Yaya.[22]

Police violence and the racial profiling of Black people in Germany is often excluded from conversations about right-wing terrorism. Many politicians refuse to acknowledge the unchecked racism within law enforcement because it is considered a tool to maintain order. The official state narrative frames right-wing terrorism as acts carried out solely by individuals, often mislabeled as "lone wolf" attacks.

On February 18, 2018, the initiative and his family memorialized Yaya by renaming a roundabout in St. Pauli, the leftist Hamburg neighborhood where Ertan carried out her protest. Nevertheless, this renaming is still not officially recognized by the city.

Abu's efforts on behalf of his brother inspired me to establish an initiative for my aunt. I owe a lot to him and the initiative, and continue to stand in deep solidarity with them. Abu says about his brother:

Many people in our family are proud of him about his hard work and honestly lovely, respect, kindness, and always smiling. Because he always wanted to help the family and the neighbours too. This is why the sad of his death is not only about the family but the neighbours too. They really liked him so much. And that's all because of his love and caring. He was someone very obedient to the people and the family. When my parents talked to him, he listened to them. When my brother talked to him, the same. And when I talked to him too. We were in a good relationship with him. We were in a good relationship with him until the end of his life. He knew that and we knew that too.[23]

Remember Yaya strives to keep the collective memory of Yaya alive through film and art. In 2023, the initiative released the short film *The Life of Yaya Jabbi*, writing: "The sudden death of Yaya as a result of the state's 'fight against alleged drug dealers' shocked many people in St. Pauli, including relatives, friends, and neighbours. But who was Yaya Jabbi as a person, beyond the crimes he was accused of? Where did he grow up, and what stages in his all too short life were important for his friends and family? The Initiative In Remembrance Of Yaya Jabbi together with his relatives has collected photos, which were turned into a motion graphic by graphic artist Whitney Bursch and filmmaker Timo Selengia."[24]

Racist Right-Wing Attack at the Olympia Shopping Center in Munich, 2016

"This is the story of Munich. But not only. This is also the history of the Federal Republic of Germany."
Hasan Leyla, 2023[25]

---

22 See the initial website of the initiative Remember Yaya Jabbi, accessed November 26, 2024, https://rememberjajadiabi.blackblogs.org/about-jaja-diabi/.
23 "Yaya Jabbi, Hamburg, February 19, 2016."
24 *The Life of Yaya Jabbi*, 2023, 11 min., 11 sec., November 26, 2024, https://www.rememberyaya.org/the-life-of-yaya-jabbi.
25 München erinnern! OEZ-Anschlag 22.07.2016, accessed November 26, 2024, https://muenchen-erinnern.de/info/.

On July 22, 2016, a right-wing extremist murdered nine teenagers—Armela Segashi, Can Leyla, Dijamant Zabërgja, Guiliano Kollmann, Hüseyin Dayıcık, Roberto Rafael, Sabine S., Selçuk Kılıç, and Sevda Dağ—at the Olympia Shopping Center (OEZ) in Munich. Today, the families are still fighting for it to be officially recognized as an act of right-wing terrorism. The police, politicians, and German state labeled it an "isolated" incident to distance it from racist motivations. At a memorial on June 22, 2022, Sibel Leyla, the mother of one of the victims, read the following letter to the public:

My dear son Can,
My life has been without you for six years. I miss you, I'm looking for you—but everywhere I look all I see is this dark emptiness. […] In these 6 years, I have learned that there is no justice and no set of values. That pains me. People who commit crimes against humanity are protected. […] The injustice in this country is shown by the fact that we have to fight for justice ourselves. And if we don't fight for it and leave it in the hands of the police and politicians, I fear that there will always be immeasurable suffering. I no longer have any trust in the judiciary and state authority. The German justice system has failed in the face of right-wing terrorist attacks. The laws have been trampled underfoot and then completely shelved. I would rather trust those people who do not close their eyes and show solidarity through their conscience and sense of fairness. People who stand up for fair and humane coexistence in society and who will not accept injustice or remain silent.[26]

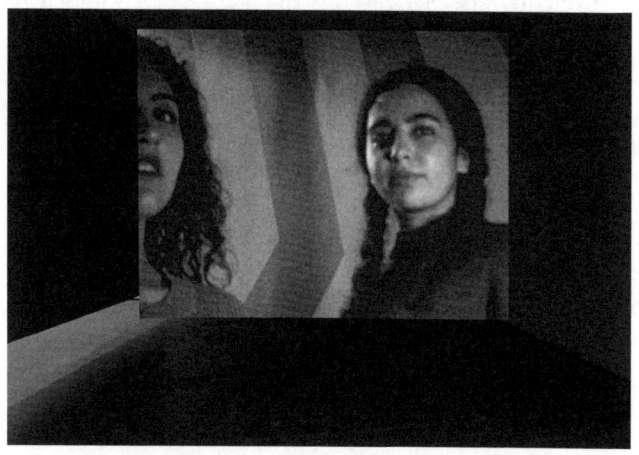

Fig. 46 Cana Bilir-Meier, *This Makes Me Want to Predict the Past*, installation view, Kunstverein Hamburg, 2019

26 Sibel Leyla, "'Wir werden nicht schweigen': Rede von Sibel Leyla zum Jahrestag des Anschlags am OEZ München," Heimatkunde: Migrationspolitisches Portal, Heinrich Böll Stiftung, July 22, 2022, https://heimatkunde.boell.de /de/2022/07/22/wir-werden-nicht-schweigen-rede-sibel-leyla-jahrestag-oez -muenchen.

On their website, the initiative München erinnern! (Remember Munich!) writes:

> Only after more than three years, in October 2019, was the right-wing, racist and anti-Roma and anti-Sinti racist attack at the OEZ recognized by the state—although and only because those affected and relatives fought for it from the outset. Despite this, the attack is barely present in the public memory, even in Munich. The disregard for the perceptions and needs of the survivors and relatives not only by the authorities, but also by large sections of society, began immediately after the attack. This was reflected not only in the police's hasty categorization of the attack as an 'assault,' but also in the way those affected were treated by the police and authorities in their shock and grief.[27]

In 2019, I made a short film titled *This Makes Me Want to Predict the Past*. The camera follows two teenagers as they explore the OEZ while discussing their dreams and fears. The film includes scenes from Erman Okay's *Düşler Ülkesi* (Land of Dreams), a play for children and youths that premiered in Munich in 1982, which are reenacted by the two protagonists. When the play was first put on, amateur actors, some with a migrant background, played everyday scenes from the life of *Gastarbeiter*, addressing these characters' unfulfilled longings, broken promises, prejudices, and misunderstandings. It was a pioneering project that brought together young people with diverse backgrounds to forge mutual understanding. The premiere of the play was overshadowed by a bomb threat at the theater, but it proceeded as planned. I learned about the play because my mother, a youth and children's behavioral therapist and social pedagogue, acted in it in 1982. The title of my film—a paradoxical statement about wanting to predict the past—refers to the intersectional experience of racism that young people in the 1980s share with the youth of today.

Initiative Semra Ertan

On April 7, 1982, Ertan wrote a letter to a publisher with a book proposal for a collection of her poetry. In her letter, she mentions that although some of her poems had been published, she did not retain the rights to them nor did she receive adequate payment, which is why she enrolled in the German Writers' Association. Her letter reads as follows:

Dear Kiper Bingöl,
I received your letter yesterday. I was very pleased with the offer you made me. I was born on 26.5.57 in Mersin, Turkey, and completed primary and secondary school there. In 1971, I came to Germany to join my family. I wanted to go to grammar school here and get an academic degree. I say "wanted" because (without making it a reproach) I wasn't allowed to. I went to a vocational school and was dismissed. I went to school in Heidelberg—as a draftswoman—and they sent me back to Kiel in the very first week. It was the same with hairdressing. This time I accepted several jobs and was dismissed again. Newspapers (the Turkish ones always had bad news... so I was angry with the people) I wrote a poem on the side. After that I only wrote. I've been writing since I was 15 and I still do today. At first, I sent my poems and writings to Hikmet Bil's section in [the newspaper] *Hürriyet*. When

27 "Info," München erinnern! OEZ-Anschlag 22.07.2016, accessed November 26, 2024, https://muenchen-erinnern.de/info/.

they were actually published, I got more courage. So I wrote to the publisher Fischerhude-Atelier in Bauernhaus: 1) *Täglich eine Reise von der Türkei nach Deutschland* [A Daily Journey from Turkey to Germany] 2) *Zuhause in der Fremde* [At Home in a Foreign Country] claiming the copyrights. As a result, my friend Robert Meerstein, who is a well-known writer, offered me the opportunity to become a member of the Writers' Association, through which you also found my name. I would like to send you a few poems, which I hope you will like. Your second offer, that you will help me publish my poems as a book, is a great thing. I have up to 350 poems and some political satires that deal with prejudice. I am waiting for your feedback. Yours sincerely,
Semra Ertan[28]

Almost a month after writing this letter and joining the Writers' Association, Ertan died in Hamburg. The letter got lost in the boxes of her personal affairs. Although I couldn't find an answer from the publisher, this letter inspired us to find a publishing house to fulfill her dreams of becoming a published author.

In 2018, my mother and I, along with other activists, initiatives, survivors, and grassroots movements in Hamburg, founded the initiative to remember Semra Ertan. Our first memorial took place in Hamburg in 2019. Every year around May 26, the anniversary of her death, we organize a memorial at the site where she died in St. Pauli. Since then, we have been calling for a memorial plaque to be installed and a square to be named after her. The politicians in the district have not accepted our demands. This refusal comes mainly from the conservative CDU and the libertarian-leaning FDP

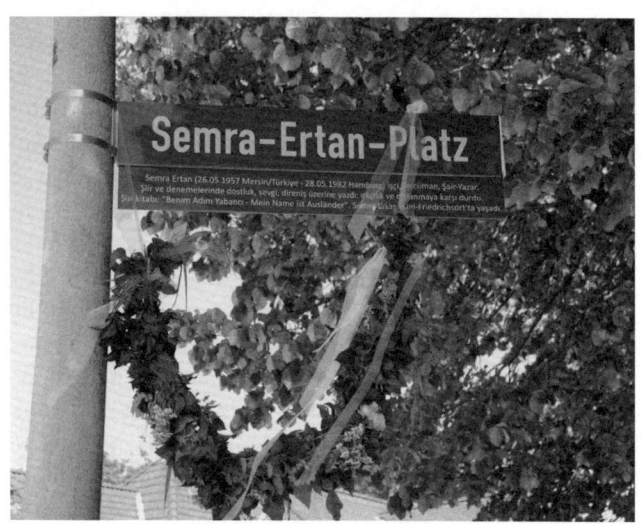

Fig. 47   Semra-Ertan-Platz in Kiel, 2024

28 Ertan, *Mein Name ist Ausländer*, 212–14.

parties, and in February 2024, the liberal SDP claimed in a city-council meeting that a street named after Ertan would "encourage or trigger" people to kill themselves. There are no studies proving the causality implied in this justification.

Publishing Semra Ertan's Book of Poetry

In 2018, a writer friend connected me and my mother to a well-known publishing house in Germany to discuss releasing a book of Ertan's poetry. After a few meetings, the editor declined the project, saying that they could not publish in Turkish—even though the manuscript was bilingual and Ertan composed all her poems about her life in Germany in German, and the publishing house had already published a poetry book in French, German, and English. In a lengthy email, the editor wrote that they focus on "high-culture" literature and claimed that Ertan was "too young," her poems "too wild," "too beautiful." In his view, they were not "reflective enough." Instead, he proposed collaborating on a book on "migrant literature" that would present Ertan as an example. I felt this proposal obscured the idea of connecting collective and individual stories.

After years searching for the right publishing house, and after numerous rejections, we came across the collectively run edition assemblage. On their website, they write: "edition assemblage is a radical, leftist, political and journalistic network. The unifying factor is the desire to create new spaces in order to realize joint projects in new constellations."[29]

In 2020, they published *Mein Name ist Ausländer*. As the book's editors, my mother and I wrote an introduction, and we included photos, Ertan's handwritten poems, and her German Writers' Association membership card. The poem that opens the book, "Wir Warten – Biz Bekliyoruz" (We Are Waiting), Ertan wrote when she was only nineteen. The poems are ordered chronologically. In the last poem, from 1982, she says: "Ich will leben / Wie ich es mir wünschen / Schmerzlos ohne Sorgen – Yasamak Istiyourm / Gönlünce / Kedersiz, Sorunsuz" (I want to live / As I dreamed / Without pain and sorrow).

In June 2023, in the Friedrichsort district of Kiel, where my grandparents lived with Ertan and her siblings, a square received the official designation of Semra-Ertan-Platz. We are still fighting for this in Hamburg, despite the continued refusal of the district authorities.[30]

Tell Your Stories Together with Others and Listen to Other Stories That Are Not Your Own

So how can we tell our own stories, and how can we listen to the stories of others? What does solidarity mean? These survivors of right-wing terrorism and anti-Semitic and racist violence are already telling their own stories, memorializing what is not recounted by dominant German society and fighting for their stories not to be forgotten. They show solidarity and empathy for others by participating in other commemorations and inviting others to theirs. Centering the perspectives of survivors also means understanding that resistance has always been present. Survivors telling their own stories motivates others to share their stories as well.

In the essay "Suspending Damage: A Letter to Communities" (2009), Eve Tuck, a scholar in Indigenous studies and educational research, reconsiders the practices within

29 "Collective," edition assemblage, accessed May 20, 2024, https://www.edition-assemblage.de/en/collective/.
30 Alexander Diehl, "Rückschlag für Gedenk-Initiative," *taz*, March 5, 2024, https://taz.de/Kein-Semra-Ertan-Platz-in-Hamburg/!5993617/.

community work that focus on the long-term impact of "damage-centered" research—namely, "research that intends to document people's pain and brokenness to hold those in power accountable for their oppression." She suggests calling for wishes of change and hope, which she names "desire-focused" research, and asks communities what they need rather than what their pain is. Although she emphasizes that it is not simply one type of research against the other, she opens up space to reflect on practices of transformative justice and collaborations within research. Tuck suggests three steps: first, reenvision our theories of change; second, establish community ethics guidelines for research; and third, create mutually beneficial roles for community and academic researchers.[31]

In my master's thesis, I wrote about the work of artists who engage with biographies of the marginalized. John Akomfrah's film *The Unfinished Conversation* (2012) about the cultural theorist Stuart Hall (1932–2014) helped me understand multi-perspective approaches and how we can recognize and respect differences within a space of empathy. Instead of trying to tell a complete story about someone, we should view the process as an "unfinished conversation," because identity is not defined or static but rather a constant, fluid becoming. The curator Julia Grosse writes, "*The Unfinished Conversation* deals with identity not as an unambiguous creature or being but instead as a 'becoming' that is in constant flux, a product of history, memories and the intersection of public and private perception."[32]

Work that emphasizes the perspective of those impacted by right-wing violence is care work, meaning that these people take the initiative to speak for themselves. Still, it's work that has to be done in a constant process of exchange, reflection, learning, and unlearning. This was made possible through the conversations with others who have motivated me throughout the years to continue remembering. To remember in a sustainable, long-lasting way must happen as an act of solidarity, empathy, and exchange. If we as individuals listen to the stories of others, we can truly recognize ourselves. The individual experiences pain, desires, and wishes in relation to others.

Trauma caused by racist, anti-Semitic, and right-wing terror has not been properly acknowledged; there are taboos around these topics in our society. We must protest all forms of group-related discrimination. Right-wing violence is misogynistic, anti-feminist, anti-queer, anti-trans, and anti-disabled. Ertan was on her own when she decided to protest racism with her death. We should work toward a society of solidarity. We are many who, through remembrance, prevent victims from being forgotten and deprived of their voices. In working with Ertan's legacy, I have often wondered how many archives of other thinkers, artists, feminists, workers, and poets have been lost because they fell out of sight or were denied a platform. How can we witness and honor their stories?

In her essay "Playfulness, 'World'-Travelling, and Loving Perception" (1989), the sociologist and philosopher María Lugones recommends that we learn to love each other by traveling to each other's worlds. The distinction of these worlds is based on the dominant white-supremacist patriarchal society (the majority) or nondominant constructions (the minority). One can travel among these worlds and inhabit more than one at the same time. Lugones views world-traveling as a practice for understanding how others perceive us and themselves in

31 Eve Tuck, "Suspending Damage: A Letter to Communities," *Harvard Educational Review* 79, no. 3 (2009): 423–24, https://doi.org/10.17763/haer.79.3.n0016675661t3n15.

32 Julia Grosse, *John Akomfrah: A Space of Empathy* (Berlin: Archive Books, 2023), 13.

their own worlds, with the goal of learning to care for them through their experiences. She writes: "We are fully dependent on each other for the possibility of being understood and without this understanding we are not intelligible, we do not make sense, we are not solid, visible, integrated; we are lacking. So travelling to each other's 'worlds' would enable us to be through loving each other."[33] The initiatives and the people named and portrayed in this essay allow us to travel to their world. We can acknowledge the story of others by the act of listening, which, as Feldman says, is a political act.

Same Sorrows	Aynı Dertler
I do earn money, how much is obvious	Kazanıyorum, ne kadar olduğu belli
Would I want to live, I have to live	Yaşamak istesem ki mecburum yaşamalıyım
It does not work…	Olmuyor…
Would I want to die, not enough money for the grave	Ölmek istesem ki mezar parası yetmez
It does not work…	Olmuyor…
My earnings obvious, even if I would want to	Kazancım belli, istesem de
I can neither live nor die	Ne yaşayabilir ne de ölebilirim

Much work, hard work, dirty work	Çok iş, ağır iş, pis iş
Little money, little money, little money…	Az para, az para, az para…
Is that a livelihood?	Geçim derdi mi?
For two, if then offspring comes	İki kişi ile bir de meyvesi gelirse
How to live?	Nasıl yaşanabilir?
Life is hard, life is hard.	Yaşamak zor, yaşamak zor.

Ertan wrote this poem in 1977. Increasingly visible in the collective memory, her legacy today is seen as an important part of the post-migrant heritage in Germany. In the words of Lugones, many people have traveled to her world and shared her experiences. This became possible through publishing her book in 2020 and naming a square in Kiel after her in 2023. The artist, rapper, scholar, and performer Reyhan Şahin (aka Lady Bitch Ray), a member of Initiative in Gedenken an Semra Ertan, said in 2024: "Today I commemorate Semra Ertan, poet, writer and anti-fascist, because her work has inspired and continues to inspire so many people—including me."[34] At the Schauspiel Dortmund, the theater director Bassam Ghazi and the choreographer Yeliz Pazar created *Working Class* (2022), a play based on Ertan's life

---

33 María Lugones, "Playfulness, 'World'-Travelling, and Loving Perception," *Hypatia* 2, no. 2 (Summer 1987): 8.

34 @semra_ertan_initative, "Warum ihr Semra Ertan kennen solltet," eighth slide in a series, August 5, 2024, https://www.instagram.com/p/C-R_5fIs6X6/?igsh=dGRjZGZ4NXg2ZHJp&img_index=8.

that links material working conditions, family histories, classism, racism, resistance, and solidarity. The director Saliha Shagasi included "Mein Name ist Ausländer" in *Drahtseilakt / Cambaz Gösterisi* (2024) at the Schauspiel Köln, a play that tells the story of strikes in North Rhine-Westphalia in the 1970s initiated by migrant workers rebelling against the racist and sexist wage system and exploitative working conditions. The artist Adi Liraz put Ertan's poem in trialogue with poetry by May Ayim and Rose Ausländer in *All Memories Flow into the Sea (And Back out Again)* (2021) to claim visibility for those who have fallen victim to ongoing right-wing terror in Germany.[35] Writers like Fatma Aydemir, Daniel Arkadij Gerzenberg, and Rabia Doğan have put Ertan's literary work in the canon of post-migrant German literature, and have dedicated poems, films, and books to her. Scholars and students are writing theses and essays on her poems and work—for example, Deborah Fallis's master's thesis, which connects poems by Black, Jewish, and post-migrant artists within the German context.[36] In 2023, the Haus der Kulturen der Welt in Berlin named a garden after Ertan, where a memorial plaque was also installed. In May 2024, the musician Berivan Kaya, based in Cologne, performed a song of Ertan's poem "Gidiyorum" in Hamburg. In April 2024, the artists, scholars, and curators Anguezomo Mba Bikoro and Fetewei Tarekegn invited me to participate in the exhibition "We Who Move the World Forward: Voices of Resistance in Germany's Migration Histories" at Kunsthaus ACUD in Berlin, and to speak on a panel about Ertan titled "Überdrüssig / My Name Is Foreigner: On Ancestral Healing." The description on the ACUD website reads: "The lives of the four protagonists Fasia Jansen, Semra Ertan, May Ayim and Sista Mimi, with their struggles within German integration and migration law and the political landscapes of West and East Germany from the post-war period to the present, are traced together with lesser-known perspectives from three waves of German migration history."[37] The panel, which also included the human-rights activist Napuli Langa and the artist Muhammad Salah, addressed "the states of displacements, mental health, and modes of de-traumatisation through models of care and solidarity in the words of Semra Ertan."[38] In 2024, Gürsoy Dogtas curated "Annem işçi / Who Sews the Red Flags?" at the Marta Herford Museum, a group exhibition based on Ertan's poem "Meine Mutter ist eine Arbeiterin – Annem işçi" (My Mother Is a Worker). The description on the venue's website reads: "This group exhibition takes up the interrelationships of artists and the guest worker movement in Germany of the 1970s. It unites the perspectives of migrants with efforts of white, German artists to show solidarity as well as personal, poetic, activist, and documentary points of departure."[39]

In 2009, when I started exploring the archive and working on my aunt's legacy, it was shortly after the death of my youngest brother, Cihan, with whom I had a very close relationship. His passing led me to ask myself what makes life valuable and peaceful. Together we can say: "Aunt Semra, I

35 Adi Liraz, "Alle Erinnerungen fließen ins Meer (und wieder Raus) / All Memories Flow into the Sea (And Back out Again)," accessed May 20, 2024, http:// adi-liraz.squarespace.com/alle-erinnerungen-flieen-ins-meer-und-wieder-raus.

36 Deborah Fallis, "Wehrhafte Lyrik: Desintegration in den Gedichten zeitgenössischer postmigrantischer und jüdischer Autorinnen" (MA thesis, Neuere Deutsche Literaturwissenschaft, Leibniz Universität, Hannover, 2021).

37 "We Who Move the World Forward: Voices of Resistance in Germany's Migration Histories," ACUD MACHT NEU, accessed November 26, 2024, https://acudmachtneu.de/projekte/we-who-move-the-world-forward-voices-of -resistance-in-germanys-migration-history/.

38 "Überdrüssig / My Name Is Foreigner: On Ancestral Healing | We Who Move the World Forward," Refuge, May 21, 2024, https://refugeworldwide .com/radio/ueberdruessig-my-name-is-foreigner-on-ancestral-healing-we-who -move-the.

39 "Annem işçi / Who Sews the Red Flags?," Marta Herford, accessed November 26, 2024, https://marta-herford.de/en/ausstellungen/annem-isci/.

imagine how you shine, how you smile when you see how your poems and your life have been brought back. So many people carry your name, your poems in their hearts, on their tongues, and into the world. Over forty years after your death, you still radiate so much love and vitality, but also sadness. With your poems and your voice, you asked many questions. I imagine how you wondered: Who makes somebody a poet? Who gives the right to write, who decides? What does it take to write? What is our desire in life? Semra Teyze, we carry on your name, your poems, your messages, your sadness, your wisdom, your thoughtfulness, your humor, your courage, your utopia, your resistance, your longing." Today I can say: we have created a bond of strength, love, courage, and understanding that will one day seem stronger than any hatred. I will always believe in that.

According to my grandfather, Ertan's favorite song was "Zeytin gözlüm" (My Olive-Eyed One), a famous Turkish love song of unknown authorship that has been recorded and reinterpreted many times.

Zeytin gözlüm

Zeytin gözlüm sana meylim nedendir?
Bu sevmenin kabahati kimdedir?
Gül olmuşsun dikenlerin bendedir
Zeytin gözlüm uzaklarda işin ne?
Şarkıları düşürürüm peşine
Zeytin gözlüm özlem ektim yollara
Rast gelirsen halimi sor onlara
Gül kurusu akşamlar senden yana
Zeytin gözlüm uzaklarda işin ne?
Şarkıları düşürürüm peşine

My Olive-Eyed One

My olive-eyed one, why do I feel so attracted to you?
Who is to blame for this love?
Oh my rose! I have moved away from your thorns
My olive-eyed one, what are you doing so far away?
I am sending you my songs
My olive-eyed one, I planted yearning on your paths
When you find it, ask it about me
The twilight by your side is tinged with the hue
of a dried rose
Oh, my olive-eyed one, what are you doing so far away?
I am sending you my songs

Telling Stories of Resistance and Resilience: "Stop. Listen. Engage."

In June 2024, I worked with Talya Feldman and the University of Düsseldorf to organize an exhibition in public space at Mehmet-Kubaşık-Platz in Dortmund. Titled "Stopp. Zuhören. Begegnen." (Stop. Listen. Encounter.), it addressed the culture of remembrance surrounding right-wing extremist violence in North Rhine-Westphalia after 1945. The exhibition narrated a story of resistance and resilience through a sculpture and sound piece created in close collaboration with local initiatives, survivors, and families of victims of right-wing, racist, and anti-Semitic violence. At the heart of the works are their experiences, struggles, demands, and wishes. The exhibition consisted of a public sculpture designed by me in collaboration with the curator Chana Boekle and the graphic designer Silvia Troian and a sound piece by Feldman and the sound designer Carlos Ángel Luppi.

My sculpture, which I later named *Zurückschauen: Stimmen die bleiben* (Looking Back: Voices That Remain, 2024), was inspired by an installation by Grupo de Arte Callejero, a Buenos Aires artist collective that critically engages with the crimes and aftermath of the military dictatorship in Argentina between 1976 and 1983. Boekle, Troian, and I developed twenty-six traffic signs in collaboration with local initiatives, survivors, and victims' families. The iconography of traffic signs was used to effectively and strategically communicate with an audience with diverse cultural backgrounds. The works' resemblance to traffic signs drew the attention of passersby, encouraging engagement with the subject matter and the perspectives of survivors and victims' families.

Feldman's sound installation for the exhibition, *Hört mir zu: Dieses Lied ist ein Denkmal* (Listen to Me: This Song Is a Monument, 2024), is a collage of protests, soundscapes, instrumental pieces, interviews, speeches, and music recordings by local musicians and legends such as Ozan Ata Canani, Berivan Kaya, and Microphone Mafia. By amplifying what is often excluded from historical archives and public spaces, this work provides an alternative narrative of the recent history of North Rhine-Westphalia. Sound and listening are presented as political tools to overcome power structures.

"Stopp. Zuhören. Begegnen." connected testimonies, struggles, and stories, showing how important it is for survivors of right-wing terror to create their own spaces. The website reads: "Right-wing, racist and anti-Semitic acts of violence are not isolated cases or exceptions in North Rhine-Westphalia either. Rather, they are an integral part of the history and present of this federal state."[40] As the participant Fatma Ceylan, who survived a parcel bomb attack in Cologne on December 22, 1992, explains: "You can't share your experiences with everyone, which is why it's all the more important for those affected to come together. Because we understand each other—we understand each other without needing to say a lot."[41] In recent years, survivors of right-wing violence across Germany have been connecting more and more. They meet regularly and create spaces to get to know one another, exchange ideas, forge bonds of solidarity, grieve together, and share their struggles. The Bündnis Tag der Solidarität and its founder Gamze Kubaşık are convinced that "the solidarity with and between those affected by right-wing, racist, and anti-Semitic violence was and is decisive in ensuring that the demands for clarification, justice, and change remain unmistakable and become ever louder."[42]

In the exhibition, a sculpture memorializes Mehmet Kubaşık. Together with Elif and Gamze Kubaşık and their family, we designed the memorial plaque in black and yellow—the club colors of the Borussia Dortmund football club, which Mehmet was a big fan of. Dortmund is shown in outline. The northern part of the city, where Mehmet lived with his family and where his kiosk was, is marked in black. His name, date of birth, and the date of the murder are also shown.

The exhibition was an open, public invitation for a society to actively engage with the stories presented. It also highlighted the fact that the perspectives depicted are incomplete. Only a fraction of the stories of individuals murdered by right-wing violence, as well as those of survivors and their families, could be shared. Gaps and questions remain.

40 "Hintergrund," Stopp. Zuhören. Begegnen., accessed November 26, 2024, https://stopp-zuhoeren-begegnen.de/hintergrund/.

41 "Schulter an Schulter," Stopp. Zuhören. Begegnen., accessed November 26, 2024, https://stopp-zuhoeren-begegnen.de/schild/schulter-an-schulter/.

42 "12. Tag der Solidarität 2024 – In Erinnerung an Mehmet Kubaşık und alle Opfer rechter, rassistischer und antisemitischer Gewalt!," Bündnis Tag der Solidarität, accessed November 26, 2024, https://tagdersolidaritaet.wordpress.com/2024/03/21/12-tag-der-solidaritat-2024-in-erinnerung-an-mehmet-kubasik-und-alle-opfer-rechter-rassistischer-und-antisemitischer-gewalt/.

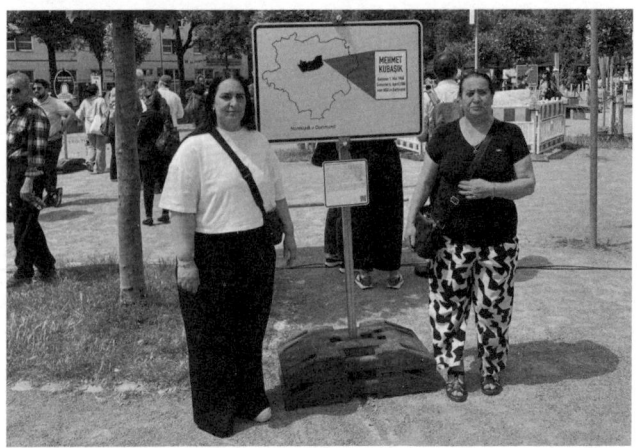

Fig. 48 Gamze Kubaşık and Elif Kubaşık, June 23, 2024

Therefore, the exhibition aimed to encourage other survivors and families to share their stories and come together in solidarity.

Tell your own stories. Tell their stories. Listen to others. Amplify their voices. Disrupt the narrative. Change conceptions. Never forget. Never forgive. Become a storyteller.

Literature

"30. Jahrestag des Gedenkens an die rassistischen Brandanschläge von Mölln." Gedenken Mölln 1992, November 7, 2022. https://gedenkenmoelln1992.wordpress.com/2022/11/07/30-jahrestag-des-gedenkens-an-die-rassistischen-brandanschlage-von-molln/.

Bilir-Meier, Cana. "Gazetelerde bir şiir karaladım tesadüfen. Güzel oldu. Poetin, Schriftstellerin, Aktivistin, Arbeiterin. Wie erinnern an Semra Ertan? Eine fragmentarische Annäherung." MA thesis, Academy of Fine Arts Vienna, 2015.

Bündnis Tag der Solidarität. *Trauer, Wut und Widerstand: Antirassistische Initiativen und Gedenkpolitik*, 2020. https://tagdersolidaritaet.wordpress.com/trauer-wut-und-widerstand/.

Diehl, Alexander. "Rückschlag für Gedenk-Initiative." *taz*, March 5, 2024. https://taz.de/Kein-Semra-Ertan-Platz-in-Hamburg/!5993617/.

Ertan, Semra. *Mein Name ist Ausländer – Benim Adım Yabancı*. Münster: edition assemblage, 2020.

Fallis, Deborah. "Wehrhafte Lyrik: Desintegration in den Gedichten zeitgenössischer postmigrantischer und jüdischer Autorinnen." MA thesis, Neuere Deutsche Literaturwissenschaft, Leibniz Universität, Hannover, 2021.

Förderzentrum Jugend Schreibt e.V., ed.. *Täglich eine Reise von der Türkei nach Deutschland: Texte der zweiten Generation in der Bundesrepublik*. Fischerhude: Atelier im Bauernhaus, 1980.

Friedrich, Sebastian, and Ibrahim Arslan. "Brandanschlag von Mölln: Es ist nichts Abgeschlossenes." *NDR Kultur*, November 24, 2022. https://www.ndr.de/kultur/Brandanschlag-von-Moelln-Es-ist-nichts-Abgeschlossenes,arslan154.html.

Grosse, Julia. *John Akomfrah: A Space of Empathy*. Berlin: Archive Books, 2023.

Hoyerswerda-1991, https://www.hoyerswerda-1991.de/.

Initiative "Pogrom 1991," last updated September 11, 2017. https://pogrom91.tumblr.com/.

Leyla, Sibel. " 'Wir werden nicht schweigen': Rede von Sibel Leyla zum Jahrestag des Anschlags am OEZ München." Heimatkunde: Migrationspolitisches Portal, Heinrich Böll Stiftung, July 22, 2022. https://heimatkunde.boell.de/de/2022/07/22/wir-werden-nicht-schweigen-rede-sibel-leyla-jahrestag-oez-muenchen.

"Listen to the Survivors! Closing Statements of Survivors at the Halle Trial." NSU Watch, December 18, 2020. https://www.nsu-watch.info/2020/12/listen-to-the-survivors-closing-statements-of-survivors-at-the-halle-trial/.

Lugones, María. "Playfulness, 'World'-Travelling, and Loving Perception." *Hypatia* 2, no. 2 (Summer 1987): 3–19.

"Möllner Rede im Exil vom 18. April 2021." Gedenken Mölln 1992, May 9, 2021. https://gedenkenmoelln1992.wordpress.com/2021/05/09/mollner-rede-im-exil-vom-18-april-2021/.

München erinnern! OEZ-Anschlag 22.07.2016, https://muenchen-erinnern.de/info/.

"Opfer und Überlebende sind die Hauptzeugen des Geschehenen, wir sind keine Statisten." NSU Watch, November 19, 2016. https://www.nsu-watch.info/2016/11/opfer-und-ueberlebende-sind-die-hauptzeugen-des-geschehenen-wir-sind-keine-statisten/.

Özkan, Hülya, and Andrea Wörle, eds. *Eine Fremde wie ich: Berichte, Erzählungen, Gedichte von Ausländerinnen*. Munich: Deutscher Taschenbuch Verlag, 1985.

"Pressemitteilung: 21. Jahrestag der rassistischen Brandanschläge von

Mölln," Gedenken Mölln 1992, October
21, 2013. https://gedenkenmoelln1992
.wordpress.com/2013/10/20
/pressemitteilung-21-jahrestag-der
-rassistischen-brandanschlage-von
-molln-gedenken-kann-nicht-an-den
-interessen-der-uberlebenden-vorbei
-gestaltet-werden/.

Remember Yaya Jabbi, https://
rememberjajadiabi.blackblogs.org
/about-jaja-diabi/.

Schaffernicht, Christian,
ed. *Zu Hause in der Fremde: Ein
bundesdeutsches Ausländer-Lesebuch.*
Fischerhude: Atelier im Bauernhaus,
1981.

Schumacher, Jennifer. "Dortmund:
Opfer rechtsextremer Gewalt
gestalten Ausstellung." *WAZ*, June
20, 2024. https://www.waz.de/kultur/
article406617223/dortmund
-opfer-rechtsextremer-gewalt-gestalten
-ausstellung.html.

Şirin, Ali. *Erinnern heißt Kämpfen:
Kein Schlusstrich unter unseren
Stimmen.* Münster: UNRAST, 2024.

Smith, Linda Tuhiwai. *Decolonizing
Methodologies: Research and Indigenous
Peoples.* London: Zed Books, 1999.

Spicker, Rachel. "'Ich möchte
mein Recht wahrnehmen, Teil der
Aufklärung zu sein.'" *Belltower News*,
September 14, 2020. https://www
.belltower.news/halle-prozess-ich
-moechte-mein-recht-wahrnehmen-teil
-der-aufklaerung-zu-sein-104161/.

Tuck, Eve. "Suspending Damage:
A Letter to Communities." *Harvard
Educational Review* 79, no. 3 (2009):
409–27. https://doi.org/10.17763
/haer.79.3.n0016675661t3n15.

Contributors

Ana de Almeida is an artist and researcher based in Lisbon and Vienna. Her practice deals with individual and collective memory, processes of remembering from a sociopolitical perspective, the intersection of family narratives and macro-political events, and the privatization of history. De Almeida is a DOC-team fellow of the Austrian Academy of Sciences and a researcher in the Institute of Art Theory and Cultural Studies at the Academy of Fine Arts Vienna.

andrea ancira is an editor and curator. Her research is situated at the crossroads of archival practice, editing, and translation as devices to probe memory, identity, and the power structures that underpin historical narratives. She is a cofounder of tumbalacasa ediciones and currently a fellow of the Fundación Jumex Arte Contemporáneo and a PhD candidate at the Academy of Fine Arts Vienna.

Cana Bilir-Meier is a filmmaker and artist who lives and works in Munich. Alongside her artistic practice, she works with art and cultural education projects. Her filmic, performative, and text-based works operate at the interface between archive work, text production, historical research, and contemporary media reflexivity and archaeology. Bilir-Meier is cofounder of the Initiative in Gedanken an Semra Ertan and coeditor of Ertan's poetry collection *Mein Name ist Ausländer – Benim Adım Yabancı* (2020).

Nina Hoechtl is a visual artist, researcher, curator, and teacher. Conceiving and practicing research as a transdisciplinary endeavor, she combines artistic, archival, and analytic practices with the study of visual culture and feminist queer_cuir, post-, and de(s)colon/ial/izing theories and practices. Hoechtl is currently a researcher at the Centro de Investigaciones y Estudios de Género (CIEG) of the National Autonomous University of Mexico (UNAM) in Mexico City.

Olena Khoroshylova is a researcher and curator specializing in educational programs related to art, architecture, and urbanism. Her work focuses on education, art, and social issues, focusing on forced migrants and the transformative power of artistic practices. Currently residing in Upper Austria as a forced migrant, Khoroshylova conducted a course at the University of Arts Linz in 2022/23 on the impact of lost routines among forced migrant women.

Sanja Lasić is a visual artist, performer, and social-work pedagogue. She is currently based in Vienna, where she works with video, performance, and drawing to create deeply intimate interventions on identity, belonging, memory, and trauma.

Mai Ling, founded in Vienna in 2019, is an anonymous artist collective and association committed to fostering dialogues on racism, sexism, homophobia, and prejudice with a focus on FLINTA* (women, lesbians, intersex, nonbinary, trans, and agender people) with Asian-descent, diasporic, and migrant backgrounds. Challenging the Western heteropatriarchal gaze and racist fantasies that continually reproduce stereotypes about "Asia," the group amplifies multilayered voices to reclaim agency through collective resistance and pleasure. Mai Ling engages in various forms of artistic practice and activism, including video and audio installations, cooking performances, community gatherings, public interventions, and protests.

Stephanie Misa is a visual artist and researcher whose work centers on decolonizing methodologies. Her artistic practice connects multicultural collaboration, curating, and feminist critique. In her work, Misa examines phenomena related to the orality and richness of multilingualism. A doctoral researcher at the University of the Arts Helsinki, she is working on projects funded by the Kone Foundation and the Finnish Cultural Foundation (SKR). She lives and works in Vienna and lectures at the Department of Artistic Strategies at the University of Applied Arts Vienna, where she leads a Philippine research program called the Island Tides Initiative.

Lena Ditte Nissen is an artistic researcher and filmmaker working at the intersection of documentary film, performance, and video installation with reference to classical experimental film and ethnographic research strategies. Since 2020, she has focused on female perpetrators and midwives' complicity in the murder of disabled children during National Socialism. Her current artistic research is based at the University of Arts Linz and is funded by the Austrian Academy of Sciences (ÖAW).

Mariel Rodríguez is a research-based artist and cultural-studies scholar interested in decolonial artistic methodologies, resistance practices, self-reflexivity, and relational research forms. In her work, she explores connections between identity construction and representation, moving between different media and aesthetic languages. She is a lecturer in the Institute of Fine Arts and Cultural Studies at the University of Arts Linz.

Ruth Sonderegger is professor of philosophy and aesthetic theory at the Academy of Fine Arts Vienna. Her main fields of research are the history of aesthetics (in the context of colonial capitalism), practice theories, and cultural as well as resistance studies. She is part of the transversal.at publishing collective.

Elif Süsler-Rohringer is a researcher, artist, and textile and graphic designer based in Vienna and Istanbul. Since 2020, she has been a doctoral student in the Design History and Theory Department of the University of Applied Arts Vienna. She has been awarded an DOC-team fellowship 2023–26 from the Austrian Academy of Sciences (ÖAW). In tandem with her academic research, she works on research-based art projects in cultural institutions, reinterpreting textile design and fashion history from a post-migrant perspective.

Verena Melgarejo Weinandt is a German Bolivian artist, researcher, curator, and educator. She is currently part of the artistic research project Repatriates, funded by the European Research Council, at the Central European University in Vienna. Her current research focuses on the significance of Indigenous stereotypes in the German-speaking context. Through performative strategies, videos, textile installations, and academic research, she investigates how cultural and institutional practices are shaped, and how our relation to the fictional, imagination, and nonhuman beings can serve as tools to (re)create the self and collective identity.

Abstracts

Ana de Almeida and
Mariel Rodríguez
*La auto-cosa: Writing Together
through Institutions, Artistic
Practices, and Critical Imagination*

A collaborative piece of writing by
the editors, the introduction is
composed in the self-reflective voice
of two Is, tracking their experiences as
students at the Academy of Fine Arts
Vienna. Alternately swapping speaking
positions, overlapping, or merging
their voices in a performative way,
the two authors intertwine personal
observations of seminars, publications, and the work of colleagues
with international positions that have
been seminal in the development of
radically self-reflexive approaches to
research. Mapping connections among
the contributions in this anthology,
the text also highlights influences
and their affective dimension, which
recognizes itself as partial and situated.
It weaves a network of perspectives
that shows what can be encompassed
by the concept of autotheory as a way
of approaching knowledge and art
production.

Keywords: autotheory, situated
writing, collaborative writing, artistic
research, art education, critical studies,
self-reflexivity, embodied knowledge,
mapping

Olena Khoroshylova
*Sofa, Zimmer, Wohnung:
Forced Migration and Women
in Partnership*

This contribution traces the winding
paths of women who have been
swept into exile as a result of Russia's
invasion of Ukraine, and the unexpected partnerships that bloom in the
spaces between survival and memory.
Through fragile networks of shared
rooms, borrowed sofas, and resilient
whispers of "home," these women craft
a new language of belonging. The essay
traces connections across generations,
contrasting today's struggles with
memories of survival from the Second
World War. It echoes past forced
migrations, told from the perspectives
of girls, mothers, and grandmothers,
threaded with desolation yet brimming
with endurance. In this essay, while
following the routes of the many road
trips she has made—and continues
to make—as a forced migrant in the
aftermath of Russia's large-scale
military offensive on Ukraine, Olena
Khoroshylova reflects on the relationship between various forms of shelter
architecture and the survival strategies
employed by forced women migrants.
Along her journey, she encounters
other women recently displaced from
Ukraine as well as art students and the
indelible memory of her grandmother,
a forced worker in a Nazi military
factory. Khoroshylova entangles her
own experience with theirs through
the practice of collaborative art and
interviews.

Keywords: forced migration,
women in partnerships, cooperation,
communal living routines, living
typologies, survival strategies, Second
World War testimonies, in-depth
interviews, memory

Sanja Lasić
Sevdah of Lost Identity

This contribution investigates the
complex interplay between individual
trauma and collective historical experience through the lens of the *sevdah*
and *sevdalinka* music genre. Grounded
in the artist's personal narrative of
displacement during the Bosnian War
in the 1990s, the project employs performative and musical methodologies
to explore the psychological and social
aftermath of the conflict. By analyzing
and reinterpreting traditional motifs
and symbols found in her native

cultural heritage within the framework of a western European education and upbringing, the artist seeks to reclaim a fragmented identity. Through embodied practice, the research examines the manifestations of intergenerational trauma, including PTSD and eating disorders. This project contributes to ongoing discourses on the role of art in trauma recovery and the construction of identity in contemporary multicultural societies.

Keywords: identity, sevdah, trauma, memory, PTSD, eating disorders, individual histories, collective histories, ethno-politics, performance art

Stephanie Misa
An altar for
the fleshy tongue

This artistic research investigation asks: How does the idea of the "multitude," of being one yet composed of many, generate new ways of positioning oneself against monolithic, essentialist representations within language? Can languages be held within the body across generations? And if so, what tools do we need to reawaken this dormant knowledge? Stephanie Misa posits these ideas to examine her own linguistic inheritance and spoken languages untethered to read-write structures that are in danger of erasure, as well as those that are all but gone aside from scattered traces. To access these different positions, Misa writes of her own fragmented "mother tongue" and the case of Fanny Cochrane Smith, the only recorded speaker of an Aboriginal Tasmanian language. Misa asks what it means for the body, voice, sound, and tongue to endure colonization, as these embodied articulations (or oralities)—acknowledged as strategies of colonial resistance—are determined by their persistence, circulation, and continuation as forms of oral communication within Indigenous communities undergoing

structural evisceration. The author also explores the different ways of "knowing" an orality and addresses the challenges of researching practices outside one's own cultural sphere, emphasizing that relationship-building and time are key for an ethical methodology. The essay follows this speculative journey to trace the tongue as the site where language leaves the body and enters the world, asking what secrets might lie within this fleshy transmitter.

Keywords: orality, language, hybridity, embodiment. mother tongue, ethical research

andrea ancira
Unlearning the Archive:
A River as Trace

This contribution explores the archive as a site to practice collective mourning. Drawing from andrea ancira's family archive, it examines questions of memory, trauma, and mourning in the context of the civil war in Guatemala (1960–96), one of the longest in Latin America. The author engages with the archival materials found in her grandparents' basement as traces that seek to document, co-construct, and poetically negotiate a narrative with multiple voices, perspectives, truths, and meanings, offering a nuanced understanding of situated and transitional accounts #of social and personal histories. From an auto-ethnographic perspective, ancira reflects on the affective economies that archives produce and circulate when generating and exchanging alternative narratives of a shared history, with a particular focus on the materials from her family archive and their donation to Riij Ib'ooy Center in Río Negro, a community that witnessed and most directly suffered the consequences of the civil war.

Keywords: archive, memory, mourning, grief, landscape, extractivism, river, trace

Nina Hoechtl
A Visual Glossary, Expanded: Delirio güero (White Delusion)

In this chapter, the artist Nina Hoechtl adds three more entries to the visual glossary first published in *Sharpening the Haze* (Ubiquity Press, 2020). Based on her film *DELIRIO GÜERO WHITE DELUSION. 2211, 2018, 1825 and Back* (2018), these entries spark a dialogue around *delirio güero* (White delusion), a concept coined by the author, which engages in a complex practice of entanglement and entitlement, implication and aspiration, innocence and ignorance, denial and delusion. The film chews over various delirio güero acts in Mexico carried out by the monarchs Maximilian of Habsburg and Charlotte of Belgium, the explorer-artist Jean-Friedrich Waldeck, the architect, researcher, and photographer Teobert Maler, and Anton "Toni" Mayr—both followers of Maximilian—and a relative of Mayr, the maker of *DELIRIO GÜERO* and author of this essay. The topics covered in this addition to the glossary include the "politics of location," which deconstructs the figure of the White savior; the practice of *autohistoria-teoría* as a way to unlearn privileges and challenge the internal and external güero; and a hauntological (auto)biography that focuses on a seemingly innocent statement in order to contemplate an approach to inheritance and heritage (personal, biological, cultural, visual, or epistemological).

Keywords: white savior, autohistoria-teoría, delirio güero (White delusion), hauntological (auto)-biography, Whiteness, mestizaje, *blanquitud* (Whiteyness)

Verena Melgarejo Weinandt
A Deep Dive into the (Collective) Self: Creating Autohistoria-teoría with the Performative Alter Ego Pocahunter

This text explores how the author's personal experiences are interwoven with her performative alter ego Pocahunter. Guided by Gloria Anzaldúa's method of *autohistoria-teoría*, Verena Melgarejo Weinandt follows the path that brought Pocahunter into existence. First, as Anzaldúa's method suggests, collective encounters and formations are fundamental to the creation of different versions of Pocahunter. Second, this method helps Melgarejo Weinandt understand her artistic practice based on her own biography as a way to position and analyze this experience within a larger societal structure. In this journey, Pocahunter focuses on how violence, especially against Indigenous people, can be contested from a decolonial and queer feminist standpoint. Finally, Melgarejo Weinandt explores how Pocahunter has been practicing what Anzaldúa calls a "deep dive" in order to create new ways and expressions of transformation and healing.

Keywords: *autohistoria-teoría*, identity, performance

Mai Ling
Who Is Mai Ling? Challenges of Anonymity and the Practice of Care

An artist collective and association, Mai Ling challenges Western hetero-patriarchy and its perpetuation of deeply embedded racist and Orientalist fantasies about Asian femininity. The group works "anonymously" to embrace a multiplicity of voices and identities. This anonymity functions as a form of nonrepresentation and an active re-fusal, resisting reduction and labeling while making space for complexities, allowing the group to exist as a hybrid entity capable of destabilizing structures and shape-shifting. It is also an open question: Who is Mai Ling? This text begins by tracing the development of the collective and examines the context of the often-overlooked experiences of Asian diasporic and migrant FLINTA* (women, lesbians, intersex, nonbinary, trans, and agender people), particularly in German-speaking society. It also addresses the lack of a discourse around oversexualized, "ornamentalized" Asian femininity, which Mai Ling incorporates within its practice. The essay then delves into the challenges presented to artistic individuality by an anonymous collective identity, particularly in terms of labor and responsibilities in art making. Furthermore, the piece discusses how to navigate a society that produces intersectional discrimination while also embracing the collective's struggles, resistance, and moments of pleasure. This reflection leads them to reorient their activities toward collective healing. Finally, they address their ongoing and honest struggle to practice mutual care within the collective, acknowledging the potential inherent in being a fluid and evolving group.

Keywords: artist collective, anonymity, care, minor feelings, ornamentalism, radical honesty

Elif Süsler-Rohringer
The Persistence of Patterns: From Strong Subjectivity to Local and Global Sartorial Exchanges

Located at the intersection of autoethnography and art and design history, this contribution focuses on the creative dimension of labor migration in the Austrian textile industry from the 1970s to the 2000s. Elif Süsler-Rohringer critically reflects on her self-situatedness as a recently migrated artist and textile designer from Turkey to Austria. The recruitment of "guest workers" from Turkey began with an official agreement in 1964 to compensate for the shortage of industrial labor in Austria. Vorarlberg and Vienna were the centers of migration, as these were the regions where the country's embroidery and textile industry was located. Through archival research, Süsler-Rohringer examines the institutional dimension of the question: How were creativity and skilled work assessed in the context of labor migration? This essay takes the example of patterns—design models for clothes—to narrate the gaps and discontinuities of the archival material. It asks how to employ patterns not just as objects of research but also as a concept and methodology to analyze the material, cultural, and social experience of creative labor migration.

Keywords: labor migration, fashion history, patterns, migrating concepts, creativity

Ruth Sonderegger
Writing Together through Institutions II: No Epilogue

This afterword of sorts is Ruth Sonderegger's attempt to examine the role of collaborations during her teaching tenure at the Academy of Fine Arts Vienna—a period that began with the "Uni brennt" protests against university reforms in 2009. It also explores how various collaborative engagements with the Academy and its history have changed the author's teaching, research, and attempts to intervene in the institution. She presents an exploration of the main reconsiderations that these institutional engagements have provided her with, starting with her role as a teacher and philosopher in an art academy and ending with her criticism of some positions within Enlightenment philosophy, an area of research she now sees from a wholly new perspective.

Keywords: Bologna Process, critical theory, colonial history of philosophical aesthetics, situated knowledges, "Uni brennt," writing together

Lena Ditte Nissen
Attempt to Situate: Speak or Let Speak?

In this contribution, Lena Ditte Nissen outlines her current artistic research project, *Chaosmos of the Personal*. She describes her research material—the writings of deceased family members who were female perpetrators in National Socialism, introduces the methodology of the "interpretation workshop," and explains how she adapted it for her inquiry. She then looks at the research project as an attempt to situate herself through shared communicative and creative processes. This reflection draws from concepts such as Donna Haraway's situated knowledge, Sandra Harding's strong objectivity, Lauren Fournier's autotheory, and the field of ethno-psychoanalysis. Nissen borrows and expands on terminology from Griselda Pollock to introduce the concept of the allo-auto-process as a way to situate oneself critically within the context of artistic research.

Keywords: National Socialism, situatedness, ethnopsychoanalysis, interpretation workshop, allo-auto-process

Cana Bilir-Meier
Becoming a Storyteller: Methodologies in Collaborative, Activist, Artistic, and Archival Work in Remembering

This essay explores the methodologies embedded in the collaborative, activist, artistic, and archival practices of commemorative initiatives addressing those affected by right-wing terror and police violence in Germany. Cana Bilir-Meier introduces her aunt Semra Ertan, a poet, worker, and political activist against racism. Bilir-Meier discusses her role as a cultural mediator in caring for and sharing Ertan's literature and life story. The piece explores the role of storytelling as an artistic practice and how to create spaces that focus on hope and desire as forms of resistance. Bilir-Meier elaborates on her family's story, the idea of listening as a political act, and the importance of sharing other stories to create collectivity within artistic practices. Through collaborative projects like art in public spaces, poetry readings, sound installations, film screenings, and exhibitions, individual and collective remembrance becomes an act of solidarity.

Keywords: poetry, remembrance, resilience, migration, art, activism, Semra Ertan, grassroots initiatives, public space, archive

Image Credits

Fig. 1 Interviewing Maria in 2004. Courtesy of Olena Khoroshylova.
p. 56

Fig. 2 My visit to Waldstraße 99, Fürth, January 2023. Courtesy of Olena Khoroshylova.
p. 59

Fig. 3 Toni Alberti, *Gravity (1/3)*, 2023. Digital collage. Courtesy of the artist.
p. 63

Fig. 4 "Sofa, Zimmer, Wohnung," exhibition view, Kyiv, October 2023. Photo: Carlotta Borcherding.
p. 63

Fig. 5 Flößaustraße 20, Fürth, January 2023. Courtesy of Olena Khoroshylova.
p. 70

Fig. 6 Sanja Lasić, *Anxiety*, 2021. Black marker on paper, 50 × 70 cm. Courtesy of the artist.
p. 80

Fig. 7 Sanja Lasić, *Jst sem*, 2007. Digital photography, 30 × 40 cm. Courtesy of the artist.
p. 94

Fig. 8 Sanja Lasić, *Sevdah of Lost Identity*, 2021. Live performance at Studio Moliere Vienna. Photo: Michel Nahabedian.
p. 101

Fig. 9 Stephanie Misa, *An altar for the fleshy tongue*, installation view, RMIT Gallery, Naarm (Melbourne), 2023. Courtesy of RMIT Gallery / Sebastian Kainey.
p. 111

Fig. 10 Stephanie Misa, *Placeholder I*, 2025. Courtesy of the artist.
p. 113

Fig. 11 Stephanie Misa, *An altar for the fleshy tongue*, installation view, RMIT Gallery, Naarm (Melbourne), 2023. Courtesy of RMIT Gallery / Sebastian Kainey.
p. 117

Fig. 12 Stephanie Misa, *Placeholder II*, 2025. Courtesy of the artist.
p. 125

Fig. 13 Fanny Cochrane Smith with William Smith and two of their sons [Nicholls Rivulet]: [publisher not identified], [between 1882 and 1893]. Courtesy of the Tasmanian Archives and the Allport Library and Museum of Fine Arts.
p. 131

Fig. 14 Gerard O'Neill holding a copy of a working wax-cylinder record and an irreparable cracked one at the recording studio of the National Film and Sound Archive of Australia, Canberra, 2023. Courtesy of the National Library of Australia.
p. 135

Fig. 15 Creating our own wax-cylinder recording at the recording studio of the National Film and Sound Archive of Australia, Canberra, 2023. Courtesy of Stephanie Misa.
p. 135

Fig. 16 Vitrine containing a wax-cylinder record, electric candles, orchids, gumnuts, and various religious paraphernalia. Stephanie Misa, *An altar for the fleshy tongue*, installation view, RMIT Gallery, Naarm (Melbourne), 2023. Courtesy of RMIT Gallery / Sebastian Kainey.
p. 137

Standpoint Autotheory
*Writing Embodied Experiences and
Relational Artistic Practices*
ISBN 978-1-915609-64-9

This is a peer-reviewed publication.
We thank the anonymous reviewers for
their in-depth comments and advice.

Editors: Ana de Almeida and Mariel Rodríguez
Editorial Coordinator: Iris Weißenböck
Copy Editor: Max Bach
Design: Beton
Typefaces: Arial, Minion Pro
Paper: MultiColor Mirabell 250 g,
Munken Print White 80 g
Printing and Binding: MMC, Memmingen,
Germany

Distributed by The MIT Press, Art Data,
Les presses du réel, and Idea Books

Every effort has been made to contact
the rightful owners with regard to
copyrights and permissions. We apologize
for any inadvertent errors or omissions.

Sternberg Press
71–75 Shelton Street
London WC2H 9JQ
www.sternberg-press.com

Sternberg Press